STUDIES IN THE HISTORY
OF CHRISTIAN MISSIONS

R. E. Frykenberg
Brian Stanley
General Editors

STUDIES IN THE HISTORY OF CHRISTIAN MISSIONS

Alvyn Austin
China's Millions: The China Inland Mission and Late Qing Society, 1832-1905

Michael Bergunder
The South Indian Pentecostal Movement in the Twentieth Century

Judith M. Brown and Robert Eric Frykenberg, *Editors*
Christians, Cultural Interactions, and India's Religious Traditions

Robert Eric Frykenberg
*Christians and Missionaries in India:
Cross-Cultural Communication Since 1500*

Susan Billington Harper
*In the Shadow of the Mahatma: Bishop V. S. Azariah
and the Travails of Christianity in British India*

D. Dennis Hudson
Protestant Origins in India: Tamil Evangelical Christians, 1706-1835

Ogbu U. Kalu, *Editor*, and Alaine M. Low, *Associate Editor*
*Interpreting Contemporary Christianity:
Global Processes and Local Identities*

Donald M. Lewis, *Editor*
*Christianity Reborn: The Global Expansion of Evangelicalism
in the Twentieth Century*

Jon Miller
*Missionary Zeal and Institutional Control: Organizational Contradictions
in the Basel Mission on the Gold Coast, 1828-1917*

Andrew Porter, *Editor*
The Imperial Horizons of British Protestant Missions, 1880-1914

Dana L. Robert, *Editor*
Converting Colonialism: Visions and Realities in Mission History, 1709-1914

Wilbert R. Shenk, *Editor*
North American Foreign Missions, 1810-1914: Theology, Theory, and Policy

Brian Stanley
The World Missionary Conference, Edinburgh 1910

Brian Stanley, *Editor*
Christian Missions and the Enlightenment

Brian Stanley, *Editor*
Missions, Nationalism, and the End of Empire

Kevin Ward and Brian Stanley, *Editors*
The Church Mission Society and World Christianity, 1799-1999

The World Missionary Conference, Edinburgh 1910

Brian Stanley

WILLIAM B. EERDMANS PUBLISHING COMPANY
GRAND RAPIDS, MICHIGAN / CAMBRIDGE, U.K.

Published 2009 by
Wm. B. Eerdmans Publishing Co.
2140 Oak Industrial Drive N.E., Grand Rapids, Michigan 49505 /
P.O. Box 163, Cambridge CB3 9PU U.K.

Printed in the United States of America

13 12 11 10   7 6 5 4 3 2

Library of Congress Cataloging-in-Publication Data

The World Missionary Conference, Edinburgh 1910 / Brian Stanley, editor.
p.   cm.   — (Studies in the history of Christian missions)
Includes bibliographical references and index.
ISBN 978-0-8028-6360-7 (pbk.: alk. paper)
1. World Missionary Conference (1910: Edinburgh, Scotland)
2. Missions — Congresses.   I. Stanley, Brian, 1953-

BV2390.W68 2009
266.009′041 — dc22

2008046918

www.eerdmans.com

In grateful memory of my parents,
Bob and Betty Stanley,
and my sister, Bridget Levick

Contents

Acknowledgments

This book has been a long time in the making, and I have incurred many debts of gratitude in the process. I first turned my attention to the World Missionary Conference when I undertook to analyse the Report of Commission VII on 'Missions and Governments' for a consultation on missions and empire during the high imperial period organised by the Currents in World Christianity Project in 1998. The resulting essay, which is reproduced as Chapter 9 of this volume, was first published in Andrew Porter (ed.), *The Imperial Horizons of British Protestant Missions, 1880-1914* (Eerdmans, 2000). It was Professor Porter who then suggested to me that I ought to go on to undertake a major study of the conference as a whole, and I am grateful to him for sowing the seeds which have now germinated in a full-length study.

The research for this book has taken me to many different libraries and archives, and I cannot list here the names of all the librarians and archivists who have helped me along the way. Nevertheless, particular mention must be made of Ruth Tonkiss Cameron, archivist of the Burke Library at Union Theological Seminary, New York, who has always been ready to make available to me the largely untapped riches of the Burke Library's collection of Edinburgh 1910 materials. The staff of the Ecumenical Centre Library, Geneva, the Day Missions Library, Yale Divinity School, and New College, University of Edinburgh, also deserve particular thanks for their assistance in giving me ready access to their respective archive collections. Professor Marcia Wright of Columbia University generously allowed me to use her apartment in New York on several occasions while I was working in the Burke Library: Marcia has saved me a great deal of money, as well as offering consistent encouragement.

Many of the chapters of this book have been tried out in draft on various audiences of conference participants and students of different universities or seminaries, and I should like to acknowledge my debt to all those whose astute questions at the end of my lectures prompted me to consider new perspectives or to re-think my conclusions. In addition to Chapter 9, some other chapters represent expansions of articles published previously, some in previous volumes in this series: I owe special thanks to Jonathan Bonk, editor of the *International Bulletin of Missionary Research,* for permission to include as Chapter 3 an expanded version of an article published in the *Bulletin* in 2006.

For permission to include photographs I am indebted to the following: Oxford University Press; the Burke Library archives (Columbia University Libraries) at Union Theological Seminary; Mission-21, Basel; the Church Mission Society; www.norway.heritage.com; Princeton Theological Seminary Libraries; Hodder & Stoughton; the Revd Rodney Ragwan; St. Colm's International Centre; National Portrait Gallery, London; Special Collections Research Center, University of Chicago; SCM-Canterbury Press; the Society for Promoting Christian Knowledge. It has not been possible in every case to trace the original copyright holder.

I also wish to express my thanks to the trustees of the Henry Martyn Trust, and to the Master and Fellows of St Edmund's College, Cambridge, for granting me a period of sabbatical leave in 2004 to work on this project. I am also deeply grateful to the Managers of the Peregrine Maitland Fund of the University of Cambridge who have generously supported the travel necessary to undertake the research.

The staff of William B. Eerdmans Publishing Company have, as always, been extremely supportive and helpful in working with me on this book: particular thanks is owed to David Bratt and Jennifer Hoffman. My fellow general editor of this series, Professor Robert E. Frykenberg, has offered continual encouragement: it has been a rich privilege of these last twelve years to know Bob as a friend and adviser.

I owe far more than I can ever express to my wife, Rosey, and my children, Jonathan, Rebecca, and Joanna, whose patience and unfailing support have been indispensable to the task of maintaining momentum in the writing of this book amidst many other responsibilities. Finally, I should like to mention with deep gratitude the encouragement offered in the earlier stages of this project by my parents, Bob and Betty Stanley, and my sister, Bridget Levick. They were all deeply committed to the cause of the world mission of the Church and had broad Christian sympathies which extended well beyond their own denomination. Sadly, none of them have lived to see the finished work, but I gladly dedicate this book to their collective memory.

BRIAN STANLEY
Edinbugh
November 2008

Illustrations

1. Randall Davidson, Archbishop of Canterbury.

2. John R. Mott, chairman of the World Missionary Conference.

3. J. H. Oldham, secretary of the World Missionary Conference.

4. The conference in session in the Assembly Hall of the United Free Church of Scotland.

5. The S.S. *Kroonland* of the Red Star Line, which transported many of the American delegates across the Atlantic.

6. Dr K. C. Chatterjee of the Presbyterian Church in India, wearing the robes of his honorary D.D. bestowed by the University of Edinburgh on the eve of the conference.

7. Lord Balfour of Burleigh, president of the conference.

8. J. H. Ritson, Bible Society secretary, clerk to the conference, and member of Commission VIII.

9. John Rangiah, delegate of the American Baptist Foreign Missionary Society.

10. Cheng Jingyi, delegate of the London Missionary Society.

11. Bishop Honda Yoitsu, invited by the American executive committee.

12. The Honourable Yun Ch'iho, invited by the American executive committee.

Abbreviations

ABCFM	American Board of Commissioners for Foreign Missions
AUL	Aberdeen University Library
BDCM	*Biographical Dictionary of Christian Missions*
BMS	Baptist Missionary Society
BSA	Bible Society Archives
CBMS	Conference of British Missionary Societies
CIM	China Inland Mission
CMS	Church Missionary Society
CUL	Cambridge University Library
CWMA	Council for World Mission Archives
ECG	Ecumenical Centre, Geneva
History and Records of the Conference	World Missionary Conference, 1910, *The History and Records of the Conference Together with Addresses Delivered at the Evening Meetings* (Edinburgh and London: Oliphant, Anderson & Ferrier; and New York, Chicago, and Toronto: Fleming H. Revell Company, n.d. [1910]).
IBMR	*International Bulletin of Missionary Research*
IMC	International Missionary Council
IRM	*International Review of Mission(s)*
LMS	London Missionary Society
LP	Lambeth Palace Library
MRL	Missionary Research Library
NCE	New College, University of Edinburgh
NZG	Nederlandsche Zendelingenootschap
ODNB	*Oxford Dictionary of National Biography*

Abbreviations

Report of Commission I, etc.	World Missionary Conference, 1910, *Report of Commission I: Carrying the Gospel to all the Non-Christian World* (Edinburgh and London: Oliphant, Anderson & Ferrier; and New York, Chicago, and Toronto: Fleming H. Revell Company, n.d. [1910]). Similarly for the reports of the other seven Commissions.
RMG	Rheinische Missionsgesellschaft
SCM	Student Christian Movement
SOAS	School of Oriental and African Studies, University of London
SPG	Society for the Propagation of the Gospel
SVMU	Student Volunteer Missionary Union
UBL	University of Birmingham Library
UCL	University of Chicago Library
UTS	Union Theological Seminary, New York
WCC	World Council of Churches
WMC	World Missionary Conference
WMMS	Wesleyan Methodist Missionary Society
YDS	Yale Divinity School
YMCA	Young Men's Christian Association
YWCA	Young Women's Christian Association

Preface

This book is intended to supply both an account of the World Missionary Conference as an event in itself and also a synthetic interpretation of the western Protestant missionary movement as it neared the apex of its size and influence. The conference was, as its title suggests, convened to address the subject of world mission, and that very obvious point has frequently been forgotten in the light of the consequences which Edinburgh 1910 had for the mutual relations of Christian churches. In addition to the published reports of its eight constituent Commissions, extensive use has been made of the surviving manuscripts which indicate the long and sometimes contested process which brought the conference into being, supplemented, in the case of some of the Commissions, by detailed analysis of samples of the replies received from working missionaries to the questionnaires issued by the Commissions. I have been able to locate, either in the Ecumenical Centre in Geneva or in the Burke Library of Union Theological Seminary in New York, sets of questionnaire replies for all of the Commissions except Commission V, but I have worked exhaustively on the replies only for Commissions II, III, IV, and VII. There remains plenty of scope for future research by other scholars, particularly on the Commission I material lodged in the Burke Library, which has the largest collection of papers relating to the Edinburgh conference. Archives in Edinburgh, Aberdeen, London, Birmingham, Cambridge, Oxford, Yale, and Chicago have also yielded rich and hitherto largely untapped resources for reconstructing the narrative of the conference.

There is a certain amount of duplication in the primary sources on the conference: for example, more or less complete sets of the replies to some or all of the eight Commission questionnaires can be found in six different locations; and the John R. Mott papers at Yale Divinity School include copies of Mott letters in the Burke Library collection. The footnotes generally refer to the locations in which I consulted a particular source: it would have been tedious and wasteful of space to have indicated every case where alternative locations may be found.

Because the book is concerned both with telling the intricate story of the conference as event and with critical analysis of the preparatory documents which preceded it, it may appear to oscillate between detailed chronological narrative and perspectival reflection on the issues thrown up by the Commission reports and their relationship to the questionnaire replies on which they were based. I have resisted the temptation to pursue the obvious course of writing a chapter on each Commission, both because two of the Commissions (V and VI) seem to me of less interest than the others to scholars of missions and world Christianity, and because such an approach would have become tediously predictable for the reader. Nonetheless, the subject-matter of some of the chapters does correspond closely to the work of particular Commissions.

The book opens with a chapter that sets the conference in the dual context of the expectations which surrounded it at the time and of the retrospective interpretations which have shaped modern understanding of the event. Chapter 2 is concerned with the origins of the conference, its relationship to its predecessors, and the process of planning the conference which was initiated in 1907. Chapter 3 is devoted entirely to an exploration of the question which nearly wrecked the conference before it assembled: namely, what were the limits of the Protestant overseas missions with which it was to be concerned — specifically, were they to include Protestant missions working among Roman Catholic, Orthodox, or ancient Oriental Christian populations? The answers given to that question reveal foundational assumptions prevailing in the Protestant world at that time about the nature and limits of 'Christendom'. Chapter 4 surveys the workings of the conference itself, and attempts to convey something of the intoxicating atmosphere of a gathering which clearly left an indelible impression on the minds of those who attended it. Chapter 5 is concerned with the group of nineteen representatives of what were then termed the 'younger churches' (all except one of them from Asia), and the major contributions that some of them made to the conference; although they were fewer in number than the organisers had hoped, their presence and what some of them said disturbed at least for a time the preconceptions which shaped the outlook of this overwhelmingly white assembly. The following four chapters step back to some extent from the conference itself and focus on the preparatory work of particular Commissions, as well as on the discussion which their reports provoked in the conference sessions. Chapter 6 is concerned with Commission II and the subject of the church on the mission field, paying particular attention to the theme of the 'three selves'. Chapter 7 examines Commission III, devoted to mission education, and expounds in particular the rationale for a multicultural Christian catholicity which the chairman of the Commission, Bishop Charles Gore, developed as a result of his work for the Commission. Chapter 8 discusses the Commission which has received more recent scholarly attention than all the others put together: Commission IV on 'The Missionary Message in Relation to Non-Christian Religions'; the evidence supplied by the questionnaire replies and the Commission's report is analyzed in relation to ongoing scholarly discussions today about the nature and meaning of 'religion'. Chapter 9 uncovers the complex process of Anglo-American bargaining and editing which lay behind the production of the Commission VII report on 'Missions and Governments', by which was meant primarily the relations that applied or should apply between western missions and colonial governments. Chapter 10 focuses on that aspect of the work of Commission VIII on 'Co-operation and the Promotion of Unity' which led to the establishment by the conference of a Continuation Committee, the body which led in 1921 to the formation of the International Missionary Council, one of the pioneering instruments of ecumenism in the twentieth century. Finally, Chapter 11 aims to sum up the many-sided legacy of the Edinburgh conference, not simply for the history of the ecumenical movement but also for Christian missions and the wider field of Christian discourse on questions of 'race' and culture.

CHAPTER 1

Visions of the Kingdom:
Edinburgh 1910 and the History of Christianity

Expectations of a New Age

On Tuesday, 14 June 1910, Randall Davidson, archbishop of Canterbury, addressed the opening evening session of the World Missionary Conference in the Assembly Hall of the United Free Church of Scotland on the Mound in Edinburgh. That the archbishop of Canterbury should be willing to speak to a non-denominational gathering in an assembly hall of a non-established church was noteworthy enough in those days, and attracted some critical comment. But what stuck in the minds of those who heard Davidson on this occasion was that the archbishop concluded his address with a prophecy. It was a conditional prophecy, whose fulfilment was made dependent on the willingness of the western churches to give foreign missions the central place which they deserved. If that condition were met, asserted Davidson with what might be deemed an appropriately Anglican lack of total certainty, '*it may well be that* "there be some standing here tonight who shall not taste of death till they see," — here on earth, in a way we know not now, — "the Kingdom of God come with power".[1] It was that closing sentence, recalled W. H. Temple Gairdner in the official history of the conference, coming as it did from 'a Scots statesman-ecclesiastic with a merited reputation for sobriety of thought

---

1. *History and Records of the Conference,* p. 150 [italics mine]. A slightly shorter version of Davidson's words is found in W. H. T. Gairdner, *'Edinburgh 1910': an account and interpretation of the World Missionary Conference* (Edinburgh and London, 1910), p. 43. For a second-hand report of the impact made by Davidson's address on an American Congregationalist delegate (Henry W. Stimson) see LP, Davidson papers, vol. 5, fol. 89, E. H. Pearce to Randall Davidson, 23 June 1910.

and word', with its bold appropriation of the words of Christ to the present, that 'gave the unforgettable thrill'.[2] Here was one of the most notable (and problematic) eschatological statements of Christ recorded in the gospels re-interpreted and applied to the current generation of his disciples.[3] Just as Christ had appeared to forecast the end of the present age within the lifetime of the disciples who had just witnessed his transfiguration, so here was the archbishop of Canterbury apparently predicting the dawning of a new age of gospel triumph within the lifetime of the conference participants. Qualified though it was, Davidson's prophecy appeared to give the highest ecclesiastical sanction to a sentiment which was in the hearts of the great majority of the 1,215 delegates at Edinburgh — the anticipation that, through the redoubled missionary endeavours of the non-Roman churches of the west, the world was on the eve of a new transfiguration destined to inaugurate the kingdom of God in its fullness and glory. It is possible that Davidson may have been in-spired by reading an article by the Scottish missionary, A. G. Hogg, in the conference *Monthly News Sheet* for January 1910, which similarly predicted that 'if at the coming Conference the Church even begins to know the Father as Jesus Christ knew Him, then will our Master's vision be fulfilled, and some of those who on that occasion will be standing by will "in no wise taste of death till they see the kingdom of God come with power".'[4]

Such eschatological language may strike the modern reader as absurdly hyperbolic, if not downright arrogant, in its expectations of Christian mis-sionary success, but Hogg and Davidson were not alone in their deployment of exceptional theological terminology in an attempt to capture the unique significance of an occasion which was supposedly destined to inaugurate the final phase of sacred history. Edinburgh 1910 was an event which was quite explicitly loaded with a weighty cargo of historical and theological meaning even before it took place. Many of the conference participants clearly shared the firm belief of the chairman and principal figurehead of the conference, the American Methodist layman, John R. Mott, that Christianity stood on the threshold of a global expansion of millennial dimensions. Mott, then forty-five years of age, was a uniquely powerful evangelist, especially among stu-dent audiences, who had developed an international renown through his work for the YMCA and World's Student Christian Federation. We shall see that Mott possessed an extraordinarily vivid sense, which was clearly im-printed on the text of the report of Commission I which he chaired, that the

2. Gairdner, *'Edinburgh 1910'*, p. 43.
3. Mark 9:1.
4. World Missionary Conference 1910, *Monthly News Sheet* 4 (Jan. 1910), p. 75.

churches of the western world stood at a *kairos* moment — a pivotal moment of unique opportunity — in which political, economic, and religious factors had combined providentially to open a whole series of doors for missionary advance, especially in East Asia. These doors would not stay open for long: this was 'the day of God's power', and the question was whether the Church would be willing and bold enough to seize the providential moment.[5] Such expectations were widely shared. As James Bashford, the American Methodist bishop of Peking, put it when addressing one of the evening sessions of the conference, 'not since the days of the Reformation, not indeed since Pentecost, has so great an opportunity confronted the Christian Church. Oh that out of this Conference may come the spiritual power for the evangelisation of the Orient!'[6]

An Evangelical Crusade Founded on 'the Science of Missions'

Numerous commentators on the conference also spoke of its potentially unique significance in reverential tones, and frequently affixed the adjective 'great' to their descriptions of the event.[7] Professor Michael Sadler, the Anglican educationalist and a member of Commission III on education, wrote to Archbishop Davidson immediately after his return home from Edinburgh, thanking Davidson for his crucial role in leading the Church of England to take a full part in the conference, and intimating that he had no doubt whatsoever that the event would prove to be of 'great historic importance'.[8] Even before the conference assembled, the *Missionary Herald*, organ of the Baptist Missionary Society, posed the question in its June 1910 issue, 'What is the meaning and the promise of this great gathering?' and answered:

> It means that Protestant Christendom is being summoned to a new consideration of the claims of Christ and the needs of the world. The Protestant Churches of all Christian lands are sending their representatives to join in a more thorough investigation of missionary problems than has ever yet been attempted. . . . The world has to be evangelised.

5. See *Report of Commission I*, pp. 5-49.
6. *History and Records of the Conference*, p. 246.
7. E.g. Alexander Smellie, *At the World Missionary Conference: a little narrative for friends who were not there* (Dundee: James P. Mathew & Co., 1910), p. 1; R. K. Hanna, *The World Missionary Conference: some impressions* (Belfast: R. Carswell & Son, Ltd., 1910), pp. 3, 32; *The Harvest Field* 30:9 (Sept. 1910), pp. 329, 346.
8. LP, Davidson papers, vol. 5, fol. 88, Michael Sadler to Randall Davidson, 21 June 1910.

God wills it. Blessed will they be who share the honour of carrying out this enterprise.[9]

The author of the *Missionary Herald* article was, whether consciously or unconsciously, evoking the distant memory of the medieval Crusades, and the popular cry of *Deus lo Vult* — 'God wills it' — which greeted the proclamation of the First Crusade by Pope Urban II at the Council of Clermont in 1095 and became the resounding slogan of the crusading armies thereafter. Edinburgh 1910 was conceived as a great deliberative council of the Church Protestant that would prepare its missionary armies to launch a concerted and final onslaught on the dark forces of heathendom that still ruled supreme beyond the frontiers of western Christendom. Those who responded with quiet determination by committing themselves anew to this militant and intensely serious calling could, like the crusaders of the medieval age, be sure of the eternal blessing of God on their united endeavours. Crusading language was often implicit and occasionally explicit at Edinburgh. Bishop Bashford's evening address on Saturday 18 June suggested that the burgeoning contemporary enthusiasm of students, young people, and the laity generally for world evangelization pointed to 'a crusade for world evangelisation quite as striking and far more providential than the crusade of Peter the Hermit for the recovery of the Holy Land.'[10]

Yet however vibrant the state of missionary passion among the evangelical public may have been in 1910, the intended appeal of the conference was not to the popular Christian imagination so much as to the concentrated attention of serious Christian minds. Almost from the outset, the conference was planned, as the Revd W. H. Findlay, a former Methodist missionary in India and a member of the British executive committee, put it, 'to be a Grand Council for the Advancement of Missionary Science'.[11] Foreign missions, once so widely ridiculed, had come of age, and their most thoughtful advocates believed that the time had come for the application of the rigorous methods of modern social science to the challenges and problems which missionaries faced on the field. This conviction was held with peculiar force by the conference secretary, J. H. Oldham, a thirty-four-year-old Scot who had served with the YMCA in India. Oldham was insistent that the call to urgent evangelistic action which would issue from Edinburgh must be based,

9. 'The World Missionary Conference. The great gathering at Edinburgh', *Missionary Herald* 93:6 (June 1910), p. 168.

10. *History and Records of the Conference*, p. 250.

11. W. H. Findlay, 'Sight, sound, and silence in Edinburgh', *London Quarterly Review* 114 (1910), p. 231.

not on emotional and stereotypical depictions of the plight of the 'heathen world', but on the 'ascertained and sifted facts'[12] minutely analyzed in the weighty reports of the eight preparatory study Commissions presented to the conference. Oldham's hope was that the eight Commission reports would become standard works of reference on world mission, distilling the best results of field experience and laying the foundations for the emergence of a new 'science of missions' that would inform all future practice.[13] Missions were becoming a matter of induction and experiment in which method was everything.

Edinburgh 1910 in Retrospect

If this is how the World Missionary Conference was widely viewed at the time, it is not how it has most often been remembered. At the inaugural assembly of the World Council of Churches at Amsterdam in 1948 the eighty-two-year-old John Mott took delight in tracing the origins of the World Council to the series of 'great conferences' that Edinburgh had initiated, marking the way towards the Amsterdam meeting.[14] Twelve years later, J. H. Oldham, looking back after the passage of fifty years on Edinburgh 1910, did not hesitate to interpret the event primarily in terms of its significance for subsequent ecumenical rather than missionary history. He described, for example, the decision of Charles Gore, then bishop of Birmingham, in 1908 to accept his invitation to attend the conference as 'the turning point in the history of the ecumenical movement': without that bold decision from the acknowledged leader of Anglo-Catholicism, Oldham believed that Randall Davidson would never have agreed to address the conference and the Church of England as a body would have remained aloof; in the longer term, therefore, William Temple as archbishop first of York and then of Canterbury would never have consented to take the prominent part in the ecumenical movement that he did, and, by extension, the Orthodox churches would not have had the confidence to take any part in what would have remained an unambiguously Protestant movement.[15] Such retrospective reflections, could, however, claim sound historical basis in

12. Smellie, *At the World Missionary Conference*, p. 1.

13. World Missionary Conference 1910, *Monthly News Sheet* 1 (Oct. 1909), p. 4; 8 (May 1910), p. 163.

14. W. A. Visser 't Hooft (ed.), *The First Assembly of the World Council of Churches Held at Amsterdam August 22nd to September 4th, 1948* (London: SCM Press, 1949), p. 22.

15. J. H. Oldham, 'Reflections on Edinburgh, 1910', *Religion and Life* 29:3 (Summer 1960), p. 333.

aspirations that were quite widely voiced in the planning of the conference that its ultimate consequences would extend even to the mutual relations of Christian churches. The first issue of the conference *Monthly News Sheet,* published in October 1909, was not afraid to note that 'another aspect of the Conference which strongly appeals to many is its possible influence in the promotion of Christian unity'. Whilst the conference could make 'no direct contribution' to the question of ecclesiastical reunion, the consideration in common by Christians of 'the great fact of the non-Christian world' and its need of salvation could prove to be a preparatory work that would pave the way for a subsequent process of church reunion.[16] As will be emphasized in Chapter 10, the formation of the Continuation Committee was not some unanticipated by-product of the conference but a response to memoranda prepared on both sides of the Atlantic before the conference assembled and to a specific recommendation from Commission VIII on 'Co-operation and the Promotion of Unity'. The re-interpretation of Edinburgh 1910 as an event whose significance transcended the foreign mission field began in the minds of some delegates at the conference itself.

The two most prominent personalities at Edinburgh 1910 understandably recalled the conference from the perspective of the major ecumenical initiatives to which it gave rise and in which they were both so intimately involved. Their long-term memories gave less prominence to the exalted ambitions and confident mood of missionary expansion which were in fact more central to the conference than the pursuit of any form of structural ecumenism, but which faded so rapidly after the First World War. The tendency to place the Edinburgh conference on the map of ecumenical history to the neglect of the history of missions is reinforced by the reference that is frequently made to the number of student leaders from the Student Christian Movement or its sister movements in the World's Student Christian Federation who were appointed to attend the conference as stewards or ushers and later achieved national or international prominence as theologians and church leaders: these included John Baillie (professor of divinity in the University of Edinburgh, 1934-56), John McLeod Campbell (principal of Trinity College, Kandy, 1924-35), Otto Dibelius (theologian of the Confessing Church and later president of the Evangelical Church in Germany), Kenneth Kirk (bishop of Oxford, 1937-54), T. W. Manson (Rylands professor of biblical criticism, University of Manchester, 1936-58), Walter Hamilton Moberly (vice-chancellor of the University of Manchester, 1926-34), Neville S. Talbot (bishop of Pretoria, 1920-33), H. G. Wood (professor of theology at the University of Birming-

16. World Missionary Conference 1910, *Monthly News Sheet* 1 (Oct. 1909), p. 5.

ham, 1940-6), and, most notable of all, William Temple.[17] W. Richey Hogg, for example, speculated that Temple's enthronement sermon at Canterbury in 1942, with its famous reference to the 'great world-fellowship' of Christians as constituting 'the great new fact of our era' may have had its roots in his youthful experience at Edinburgh. The speculation is not unreasonable, for Temple was referring to the global spread of Christianity and not simply to the recent ecumenical conversations which had led to the World Council of Churches in Process of Formation.[18] What is rarely emphasized, however, is the equivalent impact that participation in the Edinburgh conference must have had on the far larger numbers of serving missionaries who participated in the conference either as official delegates or as ticket-holders in the gallery reserved for missionaries on furlough. For many of them, Edinburgh 1910 must have been a transforming experience, enabling them to place their own geographically isolated and denominationally limited work in a broader and exciting context.

Edinburgh 1910 and the History of Ecumenism

In popular understanding, the re-interpretation of Edinburgh 1910 goes further still. Undergraduate essays and examination answers on the history of the modern movement for unity among Christian churches almost invariably begin their narrative with the World Missionary Conference. Much of the literature designed for students and general readers reinforces the debatable assumption that the ecumenical movement actually began at Edinburgh in 1910, ignoring the fact that the Edinburgh conference stands in a sequence of interdenominational and increasingly international missionary conferences that can be traced back as far as 1854. The chapter on the ecumenical movement in Alec Vidler's volume in the *Pelican History of the Church* notes at the outset that 'it is generally agreed that the movement, as it

17. R. Rouse and S. C. Neill (eds.), *A History of the Ecumenical Movement 1517-1948* (London: SPCK, 1954), p. 360; W. Richey Hogg, 'Edinburgh, 1910 — ecumenical keystone', *Religion and Life* 29:3 (Summer 1960), pp. 345-6. For a list of suggested stewards, see UBL, SCM archives, box A21, W. M. Cargin to members of SCM sub-committee, 15 March 1910. Also on this list was William Paton, secretary of the International Missionary Council, 1927-43, who was unable to attend the conference: see Margaret Sinclair, *William Paton* (London: SCM Press, 1949), p. 24.

18. Hogg, 'Edinburgh, 1910 — ecumenical keystone', p. 345; F. A. Iremonger, *William Temple Archbishop of Canterbury: his life and letters* (London: Oxford University Press, 1948), pp. 387, 391-2.

is now known, dates from the International Missionary Conference [*sic*] that was held at Edinburgh in 1910'.[19] John Kent's acerbic chapter on 'Ecumenism, the light that failed' in his *The Unacceptable Face: the modern church in the eyes of the historian* refers in its second sentence to 1910 as the year 'when the search for institutional unity was first systematically organized', which is a considerable misrepresentation of what the Edinburgh Continuation Committee was set up to do.[20] Among recently published treatments of modern Christian history, Jeremy Morris's *The Church in the Modern Age* stands out by virtue of its discussion of the Edinburgh conference on its own terms as a conference dedicated to 'the evangelization of the world in this generation', the slogan that had come to sum up the passion of a generation of Christian university students for world evangelism.[21] B. G. Worrall's *The Making of the Modern Church* similarly begins its chapter on the ecumenical movement with an account of Edinburgh 1910, though properly situating that account in the context of the developing history of co-operation in mission and evangelism by evangelical Protestants over the preceding century.[22] Most scholarly accounts give at least some such recognition to the fact that the 1910 conference was the culmination of a long tradition of pan-evangelical ecumenism deriving from the eighteenth-century evangelical revivals, and given more recent institutional embodiment internationally by the World's Student Christian Federation, formed in 1895, and its close partner, the Student Volunteer Movement for Foreign Missions.[23] The British arm of that movement, the Student Volunteer Missionary Union, gave rise to the Student Christian Movement (SCM) in the course of the 1890s. Tissington Tatlow, general secretary of the SCM, makes very clear in his history of the Movement how deeply indebted the Edinburgh conference was to the interdenominational principle embodied in the SCM which permitted practical Christian co-operation on the basis of respect for varying denominational theological convictions. Tatlow cites William Temple's verdict that 'Members of the Movement ought to know that without their movement

19. A. R. Vidler, *The Church in an Age of Revolution: 1789 to the present day* (Harmondsworth: Penguin, 1961), p. 257.

20. John Kent, *The Unacceptable Face: the modern church in the eyes of the historian* (London: SCM Press, 1987), p. 203.

21. Jeremy Morris, *The Church in the Modern Age* (London and New York: I. B. Tauris, 2007), pp. xviii-xx.

22. B. G. Worrall, *The Making of the Modern Church: Christianity in England since 1800* (London: SPCK, 1998), pp. 203-7.

23. E.g. Adrian Hastings, *A History of English Christianity 1920-2000*, 4th edn. (London: SCM Press, 2001), p. 87.

there never could have been held the Edinburgh Conference, which was the greatest event in the life of the Church for a generation.'[24]

Several authors, following a connection first made by Ruth Rouse in 1949, pay homage to the ecumenical antecedents of Edinburgh 1910 by making the wholly fortuitous connection with William Carey's chimerical proposal of 1806 that 'a general association of all denominations of Christians' should meet every ten years or so at the Cape of Good Hope, commencing in 1810, a notion famously dismissed by his Baptist colleague Andrew Fuller as 'one of bro^r Carey's pleasing dreams'.[25] By making such a connection with Carey's abortive proposal, these accounts encourage the false supposition that the Edinburgh conference was indeed 'a general association of all denominations of Christians'. One recent academic study of twentieth-century ecumenism even goes so far in a loose moment as to describe the conference as 'the first modern assembly of world-wide churches', which it emphatically was not.[26] To a possibly greater extent than any other event in modern Christian history, the conference suffers from the distortions of hindsight. Because the institutions of modern Protestant ecumenism, culminating in the formation of the World Council of Churches in 1948, can trace their descent so clearly from 1910, the temptation is irresistible to interpret the conference in the light of what followed, while paying inadequate attention to its origins in the Protestant missionary movement.

The World Missionary Conference was in fact more seriously limited in its scope than either its formal title or the ascription 'ecumenical' implies. It hardly needs to be said that the conference was representative of only one, albeit broad, segment of the world Christian community. It was a decidedly Protestant and broadly evangelical gathering, the principal exceptions being those amongst the thirty-five members of the High Church Society for the Propagation of the Gospel (SPG) who would have regarded themselves as

24. Tissington Tatlow, *The Story of the Student Christian Movement of Britain and Ireland* (London: SCM Press, 1928), pp. 404-11 (quotation at pp. 410-11).

25. R. Rouse, 'William Carey's "pleasing dream"', *IRM* 38:150 (April 1949), pp. 181-92; Norman Goodall, *The Ecumenical Movement,* 2nd edn. (London: Oxford University Press, 1964), pp. 4-5, 8; K. S. Latourette, 'Ecumenical bearings of the missionary movement and the International Missionary Council', in Rouse and Neill (eds.), *A History of the Ecumenical Movement 1517-1948,* p. 355; Hugh Martin, *Beginning at Edinburgh: a jubilee assessment of the World Missionary Conference 1910* (London: Edinburgh House Press, 1960), pp. 3-4; Ernest A. Payne, *The Growth of the World Church* (London: Edinburgh House Press and Macmillan, 1955), pp. 140-1.

26. John F. Woolverton, *Robert H. Gardiner and the Reunification of Worldwide Christianity in the Progressive Era* (Columbia and London: University of Missouri Press, 2005), p. 113.

Anglo-Catholic rather than Protestant,[27] and their supporters on the episcopal bench — principally Charles Gore of Birmingham and Edward S. Talbot of Southwark — who attended as special guests of the British executive committee. There were also some other notable individual Anglo-Catholics, such as Father H. H. Kelly of the Society of the Sacred Mission at Kelham, Father Walter H. Frere of the Community of the Resurrection at Mirfield, and the Revd Duncan Travers, secretary of the strongly Anglo-Catholic Universities' Mission to Central Africa, who attended the conference purely in a private capacity. It is noteworthy that all three of these Anglo-Catholic leaders were appointed to influential roles as members of Commissions: Kelly served on Commission V; Frere on Commission VIII; while Travers was appointed to Commission II.[28] The Anglo-Catholic participants were intensely conscious of their marginal status and theological isolation in the conference, so much so that Bishop H. H. Montgomery, the secretary of the SPG and former bishop of Tasmania, when commencing his contribution to the debate on the Commission VIII report on Co-operation and Unity, referred to himself with gentle self-mockery as belonging to 'a little band of lions in an enormous den of Daniels', pleaded with the Daniels to listen patiently to the roaring of this particular High Church lion, and promised to 'roar lovingly'.[29]

As will be emphasized in Chapter 3, the moving spirits behind the Edinburgh conference were well aware that the gathering could not claim to be 'ecumenical' in the primary sense that the word now carries (and which was coming into popular usage at the time), and for that very reason agreed in July 1908 to drop the word 'ecumenical' from the original title of the conference. One of the members of the British executive committee, C. E. Wilson, foreign secretary of the Baptist Missionary Society, freely acknowledged in his denominational newspaper that the forthcoming conference would be an assembly of Evangelical Christendom, and not an Ecumenical Council of the Church, 'because the great Romanist and Greek Churches will not be represented; and it is not summoned for the consideration of ecclesiastical polity or doctrine', for such questions were by explicit agreement excluded from the

---

27. The SPG, under pressure from many supporters opposed to the conference, initially declined to send any official delegates, but agreed to permit individual members of its committee and staff to attend if they chose. Later, in April 1910, to Bishop Montgomery's delight, the SPG standing committee finally agreed that the Society could be officially represented at Edinburgh.

28. However, Travers was prevented through illness from attending any meetings of the Commission: *Report of Commission II*, p. viii.

29. *Report of Commission VIII*, p. 213; John H. Ritson, *The World is Our Parish* (London: Hodder & Stoughton, 1939), pp. 279-80.

agenda.[30] Other commentators of Catholic sympathies were less polite in the conclusions they drew from the absence of any representation from Roman Catholic and Eastern Christendom. 'The title "World" is clap-trap', observed one Scottish Episcopalian correspondent to the *Church Times*, and he was a moderate who supported the participation of Anglo-Catholics in the conference.[31] Extreme Anglo-Catholics who opposed the conference as an expression of the wicked principle of undenominationalism were still more dismissive: 'The fact is', fulminated the Revd Bernard Moultrie from Christ Church, St Leonard's-on-Sea, 'the Conference is a gathering of Christian sects, whose very raison d'être is their bitter hatred to the Catholic Faith as taught by the Church.'[32]

The only contribution from a Roman Catholic source was a remarkable message of greeting from the seventy-nine-year-old Bishop Geremia Bonomelli of Cremona, sent at the invitation of Silas McBee, a lay American Episcopalian with an unusually clear vision for ecumenism and a member of the American executive committee, who had been introduced to the bishop in April 1910. McBee had a long-standing interest in tracking what R. E. Speer referred to as 'the liberal movement' in Italian Catholicism.[33] Chapter 10 will suggest that McBee, the editor of *The Churchman* newspaper, was one of a minority of those involved in the organization of the conference who viewed the event from the beginning as potentially significant not just for the evangelization of the non-western world but also for the unity of the churches in western Christendom. McBee regarded Bonomelli as 'one of the great evangelical preachers of the world, indeed as 'one of the greatest bishops of the world'. He read a translation of Bonomelli's lengthy letter of greeting in full to the conference in the afternoon session of 21 June, which was devoted to the discussion of the report of Commission VIII on 'Co-operation and the Promotion of Unity', of which McBee was vice-chairman.[34] Charles H. Brent, the American Episcopal bishop of the Philippines, whose attendance at Edinburgh led him to espouse McBee's expansive vision of the great ecumenical potential of the event, wrote presciently in his reflections on the conference that Bonomelli's letter was 'the little cloud not larger than a man's hand to-day, destined tomorrow to cover the Roman heavens'; for Brent it was a sign that 'the true greatness, that is to say the Ca-

---

30. *The Baptist Times and Freeman*, 3 June 1910, p. 362.

31. *Church Times*, 17 June 1910, p. 800.

32. *Church Times*, 19 May 1910, p. 667.

33. Princeton Theological Seminary, Special Collections, Robert E. Speer personal letters, box 4, vol. 9, fol. 451, R. E. Speer to Silas McBee, 5 April 1907.

34. *Report of Commission VIII*, pp. 220-3.

tholicism' of the Roman Catholic Church, was 'busy at her heart', and that 'the secondary power of the Roman Curia' could do no more than delay its eventual triumph.[35] It is worth noticing that the elderly Bishop Bonomelli was a friend of a young priest, Angelo Roncalli, later to become Pope John XXIII, the architect of the Second Vatican Council, and that in June 1908 Bonomelli specifically suggested to Roncalli that the time might be ripe for the summons of 'a great ecumenical council'.[36] Brent would surely have hailed the Second Vatican Council of 1962-5 as the eventual triumph of true Catholicism in the Roman Church which he had predicted. Brent himself was deeply affected by the experience of the conference. He later testified that at Edinburgh he 'was converted. I learned that something was working that was not of man in that conference; that the Spirit of God . . . was preparing a new era in the history of Christianity.'[37]

A Representative Conference?

Neither was the conference truly ecumenical in the sense of being geographically representative of the composition of the world church in 1910, for the simple reason that delegates represented not churches or denominations but Protestant and Anglican foreign missionary societies, and societies were allocated places strictly on the basis of their annual income (in fact, solely on that proportion of their income which was devoted to missionary work among peoples who could unambiguously be denominated as non-Christian). Hence the big battalions of the Anglo-American missionary movement, most of them denominational missions, dominated the field. Thus, of the 1,215 official delegates, 509 were British, 491 were North American, 169 originated from continental Europe, 27 came from the white colonies of South Africa and Australasia, and only 19 were from the non-western or 'majority' world (18 of them from Asia).[38] It has often been said (by this author as well as others)

35. C. H. Brent, 'The World Missionary Conference — an interpretation', *The East and the West* (Oct. 1910), p. 363.

36. J. M. Delaney, M.M., 'From Cremona to Edinburgh: Bishop Bonomelli and the World Missionary Conference of 1910', *Ecumenical Review* 52:3 (July 2000), pp. 418-31 (quotation at p. 420).

37. W. Richey Hogg, *Ecumenical Foundations: a history of the International Missionary Council and its nineteenth-century background* (New York: Harper & Bros. 1952), p. 134.

38. These figures are compiled from the list of delegates in *History and Records of the Conference*, pp. 39-71; the *Conference Daily Paper* printed names of some late withdrawals and additions, which are mostly, but not in every case, reflected in the list published in

that at Edinburgh there was not a single Christian born and bred in Africa, despite frequent reports to the contrary in the Christian press. In fact there was one such indigenous black African Christian — Mark C. Hayford from Ghana — even though his name does not appear in the main lists of official delegates. Chapter 5 will discuss at greater length the presence of Hayford and the eighteen Asian delegates. With this one exception, however, the voice of African Christianity was not heard at Edinburgh. The inhabitants of the African continent were widely regarded even by Christians as primitive, childlike, and at the bottom of the evolutionary hierarchy. They occupied a very marginal place in the visions of the future kingdom of God which so entranced the architects of the conference.

Neither was there anyone present at Edinburgh from the Christian communities of the Pacific islands or the Caribbean, nor was there any representative of the substantial North American missionary presence in Latin America, or from the tribal peoples of Southeast Asia, some of whom already had significant and rapidly growing Christian communities. As will be explained in Chapter 3, the Pacific islands of Polynesia and Micronesia, the continent of Latin America, and the Caribbean were all substantially excluded from the terms of reference of the conference on the grounds that they were, like Europe or North America, deemed to be part of the territorial entity known as Christendom, and hence beyond the horizons of Christian mission. That was part of the deal struck by the organisers of the conference with the leaders of the Anglo-Catholic wing of the Church of England, in order to encourage their participation, an important novel feature of this conference: there would have been no Anglo-Catholic attendance at all if the conference had been permitted to discuss Protestant missions to Roman Catholic territory. Anything that looked like evangelical proselytism of Catholic or Orthodox adherents was necessarily off limits. The issue of religious proselytism that is now so hotly and widely debated first surfaced in international Christian argument in 1909-10.

Christianity on the Cusp of Transfiguration

The fact that the forthcoming centenary of the World Missionary Conference in 2010 will be marked by a variety of commemorations by different interna-

---

History and Records of the Conference. Figures will vary slightly depending on how one counts a few missionaries from one region or continent who served under a mission whose home base was in another region or continent.

tional Christian bodies would not have occasioned great surprise among its delegates and principal architects. They were almost indecently conscious of taking part in an unprecedented event that promised to re-shape the course of Christian history. In Oldham's case, this consciousness took the form of a quiet but deep confidence that 'God has a great purpose for this Conference', a confidence that sustained Oldham through the many moments when he was tempted to despair that the plans for the conference would never overcome the 'hopeless confusion' in which they so often appeared to be embroiled.[39] A more flamboyant self-consciousness of the epochal significance of the event can be attributed to the infectious rhetoric of John Mott, with his insistence that this was 'a decisive hour for Christian missions'.[40] The imprint of Mott's eschatological optimism was clear throughout the text of the first and most important of the Commission reports, on 'Carrying the Gospel to all the Non-Christian World', which was presented to the conference at its first morning session on 15 June. 'Never before', proclaimed Mott in the opening paragraph of the Commission I report, 'has there been such a conjunction of crises and of opening of doors in all parts of the world as that which characterises the present decade'.[41] Appeal was made to what might now be termed 'globalisation' as evidence for the feasibility of attaining the goal of world evangelisation: the rapid expansion of railway networks was affording missionaries ready access to millions of people; and the fact that 'the vast majority' of non-Christian peoples were now under the sway either of 'Christian' (that is, western colonial) governments or of governments not antagonistic to Christian missions was identified as of peculiarly hopeful significance.[42] More disconcerting still to our ears is the confident assertion that 'The money power in the hands of believing Christians of our generation is enormous'.[43]

In country after country the report discerned signs that the world stood at the fulcrum of major religious change. China, after thousands of years of 'self-centredness and self-satisfaction', was turning her face from the past and beginning 'to go to school to the world'. Nevertheless, the report recognised that in China, as also in Korea, Japan, Turkey, and Persia, the question was whether the Church would be able to channel the strengthening currents of political, educational, and religious reform in the direction of Christianity: '. . . if the tide is not set toward Christianity during the next decade

39. NCE, Oldham papers, box I, folder 4, Oldham to Silas McBee, 13 Oct. 1909; also in UTS, MRL 12: WMC papers, series 1, box 23, folder 15.
40. *Report of Commission I*, p. 363.
41. *Report of Commission I*, p. 1.
42. *Report of Commission I*, pp. 5-6.
43. *Report of Commission I*, p. 10.

both in the Far East and the Near East, it may be turned against us in the decade following'[44] — a warning that proved to be extraordinarily accurate, as missions in China and Japan found their promise of national self-strengthening and modernization through the medium of Christianity upstaged by other ideologies that appeared to offer the same benefits at reduced cost to national identity. India also, insisted Mott, stood at the parting of the religious ways, but here the Commission I report contrived to interpret the ambiguous signs of the times in a more consistently optimistic light. The educated were turning to various forms of 'neo-Hinduism' through such movements as the Arya and Brahmo Samaj, which, for all their outward antagonism to Christianity, should be seen as 'preparing the way of the Lord'. Even the revival in certain parts of India of 'orthodox Hinduism' was viewed less as a threat than as a reaction to Christian advance and hence as a desirable development which 'will in the end hasten the progress of Christianity, as was the case in the Roman Empire'.[45] The outcastes and depressed castes were more responsive than ever before to Christianity, but equally to Islam, which had gained six million converts in the ten years preceding the last Indian census: Christians and Muslims were engaged in a race for the soul of the outcaste.[46] The Muslim world as a whole constituted both opportunity and threat: Islam was thought to be losing its grip on the educated and disintegrating philosophically into new sects and parties; yet its aggressive expansion among the uneducated posed the greatest of all challenges to Christian missions, above all in sub-Saharan Africa. 'If things continue as they are now tending', warned the report, 'Africa may become a Mohammedan continent'. Missionary enterprise in Africa was likely to become ever more difficult in the face of the southward Islamic advance. 'Paganism' was 'doomed' to crumble away before 'higher and more dogmatic' religions. As with the tribals and outcastes in India, the only question was, whether Christianity or Islam should prevail.[47]

The premise of Mott's argument was, however, not the inevitability but the realistic possibility and indeed the urgent necessity of imminent Christian triumph. As Davidson's address equally implied, everything depended on the willingness and ability of the Church to grasp the providential moment. Non-Christian nations were in an unusually 'plastic' condition, ready to be

44. *Report of Commission I*, pp. 25-30 (quotation from p. 29).
45. *Report of Commission I*, pp. 12, 16-18. The revival of Buddhism in Japan, Burma, and Ceylon, unlike the Hindu revival, was not given an optimistic gloss, but presented simply as a call for more effective Christian effort (pp. 14-15).
46. *Report of Commission I*, pp. 8, 18-19.
47. *Report of Commission I*, pp. 12-13, 18-21.

moulded by any religion or ideology that seized the chance. The door for Christian missions was open, but it might not be so for long.[48]

John Mott's conviction that the Edinburgh conference had the potential to divert the flow of Christian history into new channels appears to have been widely shared among delegates. The Boston *Missionary Herald*, for example, reported the hyperbolic judgment of one participant that this was 'the most important ecclesiastical assembly since Nicaea'.[49] It may be suggested, however, that many of those who attended the Edinburgh conference would be surprised if they were permitted to observe just how far-reaching were the long-term consequences for the mutual relations of Christian churches of a conference predicated on the total exclusion from the agenda of all questions of faith and order. Still more would undoubtedly be astonished at the radically different contours which world Christianity has assumed over the course of the century which followed 1910. The face of the world church has indeed been transfigured within the last 100 years, but not according to the pattern which was so generally predicted at Edinburgh, which presumed that the great civilizations of Asia stood on the brink of progressive transformation by a specifically Christian movement of reform and modernisation led by educated elites.

Edinburgh 1910 thus spoke with two intermingled voices. The voice most audible in the public sessions of the conference was one of boundless optimism and unsullied confidence in the ideological and financial power of western Christendom. That voice, of course, was soon to be rendered hollow and ultimately silent by the First World War and its aftermath. This book will, however, draw attention to the presence at Edinburgh of a more muted and discerning voice, heard periodically throughout the text of the Commission reports, and deriving from the more astute serving missionaries whose questionnaire replies formed the raw material for the reports. This voice spoke of crisis and opportunity, of challenge and competition, and occasionally even of threat and danger.

We are all by now well aware that the centre of gravity of world Christianity has shifted decisively from north to south and from west to east. The Christian religion has become radically de-centred, with disparate geographical foci and multiple cultural incarnations. Conversely, the tides of Christian faith have ebbed markedly in the regions that were the heartland of Christianity in 1910 and which supplied the majority of the delegates at the Edinburgh conference — Europe and the eastern seaboard of North America. In

48. *Report of Commission I*, pp. 25, 27, 49.
49. *Missionary Herald* (Boston, MA) 106 (Aug. 1910), p. 354.

some measure at least, Archbishop Davidson's prophecy of the transfiguration of Christianity has been fulfilled. Christianity is no longer primarily a religion of the western world or of the northern hemisphere. The chapters which follow tell a salutary story. The Edinburgh conference was a superbly organised and high-minded attempt to present and analyze scientifically what appeared to the best western Christian minds of the day to be the observable 'facts' of missionary expansion and policy. As an appeal to Protestant Christians to subordinate their denominational and national differences to a prayerfully and thoughtfully conceived renewed commitment to the task of world mission it was remarkably successful. Yet it managed to combine its moments of profound and bold insight with some fundamental mis-readings of the signs of the future of Christianity. The measure of missionary success enjoyed by Christianity in the century that followed arguably owed rather little to the priorities set and the objectives enunciated at Edinburgh. The Christian faith was indeed to be transfigured over the next century, but not in the way or through the mechanisms that they imagined. The most effective instrument of that transfiguration would not be western mission agencies or institutions of any kind, but rather a great and sometimes unorthodox miscellany of indigenous pastors, prophets, catechists, and evangelists, men and women who had little or no access to the metropolitan mission headquarters and the wealth of dollars and pounds which kept the missionary society machinery turning; they professed instead to rely on the simple transforming power of the Spirit and the Word.

CHAPTER 2

Origins and Preparations

The 'Third Ecumenical Missionary Conference'

What history remembers as the World Missionary Conference of 1910 was originally planned as, and formally entitled 'The Third Ecumenical Missionary Conference'. It followed two now virtually forgotten international Protestant missionary conferences held in London in 1888 and New York in 1900.[1] The 'Centenary Missionary Conference' in London in 1888 (which rather loosely commemorated the beginnings of foreign missions from the Anglo-American world in the late 1780s) took obvious Protestant pleasure on least two occasions in describing itself as an 'oecumenical council' in what were surely calculated allusions to the use of that title by the First Vatican Council of 1869-70: the chairman of one of its sessions, Sir S. Arthur Blackwood, proudly claimed that this was 'an Oecumenical Council in the truest sense of the word' because its participants were 'those engaged either in directing or carrying on Missionary enterprise throughout the world'; and the published conference volume noted in similarly hyperbolic vein that representatives hailed from an area 'little short of the habitable globe, making the Council in the highest sense oecumenical'.[2] The word 'ecumenical' was then incorporated in the official title of the New York conference in 1900, 'not be-

1. On Edinburgh's two predecessors see the two articles by Thomas A. Askew, 'The 1888 London Centenary Missions Conference: ecumenical disappointment or American missions coming of age?', *IBMR* 18:3 (July 1994), pp. 113-18; and 'The New York 1900 Ecumenical Missionary Conference: a centennial reflection', *IBMR* 24:4 (Oct. 2000), pp. 144-54.

2. James Johnston (ed.), *Report of the Centenary Conference on the Protestant Missions of the World*, 2 vols. (London: James Nisbet, 1888), I, pp. 467, xliii.

cause all portions of the Christian Church are to be represented in it by delegates', as the New England Episcopalian, William Huntington, put it when addressing the assembly, but 'because the plan of campaign which it proposes covers the whole area of the inhabited globe'.[3] 'Ecumenical' still implied global geographical reach, and not necessarily comprehensiveness of Christian affiliation or theological perspective.

The idea of holding a third such 'ecumenical conference' was mooted as early as 1905 in the Foreign Missions Conference of North America, which raised the possibility of holding such conferences on a decennial basis, commencing in 1910. The secretary of the Foreign Missions Conference, W. H. Grant, a New York Presbyterian layman, accordingly wrote on 16 September 1905 to W. B. Sloan of the China Inland Mission, inquiring 'whether it is proposed to hold an Ecumenical Missionary Conference in London on the lines of the one held in New York in 1900.'[4] Sloan, whom Grant appears to have regarded as in some way representative of the English missionary secretaries, referred the letter to the London Secretaries' Association, an informal body founded in 1819 which brought the executive secretaries of all the main English missionary societies into regular conversation. The members of the Association had some doubts whether a conference on the model of New York 1900 'would yield permanent results commensurate with the cost in money and time'[5] and appointed a sub-committee to consider Grant's letter. This concluded that 'it would not be advisable to arrange for such a Conference in London in 1910, but that probably the year 1915 would be convenient for the gathering.' At its meeting on 15 November 1905 the Association accordingly instructed its secretary, John H. Ritson (1868-1953), a Methodist minister and senior secretary of the British and Foreign Bible Society, to communicate its preference for a 1915 date to Mr Grant.[6]

It seems likely that Grant had sent a similar letter to that written to Sloan to the Scottish mission boards.[7] However, the origins of the Edinburgh conference lie more specifically in two letters written in 1906-7 from

3. *Ecumenical Missionary Conference New York, 1900*, 2 vols. (London and New York: Religious Tract Society and American Tract Society, 1900), I, p. 10.

4. CUL, BSA/F4, microfilm minutes of London Secretaries' Association, 1893-1924, minutes of 18 Oct. 1905; John H. Ritson, *The World is Our Parish* (London: Hodder & Stoughton, 1939), p. 276. Ritson incorrectly dates the approach from New York to 1907, whereas Grant's letter was written on 16 Sept. 1905.

5. Ritson, *The World is Our Parish*, p. 276.

6. CUL, BSA/F4, microfilm minutes of London Secretaries' Association, 1893-1924, minutes of 15 Nov. 1905.

7. See Ritson, *The World is Our Parish*, p. 276.

the Revd J. Fairley Daly, honorary secretary of the Livingstonia Mission Committee of the United Free Church of Scotland, to Robert E. Speer, secretary of the Presbyterian Board of Foreign Missions in New York. Daly's first letter, written early in January 1906, was principally concerned with another matter, but asked incidentally whether the American mission boards had any plans or views regarding a sequel to the New York conference (which Daly had attended). Speer referred this letter to the annual meeting of the Foreign Missions Conference, held in Nashville on 27-28 February 1906. It appears that the Conference instructed Speer to reply to Daly that it would heartily welcome the holding of a missionary conference in Great Britain in 1910. However, the meeting also referred 'all questions relating to another Ecumenical Conference on Foreign Missions' to its regular Committee of Arrangements for 1907, under the chairmanship of Dr Charles R. Watson.[8] At the request of the Committee of Arrangements, Grant then opened correspondence with various American mission leaders, informing them that the English missionary secretaries had begun consideration of the possibility of holding an international missionary conference in Britain in 1915, but seeking their views on the *additional* possibility of holding such a conference in America in 1910. The replies to Grant's inquiry revealed a considerable variety of opinion, but a new situation was created when Speer received Daly's second letter, written in response to Speer's earlier letter of reply.[9]

Daly's second letter informed Speer that following the receipt of Speer's communication, he had convened a group of Scottish representatives of seven or more missionary agencies in Glasgow in November 1906 to discuss whether the projected sequel to the New York conference, 'the Third Ecumenical Missionary Conference', might be held in Scotland, and, if so, where, and at what date. Although the meeting declined to express a formal opinion on the question, the individuals present were all in favour of the idea, and also

8. Foreign Missions Conference of North America, *Thirteenth Conference of the Foreign Missions Boards in the United States and Canada, February 27 and 28, 1906* (New York: Foreign Missions Library, n.d. [1906]), p. 5.

9. Foreign Missions Conference of North America, *Fourteenth Conference of the Foreign Missions Boards in the United States and Canada, January 9 and 10, 1907* (New York: Foreign Missions Library, n.d. [1907]), pp. 101-3. This source prints in large part the second of Daly's letters to Speer, which are not preserved in his letter-book as secretary of the Livingstonia Committee for 1909-34 in the National Library of Scotland. See John F. Piper, Jr., *Robert E. Speer: prophet of the American church* (Louisville: Geneva Press, 2000), pp. 201-2; also Andrew F. Walls, *The Cross-Cultural Process in Christian History: studies in the transmission and appropriation of faith* (New York and Edinburgh: Orbis Books and T&T Clark, 2002), pp. 53-4.

of the broader principle of holding such conferences alternately in Europe and America on a decennial basis. The Glasgow meeting agreed to invite the various Scottish mission boards to send three delegates each to an official meeting in Edinburgh on 29 January 1907 to consider the matter further.[10] At the next annual meeting of the Foreign Missions Conference of North America, in January 1907, it was unanimously agreed to endorse Daly's proposal that the third ecumenical conference should meet in 1910 in Scotland, provided that the Scottish mission leaders secured the agreement of their German counterparts (the leaders of the German *Ausschuss* had suggested that the third ecumenical missionary conference might in fact take place in Germany, but the idea was dropped owing principally to anticipated difficulties of language).[11] The meeting also set up a committee of reference and counsel under the chairmanship of the Presbyterian missionary statesman, Arthur Brown, with responsibility to promote international co-operation on missionary questions, and in particular to conduct correspondence, co-operate with the British, and perform any necessary preparatory work in North America relating to the proposed ecumenical conference.[12] From the outset John R. Mott (who was not originally a member of this committee) was determined that this should be a conference with a difference, 'a thorough unhurried conference of the leaders of the Boards of North America and Europe', and not another 'great popular convention' of the kind held in 1888 or 1900.[13]

The meeting of delegates of Scottish mission boards took place in Edinburgh on 29 January 1907, when thirty-seven delegates representing twenty mission agencies were present. At this meeting a letter was read indicating the support of the Foreign Missions Conference of North America for the idea of

10. Foreign Missions Conference of North America, *Fourteenth Conference of the Foreign Missions Boards in the United States and Canada, January 9 and 10, 1907* (New York: Foreign Missions Library, n.d. [1907]), p. 103; ECG, Third Ecumenical Missionary Conference (June 1910), minutes of general committee, 12 June 1907, pp. 3-4; Piper, *Robert E. Speer*, pp. 201-2.

11. Foreign Missions Conference of North America, *Fourteenth Conference of the Foreign Missions Boards in the United States and Canada, January 9 and 10, 1907* (New York: Foreign Missions Library, n.d. [1907]), pp. 104, 106; see World Missionary Conference 1910, *Monthly News Sheet* 5 (Feb. 1910), p. 96. On the *Ausschuss* see Chapter 10 below, p.281.

12. C. H. Hopkins, *John R. Mott 1865-1955: a biography* (Grand Rapids: Eerdmans, 1979), p. 343; ECG, Third Ecumenical Missionary Conference (June 1910), minutes of general committee, 10 Oct. 1907, pp. 13-14; UTS, MRL 12, WMC papers, series 1, box 24, folder 12, Report of the Executive Committee for the United States and Canada . . . presented to the Conference of Foreign Mission Boards, New York, January 14, 1909, p. 3.

13. Hopkins, *John R. Mott*, p. 343.

holding the next conference in Scotland.[14] In the light of this letter, the Scottish representatives at their meeting on 29 January 1907 accordingly agreed formally to invite the 'Third Ecumenical Missionary Conference' to meet in Edinburgh in the Assembly Hall of the United Free Church of Scotland in June 1910. A list of sixty-three British and Irish foreign missionary societies was drawn up, which were to be asked by printed circular letter to nominate delegates to attend a meeting to constitute a general committee to issue invitations and plan the conference.[15] When copies of this circular letter reached the secretaries of the English societies in March, there was some surprise, even consternation, in the words of the minutes of the London Secretaries' Association, that the matter had 'advanced so far without any preliminary communication with this Association, or, so far as was known, with any leading Foreign Missionary Societies in London.' The acting secretary of the Association was asked to make enquiries and to refer to the 1905 correspondence with Grant expressing preference for a 1915 date.[16] By their April meeting, however, the English society secretaries had calmed down sufficiently to regard the idea of holding the conference in 1910 as 'an open question' until the promised delegates' meeting.[17]

The 'general committee' met for the first time on 12 June 1907 in Edinburgh. Thirty-four delegates from Scottish and English missions attended under the chairmanship of Sir Archibald Campbell of Succoth, owner of the Garscube landed estate near Glasgow and a well-known lawyer, philanthropist, and evangelist.[18] Although most of the major English societies were represented, their representatives were mostly their Scottish agents; no senior secretary of a London-based society was present. The meeting reconsidered the date for the conference, settled on 'the latter half of 1910', established procedures for the appointment of an executive committee, and appointed two Scotsmen as conference secretaries — the Revd James Buchanan, of the

14. ECG, Third Ecumenical Missionary Conference (June 1910), minutes of general committee, 12 June 1907, p. 4; UTS, MRL 12, WMC papers, series 1, box 24, folder 12, Report of the Executive Committee for the United States and Canada . . . presented to the Conference of Foreign Mission Boards, January 14, 1909, p. 2.

15. ECG, Third Ecumenical Missionary Conference (June 1910), minutes of general committee, 12 June 1907, pp. 4-5.

16. CUL, BSA/F4, microfilm minutes of London Secretaries' Association, 1893-1924, minutes of 20 March 1907.

17. CUL, BSA/F4, microfilm minutes of London Secretaries' Association, 1893-1924, minutes of 17 April 1907.

18. On Campbell see http://www.theglasgowstory.com/image.php?inum=TGSA05160 and http://www.nahste.ac.uk/cgi-bin/view_isad.pl?id=GB-0248-DC-080&view=basic (accessed 18.12.07).

United Free Church of Scotland Foreign Mission, and the Revd Andrew Wann of the Church of Scotland Foreign Mission.[19] The planning of a conference which, like its predecessor in New York, was to be designated as 'ecumenical' in the sense that it purported to include the whole human race in its scope, had been assumed by a select band of senior Scottish churchmen.

J. H. Oldham and George Robson Make Their Presence Felt

The general committee met for a second time on 10 October 1907 in Edinburgh. It appointed an executive committee and various special committees: a finance committee, publication and press committee, programme committee, and women's committee. In every case Scots or those resident in Scotland were in the majority: by 17 to 12 in the case of the executive committee.[20] Most of those present were venerable gentlemen in their seventies or even eighties. But one of those in attendance, and a member of the 17-strong Scottish contingent on the executive committee, was celebrating his thirty-third birthday that very day. His name was Joseph Houldsworth Oldham. 'Joe' Oldham had spent the first seven years of his life in India and had returned to India in 1897 as a missionary of the YMCA. After only three and a half years of student work in Lahore, he had been forced to return to Scotland by ill health. Following theological studies at New College, Edinburgh, and then in Halle under the father of German missiology, Gustav Warneck, Oldham had been appointed secretary of the newly-formed Mission Study Council of the United Free Church of Scotland, a body established to promote mission education in the United Free Church. It was in this representative capacity that he found himself elected to the general committee charged with planning the Edinburgh conference, 'though very junior in age to all my colleagues'.[21] The chairman of the Council and the person responsible for Oldham's nomination to the executive committee was the Revd Dr George Robson, editor of the United Free Church's *Missionary Record* and the translator into English of Warneck's *History of Protestant Missions* (1901); the Council's office was at Windsor Buildings, 100 Princes Street, Edinburgh. Robson, the Princes Street office, and above all Oldham himself, were each to play their part in the history of the World Missionary Conference.

19. ECG, Third Ecumenical Missionary Conference (June 1910), minutes of general committee, 12 June 1907, pp. 1-6.

20. ECG, Third Ecumenical Missionary Conference (June 1910), minutes of general committee, 10 Oct. 1907, pp. 8-9.

21. J. H. Oldham, 'Reflections on Edinburgh, 1910', *Religion and Life* 29:3 (Summer 1960), p. 329.

Oldham, who had been intimately involved in the frenetically evangelical ecumenism of the Student Christian Movement and the World's Student Christian Federation, recalls that he was dismayed at finding the preparations for a supposedly international conference lodged in the hands of what was in practice almost exclusively a Scottish committee, 'consisting largely of fossils'. He therefore got Robson to move a motion, which he himself seconded, that future meetings of the general committee should be held in York to give Londoners a better chance of attending (the railway journey from London to Edinburgh at that time routinely took a forbidding eight and a half hours). The motion was overwhelmingly defeated, but Robson encouraged Oldham by saying that 'we have not seen the end of this yet', and Oldham responded by proposing that they consult John Mott about the plans for the Edinburgh conference at the forthcoming quadrennial convention of the Student Volunteer Movement, due to take place in Liverpool in January 1908.[22] The October meeting did, however, take one decision that in time was to prove highly significant in loosening the grip that Scottish ecclesiastics had established on the early stages of the conference planning: all members of the general, executive, and special committees resident in England were constituted as an English local committee, and John H. Ritson as secretary of the London Secretaries' Association was appointed as its convener.[23] Ritson, whose role in the Association gave him unrivalled access to the secretaries of all the London-based missionary societies, accepted his commission with enthusiasm on 5 November. An Oxford graduate with a first-class degree in chemistry and a former tutor at Didsbury College in Manchester, he was to play a role in preparing the ground for the Edinburgh conference that was eclipsed only by Oldham and Mott. He had been one of the two secretaries of the Bible Society since 1 January 1900, and was also a

22. NCE, Oldham papers, box 10, folder 9, Oldham to Bliss, 11 Sept. 1962; Oldham, 'Reflections on Edinburgh, 1910', pp. 329-30; Keith Clements, *Faith on the Frontier: a life of J. H. Oldham* (Edinburgh and Geneva: T&T Clark and WCC Publications, 1999), p. 75. Oldham gave two mutually contradictory accounts of this meeting. In his 1960 'Reflections' he wrote that the motion was put at the 'next meeting' after his election, i.e. at the general committee on 13 Feb. 1908, and that it was defeated by about 40 votes to 2. In his 1962 letter he dates the meeting as taking place in 1907, and gives the voting figures as 46 (though he is not certain about that figure) to 2. There is no record of this motion in the minutes of either meeting, and the attendance was only 34 persons on 10 Oct. 1907 and 25 persons on 13 Feb. 1908. Since Oldham suggested to Robson that they should raise the matter with Mott at the forthcoming Liverpool convention, the 10 Oct. 1907 date must be the correct one.

23. ECG, Third Ecumenical Missionary Conference (June 1910), minutes of general committee, 10 Oct. 1907, p. 13.

committee member of the WMMS, the Christian Literature Society for China, and the China Emergency Committee.[24]

Robson and Oldham duly spoke with Mott at the Liverpool Student Volunteer Movement conference in January 1908. Mott speedily grasped their point that it was inappropriate for an international conference not to be planned on an international basis, and promised to act. As it happened, the Foreign Missions Conference of North America was due to meet for its annual meeting in New York immediately after Mott returned from Liverpool. There is second-hand evidence that Robson and Oldham submitted to Mott a draft of the letter they should like to see sent from the Foreign Missions Conference to the Scottish committee.[25] The Conference responded to Mott's intervention, resolving that 'in view of the magnitude of the task of arranging for a large convention', the committee of reference and counsel set up a year earlier be relieved of its responsibility for liaison with the Scottish committee. A specially designated committee was now created for this purpose: its membership was much the same as that of the committee of reference and counsel, but with the crucial additions of Mott himself and the Presbyterian missionary leader, Robert E. Speer.[26] This expanded committee (which was to evolve into the American executive committee of the World Missionary Conference) duly produced a letter to James Buchanan in Edinburgh, issued under the signatures of Arthur J. Brown and Mott. The opinions advocated in the letter were clearly those of Mott, but they were almost certainly Robson's and Oldham's as well: the forthcoming conference was not to be 'devoted primarily to educational and inspirational purposes, as was perhaps necessarily and wisely the case with the London and New York Ecumenical Conferences'; rather the emphasis was to be on 'study and consultation by the leaders of the foreign missionary forces of the world concerning the large and most vital questions of missionary opportunity and policy'. Prayer, education, and inspiration would

24. ECG, Third Ecumenical Missionary Conference (June 1910), minutes of executive committee, 12 Dec. 1907, p. 5. On Ritson see his autobiography, *The World is Our Parish*; James Moulton Roe, *A History of the British and Foreign Bible Society 1905-1954* (London: British & Foreign Bible Society, 1965), pp. 32-7; and CUL, BSA F4/3/1, fols. 99-100, Ritson to Oldham, 28 Sept 1909.

25. Clements, *Faith on the Frontier*, p. 76, citing NCE, Oldham papers, box 22, folder 2, unpublished manuscript by Kathleen Bliss on J. H. Oldham, pp. 57-8. Oldham's memory was at fault in writing in 1955 that Mott promised to 'call a meeting' of the American mission boards on his return from Liverpool: J. H. Oldham, 'John R. Mott', *Ecumenical Review* 7:3 (April 1955), p. 257.

26. *Foreign Missions Conference of North America, Fifteenth Conference of the Foreign Missions Boards in Canada and in the United States at New York January 29th and 30th 1908* (New York: Foreign Missions Library, n.d. [1908]), pp. 8, 68-9.

have their rightful place, for Brown and Mott commended the practice followed at the Liverpool conference of devoting twenty minutes each day to united intercession, and suggested that the evening sessions should be devoted to 'inspirational addresses' by 'the greatest missionary speakers in the English language'. But the bulk of the conference — the morning and at least some of the afternoon sessions — was to be taken up with thorough discussion of reports produced well in advance by a series of study Commissions. The document made some illustrative suggestions for the topics that the Commissions might address, but was more directive in suggesting a mode of procedure for setting up the Commissions, recommending that *'within a few months'* a 'Consolidated Committee' of twelve of 'the wisest and most experienced missionary thinkers and workers' be assembled in Britain, six from Britain and three each from North America and continental Europe, to determine the number, subject-matter, and appoint the membership of the Commissions.[27]

Deciding on the Model for Edinburgh 1910

When the executive committee met in Edinburgh on 13 February 1908, it had before it two documents: the letter from the Foreign Missions Conference of North America and the report of a sub-committee appointed by the executive committee at its previous meeting on 12 December 1907, which took the form of a memorandum suggesting guidelines for the constitution and procedure of the conference. The members of the sub-committee were: W. H. Findlay (convener), secretary of the Wesleyan Methodist Missionary Society, J. Fairley Daly, secretary of the United Free Church's Livingstonia Committee, Duncan M'Laren (joint chairman of the executive committee, and a leading figure on the United Free Church's Foreign Mission Board), George Robson, and R. Wardlaw Thompson, foreign secretary of the London Missionary Society. The two ostensibly independent documents were in agreement on the essential point, a convergence that is less surprising if it is indeed the case that the hands of Robson and Oldham lay behind the American letter: they were both emphatic that the 1910 conference was not to be an inspirational jamboree for mission enthusiasts, but a serious business gathering of appointed experts. The American letter and the British memorandum both identified two possible models for a missionary conference: the New York 1900 model of an open

27. UTS, MRL 12, WMC papers, series 1, box 8, folder 20, item 540, Arthur J. Brown and John R. Mott to James Buchanan, 31 Jan. 1908; reprinted in ECG, Third Ecumenical Missionary Conference (June 1910), report from North American committee, 31 Jan. 1908.

'demonstrational conference', designed to impress and enthuse the Christian public; and the model of a 'consultative conference' of authorised delegates, as exemplified by the fourth Indian Decennial Missionary Conference held in Madras in 1902 and the Shanghai Missionary Conference of 1907. Both submissions were unambiguous in recommending that the second of these two models be followed. As the American letter expressed it, the 1910 conference was to 'translate into terms of the entire non-Christian world the plan recently carried out with such marked success and helpfulness in connection with the Shanghai Conference'.[28]

The Madras conference (itself following a pattern pioneered on a smaller scale by the regional South India Missionary Conference in 1900) had proceeded by allocating all delegates to eight subject committees, each with its own convener, who was charged to gather information and opinions well in advance from his apportioned delegates and more widely. Each committee then drafted a series of resolutions, usually preceded by preliminary remarks, for discussion and adoption by the conference in session.[29] Five years later, the much larger Shanghai conference adhered to a modified version of the same pattern, drawing a clear distinction between the members of the preparatory committees and the rest of the delegates: twelve programme committees were established in advance, but in this instance with a limited membership of ten to thirteen persons; the chairman of each programme committee was responsible for preparing a paper in consultation with his committee, which was to be printed in advance of the conference, and for introducing the paper and its accompanying resolutions to the conference. Four members of the North American committee (James L. Barton, Walter R. Lambuth, Alexander Sutherland, and W. H. Grant) and two of the British sub-committee (Duncan M'Laren and Ralph Wardlaw Thompson) had been present at Shanghai in 1907 and could thus testify first-hand to the success of this mode of operation.[30] It may also be significant that W. H.

28. ECG, Third Ecumenical Missionary Conference (June 1910), Memorandum suggesting Constitution and Procedure of Conference (report of sub-committee appointed by executive committee, 12 December 1907); Third Ecumenical Missionary Conference (June 1910), Report from North American committee, 31 Jan. 1908; also in UTS, MRL 12, WMC papers, series 1, box 8, folder 20, item 540, Arthur J. Brown and John R. Mott to James Buchanan, 31 Jan. 1908.

29. *Report of the Fourth Decennial Indian Missionary Conference Held in Madras December 11th-18th, 1902* (London and Madras: Christian Literature Society, n.d. [1903?]), pp. xx-xxvii and *passim*. George Robson had in his personal library a copy of this report, which is now in the library of the Henry Martyn Centre, Cambridge.

30. *Records: China Centenary Missionary Conference Held at Shanghai, April 25 to May 8, 1907* (Shanghai: Centenary Conference Committee, 1907), pp. 784, 791, 795, 798, 804, 805.

Findlay had been present at the South Indian Missionary Conference in 1900, where he gave the closing address.[31]

The executive committee endorsed the main recommendations of the two documents submitted to it. It accordingly resolved to recommend to the general committee that 'the approaching Conference shall be organised as a Consultative Conference of duly appointed delegates, with which, however, public meetings will be associated.' It further recommended that the number of delegates should not exceed 1,100 (up to 100 of whom could be individually invited by the executive), that the basis of representation should be the home income of the missionary societies, and crucially endorsed the North American proposal that an international ('consolidated') committee should meet in Britain 'within the next few months'; the composition of the committee was, however, altered to ten members from Britain, five from North America, and three from Europe.[32] The general committee, meeting immediately after the executive committee, approved all these recommendations. The decision was thus taken to use two recent conferences of working missionaries in Asia — Madras 1902, and, more immediately, Shanghai 1907 — as the template for Edinburgh 1910. The World Missionary Conference, which is so often credited with instigating ecumenical formation in Asia, was in fact deeply indebted from the outset to ecumenical missionary precedents from India and China for its mode of proceeding. In marked contrast to the two preceding missionary conferences held in the western world, the third 'ecumenical missionary conference' was to proceed on the basis of discussing detailed reports prepared in advance by appointed study commissions, and its principal sessions were not to be open to the public.

Broadening the Base of Planning

The decisions taken at the meetings on 13 February 1908 decisively altered the tenor of plans for the Edinburgh conference in the direction that Robson and Oldham desired. Although Oldham in retrospect gave the credit to Mott's intervention,[33] it would not have been unreasonable for Oldham and Robson to claim that it was their priming of Mott at Liverpool which had

31. W. Richey Hogg, *Ecumenical Foundations: a history of the International Missionary Council and its nineteenth-century background* (New York: Harper & Bros., 1952), p. 107.

32. ECG, Third Ecumenical Missionary Conference (June 1910), minutes of executive committee, 13 Feb. 1908, pp. 9-10. The ceiling of 1,100 delegates was presumably dictated in part by the capacity of the Assembly Hall of the United Free Church of Scotland.

33. Oldham, 'Reflections on Edinburgh, 1910', p. 330.

been crucial. The two Scotsmen made further progress in broadening the international basis of the conference at the next meeting of the executive committee on 12 March, which took place, significantly, in York — perhaps a belated response to their defeated motion in the general committee.[34] For the first time, equal numbers of Scots and English were in attendance (six of each). The committee agreed to allocate the ten British places in the forthcoming international committee meeting (to take place in mid-July) in the ratio of six to four in favour of the English, thus leaving the Scots with only four representatives out of a total of eighteen. It was also resolved to give special consideration to representatives of the Student Volunteer Movement in the allocation of the executive's 100 nominated delegates; it may not be coincidental that Tissington Tatlow, general secretary of the Student Christian Movement, had been added to the executive at its previous meeting.[35] Oldham's father-in-law, Sir Andrew Fraser, the lieutenant-governor of Bengal, was appointed as one of the three vice-presidents of the conference in place of Lord Overtoun, for long the bank-roller of the Livingstonia Mission, who had died in February.[36] Perhaps most important of all, the committee accepted the report of a sub-committee on the basis of representation, drawn up by Oldham and E. A. Wareham, the long-serving district agent for Scotland and Ireland of the LMS. The report, which clearly expressed Oldham's personal convictions, contained two clauses which were to prove determinative for the scope of the conference:

> Societies and Boards administering funds and sending out missionaries for the propagation of the Gospel among non-Christian peoples, and possessing an annual income of £2000 and over, shall be entitled to representation.
>
> In the case of Societies, part of whose work is carried on in professedly Christian countries, only that portion of the income shall be taken into account which is estimated to be expended on work among non-Christians.[37]

34. This paragraph is based on ECG, Third Ecumenical Missionary Conference (June 1910), minutes of executive committee, 12 March 1908, pp. 12-15.

35. ECG, Third Ecumenical Missionary Conference (June 1910), minutes of executive committee, 13 Feb. 1908, p. 10.

36. The other two vice-presidents were Sir John Kennaway of the CMS and Lord Reay, formerly governor of Bombay and under-secretary of state for India.

37. ECG, Third Ecumenical Missionary Conference (June 1910), minutes of executive committee, 12 March 1908, pp. 14-15.

In the wake of the York meeting, the locus of planning for the 1910 conference shifted perceptibly. Edinburgh was still the seat of the conference secretaries, but now they had to communicate regularly with London. Goaded by Ritson, the London Secretaries' Association, which had studiously ignored the subject of the conference between April 1907 and February 1908, sparked back into life and took steps to appoint the permitted number of English representatives on the forthcoming international committee: six heavyweights were elected at a meeting held at Bible House on 30 March: Ritson himself, R. W. Thompson of the LMS, W. H. Findlay of the WMMS, Prebendary H. E. Fox of the CMS, C. E. Wilson of the BMS, and Tissington Tatlow.[38] Ritson began to correspond regularly with Buchanan in Edinburgh. Progress was still far from smooth. A meeting of Scottish and English representatives was planned in York on 10 April to prepare for the international committee, but poor communications between Edinburgh and London meant that only Thompson and Fox turned up from the English side, and the meeting accomplished little.[39] Ritson offered his own society headquarters, Bible House in London, as the venue for the international committee, but then had to withdraw the offer because the date clashed with a projected visit to the House from delegates to the forthcoming Lambeth Conference.[40] Undaunted, Ritson kept up the pressure. He was keenly aware, as he wrote to more than one correspondent, that 'our friends in America are throwing themselves into the Conference preparations with extraordinary enthusiasm', and urged Buchanan that 'we must not be behind them, but must strive all in our power to make things a success on this side'.[41]

With Bible House no longer a possibility as the main venue for the international committee, a meeting on 8 May in Baslow, Derbyshire (then the site of the SCM summer conference), attended by five of the six English members of the Committee, took the decision to look for a suitable location in Oxford rather than London.[42] Through the good offices of Prebendary Fox, W. H.

---

38. CUL, BSA/F4, microfilm minutes of London Secretaries' Association, 1893-1924, minutes of 19 Feb. and 18 March 1908; and BSA/F4/3/1, fols. 1-2, John H. Ritson to James Buchanan and W. H. Findlay, 30 March 1908.

39. CUL, BSA/F4/3/1, fol. 14, Ritson to J. R. Hill, 13 April 1908; and fol. 20, Ritson to C. E. Wilson, 29 April 1908.

40. CUL, BSA/F4/3/1, fol. 19, Ritson to Buchanan, 28 April 1908.

41. CUL, BSA/F4/3/1, fols. 16-17, Ritson to R. W. Thompson and James Buchanan, 25 April 1908; UBL, SCM archives, A21, Ritson to Tissington Tatlow, 25 April 1908. R. W. Thompson was absent.

42. CUL, BSA/F4/3/1, fol. 21, Ritson to Duncan M'Laren, 4 May 1908; UBL, SCM archives, A21, Tissington Tatlow to J. H. Oldham, 18 May 1908, pp. 6-7.

Griffith Thomas, the principal of Wycliffe Hall, an evangelical Anglican theological college, offered his premises for the purpose, and a booking was made for 14 to 18 July (though the meeting would in fact continue on Monday 20th at Bible House in London).[43] Ritson set about making the necessary arrangements. His correspondence shows him worrying about how to accommodate the wives of the overseas visitors given the nature of theological college premises,[44] and over whether or not to charge overseas members the six shillings per head per day for their board and lodging: in the event, the Americans had their expenses met from conference funds, whilst the three continental representatives (Julius Richter, Karl Fries, and F. Frohnmeyer) had to pay for themselves:[45] a distinction that betrays certain assumptions about the marginality of continental Europe to the whole process. Ritson became more concerned still when Wardlaw Thompson, the most senior of the British missionary society secretaries, indicated that he could not be present for the whole occasion: 'I am very anxious', responded Ritson, 'that our American friends should not unduly predominate, and we cannot well spare our strongest representative for England. Give us, therefore, all the time you possibly can': 'I am not afraid of the Conference being captured by the Scotch', Ritson confessed to Thompson; 'I fear our American friends more than them'.[46] The juxtaposition between Scottish and English influence that had appeared so sharp in the initial stages of planning now appeared of secondary importance. From now on, the tussle between British and American perspectives on church and mission was to be the primary axis on which debate and policy would turn.

Ritson's final problem arose when news came on 8 July that James Buchanan was seriously ill and unable to take part.[47] This unfortunate development proved pivotal for the course of the ecumenical movement. The other conference secretary, Andrew Wann, had already laid down his office in order to take up a post as principal of the newly united Scottish Churches' College in Calcutta. George Robson had originally nominated Oldham as one of the four allotted Scottish representatives, but he had lost his place to another more senior delegate.[48] With just two days to go before the Oxford meeting

43. CUL, BSA/F4/3/1, fols. 27 and 31, Ritson to Buchanan, 22 May and 1 June 1908.

44. CUL, BSA/F4/3/1, fols. 32, 45, 50, Ritson to Buchanan, 3 and 29 June 1908; Ritson to W. H. Griffith Thomas, 1 July 1908.

45. CUL, BSA/F4/3/1, fols. 55 and 60, Ritson to W. H. Findlay and F. Frohnmeyer, 8 July 1908.

46. CUL, BSA/F4/3/1, fols. 47 and 57, Ritson to Thompson, 29 June and 8 July 1908.

47. CUL, BSA/F4/3/1, fols. 55 and 64, Ritson to Findlay, 8 July 1908; Ritson to W. Valentine, 11 July 1908.

48. Oldham in NCE, Oldham papers, box 10, folder 9, Oldham to Kathleen Bliss, 11

began, Oldham was drafted in as an emergency measure to serve as secretary of the meeting in Buchanan's place. Joe Oldham thus took his place as one of the nineteen members of the international committee who assembled at Wycliffe Hall on 14 July: there were in all five North Americans (including one Canadian), five Scots, six English, and three from continental Europe.[49] Duncan M'Laren as joint chairman of the executive committee was elected chairman. Oldham's memory in old age deceived him into thinking that at the Oxford meeting John Mott had been unanimously elected as chairman of the committee.[50] In fact Mott was given no official leadership status in the conference itself until as late as January 1910:[51] his dominance of the sessions when the conference assembled, coupled with his undoubted unofficial leadership at Oxford, mis-led Oldham into recollecting that he had chaired the crucial planning meeting. Nevertheless, under M'Laren's chairmanship, the Oxford international committee made important advances in four main areas of conference planning.

Shaping the Eight Commissions

The first and most onerous task of the Oxford meeting was to determine the number, subject matter, personnel, and constitution of the Commissions which both the American and the British documents presented to the February 1908 executive committee had commended as the most efficient way to organise the conference. Following submissions from Mott and Robson, detailed deliberation in a sub-committee, and 'prolonged discussion' over two full days,[52] eight Commissions were eventually appointed on the following topics:

Sept. 1962, cited in Clements, *Faith on the Frontier,* p. 77, says that this was Dugald Mackichan, but he is not listed as present in the minutes of the international committee: the rival candidate may have been W. H. Rankine of the Church of Scotland.

49. The nineteen were: James L. Barton (Boston), John R. Mott (New York), Silas McBee (New York), Norman Tucker (Toronto), Arthur Brown (New York), W. H. Rankine (Glasgow), George Robson (Edinburgh), J. Fairley Daly (Glasgow), Duncan M'Laren (Edinburgh), F. Frohnmeyer (Basel), J. Richter (Schwanebeck, Belzig, Germany), Karl Fries (Stockholm), R. Wardlaw Thompson, W. H. Findlay, J. H. Ritson, H. E. Fox, T. Tatlow, C. E. Wilson (all London), and J. H. Oldham (Edinburgh).

50. ECG, Third Ecumenical Missionary Conference (June 1910), minutes of international committee, 14-20 July 1908, p. 2. For Oldham's inaccurate recollection see NCE, Oldham papers, box 10, folder 9, Oldham to Kathleen Bliss, 11 Sept. 1962.

51. ECG, World Missionary Conference (1910), minutes of executive committee, 1 April 1910, p. 71, approval of minutes of international committee held on 29 Jan. 1910.

52. World Missionary Conference 1910, *Monthly News Sheet* 6 (March 1910), p. 119.

I. Carrying the Gospel to all the World
II. The Native Church and its Workers
III. Education in relation to the Christianisation of National Life
IV. The Missionary Message in Relation to Non-Christian Religions
V. The Preparation of Missionaries
VI. The Home Base of Missions
VII. Relation of Missions to Governments
VIII. Co-operation and the Promotion of Unity[53]

An initial list of chairmen and members to be invited to serve on each Commission (160 names in all) was agreed — a task that occupied more than another day of the committee's attention.[54] Mott was appointed chairman of Commission I. There were major divergences of view to overcome. The nomination of Anglican members of the Commissions was entrusted to a subcommittee comprising H. E. Fox, the strongly evangelical honorary clerical secretary of the CMS, and Tissington Tatlow of the SCM. Fox presented a list drawn exclusively from the evangelical wing of the Church of England; Tatlow's list, on the other hand, was designed to be comprehensive of the whole church and included some of the most notable figures from the Anglo-Catholic party: Bishop Gore of Birmingham, Bishop Talbot of Southwark, Father H. H. Kelly, Father Walter H. Frere, Professor Michael Sadler, Mrs Louise Creighton, and the dean of Westminster, J. Armitage Robinson. Fox and Tatlow contended 'for a long time' in one of the bedrooms at Wycliffe Hall before Tatlow in the end got his way; Fox declined to be involved in proposing the names to the full meeting of the committee.[55] This was a defining victory for Tatlow and Oldham, both of whom were determined that the Edinburgh conference should encompass a broader range of theological opinion than its predecessors. Almost all of these Anglo-Catholic names on Tatlow's list were to play seminal roles in the Commissions, and some, as we shall see in the next chapter, were to shape the terms of reference of the conference itself.

It was also necessary for the Oxford meeting to arbitrate between widely differing ideas of the mode of operation of the Commissions that had been in circulation before the meeting. At Baslow on 8 May, W. H. Findlay had sought to persuade his English colleagues to adopt a version of the Madras 1902 pat-

53. ECG, Third Ecumenical Missionary Conference (June 1910), minutes of international committee, 14-20 July 1908, pp. 3-5.
54. *Ibid.*, p. 8; World Missionary Conference 1910, *Monthly News Sheet* 6 (March 1910), p. 119.
55. Tissington Tatlow, *The Story of the Student Christian Movement of Great Britain and Ireland* (London: SCM Press, 1933), p. 407.

tern, whereby all conference delegates would be allocated to a Commission: he wanted ten Commissions with 100 members each. Tatlow had strongly opposed this scheme as hopelessly impractical, and argued instead for the Shanghai pattern of small Commissions of no more than twenty members each, that should meet as soon as possible and continue to do so on a periodic basis over the two years before the conference itself.[56] At Oxford Tatlow, Ritson, James L. Barton of the ABCFM and F. Frohnmeyer of the Basel Mission were appointed as a sub-committee charged with recommending the constitution and procedures of the Commissions, and it was Tatlow's ideas as presented at Baslow and supported by Ritson which triumphed. The Commissions were to be working bodies, comprising between ten and twenty members, 'not necessarily limited to residents in Europe and America'. Each Commission was to have a chairman and vice-chairman, who were to be from 'different countries'; in practice this would be generally interpreted as meaning from Britain and the USA, or vice-versa, though Commissions I and VI had more than one vice-chairman.[57] The Commissions were to elicit information on a detailed list of topics on which questions were to be addressed to existing organisations in the various mission fields, and to a 'list of natives and missionaries' who would serve as corresponding members. The chairman of each Commission was given responsibility for producing a draft report with specific 'findings' by the end of December 1909, so that final copies of the reports could be available for sale by 1 May 1910.[58] This objective imposed an extremely tight timetable on the operation of the Commissions: Oldham issued instructions that any reports of sub-committees should be in the hands of Commission chairmen by 30 September 1909; and that a draft report should be in hands of the vice-chairman by early January 1910 in order that it could be considered by his advisory council on the other side of the Atlantic during January-February 1910; this in turn meant that replies from the mission field should be asked for by 30 June 1909 if possible.[59]

56. UBL, SCM archives, A21, T. Tatlow to J. H. Oldham, 18 May 1908.

57. Commission I had two vice-chairmen: George Robson and Julius Richter. Commission VI had three vice-chairmen: Friedrich Würz, *Missionsinspektor* of the Basel Mission, Sir George Macalpine, chairman of the Baptist Missionary Society, and the Rev. J. P. Maud, vicar of St Mary Redcliffe, Bristol, who were entrusted with responsibility for, respectively, the continental European, Nonconformist, and Anglican sections of the Commission.

58. ECG, Third Ecumenical Missionary Conference (June 1910), minutes of international committee, 14-20 July 1908, pp. 5-6, 9.

59. UTS, MRL 12, WMC papers, series 1, box 17, folder 1, microfilm copy of Hartford Theological Seminary archives of Commission V, circular letter from J. H. Oldham to chairmen and vice-chairmen of Commissions, 28 Dec. 1908.

The Central Advisory Committee and Its Secretary

The second principal achievement of the Oxford meeting was to create an administrative structure that would facilitate efficient day-to-day planning. A small central advisory committee, made up entirely of six British members (M'Laren, Robson, and Oldham from Scotland; Fox, Thompson, and Findlay from the 'English local committee'), was therefore established. The committee was entrusted with co-ordinating the work of the Commissions: it was to oversee the process of appointment of their members, fill vacancies that might arise to the chairmanship and vice-chairmanship of Commissions, check the drafting of the questionnaires for points of omission or overlap, and receive and comment on the drafts of the Commission reports. Such an extensive brief required more than a nominal executive officer. Mott in particular was insistent that nothing less than a full-time salaried officer would do if his vision of a serious study conference were to be realised, and called Oldham to his room to persuade him that he was the only possible candidate for the job. As the letter from Duncan M'Laren as chairman to the SCM seeking approval for Oldham's appointment put it,

> It is essential to this purpose that there should be at the centre one man, at least, who, acting as Secretary of the Executive Board, should be able to give direction and impulse, as well as unity to the preparatory work. He must be a man, who by spiritual experience and power, by natural capacity and by organising gifts, will command the cordial respect, not only of his own countrymen, but of those associated with him from other lands.[60]

The meeting agreed to appoint Joe Oldham to the salaried post of secretary to the new central advisory committee of the conference, plus acting secretary (during Buchanan's illness) to the executive and general committees,

---

60. UBL, SCM archives, A21, M'Laren to Tatlow, n.d. [c. 20 July 1908]. For Mott's persuasion of Oldham at Oxford see NCE, Oldham papers, box 10, folder 9, Oldham to Kathleen Bliss, 11 Sept. 1962; see also Clements, *Faith on the Frontier*, p. 78; Hopkins, *John R. Mott*, p. 345. Since Easter 1908 one-third of Oldham's time was contracted to the SCM/SVMU, with the other two-thirds remaining at the disposal of the United Free Church of Scotland. A letter was also sent to the Church seeking Oldham's release. In response to M'Laren's letter, the SVMU asked that it should continue to have Oldham's services for six weeks a year, and this was agreed to: UBL, SCM archives, A21, unsigned letter to the secretary, Ecumenical Missionary Conference, 22 Sept., 1908. ECG, World Missionary Conference (1910), minutes of executive committee, 23 Sept. 1908, p. 19.

for the period of two years until the conference took place.[61] Of all the decisions made at Oxford, this was perhaps the most prescient, and one which had no precedent in the history of previous missionary conferences. In the event, Buchanan proved to be a dying man, and resigned his post as conference secretary on 11 September, so that Oldham became full secretary of the executive and general committees as well.[62] The American executive committee, reporting the appointment to the Foreign Missions Conference of North America in January 1909, enthusiastically described Oldham as 'a man of ability, consecration and knowledge of missions. We believe him to be admirably qualified for this responsible post, and he has begun this work in a way which amply justifies the expectations of his friends.'[63]

Changing the Title of the Conference

The third and extremely significant decision taken at Oxford was to recommend the abandonment of the original title of 'The Third Ecumenical Missionary Conference' and substitution of the new title of 'World Missionary Conference, 1910'. The recommendation to drop the term was on the basis of 'the fact that the word "Ecumenical" has acquired a technical meaning, and has been found in some instances to lead to misunderstanding'.[64] By 1908 the term was acquiring something like its modern meaning, and open-minded Protestants were becoming more cautious than they had been in 1900 in claiming the title for their own assemblies. As John H. Ritson explained in a letter to Harry Smith, the treasurer of the Edinburgh conference, those present at Oxford in July 1908 had felt compelled to drop the term 'ecumenical' 'as it cannot be used truthfully while great sections of the Church are in no way connected with the Conference'.[65] What might appear today as the more pretentious 'global' title was in fact adopted out of appropriate Christian modesty. The recommended change of name was confirmed when the executive

61. ECG, Third Ecumenical Missionary Conference (June 1910), minutes of international committee, 14-20 July 1908, p. 8.
62. ECG, World Missionary Conference (1910), minutes of executive committee, 23 Sept. 1908, p. 18. Buchanan died on 24 Sept. 1908.
63. UTS, MRL 12, WMC papers, series 1, box 24, folder 12, Report of the Executive Committee for the United States and Canada . . . presented to the Conference of Foreign Mission Boards, New York, January 14, 1909, p. 12.
64. ECG, Third Ecumenical Missionary Conference (June 1910), minutes of international committee, 14-20 July 1908, p. 9.
65. CUL, BSA/F4/3/1, fol. 69, Ritson to Harry Smith, 24 July 1908.

and general committees of the conference met in Edinburgh on 23 September 1908.[66] From this point on, the notepaper and printed minutes issued by the preparatory committees and their officials bore the heading 'World Missionary Conference (1910)'.

The Inclusion of National Christians
and the Exclusion of Faith and Order

A fourth concern of the Oxford meeting, though much less prominent on the agenda, was the nature of the representation and the conduct of the conference itself. The basis of representation at Edinburgh had already been decided at the executive committee meetings in February and March, but it should be noted that the Oxford minutes contain for the first time reference to the desirability of missionary societies including in their delegations 'if practicable, one or two natives from mission lands.'[67] This statement was almost certainly a result of Mott's personal intervention, and there is evidence that at least in the early stages of planning this injunction was taken very seriously. Robert E. Speer, who was made chair of the American sub-committee on the appointment of delegates, informed officials of the various American mission boards in October 1908 that 'it is hoped that the larger organizations will not fail to include among their representatives strong native leaders, as well as some of their ablest missionaries', and that financial assistance would be 'absolutely necessary' to make their attendance possible.[68] Efforts were also made to persuade missionary societies to include leading national Christians in their list of suggested names to serve as corresponding members of the Commissions.[69] The executive committee for the United States and Canada continued into 1909 to express the hope that the missionary delegates would be 'accompanied by native Christians from the various missions so that the Conference will be something of an interdenominational Congress of the nations of the world in the name of the one God, the one Gospel, and the one cause'.[70] How-

66. ECG, World Missionary Conference (1910), minutes of executive committee, 23 Sept. 1908, p. 18, and minutes of general committee, 23 Sept. 1908, p. 21.

67. ECG, Third Ecumenical Missionary Conference (June 1910), minutes of international committee, 14-20 July 1908, p. 9.

68. UTS, MRL 12, WMC papers, series 1, box 10, folder 16, R. E. Speer to H. P. Andersen, 21 Oct. 1908.

69. UTS, MRL 12, WMC papers, series 1, box 8, folder 20, circular letter from W. Henry Grant to North American mission boards, 10 Nov. 1908.

70. UTS, MRL 12, WMC papers, series 1, box 24, folder 1, item 427, Second General An-

ever, as will be emphasized in Chapter 5, the hope of inclusion of national Christians in the conference was to be only imperfectly realized. Initial consideration was also given at Oxford to the provision of space in the galleries of the Assembly Hall for missionaries and members of mission boards who were not official delegates.[71]

At this stage, it was envisaged that the conference, like its predecessors in Madras and Shanghai, would pass resolutions, but it was minuted at Oxford that 'no resolution shall be allowed which involves questions of doctrine or Church polity with regard to which the Churches or Societies taking part in the Conference differ among themselves.'[72] The potentially divisive issues of doctrine and church order were declared to be off limits when it came to the process of making formal public resolutions, but they were not originally excluded, it should be noted, either from being the subject of attention by the Commissions or from discussion in the conference itself. Within a few months, however, Oldham had received a letter from Bishop Charles Gore of Birmingham, the leader of Anglo-Catholic opinion, pointedly asking whether the Oxford minute was intended to apply also to the recommendations of the Commissions, and in particular whether the work of Commission VIII on Co-operation and Unity was likely to lead to any infringement of the principle. Oldham sought the advice of the central advisory committee and replied on 5 October that 'it is the opinion of the Central Advisory Committee that the principle referred to applies to any recommendations made by the Commissions in their Reports' and that therefore it would be 'entirely outside the scope of the work' of Commission VIII 'to make any recommendations or express any opinion regarding any possible basis or terms of ecclesiastical union between different Churches'.[73] When Oldham sent a copy of this letter to the American executive committee, with a printed set of Instructions to Commissions which included a sentence added by the central advisory committee extending the principle of exclusion to the Commission reports, the Americans registered a decided objection.[74] Silas McBee, the leading American

nouncement World Missionary Conference, issued by the North American Committee on Leaflets and Preliminary Announcements, n.d. [early 1909].

71. ECG, Third Ecumenical Missionary Conference (June 1910), minutes of international committee, 14-20 July 1908, p. 10.

72. ECG, Third Ecumenical Missionary Conference (June 1910), minutes of international committee, 14-20 July 1908, p. 9.

73. LP, Davidson papers, vol. 269, fols. 5-6, copy of Oldham to Gore, 5 Oct. 1908; see also Kathleen Bliss's account in NCE, Oldham papers, box 22, folder 2, pp. 66-7.

74. ECG, World Missionary Conference (1910), minutes of executive committee, 11 Dec. 1908, pp. 22-23.

Episcopal layman and editor of *The Churchman* newspaper in New York, wrote immediately to Oldham expressing his concern that the broad vision delineated at Oxford was being narrowed, namely that:

> the Conference was to concentrate its attention and if possible, the attention of the whole Christian Church at home upon the mission field and upon Christ's purpose for the Church at home for that field, and thus to find a message from Him through the field to the home Church. There was to be no effort by resolution or otherwise to interfere with the autonomy and independence of the Churches, but the idea was to let the message bear its own inherent witness to the divided Churches of Christendom in the sure confidence that they would be drawn together in their witness for Christ.[75]

On 29 October, the American executive committee minuted its unanimous refusal to assent to the abridgement of the freedom of action of the Commissions implicit in Oldham's letter to Gore: in the committee's view, the facts and judgments presented in the Commission reports 'should be allowed to bear their own witness to the Churches of Christendom, in the sure confidence that they will thus be drawn together in the common service of Christ.'[76] In his reply, Oldham sought to explain the divergence of view as a misunderstanding caused by lack of clarity on his part, but gave no ground on the principle at stake, which was non-negotiable if the support of Bishop Gore and his party were to be obtained.[77] Oldham's extension of the exclusion of doctrine and church order to the findings of the Commissions won the backing of the executive committee in December.[78] He also followed up his letter to Gore by a personal visit to Birmingham, staying overnight in the bishop's home, a visit which bore the desired fruit in a promise by Gore to attend the conference — an undertaking which Bishop Montgomery had intimated was a necessary precondition for the fulfilment of Oldham's goal of securing the official support of the SPG for the conference.[79]

75. UTS, MRL 12, WMC papers, series 1, box 8, folder 1, S. McBee to J. H. Oldham, 14 Oct. 1908.

76. UTS, MRL 12, WMC papers, series 1, box 24, folder 13, minutes of American executive committee, 29 Oct. 1908, p. 3.

77. UTS, MRL 12, WMC papers, series 1, box 8, folder 20, item 558, Oldham to A. J. Brown, 19 Dec. 1908.

78. ECG, World Missionary Conference (1910), minutes of executive committee, 11 Dec. 1908, pp. 22-4.

79. NCE, Oldham papers, box 10, folder 9, Oldham to Kathleen Bliss, 11 Sept. 1962; and box 22, folder 2, unpublished manuscript on Oldham by Kathleen Bliss, p. 67.

The divergence between the British and American positions on this question was not, however, to be easily or rapidly bridged. It was one of the issues that had to be addressed in April 1909 when Oldham visited New York, primarily to persuade the Americans of the British view on the geographical scope of the conference and its statistics.[80] The solution proposed at the New York meetings was that no resolutions on *any* topic should be proposed for adoption by the conference. The Americans felt that this would keep Anglo-Catholic fears at bay while preserving what they wanted, namely 'untrammeled liberty' for the Commissions in their investigations and in the presentation of their views and 'entire freedom of discussion' for the conference itself.[81] The American proposal was the subject of 'prolonged discussion' by the central advisory committee at its meetings on 7-8 June 1909, when it was 'finally agreed' to recommend to the executive committee that 'the findings of the Commissions shall not as a rule be submitted to the Conference for vote', although provision was still to be made for the conference to pronounce its view on any question raised by a Commission or on 'any matter of general and public interest touching the missionary enterprise', provided that such a course was supported by a two-thirds majority of the business committee.[82] This compromise solution represented a significant dilution and modification of the American proposal and was endorsed by the executive committee on 30 June 1909.[83] The limited freedom thus given to submit exceptional resolutions for formal adoption by the conference would be used sparingly when the conference assembled a year later, but without such permission, it would not have been possible for the conference formally to authorise the setting up of the Continuation Committee, and Edinburgh 1910 would not occupy the place in the history of ecumenism that it now does.

Although relatively few, even on the American side, were quite as specific as Silas McBee in thinking of the conference as an event of major potential significance for the mutual relations, not just of missionary societies and the Christian communions they had planted in Asia and Africa, but of western churches, the disagreement on the issue of how absolute should be the exclusion of matters of faith and order is revealing. The Americans held consistently to a more expansive vision of the purpose of the conference than the

80. See Chapter 3 below.
81. UTS, MRL 12, WMC papers, series 1, box 24, folder 13, minutes of the American executive committee, 8 April 1909, p. 1.
82. UTS, MRL 12, WMC papers, series 1, box 24, folder 6, minutes of the central advisory committee, 7-8 June [1909], p. 5.
83. ECG, World Missionary Conference (1910), minutes of executive committee, 30 June 1909, p. 40.

British and stoutly resisted any attempt to restrict the freedom of manoeuvre of the Commissions. The American executive committee testified in January 1909 that 'from the outset', it had been their hope and prayer that the Edinburgh conference should make 'a moral and spiritual contribution' to 'the cause of cooperation and Christian unity.'[84] The more polarized nature of British ecclesiastical politics made any declaration of such an exalted aim impossible within Britain. The tensions that surfaced in October 1908 presaged the more fundamental battles that would shortly erupt over the geographical scope of the conference. This episode was also the first of several occasions on which the innocuously entitled 'central advisory committee' set up at Oxford proved its capacity to exercise a decisive influence on conference policy. This little band of Scotsmen and Englishmen was beginning to wield an executive power that was denied to both the official (British) executive committee (on which elderly Scotsmen continued to predominate, though not to the same degree as hitherto) and the American executive committee.

Oldham Gets to Work

The executive committee at its meeting on 22 September 1908 accepted the recommendations of the international committee *en bloc,* and fixed the date of the opening of the conference as 14 June 1910.[85] In the wake of the Oxford meeting, Oldham set about his new duties with alacrity. He wrote a phenomenal number of letters. He attended the October meeting of the London Secretaries' Association and there appealed to the English missionary secretaries for their help and prayers 'to make this Conference a great force in the evangelisation of the world'.[86] He issued invitations to prospective members of the Commissions, drafted instructions for Commission chairmen, and sought nominations from missionary society secretaries of names of suitable correspondents for the Commission questionnaires. Although appointment of members of the Commissions was formally the responsibility of the international committee, in practice this duty fell largely to Oldham on the British side (guided by the central advisory committee) and on the American side to Arthur Judson Brown and W. Henry Grant, respectively chairman and assistant secretary of the American executive committee. By the end of October

84. UTS, MRL 12, WMC papers, series 1, box 24, folder 13, minutes of the American executive committee, 12-13 Jan. 1909, p. 3.

85. ECG, World Missionary Conference (1910), minutes of executive committee, 23 Sept. 1908, pp. 18-19.

86. CUL, BSA/F4, microfilm minutes of London Secretaries' Association, 21 Oct. 1908.

1908 the American executive committee had nominated a first batch of six-teen names of North Americans to serve as members of the Commissions, fif-teen of whom duly became members of the Commissions for which they were nominated.[87] It was a pleasant surprise to the conference organisers to find that of the 160 names decided on at Oxford as prospective members of the Commissions, only 11 declined, confounding the gloomy predictions of those who had supposed that eminent people would be too busy to serve in this capacity.[88]

The work involved in compiling and dispatching the Commission ques-tionnaires, processing the returns, and copying them for the members of the Commissions, was also very considerable. The great majority of the question-naires for the various Commissions had been sent out by the end of February 1909. Statistics do not survive of how many such papers were distributed, but over 1,000 completed questionnaires were received from serving missionar-ies, and almost as many again from home officials or retired missionaries.[89] Oldham's escalating work-load required the recruitment of an assistant con-ference secretary, Kenneth Maclennan, who was seconded from the Scottish branch of the Laymen's Missionary Movement early in 1909. Oldham and Maclennan were assisted by a growing army of typists and clerks; for the pe-riod from the spring of 1909 to the spring of 1910 the total staff complement of the conference office was between twenty and thirty people. To accommo-date this workforce, the conference office at 100 Princes Street had to expand from its original two rooms to an eventual seven, and eventually three further offices were taken in an adjacent building.[90]

Oldham was not afraid to use the central advisory committee to shape the conference programme, a function that was not part of the brief given to it at Oxford. At its meeting in York on 17-18 December 1908, at which Mott was able to be present throughout, the central advisory committee drafted pro-posals for a series of parallel meetings in the Synod Hall, to accommodate those among 'the large number of missionaries on furlough and other friends of missions' who would desire to be present at the conference but who could not be accommodated in the galleries of the Assembly Hall. The committee also anticipated that a third hall would be needed for evening meetings of a

87. UTS, MRL 12, WMC papers, series 1, box 24, folder 13, minutes of American execu-tive committee, 29 Oct. 1908, pp. 2-3. The only nominee who did not become a Commis-sion member was Miss Helen Richardson, head of the Southern Methodist Girls' School, Shanghai, who was nominated for Commission III.

88. World Missionary Conference 1910, *Monthly News Sheet* 6 (March 1910), pp. 119-20.

89. World Missionary Conference 1910, *Monthly News Sheet* 7 (April 1910), p. 140.

90. *Ibid.*, p. 141.

more public kind. Detailed plans were laid for the programme. It was suggested that each of the eight full days of the conference from Wednesday 15 to Thursday 23 June (with the exception of Sunday 19 June, when there would be an evening meeting only) should follow a standard pattern, beginning with united intercessory prayer at 9.30 a.m., followed by discussion of the Commission reports (roughly on a one per day basis) from 10.15 a.m. to 1 p.m. and 2 to 4 p.m., and concluding with an evening meeting at 7 p.m. Topics and possible speakers for the ten evening meetings were suggested, beginning with the archbishop of Canterbury at the opening meeting on Tuesday 14 June. It was envisaged that four evenings should be given a specific geographical or religious focus — on 'The Awakening in the Far East', India, Africa, and Islam respectively — and that on each of these evenings a relevant national Christian should if possible be invited to speak. Mott's influence and international student contacts were apparent in the names suggested: President Kajosine Ibuka, Bishop Yoitsu Honda, and Dr S. Motoda from Japan; Dr K. C. Chatterjee, Miss Lilavati Singh, and Mrs Pandita Ramabai from India; C. T. Wang (Wang Cheng-ting) from China; and Yun Ch'iho from Korea.[91]

It is a mark of the rapidity with which Oldham had seized the initiative in the complex preparatory work for the conference, and of the convergence between his ideas and those of Mott, that so many of these early plans came to fruition: notably, the three-tier structure of Assembly Hall, Synod Hall, and Tolbooth meetings; the opening address by Archbishop Randall Davidson; the pattern of the daily programme (which was adopted with only minor amendment); and even the identities of some of the suggested Asian speakers — Ibuka, Honda, Chatterjee, and Yun Ch'iho, all spoke at Edinburgh, though not necessarily in the evening sessions as originally envisaged.[92] At a subsequent meeting, the central advisory committee extended its reach still further, recommending to the executive the publication of a monthly conference *News Sheet* (which was duly published from October 1909 to May 1910, attaining a circulation of over 8,000), and making detailed proposals for the length and purchase price of the Commission reports (which proved roughly accurate).[93]

91. UTS, MRL 12, WMC papers, series 1, box 24, folder 6, Extract from minutes of central advisory committee, 17-18 Dec. 1908. The committee was confused over dates, and in fact talked of a conference opening on 'Tuesday 10th' and concluding on Thursday, 23rd.

92. C. T. Wang did not attend the Edinburgh conference, although some accounts, such as that of Temple Gairdner (pp. 164-5), confuse him with Dr C. C. Wang of Shanghai, who did attend and address the conference. See Chapter 5.

93. UTS, MRL 12, WMC papers, series 1, box 24, folder 6, minutes of central advisory committee, 7-8 June 1909.

The Financing of the Conference

The responsibility for financing 'the third ecumenical missionary conference' as originally conceived lay with the host churches of the British Isles
and with the Scottish churches in particular. In October 1907 the general
committee had appointed a cumbrous finance committee comprising
thirty-six Scotsmen (all except two were laymen), eight English, and six
Irish representatives. It was instructed to consider raising a guarantee fund,
plus a fund for preliminary expenses, and was given powers to appoint local
fund-raising committees, but appears to have accomplished little or nothing over the next twelve months.[94] Resources for the early stages of conference planning in Britain were meagre. The English members of the executive committee had to ask for reimbursement of their expenses incurred
through attendance at the meeting in York of 12 March 1908, when a treasurer for the conference, Mr Harry W. Smith of Edinburgh, was appointed.[95] At the Oxford international committee meeting in July, finance
seems to have occupied remarkably little attention in comparison with the
time devoted to the administrative support for the conference: the minutes
record simply a recommendation to the British and American executive
committees that the Commissions should be provided with all necessary financial help for the discharge of their duties.[96] John Ritson felt obliged to
ask Oldham whether he would be justified in taking an overnight sleeper to
enable him to attend the morning session of the September 1908 meeting of
the executive committee in Edinburgh, and to reassure him that he would
deduct from his expense claim the cost of a third-class return from London
to Darlington, since he had Bible Society commitments to fulfil in that
town later the same day.[97] At this meeting Smith was able to report a total
expenditure to date of no more than £131. However, the conference now had
a full-time secretary to support, and a shoestring budget would no longer
suffice. The executive accordingly asked the finance committee 'to make
suitable financial arrangements' for Oldham's remuneration, and the general committee, meeting immediately afterwards, empowered the executive

94. ECG, Third Ecumenical Missionary Conference (June 1910), minutes of general
committee, 10 Oct. 1907, pp. 10, 14.
95. ECG, Third Ecumenical Missionary Conference (June 1910), minutes of executive
committee, 12 March 1908, pp. 12-13.
96. ECG, Third Ecumenical Missionary Conference (June 1910), minutes of international committee, 14-20 July 1908, p. 8.
97. CUL, BSA/F4/3/1, fol. 75, Ritson to Oldham, 14 Sept. 1908.

committee to construct a budget for the conference and make a public appeal for the necessary funds.[98]

In December 1908 the executive committee declared itself unable, 'on the present data, to frame any exact estimate of the probable cost of the Conference', but suggested that the finance committee should aim to raise the sum of about £10,000. It also endorsed the finance committee's proposal that a meeting comprising treasurers of English missionary societies and others should be convened in London, with a view to forming an English auxiliary of the finance committee.[99] The finance committee evidently judged the target of £10,000 to be unnecessarily or unrealistically ambitious, and revised the target downward to £7,000. No public appeal for funds was launched, but private application was made via a printed circular letter directed at the well-to-do — 'those who might be expected to give considerable amounts'.[100] However, progress in meeting even the more modest goal of £7,000 was slow. In March 1909, pledges for only £1,329 had been received; by the end of June, the figure had risen to £2,073; by the end of October, it stood at no higher than £2,701.[101] Funds actually received then amounted to £2,014, of which about 40% (about £800) had been received from English sources.[102] The relatively low level of contributions from English sources was doubtless one reason for the establishment in January 1910 of a sub-committee for the development of interest in England and Wales. J. H. Ritson and a retired businessman from Northwood, Frederic S. Bishop, were appointed joint honorary secretaries; the Bible Society agreed to release Ritson part-time for the task, and provided an office at Bible House free of charge.[103] Nevertheless, by 1 April 1910, with just ten weeks remaining before the conference opened, the level of pledged subscriptions stood at only £4,463, though a further £1,005 had been received from sales of the conference *Monthly News Sheet* and of tickets for the public meetings. With a shortfall of £2,537 in view, the finance committee inserted a new appeal in

98. ECG, World Missionary Conference (1910), minutes of executive committee, 23 Sept. 1908, p. 19; minutes of general committee, 23 Sept. 1908, p. 22.

99. ECG, World Missionary Conference (1910), minutes of executive committee, 11 Dec. 1908, p. 25.

100. World Missionary Conference 1910, *Monthly News Sheet* 1 (Oct. 1909), p. 12; 7 (April 1910), p. 143.

101. ECG, World Missionary Conference (1910), minutes of executive committee, 25 March 1909, p. 33; 30 June 1909, pp. 36-7; 29 Oct. 1909, p. 49.

102. CUL, BSA/F4/, microfilm minutes of London Secretaries' Association, 20 Oct. 1909.

103. ECG, World Missionary Conference (1910), minutes of executive committee, 28 Jan. 1910, p. 63; CUL, BSA/F4/3/1, fols. 112-113, Ritson to Harry W. Smith, 29 Dec. 1909, and fols. 117-18, Ritson to Oldham, 13 Jan. 1910.

the *News Sheet* aimed at eliciting small donations.[104] This appeal brought in a further £435 in small sums, but the final *Monthly News Sheet,* published in May 1910, still had to report a short-fall of £1,835 on the target figure of £7,000, and invited eleventh-hour subscriptions.[105] The target of £7,000 from public subscriptions in Britain was never reached.[106] Nevertheless, the final balance sheet for the conference showed a total income of £10,475 (not including sales of the Commission reports), and a healthy surplus over expenditure of £1,175, which was transferred to the use of the Continuation Committee.[107] It is unclear where the additional income had come from. It is possible that offerings taken at the different conference venues proved generous. Delegates' fees may also have proved more than sufficient to cover the costs of hire of premises: official delegates were charged ten shillings each, their spouses six shillings and three pence (they were allowed admission to the Assembly Hall on alternate days only); while tickets for the Synod Hall meetings were available for seven shillings and sixpence.[108] There is also evidence, supplied many years later by John Mott in a personal interview with W. Richey Hogg, that he had played his own part in raising funds within Britain.[109]

If sales of the final bound versions of the Commission reports are included, the final surplus becomes still more handsome. The reports were sold after 23 June 1910 at eighteen shillings for the set (or three shillings and sixpence per volume); pre-publication orders received before the conference attracted discounted prices of thirteen shillings a set from the United Kingdom, or fifteen shillings from overseas (excluding North America), or four dollars from North America. Whereas 5,000 sales were needed to cover printing costs, and 10,000 to meet the total cost of producing the reports, pre-publication orders amounted to nearly 8,000 sets and in all some 15,000 sets were sold in Britain alone.[110] The financial picture was in the end so favourable that the executive committee was able to authorise the payment of addi-

104. World Missionary Conference 1910, *Monthly News Sheet* 7 (April 1910), p. 143; ECG, World Missionary Conference (1910), minutes of executive committee, 1 April 1910, p. 68, gives a slightly different figure for subscriptions received.

105. World Missionary Conference 1910, *Monthly News Sheet* 8 (May 1910), p. 167.

106. *History and Records of the Conference,* p. 16.

107. Hogg, *Ecumenical Foundations,* p. 147; ECG, World Missionary Conference (1910), minutes of general committee, 15 July 1910, minute 58.

108. CUL, BSA/F4/3/1, fols. 293 and 306, Ritson to C. Hay Walker, 27 and 30 May 1910.

109. Hogg, *Ecumenical Foundations,* pp. 115, 394 n. 63.

110. World Missionary Conference 1910, *Monthly News Sheet* 2 (Nov. 1909), p. 45; and 5 (Feb. 1910), p. 106; UTS, MRL 12, WMC papers, series 2, box 3, folder 11, circular letter from Mott and Oldham, n.d. [1910]; Clements, *Faith on the Frontier,* p. 103.

tional honoraria of £150 to Oldham and £100 to his assistant, Kenneth Maclennan, 'in respect of the valuable service they have rendered to the Conference. The fact that so large a revenue had been secured, and that the work had been so economically conducted, had to a very large extent arisen from the unwearied labour so ungrudgingly bestowed by them'.[111]

Across the Atlantic a very different financial scenario applied throughout. The American executive committee had no financial responsibility for the conference itself, but was required to meet its own expenses and those of the three Commissions (I, V, and VI) which were primarily based in the United States, having been allocated Americans as chairmen. In addition, the American executive committee (as also the continental executive committee) undertook to pay the expenses of all members of Commissions resident within their respective countries. A sum of $1,000 was available for immediate use, being the surplus remaining from the New York conference of 1900. A budget committee was promptly appointed by the American executive committee at its first meeting after the York international committee, in September 1908, and at the next meeting on 29 October it submitted a budget for approval amounting to $16,500, of which $1,000 were set aside for the executive committee's own expenses, and 2,000 for miscellaneous purposes. The remainder was divided among the three Commissions with American chairmen, but in markedly unequal shares: W. Douglas Mackenzie's Commission V on 'The Preparation of Missionaries' was given $700; John Barton's Commission VI on 'The Home Base of Missions', $950; while the remaining $9,900 was apportioned to John Mott for the sole use of his Commission I on 'Taking the Gospel to all the World'.[112] The bulk of this large sum was to be spent on the statistical survey and atlas to be compiled by Dr James S. Dennis of New York and Professor Harlan P. Beach of Yale Divinity School, which Mott saw as integral to his vision for Commission I. The meeting on 29 October decided that confidential application should be made to the various American mission boards for lists of names of persons who might be approached for contributions.[113]

By the end of February 1909 some $5,000 had been promised by private donors towards the total required. Fortified by these promises, the chairman of the American finance committee, William Jay Schieffelin of Hartford,

111. ECG, World Missionary Conference 1910, minutes of executive committee, 15 July 1910, pp. 80-1.

112. UTS, MRL 12, WMC papers, series 1, box 24, folder 13, minutes of the American executive committee, 29 Oct. 1908, p. 1.

113. UTS, MRL 12, WMC papers, series 1, box 10, folder 13, W. Henry Grant to John R. Mott, 21 Nov. 1908.

Connecticut, sent out 450 printed circular letters to American church leaders, asking them to give or raise $200 as their contribution towards making 'this conference the most representative assemblage of Christian leaders in the history of the Church': the survey, Schieffelin confidently predicted, 'will prove indispensible [*sic*] to the work of the conference in planning a campaign for the evangelization of the world.'[114] W. Douglas Mackenzie also fed Schieffelin with names of wealthy laymen who could be approached for substantial donations.[115] W. Richey Hogg records that, on the basis of testimony received long afterwards from Mott himself, Mott was personally instrumental in raising a sum of $55,000 made up of eleven individual gifts of $5,000 each, most of which must have been raised before Mott knew that he was to exercise a leadership role at Edinburgh.[116] If these recollections are correct, the budget set by the American executive committee must have been far exceeded by the income received, and the resulting surplus was very probably used to remedy the serious shortfall on the British side. Operating in a very different philanthropic climate, the American executive committee seems to have had relatively little difficulty in raising and probably surpassing the necessary budget. Edinburgh 1910 had to operate within the constraints imposed by a disjunction between the primary seat of administrative responsibility — which was in Britain — and the most promising constituency of financial support — which was in the United States. All things considered, Oldham and his colleagues accomplished a remarkable achievement in negotiating their way through this disjunction to a successful financial outcome.

114. YDS Special Collections, RG 45, Mott papers, box 80: Schieffelin to Mott, 26 Feb. 1909.

115. UTS, MRL 12, WMC papers, series 1, box 8, folder 20, Mackenzie to Schieffelin, 28 Dec. 1908.

116. Hogg, *Ecumenical Foundations*, pp. 115, 394 n. 63.

CHAPTER 3

Carrying the Gospel to All the World?
Defining the Limits of Christendom

A Mission to All Humanity?

The Edinburgh conference, like its predecessors in London and New York, was originally designated as 'Ecumenical' in the original sense of the word that it would include the whole human race in its scope. It was to be concerned, according to the December 1907 'Memorandum Suggesting Constitution and Procedure of Conference', with 'problems of supreme moment for the missionary future of the world'.[1] The first of its eight commissions originally bore the title 'Carrying the Gospel to all the World'.[2] In September 1908 it was decided that the title of the conference be changed from 'Third Ecumenical Missionary Conference' to 'The World Missionary Conference' in order to avoid any misunderstanding arising from the fact that 'the word "Ecumenical" has acquired a technical meaning' — in other words, its modern meaning, associated, ironically, with the very movement for church unity to which Edinburgh gave birth.[3]

Formally, therefore, Edinburgh 1910 might appear to have been originally summoned to discuss how the good news of Jesus Christ could be more effectively proclaimed to the whole world, to humanity in its entirety. If such had been substantially the case, it could hardly be faulted on theological grounds.

---

1. ECG, Third Ecumenical Missionary Conference (June 1910), memorandum suggesting constitution and procedure of conference, 12 Dec. 1907, pp. 5-6.

2. ECG, Third Ecumenical Missionary Conference (June 1910), minutes of international committee, 14-20 July 1908, p. 3.

3. ECG, World Missionary Conference (1910), minutes of general committee, 23 Sept. 1908, p. 21.

In reality, however, the scope of the conference was implicitly limited from the outset by a decision taken by the executive committee in York on 12 March 1908 that representation at the conference was not simply to be on a financial basis but also confined to 'Societies and Boards administering funds and sending out missionaries for the propagation of the Gospel among non-Christian peoples'. In the case of societies which worked in part in 'professedly Christian countries', only that portion of their income 'expended on work among non-Christians' could be counted.[4] In September 1908 the first (American) meeting of Commission I, supposedly entrusted with the topic 'Carrying the Gospel to all the World', accordingly took a decision that its sub-committee on statistics should exclude 'missionary work carried on on the Continent of Europe, with the exception of the Turkish Empire and southeastern Europe'. The meeting considered the possibility of excluding *all* missions in Catholic and Orthodox countries, but unanimously rejected the idea, ostensibly on the grounds of 'practical difficulty', though one suspects more substantial reasons for the American decision.[5] It is important to note that even before the question of the geographical scope of the conference became a bone of contention between Anglo-Catholics and evangelical Protestants, the principle had been conceded by all, including the Americans, that most of Europe (and also, implicitly, North America itself) should be excluded from its purview as being 'Christian' lands. In practice, therefore, it had been decided that the conference was not in fact to be about *world* mission but rather about mission from 'Christendom' to 'heathendom'. There was no dispute that the two could be differentiated on a territorial basis: the only issue was where to draw the boundaries.

Commission I and the Problem of Statistics

Just how problematic that issue was became clear in the course of February 1909. The Oxford meeting of the international committee in July 1908 had commissioned Oldham to approach leading Anglo-Catholics in the Church of England to seek their agreement to participate in the conference. Oldham, who was at that stage still a Presbyterian, felt the need of Anglican aid in this task and turned to his friend, Tissington Tatlow, for assistance. Over the next

4. ECG, Third Ecumenical Missionary Conference (June 1910), minutes of executive committee, 12 March 1908, pp. 14-15.

5. UTS, MRL 12, WMC papers, series 1, box 7, folder 5, minutes of Commission I, 9-10 Sept. 1908.

few months Tatlow and Oldham between them secured the support for the conference of most of the key Anglo-Catholics whose names Tatlow had successfully proposed at the Oxford meeting. The two most crucial figures were the two bishops, Gore and Talbot. Their support was conditional upon a promise that the conference would not be '*un*denominational' but rather *inter*-denominational, and that questions of doctrine and church order were not to be brought before the conference either for debate or for resolution. On this basis Gore and Talbot began in early November 1908 to apply pressure on the SPG standing committee to reverse its earlier decision not to take part in the conference.[6] But in early February events took a turn that threatened to wreck all the careful diplomacy of Tatlow and Oldham.

On 3 February the British advisory council of Commission I considered a long letter written by John Mott to George Robson on 11 January in which Mott communicated proposals from the American 'executive committee' of the Commission regarding its mode of operation.[7] The British advisory council readily agreed to the American proposal that the British side of the Commission should accept full responsibility for processing replies received from Africa (leaving Asia to the Americans, and Australasia to the four continental European members of the Commission).[8] However, the British council made a significant change to the Commission I questionnaire as drafted by the Americans. It was insisted that an explanation be added to the questionnaire instructing respondents when answering the questions concerning missionaries and missionary agencies to bear in mind the work of other Christian missions than their own, but that these answers should not include those of the Roman Catholic or Orthodox churches; the American draft had been less consistent and explicit in its exclusion of non-Protestant missions.[9] From the outset, it was clear that the work of Commission I was going to be complicated by some fundamental divergences of ecclesiastical perspective between the American and British sections of the Commission.

6. Oxford, Rhodes House, USPG archives, minutes of standing committee, vol. 59 (1908-), pp. 1445-7, minutes of 26 Nov. 1908; Tissington Tatlow, *The Story of the Student Christian Movement of Britain and Ireland* (London: SCM Press, 1933), pp. 407-9; Tatlow, 'The World Conference on Faith and Order', in Ruth Rouse and Stephen C. Neill (eds.), *A History of the Ecumenical Movement 1517-1948* (London: SPCK, 1954), p. 406.

7. YDS, RG45, Mott papers, box 74, folder 1358, Letter 474, Mott to Robson, 11 Jan. 1909.

8. Mott's letter refers to giving 'the Continental Advisory Council' responsibility for Australasia. No records have yet come to light of a meeting of the four continental members (Julius Richter, A. Boegner, Bishop La Trobe, and Vilhelm Sörensen).

9. UTS, MRL 12, WMC papers, series 1, box 7, folder 4, Commission I, minutes of British advisory council, 3 Feb. 1909. The Commission I questionnaire is to be found in UTS, MRL 12, WMC papers, series 1, box 7, folder 9.

At the 3 February meeting Bishop H. H. Montgomery of the SPG (the sole Anglo-Catholic member of Commission I) asked a question regarding the section of Mott's letter which alluded to the brief given to the sub-committee on statistical survey, maps, and charts: Mott had written that the range of Dr James S. Dennis's work in the compilation of statistics would 'correspond largely' to his similar work done for the New York Missionary Conference of 1900.[10] Montgomery was evidently aware, or was made aware by others present, that Dennis's statistical summary of Protestant missions prepared for that conference had treated South America, Palestine, Syria, and Turkey as mission fields alongside Africa, Asia, and Oceania.[11] Montgomery apparently asked the meeting 'whether missions of Protestant Bodies among Roman and Greek Churchmen were to be considered as coming within the province of the Conference, as Foreign Missions'. No clear answer was forthcoming. According to Robson, he then informed the advisory council that he was due that same afternoon to see Randall Davidson, the archbishop of Canterbury, and Edward Stuart Talbot, bishop of Southwark, and would consult them on the matter.[12] Whether such a meeting took place is doubtful; the Davidson papers suggest rather that Montgomery immediately wrote a memorandum recording the main points at issue in the advisory council meeting, and sent this for comment to Davidson, Talbot, and probably also to Charles Gore, bishop of Birmingham.[13]

One of the central questions facing the Commission, Montgomery noted, was how 'to define "Christendom", in order to settle from all the countries where to get statistics of foreign Missions, "foreign" meaning outside Christendom. . . . Again the definition of the word "foreign" is not yet settled. Some of us feel that the word ought not to exist in the Church of God'.[14] Montgomery's concern had been triggered by two particular allusions in the meeting: one was a statement in a letter from Julius Richter that 'Roman Catholics

10. YDS, RG45, Mott papers, box 74, folder 1358, Mott to Robson, 11 Jan. 1909 [letter 474]. On Montgomery (1847-1932), former bishop of Tasmania, see BDCM; M. M. [Maud Montgomery], Bishop Montgomery: a memoir (London: SPG, 1933); and D. O'Connor and others, Three Centuries of Mission: The United Society for the Propagation of the Gospel (London and New York: Continuum, 2000), pp. 358-70.

11. Ecumenical Missionary Conference, New York, 1900, Report of the Ecumenical Conference on Foreign Missions . . . , 2 vols. (London and New York: Religious Tract Society and American Tract Society, 1900), II, pp. 428-33. On Dennis (1842-1914) see BDCM.

12. NCE, Oldham papers, box 1, folder 2, Robson to Dennis, 2 March 1909; copy in YDS, RG45, Mott papers, box 74, folder 1358.

13. LP, Davidson papers, vol. 269, fols. 18-20.

14. LP, Davidson papers, vol. 269, fol. 19, memorandum from Bishop Montgomery, n.d. [3 Feb. 1909].

were semi-Christians who had to be evangelized'; the other was a reference to the Archbishop's Mission to the Assyrian Christians (the Mission to the Church of the East) as being 'a Mission to non-Christians'. Montgomery's memorandum urged that all missions to existing Christian communions should be put into a separate category and called 'Missions of Help'. If this were not done, he anticipated the need for a minority report or even the complete withdrawal of the Anglican representatives.[15] His covering note to Davidson's domestic chaplain put the formal question whether the archbishop considered his Assyrian Mission to be a foreign mission and to non-Christians, while giving the assurance that he had informed the meeting that the archbishop's answer would be that it was 'a Mission of Help to a Christian Church'.[16]

The following morning, 4 February, Montgomery was granted an audience with the archbishop. As anticipated, Davidson took the view 'that this mission must in no case be placed amongst those which have for their object conversion to Christianity, or conversion to another Church. 'It is a Mission of Help to a Christian Church to renew itself on its own lines.'[17] Montgomery promptly wrote to Robson communicating this information and gently voicing anxiety over the larger question of the designation that would be applied to 'Missions of other Churches to other Christians, such as Roman Catholics and Greek Churchmen.' The wording of his letter led Robson and Oldham initially to suppose that Anglo-Catholic concerns could be met provided that a clear distinction was made in the statistics between mission work among non-Christians and that carried on among Roman Catholics and the Eastern churches.[18] Robson wrote immediately to James Dennis requesting that such a distinction should be made, and on 19 February received a cable in reply indicating 'that the discrimination we desire in the statistics would be made'.

The next day Robson wrote a letter to Montgomery reassuring him that all gathering of statistics for the Conference would adhere to this principle.[19]

15. LP, Davidson papers, vol. 269, fols. 19-20, memorandum from Bishop Montgomery, n.d. [3 Feb. 1909]. On the archbishop of Canterbury's Assyrian Mission (established in 1886), an Anglo-Catholic mission of help to the 'Nestorian' church of the ancient Persian empire, see J. F. Coakley, *The Church of the East and the Church of England: a history of the Archbishop of Canterbury's Assyrian Mission* (Oxford: Clarendon Press, 1992).

16. LP, Davidson papers, vol. 269, fol. 18, Montgomery to [W. G.] Boyd, 3 Feb. 1909.

17. Oxford, Rhodes House, USPG archives, Montgomery to Robson, X 366, fols. 755-6, 4 Feb. 1909. See also YDS, RG45, Mott papers, box 74, folder 1358, Robson to Mott, 5 Feb. 1909.

18. NCE, Oldham papers, box 1, folder 2, Robson to Dennis, 2 March 1909; copy in YDS, RG45, Mott papers, box 74, folder 1358.

19. UBL, SCM archives, box A21, copy of Robson to Montgomery, 20 Feb. 1909.

It soon became evident, however, that the Anglo-Catholic bishops would not be satisfied merely by the separate tabulation of Protestant missions aimed at other Christian populations. As a result, Montgomery's suggestion of making 'Missions of Help' a separate category in the statistics was lost, and with it the opportunity of affirming any variety of Christian mission that was not evangelistic in ultimate intent. Within a matter of days J. H. Oldham had received letters from Talbot and Gore protesting against the intention to include in the conference statistical atlas (which was to contain both maps and tables) statistics of Protestant missions working among Catholic, Orthodox, or Oriental Christian populations. Unless such an intention were revoked, it became clear that all Anglo-Catholic participation in the conference would be forfeited, and the earnest endeavours of Oldham and Tissington Tatlow, secretary of the Student Christian Movement, to ensure that this conference, unlike its forbears in 1888 and 1900, could claim the full endorsement of the Church of England, would be dashed.[20] Talbot informed Oldham on 20 February that he, Gore, and Montgomery also were agreed that any departure, whether in statistics or in agenda, from the principle that the conference was concerned solely 'with Christian efforts to communicate the Gospel to non-Christians' would 'lead to the entire secession from the Conference of a large section of members of the Church of England, and very probably of others with them'.[21]

In response Oldham cited the relevant minutes of the York executive committee of 12 March 1908 and assured Talbot that, whilst the detail of the statistics was a matter for the sub-committee on statistics, 'any mission work which is immediately and predominantly directed towards Christian communities will be excluded from the returns'.[22] Oldham initially sought to persuade Mott that the issue, though 'of considerable moment', was not 'really serious', and informed him that he thought the bishops were 'unnecessarily scared'. His hope was that they would be content with the exclusion of missions directed explicitly at Catholic populations in Europe, and accept his suggestion that the Christianity of Latin America was 'to a large extent . . . merely nominal'.[23] Oldham's anxiety, however, turned into alarm when on 24 February Bishop Gore wrote a second letter stating explicitly that his terms

20. See Clements, *Faith on the Frontier*, pp. 81-5; T. Tatlow, *The Story of the Student Christian Movement of Great Britain and Ireland* (London: SCM Press, 1933), pp. 404-10.

21. NCE, Oldham papers, box 1, folder 2, Bishop of Southwark to Oldham, 20 Feb. 1909. Gore's first letter to Oldham does not appear to be extant.

22. NCE, Oldham papers, box 1, folder 2, Oldham to Bishop of Southwark, 23 Feb. 1909.

23. NCE, Oldham papers, box 1, folder 2, Oldham to Mott, 23 and 25 Feb. 1909.

were that all missions to Catholic populations, whether in Latin America or elsewhere, should be excluded from the conference, and suspending his membership of Commission III on Education in relation to the Christianisation of National Life.[24] The covering letter to missionaries, seeking their responses to the Commission III questionnaire, was at that very moment being prepared for dispatch under Gore's signature as chairman of the Commission. Influenced by Gore's ominous words that his 'friends among Churchmen will be very much "awake" and alert on this subject,' Oldham warned Mott that they faced the prospect of the resignation of twenty leading members of the Commissions, with the result that 'the Church of England, so far as its real authorities are concerned, will be out of the conference'. The consequences for the public standing of the conference looked very serious indeed.[25]

The Conference Hangs in the Balance

With the comprehensiveness and hence prestige of the conference hanging in the balance, Oldham wrote a long letter to Gore, giving the desired assurance that 'all work that aims at the conversion of persons from one form of Christianity to the other is necessarily excluded from the purview of the Conference', and pleading with him to allow his name still to be printed at the head of the Commission III circular letter and re-consider his refusal to sign the letter.[26] Gore's reply professed to accept Oldham's reassurance, agreed to let his name stand at the head of the letter, yet declined to sign it, leaving the acting chairman, Professor Michael Sadler of the University of Manchester, to sign it in his stead. Gore gave Oldham a month to obtain from the sub-committee on statistics a guarantee that their statistics would conform to the desired principle.[27] In effect Gore had kept his resignation from Commission III in abeyance, while declining to resume his role as chairman pending full satisfaction on the central issue for the Anglo-Catholic party.

Oldham's reports to Mott still warned bleakly of potential 'disaster'. He feared that the membership of the Commissions would be decimated, and

24. NCE, Oldham papers, box 1, folder 2, bishop of Birmingham to Oldham, 24 Feb. 1909.

25. NCE, Oldham papers, box 1, folder 2, Oldham to Mott, 25 Feb. and 2 March 1909.

26. NCE, Oldham papers, box 1, folder 2, Oldham to bishop of Birmingham, 26 Feb. 1909.

27. NCE, Oldham papers, box 1, folder 2, bishop of Birmingham to Oldham, 1 March 1909.

Commission III wrecked entirely. He had received a letter from Sadler indicating that he felt bound to follow the line taken by Gore and Talbot, not from any particularly strong conviction on the issue, but simply because he was not inclined to participate in a gathering which did not have the co-operation of the national church. If Sadler, 'probably the ablest Educationalist in England',[28] were to resign from Commission III, Oldham anticipated that other members of similar stature and central churchmanship would follow: the Revd Lord William Gascoyne-Cecil, Dr George Parkin, the Canadian educationist and fervent Christian advocate of imperial federation, and the Revd Lionel Ford, the headmaster of Repton School.[29] Even before this crisis arose, Oldham had contemplated a visit to America in connection with preparations for Edinburgh. He now brought forward his plans with a view to crossing the Atlantic between the meeting of the British executive committee on 25 March and that of the American Executive on 7 April.

The seriousness of the situation was quickly grasped on the other side of the Atlantic on 12 March when Arthur Brown, as chairman of the American executive, received a letter from Oldham (dated 2 March), alerting him to the problem. Brown, by his own confession 'startled', immediately convened an emergency informal meeting of the New York members of the executive and Commission I, including the sub-committee on statistics. There was a divergence of views. Some of the nine members present expressed full support for the Anglican case, indicating surprise that there had been any intention of including missions to Christian populations in the statistical survey. Others felt that the exclusion of all such missions 'would involve many perplexities'. All, however, were agreed that the success of the conference was more important than the scope of its statistics, and that some signal had to be given to Oldham pending a full meeting of the executive and consultation with Mott (then in Moscow) as chairman of Commission I. It was accordingly resolved that Brown should send Oldham a cable saying 'New York members Execu-

28. On Sadler (1861-1943) see *ODNB;* Michael Sadler, *Michael Ernest Sadler . . . : a memoir by his son* (London: Constable, 1949); Lynda Grier, *Achievement in Education: the work of Michael Ernest Sadler 1885-1935* (London: Constable, 1952).

29. NCE, Oldham papers, box 1, folder 2, Oldham to Mott, 10 March 1909. William Gascoyne-Cecil (1863-1936) was the second son of the former prime minister, Lord Salisbury, and rector of Bishop Hatfield, Herts. In 1916 he was made bishop of Exeter. On Parkin (1846-1922) see *ODNB* and Sir John Willison, *Sir George Parkin: a biography* (London: Macmillan, 1929). On Ford see Alec MacDonald, *A Short History of Repton* (London: Ernest Benn, 1929). Ford did not in fact serve on Commission IV, possibly because he was appointed headmaster of Harrow School in 1910, being succeeded at Repton by William Temple.

tive and Statistical Committee personally willing to conform to judgment of British Executive on statistics Confer Mott.'[30]

Armed with this cable, Oldham met in turn Talbot, Gore, and Montgomery between the evening of Sunday, 14 March and Tuesday the 16th. The generous response from New York proved to have 'helped matters enormously'. He found all three bishops 'extraordinarily cordial and friendly'. Oldham informed Mott that the way was now clear for the unprecedented phenomenon of an ecumenical missionary conference supported fully by the Church of England as a national church, provided that two essential points were scrupulously observed: the exclusion of all reference to work among Roman Catholics or other Christians; and that 'no surrender of conscientious conviction' be demanded of any participant in the conference. Oldham added:

> This is the principle which we have always claimed for the Student Movement in this country, and it is largely through the influence which the assertion of this principle in the Student Movement has had upon leading members of the Church of England that we have secured their cooperation in the Conference. If this principle is clearly defined and loyally adhered to, I do not think we need anticipate any difficulty from the High Church party. As Bishop Montgomery said to me, 'Once that principle is secured, you will find us as easy to get on with as anyone. We shall make no objection if a Calvinist or Baptist is allowed to say what he likes.'[31]

With the ecclesiastical stakes as high as they were, there was little doubt that Oldham would receive the backing he wanted from the British executive committee. On 25 March it duly resolved unanimously that the statistics of the conference should relate only to work among non-Christians.[32] What was rather less predictable was Mott's response. There is no doubt that he shared Oldham's desire to maintain the ecumenical breadth of the conference. Although convinced of 'the essential non-Christian character of whole sections of the nominally Roman Catholic parts of Latin America', he was willing for the sake of a united front to concede that the conference should concentrate its forces on what all could agree were non-Christian fields. His principal anxiety, however, was of significant corporate defections from the conference

30. NCE, Oldham papers, box 1, folder 2, Arthur J. Brown to Oldham, 13 March 1909; Oldham to Mott, 15 March 1909.

31. NCE, Oldham papers, box 1, folder 2, Oldham to Mott, 17 March 1909.

32. ECG, World Missionary Conference (1910), minutes of executive committee, 25 March 1909, p. 33. The continental executive committee had passed a similar resolution on 17 March.

ranks at the other (American) end of the ecclesiastical spectrum. He advised Oldham to give the American mission leaders when he met them in New York

> the impression that you are quite as solicitous about holding their co-operation as you are that of the Church of England leaders. Avoid, if at all possible, giving the impression that the whole British Committee and Continental leaders have made up their minds finally on the subject. Even if this is true it will not make a favourable impression to say it because some of the American leaders will think that this has been done without adequate time and effort being taken to understand their point of view.[33]

Yet, at the same time as offering this advice to Oldham, Mott was instructing his trusted lieutenant in the American YMCA, Hans P. Andersen, 'to cultivate Oldham very thoroughly while he is in America'. Oldham was 'by odds the deepest thinker and most influential worker in the British Student Movement', but he had never been 'fully converted to our Student Association Movement, to the Foreign Association work and to some of our foreign missionary views', and was not a man to be 'easily changed'. Andersen was given strict instructions to confer individually with Arthur Brown and with each American member of Commission I before Oldham got to them; Oldham was not to be permitted to see any of the members on his own; and Andersen was to act in meetings attended by Oldham as Mott's appointed representative and report to him.[34] Clearly Mott did not yet trust Oldham, if permitted to operate without close 'cultivation', to reach conclusions that were in harmony with his own priorities, which in 1909, and for some years thereafter, were shaped primarily by the distinctive vision and interests of the American YMCA.[35] Mott was unwilling to abandon altogether those parts of the globe which had caused the controversy: 'the admittedly non-Christian part of the population' in Latin America, the Levant, and Russia must remain part of the investigations of his Commission. The controversy over statistics was for him only one expression of a broader divergence of view which set some of the British and Continental members of the Commission apart from the activist concerns of the American half of the Commission.[36]

33. NCE, Oldham papers, box 1, folder 2, Mott to Oldham, 15 March 1909.

34. YDS, RG45, Mott papers, box 2, folder 26, Mott to Andersen, 16, 18, and 27 March 1909; for a rather guarded commentary on these instructions see Hopkins, *John R. Mott*, p. 347.

35. See Clements, *Faith on the Frontier*, pp. 254-5.

36. See UTS, MRL 12, WMC papers, series 1, box 10, folder 16, Mott to Andersen, 16 March 1909, p. 2.

Oldham in New York

Oldham landed in New York on the morning of Palm Sunday, 4 April. A three-day series of meetings with the American executive committee and Commission I had been arranged to begin on Tuesday the 6th. On that day, Hans Andersen wrote pessimistically to Mott (in London) saying that it would not be easy to reach an agreement, since 'the underlying assumptions on the part of Anglicans in Great Britain and the assumptions underlying our thinking have been so different that we have not understood each other'. Andersen indicated that one of the embarrassments from the American point of view was how to square the title of Commission I with the more limited scope of investigation now envisaged for it. He made a suggestion that proved to be pivotal for the character of the conference:

> In reality it is not a Commission on Carrying the Gospel to All the World but a Commission on Carrying the Gospel to the Non-Christian World. It would help us very materially if the title of this Commission could be changed so as to avoid the implication that countries occupied by Roman Catholic and Eastern Churches are not to be considered in contemplating carrying the Gospel to all the world. This of course would imply that they are adequately occupied. I am wondering whether it is too late to make a change in the title of our Commission. We could then clearly indicate that the scope of the Conference is limited and that the title 'World Missionary Conference' does not have reference to the field but to the participants.[37]

Oldham's first meeting, on the morning of the 6th, was with the American executive committee. He was accompanied by his father-in-law, Sir Andrew H. L. Fraser, former lieutenant-governor of Bengal and one of the three vice-presidents of the conference, who had stopped off in New York on his way to attend the Convention of the Laymen's Missionary Movement in Toronto.[38] Oldham addressed the Committee at length, reviewing the progress made by the various Commissions, and making proposals for the format of the Commission reports. The statistical question was not on

37. YDS, RG45, Mott papers, box 2, folder 26, Andersen to Mott, 6 April 1909.
38. UTS, MRL 12, WMC papers, series 1, box 17, folder 1, microfilm copy of Hartford Theological Seminary archives of Commission V, Arthur J. Brown to W. Douglas Mackenzie, New York, 22 March 1909. On Fraser (1848-1919) see *ODNB;* and his *Among Indian Rajahs and Ryots: a civil servant's recollections & impressions of thirty-seven years of work & sport in the central provinces & Bengal* (London: Seeley, 1911).

the agenda.[39] At 10 a.m. on Wednesday the 7th, two simultaneous meetings took place. The American executive resumed its meeting with Oldham at the conference's American office at 156 Fifth Avenue, and various items of conference procedure were discussed.[40] Meanwhile, at Mott's YMCA office at 124 East 28th Street, the American members of Commission I met to agree on a series of five questions regarding the basis of gathering statistics, to be raised with Oldham in a joint meeting of the Commission and the American executive committee. The questions were of a detailed nature and imply that the essential principle had already been conceded.[41]

At 2 p.m. the executive committee reassembled, together with the members of Commission I, Oldham, and Fraser. Oldham stated the unanimous British view that the scope of the statistics must conform to the basis of the conference, warned the meeting that any other position would result in the withdrawal of the Anglican members, and expressed great appreciation for the spirit shown by the American brethren in the cable sent on 12 March. In response members of Commission I expressed their willingness to confine their statistical enquiries to the conference basis, but Professor Harlan P. Beach, the first professor of missions at Yale Divinity School,[42] and Dr Charles Watson, acting chairman of the Commission in Mott's absence, proceeded to expound the 'very serious' practical obstacles which this principle raised. Egypt, for example, had a million Copts living among about 15 million Muslims — did it fall in the Christian or the non-Christian world? In Turkey, the students of the Syrian Protestant College included Muslims as well as Oriental Christians: the British principle required that the former should be included in the returns but the latter excluded. Beach, on behalf of Commission I, proposed that where mission work was almost entirely among Roman or Eastern Christians, it should be excluded and reserved for a later, unofficial volume, but where the two classes of work were intermingled, full statistics should be given without attempting separation. It seems likely that this last proposal was opposed by Oldham as being inadequate to meet the Anglican case. 'Much discussion' then ensued. North American Episcopalians on the committee, such as Silas McBee and Canon Norman Tucker, insisted that the difference of opinion was not one between Britain and North America, and

39. UTS, MRL 12, WMC papers, series 1, box 24, folder 13, minutes of American executive committee, 'Tuesday 7' [in fact 6] April 1909.

40. UTS, MRL 12, WMC papers, series 1, box 24, folder 13, minutes of American executive committee, 7 April 1909.

41. UTS, MRL 12, WMC papers, series 1, box 7, folder 5, minutes of Commission I, 7 April 1909.

42. On Beach (1854-1933) see BDCM.

that many Americans were in fact in agreement with the Anglican position. Others present, such as Watson, who was secretary of the Board of Foreign Missions of the United Presbyterian Church of North America, or Thomas Barbour, foreign secretary of the American Baptist Missionary Union, found the prospective exclusion of much of their mission work far harder to swallow, but felt that no other course was possible. Robert E. Speer, who was firmly in favour of making the desired concession, put forward a resolution expressing approval of the cable of 12 March and full acceptance of the British position. With some modification, and after several amendments had been voted down, this was eventually adopted. Speer, Beach, and Oldham were appointed as a sub-committee to consider and report on the atlas and proposed unofficial statistical volume.[43]

At 10 a.m. on Thursday 8 April the meeting re-convened. American concerns focussed on two practical questions. One was how to explain to the Christian public in America an unexpected substantial restriction in the scope of the conference, involving the elimination of substantial tracts of the American Protestant mission field. The other was simply the enormous amount of statistical work that James Dennis and Harlan Beach had already devoted to the statistics and the atlas, which must now be done all over again in a way that overcame the dilemma of how to define the boundary between the Christian and non-Christian worlds.[44] To ameliorate the first difficulty, it was agreed, on the motion of Charles Watson as acting chairman of Commission I, to recommend to the British executive committee the adoption of Andersen's suggestion that the title of the Commission be amended to 'Carrying the Gospel to All the Non-Christian World'. The response to the second problem was twofold, but less clear-cut. First, the meeting endorsed the proposal of the sub-committee on statistics that the American members of Commission I should be granted the right to issue their own comprehensive statistical volume after the conference.[45] Second, Beach presented a proposal containing the view of the American members of Commission I on which countries were now 'in' and which were 'out'. Sir Andrew Fraser, however, felt that Beach had cut out countries that ought to be included, and, with Oldham, suggested that the detailed implementation of the principle now agreed upon should be delayed

43. UTS, MRL 12, WMC papers, series 1, box 24, folder 13, minutes of American executive committee, 7 April 1909; NCE, Oldham papers, box 1, folder 3, Oldham to Mott, 13 April 1909.

44. NCE, Oldham papers, box 1, folder 3, Oldham to Robson, 9 April 1909.

45. This was eventually published as H. P. Beach et al. (eds.), *World Statistics of Christian Missions* (New York: The Committee on Reference and Counsel of the Foreign Missions Conference of North America, 1916).

until he and Oldham could consult the British section of the Commission. Beach and Dennis were understandably anxious at the prospect of undertaking further statistical work which might still fall foul of British scruples. They were clearly also determined to avoid the statistical nightmare of having to separate all mission operations and personnel in any single locality into two categories. Beach therefore successfully moved that

> It is the judgment of the American executive committee that the statistical and atlas work of Commission I be geographical and that the British representatives present be asked to secure the judgment of the American and British members of Commission I as to whether the countries in which missions for both Christians and non-Christians are combined should be included or excluded and, if possible, a definite statement of the territory which should be excluded.[46]

Since the Americans had just had their own list of suggested exclusions turned down, what Beach and Dennis were insisting on, as Oldham reported to Mott, was that the British section of Commission I must take responsibility for adjudicating all doubtful cases. The Americans had, with varying degrees of reluctance, accepted the necessity of conforming to the Anglican definition of what constituted legitimate evangelistic endeavour, but were now throwing it back to the British for detailed application on the basis of specifically territorial lines of division.[47]

Later the same day the American members of Commission I presented Oldham with a memorandum which included a list of hard questions to be submitted to the British advisory council. They included questions about the admissibility in the atlas of missions to the Jews, both within and without Christendom, and of work among 'negroes' in the United States and West Indies. Probably the two most crucial questions were:

1. What percentage of Christians, whether Protestant, Roman Catholic, or of Oriental churches, shall be deemed sufficient to change the country from the non-Christian to the Christian class?
2. Shall Persia, Turkey, Syria, and Egypt, where the ultimate aim of the boards at work is to reach non-Christians, have all their statistics included?[48]

46. UTS, MRL 12, WMC papers, series 1, box 24, folder 13, minutes of American executive committee, 8 April 1909.
47. NCE, Oldham papers, box 1, folder 3, Oldham to Mott, 13 April 1909.
48. UTS, MRL 12, WMC papers, series 1, box 7, folder 5, minutes of Commission I, 8

Resolving the Hard Cases

Oldham was well satisfied with the fruits of his ecumenical diplomacy in New York. He told Mott that the meetings with the American executive had been 'of a delightful character', and saw the spiritual generosity of the Americans as 'a great object lesson' in Christian brotherhood which would 'greatly increase the spiritual power of the conference'.[49] He also took the opportunity to travel to Yale for further consultations with Harlan Beach and to Hartford for a meeting with W. Douglas Mackenzie, the chairman of Commission V.[50] A further meeting with the New York advisory council of the American executive followed on 20 April, at which Oldham urged that the chairmen of Commissions V and VI (Mackenzie and James L. Barton) and the vice-chairman of Commission III (Edward C. Moore) should cross the Atlantic during the coming summer to confer with their British counterparts.[51]

On 4 May the British advisory council of Commission I gathered at Bible House in London under George Robson's chairmanship. Talbot, Gore, Oldham, Sir Andrew Fraser, and Julius Richter were present by invitation. Oldham reported on his visit to New York. The proposals of the American executive to change the title of Commission I and permit the American members to compile their own unofficial statistical survey were endorsed, despite Robson's personal lack of enthusiasm for the new title.[52] Consideration was then given to the memorandum containing the list of hard cases compiled by the American section of Commission I. Missions to Jews were to be included, but tabulated separately, as were statistics of Catholic and Orthodox missions. In the cases of the Ottoman empire, Egypt, and Persia, a compromise of strange logic was reached. Statistics of *all* Protestant missionaries and their institutions in these territories were to be included 'in view of the direct bearing of the work in these countries upon the Mohammedan population' and 'as indicating the agencies and forces which are influencing, and in a measure are

---

April 1909. It was also agreed to send letters to Mott and Robson seeking approval of the change in the title of the Commission. For the memorandum itself see UTS, MRL 12, WMC papers, series 1, box 8, folder 3, item 325.

49. NCE, Oldham papers, box 1, folder 3, Oldham to Mott, 13 April 1909.

50. UTS, MRL 12, WMC papers, series 1, box 17, folder 1, microfilm copy of Hartford Theological Seminary archives of Commission V, Oldham to W. Douglas Mackenzie, New York, 8 April 1909; Mackenzie to Oldham, 16 April 1909.

51. UTS, MRL 12, WMC papers, series 1, box 24, folder 11, minutes of the New York advisory council, 20 April 1909.

52. For Robson's view see YDS, RG45, Mott papers, box 74, folder 1358, Robson to Mott, 19 April 1909.

directed to effect the ultimate conversion of the non-Christian populations'. Yet all statistics of the Protestant church members converted through the agency of these same missionaries were to be omitted, on the grounds that these Christians were primarily proselytes from the ancient Oriental churches.[53] The origins of this compromise are to be found in a proposal put forward by Eugene Stock, the former editorial secretary of the CMS, 'that in the Near East the living agents who were there for Mahommedan work should be included, but that the whole of their congregations drawn from other Christian bodies should be deleted'.[54] If Stock had meant to include only those missionaries who were specifically engaged in Muslim work, his proposal had some logical basis; but the decision to include all foreign missionaries but exclude all their converts was anomalous in the extreme. All Protestant work in Latin America was to be excluded from the statistics, with the exception of missions among the aboriginal tribes and 'non-Christian immigrants'; Oldham supposed that this exception would permit the inclusion of the work of the South American Missionary Society, and also of most Protestant work in British and Dutch Guiana (the former also being a field where a British mission, the LMS, worked).[55] All missions among African American people in North and South America and even the West Indies were to be excluded on the grounds that these peoples now formed part of Christendom, though work among Asian immigrants to the Caribbean was to be included. Protestant missions working in Madagascar, Portuguese Africa, and Portuguese India, territories which were predominantly or even overwhelmingly Catholic in their missionary complexion, were to be included, presumably on the grounds that they, unlike Latin America, were deemed insufficiently Christianised to be part of Christendom. No explicit answer was apparently given to the American question about what percentage of the population had to be Christian for a country to be counted in Christendom, but it is evident that the percentage was deemed high enough in, for example, Brazil, but too low in Goa.[56]

53. UTS, MRL 12, WMC papers, series 1, box 7, folder 3, minutes of the British section of Commission I, 4 May 1909; NCE, Oldham papers, box 1, folder 3, Oldham to Dennis, 8 May 1909; *Statistical Atlas of Christian Missions* (Edinburgh: World Missionary Conference, 1910), p. 61.

54. LP, Davidson papers, vol. 269, fol. 24, memorandum from Bishop Montgomery, 6 May 1909.

55. NCE, Oldham papers, box 1, folder 3, Oldham to Dennis, 8 May 1909. The South American Missionary Society did indeed have two delegates at Edinburgh, H. S. Acworth and J. M. Harris.

56. UTS, MRL 12, WMC papers, series 1, box 7, folder 3, minutes of the British section of Commission I, 4 May 1909.

The Anglican Position Clarified

Bishop Montgomery produced a memorandum of the 4 May meeting which he sent to Davidson and other Anglican leaders. He indicated that they could be quite happy with the outcome. Nevertheless, the memorandum makes clear that the Anglican position as he defined it was less sympathetic to the rigidly territorial definition of Christendom that was emerging than might be imagined:

> One very extraordinary fact came out. All Mission work in the United States is done by the Home Missionary Societies, and all work outside the States is done by the Foreign Missionary Societies. In order to obtain statistics in the States itself of work among non-Christians, it will be necessary for the Foreign Missionary Society to approach the Home Missionary Society. This is impossible. There is such a strong feeling between the two, that the Foreign Society cannot even ask the Home Society for facts. This refers to all sorts of denominations, not only to one, but chiefly I gather to what we call nonconformists. The Home Societies won't give the facts, so the whole of the work among non-Christians in the States has to be ignored, and all work among Red Indians, Chinese, Malays, Japanese, etc. We passed a Resolution saying it was a great pity, but of course if it is necessary, we could say no more. The Committees in America begged us not to press this point. They had said they had given way to us so much, that they asked us to give way to them in this matter. In consequence, all work in Alaska is left out. Again, South America by census is Roman Catholic, and therefore the whole Continent is almost entirely ruled out, except for a certain amount of work done by Moravians and by ourselves.[57]

Contrary to what appeared on the basis of the consequences of their intervention to be the case, Catholic Anglican leaders did *not* wish to see all of North and South America classified without differentiation as falling within Christendom. Indeed, the British members of Commission I, with Montgomery apparently in the lead, had urged the inclusion in the statistics of home missionary activity within the United States directed towards Native Americans, Asian immigrants, and the Inuit peoples of Alaska. Opposition to such a course had come from the Americans themselves, and can be traced to the or-

57. LP, Davidson papers, vol. 269, fols. 23-4, memorandum [from Bishop Montgomery], 6 May 1909.

ganisational gulf within American Protestantism between denominational church structures (into which the home missionary societies had mostly been absorbed) and the still autonomous foreign missionary societies. An additional factor was simply the practical reluctance of the American statisticians, so evident in the April meetings in New York, to have to make repeated distinctions in the statistics on the basis of a theological judgment as to which sections within a given population were, or were not Christian. Confronted by the Anglican insistence that, if Christian mission were indeed to be equated with evangelism, then only enterprises directed at non-Christian populations could be denominated as mission, the Americans had fallen back on what seemed the only possible course, namely to adopt a crudely geographical line of division between the Christian and non-Christian worlds. This accentuated the feeling among some of the British mission leaders, in Montgomery's words, that the terms of the conference had erected into a central principle a category — that of 'foreignness' — that ought to have no place in Christian vocabulary.[58]

Anglo-Catholic theological conviction had dictated that the conference must exclude from its scope Protestant activity in contexts where baptised Catholics, Orthodox, or even Protestants (as ostensibly in the West Indies), represented the overall majority of the population. Such endeavours could be included only when, as in certain parts of Latin America, they were directed towards statistically identifiable ethnic groups of aborigines or recent immigrants — islands of heathenism within the boundaries of Christendom. Conversely, the conference was being permitted to include in its purview Protestant efforts to compete with Catholics or Orthodox for the conversion of Muslims, Hindus, or animists, even in situations where Protestant missions were, from the standpoint of their Catholic counterparts, interlopers in a Catholic mission field. The nature of the American response to the principle contended for by the Anglican bishops meant that only missions operating within large territorial units where the majority of the population were recipients of Christian baptism were to be excluded: all other conversionist efforts were by implication either legitimated or condoned. Hence Oldham could observe in a letter to Dennis that the outcome demonstrated how liberal an interpretation the bishops were willing to place on their central principle, reassuring him that they were not going to quibble over any particular application, so long as the principle itself was respected.[59]

58. See Montgomery's earlier memorandum of 3 Feb. 1909; see above, p. 52.
59. NCE, Oldham papers, box 1, folder 3, Oldham to Dennis, 8 May 1909.

Evangelical Reactions

Despite his observations to Dennis, Oldham himself was left with a lingering unease that for a time sharpened to anxiety. As he commented in a letter to Mott on 21 May, it was impossible to avoid giving the public impression that all work that was included in the statistics was endorsed, and all that was excluded was thereby discredited. The latter implication was indeed one that the bishops desired to give. However, because evangelical Protestants believed passionately in the theological legitimacy of the mission work they were doing in Latin America, the Caribbean, or indeed Europe, Oldham recognized that its exclusion marked 'the one point in which we depart from the fundamental principle of the conference, that we ask from none of those who cooperate any surrender of conviction'.[60] Adhering to that fundamental principle as far as High Anglicans were concerned had meant infringing it in relation to evangelicals. The decision to restrict the territorial scope of the conference had drawn strong and immediate criticism in Britain from the leaders of the Baptist and Wesleyan Methodist Missionary Societies, and the China Inland Mission. Their reaction, Oldham explained to Mott, was symptomatic of an atmosphere in England of 'suspicion between the Church and Nonconformity which makes things very difficult'.[61] Other British missionary leaders accepted the decision as unavoidable, but privately expressed their regret. John H. Ritson, for example, who was intimately involved in planning the conference and was a member of Commission VIII, pointed out in a letter designed to mollify William Wilkes of the Regions Beyond Missionary Union, which had work in Latin America, that 'The decision hits no one harder than the B.F.B.S., as we spend half our money on the Continent of Europe.'[62] It was ironic that the Bible Society, the most comprehensively ecumenical of all Protestant missionary agencies, should have suffered perhaps more than any other body as a result of a decision taken in the name of Christian unity.

Oldham's unease may, however, have been exaggerated. The majority of leaders of denominational Protestant missions appear to have regarded the limitations imposed by Anglican convictions as a price worth paying, perhaps because they were themselves more or less ambivalent about the acceptability of the notion of Christendom. R. Wardlaw Thompson of the LMS, for instance, in defending to Lord Kinnaird the concession made to the Anglo-

---

60. NCE, Oldham papers, box 1, folder 3, Oldham to Mott, 21 May 1909.

61. NCE, Oldham papers, box 1, folder 3, Oldham to Mott, 21 May 1909.

62. CUL, BSA/F4/3/1. fol. 93, John H. Ritson to William Wilkes, 7 April 1909. Nevertheless, the RBMU participated in the Edinburgh conference, sending three representatives.

Catholics, referred to his regret at the necessity for restricting the sphere of the conference to missions 'working among non-Christian peoples'.[63] Yet Thompson appears himself to have subscribed to a strongly territorial understanding of Christendom and heathendom, an understanding that made fundamental objection to the Anglican case ultimately untenable.[64] Given the widespread acceptance of such premises among evangelical Protestants, there was little doubt that the Anglo-Catholic case would ultimately triumph, because, if Europe and North America were deemed to be within Christendom and hence beyond the scope of evangelistic mission, how could the same status logically be denied to Latin America? As Oldham had commented to Mott at an early stage of the controversy, 'If you admit work among the Roman Catholics in South America why should we exclude such work in papal Europe?'[65] When the British executive committee met in York on 30 June 1909, there was no dissent from Oldham's proposal that, 'in order to remove misconception', a sub-title should be added to the words 'World Missionary Conference': 'to consider Missionary Problems in relation to the Non-Christian World'.[66]

Negotiations with the Archbishop of Canterbury

The way was now clear for an official approach to be made to the archbishop of Canterbury. On 5 July 1909 a deputation comprising Oldham, Mott, Tissington Tatlow, and Prebendary H. E. Fox of the CMS, with Bishop Montgomery additionally present, waited on Randall Davidson at Lambeth Palace to invite him to address the opening meeting of the conference on 14 June 1910. The archbishop expressed polite interest, but pointed out the difficulties of his position which prevented him from making an immediate decision:

> how my going thither might compromise some people who are quite willing to keep silence, although they disapprove of the joint action, but who would not keep silence if they thought that by the Archbishop's presence the whole Church was committed. I told them that I must

63. SOAS, CWMA, LMS Home Office Outward Letters, box 2, Thompson to Lord Kinnaird, 24 May 1910.

64. For Thompson's belief that the time was not ripe to include delegates from churches 'in non-Christian lands' see below, Chapter 5, pp. 103-4.

65. NCE, Oldham papers, box 1, folder 2, Oldham to Mott, 10 March 1909.

66. ECG, World Missionary Conference (1910), minutes of executive committee, 30 June 1909, p. 44.

think the whole matter over and take counsel with those who can advise me best.[67]

The deputation indicated that they could wait for two to three months for a decision. A week after the Lambeth meeting Cosmo Lang, archbishop of York, whom Oldham had also invited to address the conference, sought Davidson's advice on whether he should accept.[68] Davidson replied that, whilst he did not think it possible that he could attend himself, Lang should certainly accept.[69] Oldham remained pessimistic, writing to Silas McBee on 28 July 1909 that, whilst it would be 'a great triumph for Christian unity' if both Lang and Davidson were to be secured to speak at Edinburgh, he feared that the latter was 'not very likely to accept'.[70] Several months passed, and Oldham wrote to Davidson seeking a definite response. Davidson's reply was tetchy: 'I have been, and am, under continuous pressure. Surely I have done enough for you without coming?'[71] With the standing committee of the SPG taking a hostile stance to the conference, and the *Church Times* full of dire warnings against the surrender of church principles to undenominationalism, there were grounds for Davidson's hesitation.[72] His room for manoeuvre was, however, expanded on 24 February 1910, when the lower house of the convocation of Canterbury voted, after initial hesitation and despite vocal opposition from a group of SPG supporters, to send a message of cordial greeting to the conference, followed a day later by the unanimous backing of the upper house, led by Davidson in the chair.[73] Yet still the archbishop hung back.

Matters came to a head as a result of an unauthorised report in the *Daily*

67. LP, Davidson papers, vol. 269, fol. 25, notes by Randall Davidson of deputation dated 5 July 1909, cited in G. K. A. Bell, *Randall Davidson Archbishop of Canterbury*, 2nd edn. (London: OUP, 1938), pp. 573-4; see also rough notes of the meeting, presumably taken by one of Davidson's staff, at fols. 26-7.

68. LP, Davidson papers, vol. 269, fol. 32, Lang to Davidson, 12 July 1909.

69. LP, Davidson papers, vol. 269, fol. 33, note from 'AS' [A. Sheppard, Esq., the archbishop's private secretary] to Lang, 15 July 1909. Archbishop Lang did accept and addressed the conference on the evening of 19 June. See UTS, MRL 12, WMC papers, series 1, box 23, folder 15, Oldham to Silas McBee, 22 Sept. 1909.

70. UTS, MRL 12, WMC papers, series 1, box 23, folder 15, Oldham to Silas McBee, 28 July 1909.

71. NCE, Oldham papers, box 22, folder 2, unpublished manuscript on Oldham by Kathleen Bliss, pp. 76-77, cited in Clements, *Faith on the Frontier*, p. 88. I have been unable to locate the original of this letter in either the Davidson or the Oldham papers.

72. *Church Times*, 4 March 1910, p. 285.

73. *The Chronicle of the Convocation of Canterbury*, 23-25 Feb. 1910, pp. 40-2, 64-70, 84; *Church Times*, 25 Feb. 1910, p. 215, 4 March 1910, p. 305; Clements, *Faith on the Frontier*, p. 87.

Graphic which was interpreted as saying that Davidson had consented to take part in the conference. In fact the newspaper had said merely that the conference was 'now engaging the support and co-operation of so many excellent Churchmen like the Archbishop of Canterbury, the Bishop of Birmingham, the Rev. the Lord Gascoyne Cecil, and many distinguished laymen'.[74] Embarrassed, Oldham wrote to the archbishop on 4 March 1910 disclaiming any responsibility for the report, but taking the opportunity to intimate that 'we should like to be able to make a statement before long regarding those who hope to take part in the Conference'.[75] Davidson replied warmly, but indicating that 'I think on the whole that I ought not to accept the invitation'. He pleaded a full diary, the unpredictable state of public affairs, and the fact that the Church of England would be well represented through Lang, Gore, Talbot, Montgomery, and many more.[76] Oldham brought the archbishop's letter before his committee on 1 April. The committee seized on the tentative tone of Davidson's refusal, and instructed Oldham to write again, inquiring 'whether we must regard this decision as altogether final'.[77] As Davidson considered Oldham's renewed inquiry, he also received word from a jubilant Bishop Montgomery that he had finally persuaded the SPG, after a good deal of wavering in the face of a determined campaign of opposition by a large group of extreme High Churchmen, to lend its official support to the conference.[78] That news appears to have been decisive for the archbishop. On 18 April he wrote to Lang 'I do feel the uniqueness of the Edinburgh Conference, and I should feel it horribly were I supposed to have treated it with lukewarmness or mere external sympathy. You know that S.P.G. has now consented officially to take part. I thank God for this'.[79] At the same time Davidson informed Oldham of his agreement to speak at the opening session of the conference on the evening of Tuesday, 14 June.[80] Oldham finally had his prize.

74. *Daily Graphic*, 26 Feb. 1910, p. 12.

75. LP, Davidson papers, vol. 269, fol. 54, Oldham to Davidson, 4 March 1910.

76. LP, Davidson papers, vol. 269, fol. 55, Davidson to Oldham, 8 March 1910.

77. LP, Davidson papers, vol. 269, fols. 59-60, Oldham to Davidson, 13 April 1910. There is no minute to this effect in the minutes of the executive committee of 1 April 1910. Oldham's letter refers to 'the Committee which has charge of the programme for the Conference'.

78. LP, Davidson papers, vol. 269, fol. 61, Montgomery to Davidson, 14 April 1910. H. P. Thompson, *Into All Lands: the history of the Society for the Propagation of the Gospel in Foreign Parts 1701-1950* (London: SPCK, 1951), p. 487, is incorrect to state that the SPG delegates at Edinburgh were only unofficial representatives of the Society. See below, Chapter 10, p. 290.

79. LP, Davidson papers, vol. 269, fol. 66, Davidson to Lang, 18 April 1910.

80. LP, Davidson papers, vol. 269, fols. 67-69, Davidson to Oldham, 18 April 1910.

The Unity of Christendom Preserved — But at What Price?

Whilst in Britain the course of the controversy was dictated by the pressures of ecclesiastical politics, in the United States the responses of mission leaders to the controversy were essentially pragmatic throughout. With the exception of the Episcopalians, few welcomed the conditions imposed by the Anglicans. There was rather a resigned and somewhat bemused acceptance of the situation as a regrettable necessity imposed by British peculiarities. Such appears to have been Mott's own view, although as an absentee from New York in April 1909, he had exerted little influence on the crucial meetings with Oldham, despite his specific instructions to Andersen. Mott regarded the issues of principle at stake in the controversy as significant mainly in regard to their potentially divisive consequences. In his efforts to avert such consequences, he appeared to vacillate over the issues themselves. To a correspondent such as Julius Richter who had from the beginning favoured making a clear distinction in the statistics between missions to non-Christian and nominally Christian peoples, Mott could comment on 2 April 1909 that the decision to accede to Anglican wishes was one that personally he had favoured from the beginning.[81] His acceptance of the title change to Commission I was, however, only grudging.[82] Only eight weeks later, writing to the American student leader, R. P. Wilder, who had reported the widespread feeling even in Britain that too much had been conceded to Anglo-Catholic scruples, Mott confessed 'I have come to the conclusion that possibly our Committee have gone too far — that we have been led beyond where we intended to go'.[83] Mott promised to take the matter up when he met the British executive in York on 30 June, but if he did so, it was without success.[84] In reality there was little that Mott could do to reverse the undermining of his global vision for his Commission. On 20 May the American members of Commission I, meeting in New York in his absence, had considered 'with great care' the responses of the 4 May meeting of the British advisory council to the list of questions they had submitted, and accepted the British recommendations with only one hesitation. That was with respect to the status of the black population of Central America and the Caribbean, whom the Americans felt 'have had so much less of Christian influence than the negroes in the United States as to justify their classification as non-Christian'. The Americans even

81. YDS, RG45, Mott papers, box 74, folder 1348, Mott to Richter, 2 April 1909.
82. YDS, RG45, Mott papers, box 74, folder 1358, Mott to Robson, 27 April 1909.
83. YDS, RG38, R. P. Wilder papers, box 10, folder 109, Mott to Wilder, 3 June 1909.
84. ECG, World Missionary Conference (1910), minutes of executive committee, 30 June 1909.

adopted the quixotic British solution on the Levant — including missionaries but excluding their converts — and applied it to the Philippines.[85]

From the standpoint of present-day ecumenical orthodoxy, the overall outcome may appear highly desirable. Edinburgh 1910 implicitly declared Protestant proselytism of Roman Catholics, and, rather less clearly of Orthodox and Oriental Christians, to be no valid part of Christian mission. The principle of the unity of Christendom had been preserved, as the Anglican leaders had been determined that it should be. But this had been achieved only at a price which Bishop Montgomery at least regarded as regrettable though still necessary — the division of humanity into two along lines that were not strictly confessional, but primarily geographical. The centuries-old gulf in western Christian thinking between territorial Christendom and the so-called 'non-Christian world' was now wider than ever. From the perspective of most present-day theologies of mission, the stance taken by the conference was indefensible in that it had restricted the mission of the Church (and by ultimate implication also the mission of God) to certain geographically demarcated portions of humanity. The deleterious consequences of that restriction are still being played out. The exclusion of Latin America from the conference agenda had the further effect of accentuating the existing Protestant tendency to identify the West with Christianity and the Orient with heathendom. Ironically, just two years after the Vatican had removed the United States from the jurisdiction of Propaganda Fide, and hence recognized that the United States now belonged within Christendom, the leaders of global Protestantism had drawn the boundaries of their own version of the Christian world.

85. UTS, MRL 12, WMC papers, series 1, box 7, folder 5, minutes of Commission I, 20 May 1909. The Commission deputed Prof. Beach to take up with the British advisory council the classification of African Americans in Central America and the West Indies, but the British recommendation on the matter was upheld in the *Statistical Atlas*, p. 75, which includes figures for these regions only for Indians and Asiatic immigrants.

CHAPTER 4

The Conference in Session

Conference Logistics

The Edinburgh conference, despite its much greater prominence in current historical memory, was on a noticeably smaller scale than its predecessors in London in 1888 and New York in 1900. The former had 1,579 delegates; the latter over 2,500, in comparison with Edinburgh's list of 1,215 official delegates.[1] 1,008 of the official delegates in 1910 were men, and 207 were women. The majority, according to one observer, 'seemed to have gone gray in their service':[2] the missionary society committees who determined the composition of the delegations gave priority to those of long experience and mature years. Total attendance at the 1910 conference and its penumbra of events was of course, larger than the number of official delegates, but probably still on a smaller scale than that witnessed in 1888 or 1900. By February 1910 John H. Ritson was anticipating a total attendance in Edinburgh of about 4,800 persons, and warning that 'thousands more' would be disappointed on account of the intense demand for tickets for the public meetings.[3] If one includes the numbers (a large proportion of whom were women)[4] who at-

---

1. Thomas A. Askew, 'The 1888 London Centenary Missions Conference: ecumenical disappointment or American missions coming of age?', *IBMR* 18:3 (July 1994), p. 113; *Ecumenical Missionary Conference New York, 1900*, 2 vols. (London and New York: Religious Tract Society and American Tract Society, 1900), I, pp. 22, 25.

2. *Missionary Herald of the Presbyterian Church of Ireland*, 1 Aug. 1910, p. 189.

3. CUL, BSA/F4/3/1, fols. 133-4, John H. Ritson to A. T. Dence, 5 Feb. [1910].

4. 'James Adamson, 'The World Missionary Conference. Synod Hall meetings', *Missionary Record of the United Free Church of Scotland* 117 (Sept. 1910), p. 393.

tended the 'parallel conference' for home workers for foreign missions in the Synod Hall, Castle Terrace, and also those attending the various public meetings held during the second week of the conference in the Tolbooth Church, aggregate daily attendances in the three venues of the Assembly Hall of the United Free Church of Scotland, the Synod Hall, and the Tolbooth Church reached between 6,000 and 7,000.[5] There was also a sectional conference on medical missions held in two Edinburgh venues (the Edinburgh Café and the Hall of the Royal College of Physicians) on 20-21 June, which was attended by twenty-seven local medical practitioners and forty-six medical missionaries who were not delegates at the main conference, as well as by fifty-seven medical missionaries who were. Further public meetings addressed by leading figures at the conference were also held in Glasgow during the second week at St George's Church, Buchanan Street, St Andrew's Hall, and in the Queen's Rooms.[6]

Organizing an event of this size in an era before the invention of modern electronic communication posed a considerable logistical challenge embracing everything from transportation to accommodation. A modern 12,760-ton steamer of the Red Star Line, the *Kroonland,* was chartered to ship North American delegates across the Atlantic at a 10% discount fare. The *Kroonland* sailed from New York on 31 May and docked at Southampton on 9 June in time for members of the Commissions to reach Edinburgh by rail by the early date of 10 June. For ordinary delegates who wished a more leisurely progression to Edinburgh, a special tourist rail itinerary was arranged from Southampton that encompassed Oxford, Stratford-on Avon, Chester, the Lake District, and Melrose.[7] After the conference attractive travel options were on offer to North American visitors which permitted a trip to Oberammergau to see the Passion Play, followed by either Switzerland and Paris or a Mediterranean cruise on a chartered steam yacht to Greece, Turkey, and the Holy Land.[8] All delegates were provided with travel vouchers which entitled them to purchase return rail fares to Edinburgh from the principal railway companies at the advantageous rate of a single fare plus a quarter. Those attending the conference in capacities other than as official delegates were expected to find hotel or boarding house accommodation, although a member of the conference office staff, W. L. H. Paterson, was set aside to assist

5. *History and Records of the Conference,* p. 29; *Missionary Herald of the Presbyterian Church of Ireland,* 1 Aug. 1910, p. 189; *Women's Missionary Magazine of the United Presbyterian Church* 24: 2 (Sept. 1910), p. 42.

6. *History and Records of the Conference,* pp. 30, 113, 130-2.

7. World Missionary Conference 1910, *Monthly News Sheet* 3 (Dec. 1909), p. 63.

8. UTS, WMC papers, box 24, folder 10, brochure for *Kroonland.*

visitors with booking their lodging.[9] Between seventy and eighty members of the British and American press were sent to Edinburgh to cover the conference, including no less than three reporters from *The Times*.[10] Most of the 1,215 official delegates and their wives were accommodated in private homes in Edinburgh for the period from 13 to 24 June, which must have imposed a considerable demand on the hospitality of Edinburgh church members. A few exceptions were made for the most important delegates, who were allocated hotel accommodation. Oldham ensured that Mott, who described himself as a notoriously poor sleeper, was given two quiet rooms for his secretary and himself at the Caledonian Station (now Caledonian Hilton) Hotel on Princes Street; Oldham also reserved a room for his own use there, to obviate the necessity for constant journeys to and from his home at 23 Murrayfield Gardens.[11] W. Jennings Bryan, the Democrat politician and later champion of fundamentalism, who had thrice stood unsuccessfully for the American presidency, was also accommodated in the same hotel. Another guest of political eminence, the Hon. Yun Ch'iho, former vice-minister of foreign affairs in the Korean government, was also placed in a hotel (the Balmoral), along with his missionary minder, Bishop W. R. Lambuth, secretary of the Board of Missions of the Methodist Episcopal Church, South. The president of the conference, Lord Balfour of Burleigh, who had served as secretary of state for Scotland in A. J. Balfour's Conservative administration from 1902 to 1903 and was 'perhaps the most outstanding figure in the public life of Scotland',[12] was accommodated at the New Club, 85 Princes Street. Four of the Asian delegates (V. S. Azariah, Harada Tasuku, Thang Khan Sangma, and Tong Tsing-En) were among a small group of delegates accommodated in the recently opened United Free Church Women's Missionary Institute (now the St Colm's International Centre) at 23 Inverleith Terrace: with six other delegates, they commemorated their visit by the gift of a picture which hangs in St Colm's to this day.[13] Some of the Edinburgh church members who were allocated overseas

---

9. World Missionary Conference 1910, *Monthly News Sheet* 8 (May 1910), p. 172.

10. *Missionary Record of the United Free Church of Scotland* 116 (Aug. 1910), p. 342; *History and Records of the Conference*, p. 20.

11. NCE, Oldham papers, box I, folder 4, Oldham to Mott, 23 Nov. 1909, and Mott to Oldham, 9 Dec. 1909; YDS, Record Group 45, Mott papers, box 63, folder 1169, Mott to Oldham, 3 Feb. 1910.

12. *ODNB*, vol. 8, p. 281.

13. For the Women's Missionary Institute see David F. Wright and Gary Badcock (eds.) *Disruption to Diversity: Edinburgh Divinity 1846-1996* (Edinburgh: T&T Clark, 1996), p. 255. The other delegates accommodated at the Institute were Bishop and Mrs J. W. Bashford, Miss M. C. Gollock, Miss Ruth Rouse, and the Revd and Mrs Nicol MacNicol. The picture, depicting a pastoral scene, and labelled 'Other sheep I have' [John 10:16],

visitors as guests must have had memorable experiences: for example, a Mrs Simpson of 'Highbury', 20 Stanley Road, Trinity, had both Bishop Honda Yoitsu from Japan and the Rev. W. W. Beckett, an African American delegate from the African Methodist Episcopal Church, staying in her home.[14] The archbishop of Canterbury elected to stay at his boyhood home at Muirhouse on the shore of the Firth of Forth, with his relative, J. H. Davidson.[15]

All official delegates paid a registration fee of ten shillings. Registration entitled them to free delivery of a proof set of the eight Commission reports and a copy of the printed and illustrated conference handbook.[16] The proofs were so voluminous that few delegates can have had time to read them in advance of the conference.[17] The handbook contained full information on arrangements for transportation and accommodation, the conference programme for both the Assembly Hall and Synod Hall meetings, and two complete lists of delegates' names and addresses arranged first by missionary society and then by nationality. It also included a hymnal containing forty-five hymns for use in the sessions of worship, and numerous advertisements for missionary and other agencies.[18] Delegates were issued with a small cardboard badge on which to write their names and church affiliation, as has since become *de rigueur* with conferences. The majority of delegates, however, apparently declined to wear their badges, despite repeated entreaties in the *Conference Daily Paper* for each delegate to do so.[19] The ground floor of the conference office at 100

---

hangs in the Moinet Room at St Colm's International Centre with a plaque that records the presence of these delegates for the conference. They donated the picture in gratitude for their stay (St Colm's archives, *Journal of the Women's Missionary Training Institute, 10-27 June 1910*, pp. 141-6). L. T. Ah Sou, K. C. Chatterjee, Cheng Jingyi, Yugoro Chiba, J. R. Chitambar, S. A. C. Ghose, Honda Yoitsu, Kajinosuke Ibuka, Shivram Masoji, John Rungiah, R. K. Sorabji, and Tsang Ding Tong were accommodated at various private addresses. UTS, WMC papers, series 1, box 24, folder 5, item 532, 'List of Addresses Registered by Delegates During the Conference'. No address is listed for Johannes Awetaranian.

14. UTS, WMC papers, series 1, box 24, folder 5, item 532, 'List of Addresses Registered by Delegates During the Conference', pp. 6, 25.

15. The Davidson family home is described in G. K. A. Bell, *Randall Davidson Archbishop of Canterbury*, 2nd edn. (London: OUP, 1938), pp. 9-10.

16. World Missionary Conference 1910, *Monthly News Sheet* 7 (April 1910), p. 146.

17. See R. E. Speer's comment in Princeton Theological Seminary, Special Collections, Robert E. Speer personal letters, box 6, vol. 17, fol. 308, R. E. Speer to Paul Barnhardt, 13 June 1910 (dictated 3 June 1910).

18. *World Missionary Conference 1910, Edinburgh, June 14-23 [Official Handbook]* (Edinburgh: World Missionary Conference Office, 1910).

19. *Missionary Herald of the Presbyterian Church of Ireland*, 1 Aug. 1910, p. 194; World Missionary Conference 1910, *Conference Daily Paper* 5 (18 June 1910), p. 69, and 6 (20 June 1910), p. 89, etc.

Princes Street was devoted to a showroom, in which an assortment of publishers displayed their wares of missionary books. A conference daily newspaper was produced, which contained conference announcements, the minutes of the previous day's proceedings, and the agenda for the day. The nine issues of the paper were delivered to each delegate at their registered Edinburgh address by first post in time for each morning session, a feat of postal delivery which the Post Office today would struggle to emulate.[20]

The Opening of the Conference

Before the conference itself got fully under way, five preliminary gatherings of very different kinds took place. The first was a prayer meeting in the Assembly Hall on the afternoon of Monday, 13 June, presided over by Sir Andrew Fraser; it was 'very largely attended'.[21] The second was a grand civic reception held at 8.10 pm that evening in the Great Hall of the Royal Scottish Museum in Chambers Street (now known as the Royal Museum).[22] Up to 5,000 people attended, made up of conference delegates, their hosts and hostesses, and the large number of mission workers who had come to Edinburgh to attend the parallel sessions in the Synod Hall. The Great Hall, its galleries and staircases were packed to capacity. All the movable exhibits in the Great Hall were pushed to one side to create a wide thoroughfare running the whole length of the museum. Flowers and palms from the City Gardens decorated the Hall and the corridors. The reception was hosted by the lord provost of Edinburgh, magistrates, and city councillors, resplendent in their scarlet robes. The lord provost, Sir William Slater Brown, was attended by uniformed halberdiers, and the kilted band of the Edinburgh Police Pipers played. It was an impressive occasion. The chief city officer solemnly announced the names and nationalities of each of the guests, until it was realized at about nine o'clock that this procedure would protract the ceremony unduly if continued. One awed American commentator observed, 'one could see why it is that the cities of Great Britain are so much better governed than ours and why it is regarded as high honor to render unpaid service as member of council.'[23] But the English seem to have been no

20. *World Missionary Conference 1910, Edinburgh, June 14-23 [Official Handbook]*, p. 27; World Missionary Conference 1910, *Conference Daily Paper* 1-9 (14-23 June 1910), (Edinburgh, 1910).

21. *History and Records of the Conference*, p. 22.

22. See the report in *The Scotsman*, 14 June 1910, p. 8.

23. Howard B. Grose, 'The Edinburgh conference: a pen picture of the world meeting', *Missions* 1:9 (Sept. 1910), p. 567.

less entranced by the ceremony. The correspondent of *The Baptist Times and Freeman* gave his pen free course as he lyrically described the exotic global miscellany of humanity arrayed before his eyes against the background of the no less exotic exhibits of natural history on display in the museum:

> The delegates came by in their thousands from the ends of the earth and the ultimate islands of the sea. The first delegate presented came from Constantinople. Others followed from Peking and Toronto, Boston and Benares, Dublin and Delhi, Moscow, Tokyo, Shanghai and Samoa, Christiania, New York and Papua, Jerusalem, Berlin, Cairo, and Capetown. The cosmopolitan animals and relics in the Museum had also a quaint appropriateness. One would see a Baptist missionary from Congo side by side with an African negro, gazing up at a mighty elephant, while zebras, hyenas, kangaroos, bisons, and wolves formed a background to men and women from the very lands whence the animals came.[24]

In fact, as will be explained in Chapter 5, what the Baptist journalist saw was most probably not a black African (only one such was present), but more likely one of the six or more African American delegates. Addresses were given by the lord provost; the chairman of the American executive committee, Dr Arthur Judson Brown; Lord Balfour of Burleigh; and Bishop La Trobe of the Moravian Church. Lord Provost Brown expressed his satisfaction that Edinburgh — 'the finest city in the world, not excepting Washington! — had been chosen for the great gathering.' Arthur Judson Brown aptly quoted Robert Burns's 'Address to Edinburgh' to describe the welcome which the overseas delegates had received:

> Thy sons, Edina, social, kind,
> With open arms the stranger hail.

Lord Balfour and Bishop La Trobe returned thanks to the provost and corporation of Edinburgh for the city's hospitality to the conference, and Bishop La Trobe brought a fulsome message of greeting from the German Colonial Office, which noted 'with satisfaction and gratitude that the endeavours for the spread of the Gospel are followed by the blessings of civilisation and culture in all countries'.[25]

24. *Baptist Times and Freeman*, 17 June 1910, p. 393.
25. *Ibid.*, p. 393; *History and Records of the Conference*, p. 20; Gairdner, *'Edinburgh 1910'*, p. 45.

The third preliminary event was a service of worship held in St Giles' Cathedral at 12 noon on Tuesday 14 June. The sermon on the text from Matthew 13:38 'The field is the world' was preached by the Revd Dr Andrew Wallace Williamson, minister of St Giles', who was one of the special delegates appointed by the British executive committee. Williamson compared the coming conference — 'met in a unique fashion under a veritable truce of God for the practical purposes of the Kingdom' — with the great ecumenical councils of the early centuries, which had so often been the scene of strife and disorder.[26] This was followed at 3 p.m. by the preliminary business session of the conference, which within the space of thirty minutes approved the standing orders and rules of debate of the conference that had been prepared by the business committee, and unanimously elected the conference's officers: Mott as chairman; Oldham as secretary; and J. H. Ritson and his fellow-Methodist, Newton W. Rowell, K.C., a Toronto barrister and later chief justice of Canada, as recording clerks.[27] During the business session a telegram, sent from the noon prayer meeting of the CMS general committee, was handed to the president, asking that the petition of Christ in John 17:21 — 'that they all may be one . . . that the world might believe that thou hast sent me' — might be fulfilled for the conference. Lord Balfour read the telegram and the text to the assembly 'with great solemnity amid profound silence'. It was, in the judgment of one commentator, a symbolic moment that set the tone for the conference.[28]

At 5 p.m. the fifth and final preliminary function took place, when the University of Edinburgh held an honorary degree ceremony in the McEwan Hall in Teviot Place, presided over by the vice-chancellor, principal Sir William Turner. No less than fourteen conference delegates, two of whom were Asians, received honorary doctorates in an unprecedented outpouring of academic recognition towards the missionary movement. Honorary doctorates of divinity were bestowed on the following eight delegates: K. C. Chatterjee, moderator of the General Assembly of the Presbyterian Church in India; W. Douglas Mackenzie, president of Hartford Seminary in Connecticut and chairman of Commission V; F. L. Hawks Pott, Protestant Episcopal missionary in China and principal of St John's University, Shanghai; Pastor Julius Richter of Belzig, Germany; C. H. Robinson, the Hausa scholar and editorial secretary of the SPG; Robert E. Speer, the American Presbyterian mission leader; Ralph Wardlaw Thompson, veteran foreign secretary of

26. W. Nelson Bitton, 'Report of the proceedings of the World Missionary Conference in Edinburgh', *Chinese Recorder* (Aug. 1910), p. 531.

27. *History and Records of the Conference,* pp. 23, 72-7.

28. Grose, 'The Edinburgh conference', pp. 559-60.

the LMS; and Johannes Warneck, foreign secretary of the Rhenish Mission, and son of Professor Gustav Warneck of Halle. The award of the honorary doctorates was only made public a few days beforehand; Speer knew nothing of his impending honour until the night before.[29] Six delegates received the degree of honorary doctor of laws: Archbishop Randall Davidson; General James Addams Beaver, former governor of Pennsylvania and a delegate of the Board of Foreign Missions of the Presbyterian Church in the USA; Revd Dr Harada Tasuku, president of the Doshisha institution and one of the foremost leaders of Japan's small Protestant community; the Hon. Seth Low, New York businessman, civic politician, and vice-chairman of Commission VII; Karl Meinhof, professor of African languages at the Colonial Institute in Hamburg, who was a special delegate appointed by the continental executive committee; and, finally, John Mott himself.[30] The archbishop of Canterbury, 'as an Edinburgh-born man, received a great ovation', but the names of Mott and Speer, according to one source, were greeted by the students present with 'by far the heartiest applause . . . being hailed with tumultuous cheering', on account of their renown among university students.[31] Another source, paradoxically, says precisely the opposite so far as Speer was concerned: when Speer's name was called, 'dead silence fell upon the student group'; 'it was eloquent tribute of the student body of the University of another country, to one whom they regarded as doing most for the student life of the world'.[32] The principal of Edinburgh University broke with precedent by inviting several of the recipients of the degrees to make a short speech each. Harada Tasuku made a particular impression by speaking of the debt which Japan owed to the great men of Scottish intellectual history and of the work they had done to cement the sympathies of Asia and Europe. Davidson, Low, Meinhof, and Mott also spoke.[33]

The first full session of the conference assembled at 8 p.m. that evening under the imposing chairmanship of Lord Balfour, 'towering gigantic above the desk' (he measured some 6 foot 5 inches in height), and resplendent in his decorations and the silver star and green sash of a knight of the Thistle, worn 'to salute the missionaries of Christ, as he would have worn them at some

29. Princeton Theological Seminary, Special Collections, Robert E. Speer papers, box 6, vol. 17, fol. 357, Robert E. Speer to Professor John Meigs, 23 Aug. 1910.

30. *Ibid.*, pp. 22-3.

31. Bitton, 'Report of the proceedings', p. 532; R. K. Hanna, *Some Impressions of the World Missionary Conference* (Belfast: R. Carswell & Son, 1910), pp. 3-4.

32. Cited in John F. Piper, Jr., *Robert E. Speer: prophet of the American church* (Louisville: Geneva Press, 2000), p. 204.

33. Bitton, 'Report of the proceedings', p. 532.

high ceremonial in Windsor Castle or Buckingham Palace'.[34] After an opening hymn ('All people that on earth do dwell') and prayer offered by Dr Alexander Whyte, principal of New College, and formerly Oldham's senior minister at St George's Church in Edinburgh, Lord Balfour began his address by reading a message of greeting from the still-uncrowned new King, George V. King Edward VII had agreed in early 1909 to send such a message of greeting to the conference, if Lord Balfour could draft it for him. Within a week of his sudden death on 6 May 1910, Balfour had contacted the Buckingham Palace staff and at their request produced a draft which he sent to the Palace and to Archbishop Davidson for comment. The message as read to the conference represented Balfour's own draft with only minor alterations.[35] As the conference stood at Lord Balfour's bidding 'in the royal capital of a Christian king' to receive this royal greeting, Temple Gairdner was reminded of the historic role of the Roman emperor in opening the ecumenical councils of the early church.[36] In response, someone began singing the National Anthem, and the conference joined in, 'monarchists and republicans alike', Americans apparently included.[37] *The Missionary Record of the United Free Church of Scotland* was pleased to observe that 'the great-great-grandsons of the men who threw George III's chests of tea into Boston Harbour' sung as heartily as his own subjects.[38] The accuracy of such reports may have been stretched by imperial sentiment, but an American source paints a markedly similar picture:

> Everybody joined and made the rafters ring. The effect was electrical, and nothing could have drawn that mixed throng so close together. There they stood, British and American, Continentals and Indians, Chinese and Japanese, white, black, and brown, singing with one voice and soul, "God save the King!"[39]

The infectious power of British imperial motifs thus ironically played its part in making unity from the outset a dominant theme of the Edinburgh

---

34. *Missionary Record of the United Free Church of Scotland* 116 (Aug. 1910), p. 343; Alexander Smellie, *At the World Missionary Conference: a little narrative for friends who were not there* (Dundee: James P. Mathew, 1910), p. 13.

35. LP, Davidson papers, vol. 269, fols. 1-3, Lord Balfour of Burleigh to private secretary to the archbishop of Canterbury, 17 Dec. 1908; and fols. 71-5, Lord Balfour of Burleigh to Archbishop Davidson, 26 May 1910, and draft message of greeting from King George V to the World Missionary Conference.

36. *History and Records of the Conference*, p. 141; Gairdner, *'Edinburgh 1910'*, p. 38.

37. Gairdner, *'Edinburgh 1910'*, p. 39.

38. *Missionary Record of the United Free Church of Scotland* 116 (Aug. 1910), p. 343.

39. Grose, 'The Edinburgh conference', p. 564.

conference. Lord Balfour then went on in his address to strike repeatedly the note of the underlying and deepening unity which the delegates shared in the fulfilment of their common missionary task: 'we are drawing together now as perhaps we have never before been drawn together, in the prosecution of the great enterprise in which we are all interested.' He concluded by expressing the hope that 'a unity begun in the mission field may extend its influence and react upon us at home . . . that it may bring to us increased hope of international peace among the nations of the world, and of at least fraternal co-operation and perhaps a greater measure of unity in ecclesiastical matters at home.'[40]

Balfour was followed by the archbishop of Canterbury, in the memorably prophetic address described in Chapter 1 and whose complex background in Anglican ecclesiastical politics has been narrated in Chapter 3. The evening concluded with an impassioned oration by Robert E. Speer on 'Christ the leader of the missionary work of the church', an exposition of the evangelical theme of the Lordship of Christ and its implications for the church's mission. 'No one', insisted Speer, 'can follow Christ without following Him to the uttermost parts of the earth'. If only the church were to become alert to the full meaning of Christ's leadership, that living faith would then 'make it possible for Him to make use of us for the immediate conquest of the world'.[41] Both Davidson's and Speer's addresses appeared to make the missionary conquest of the world dependent on the measure of faith and obedience displayed by the Christian armies gathered that night on the Mound.

The Assembly Hall of the United Free Church of Scotland

Admission to the Assembly Hall, the venue for all the main conference sessions, was by ticket only, a rule which was strictly enforced by the student stewards at the main entrance. Stewards were given instructions to admit nobody to the premises without a ticket, with the sole exception of 'half-a-dozen distinguished people (e.g. the Presidents of the Conference and the Archbishops)'.[42] Seating arrangements were also carefully controlled. Official delegates were accommodated on the floor of the Hall and in the Moderator's gallery, immediately behind the speakers' platform, where the conference president and vice-presidents were seated. The square railed enclosure in

40. *History and Records of the Conference*, pp. 142, 145.
41. *Ibid.*, p. 154.
42. UTS, WMC papers, series 1, box 24, folder 5, *Instructions to Stewards*, p. 5.

front of the platform housed members of the conference business committee arranged around the clerks' table — among them, George Robson, Arthur Judson Brown, and, of course, J. H. Oldham, who, apart from the giving of notices, never opened his mouth to speak during the whole conference.[43] There also sat the two recording clerks of the conference, J. H. Ritson and Newton W. Rowell, and the stenographers responsible for recording the speeches. Immediately in front of the enclosure were seats reserved for the press, and on either side, in the central section to the right and left of the platform, were blocks of seats reserved for the continental delegates, who were perhaps given this privilege to assist their linguistic comprehension of proceedings which were invariably conducted in English. Two rows of seats near the platform were also reserved each day for members of the Commission whose report was under discussion that day. No other seats in the main body of the hall were reserved. The west gallery on the chairman's right was set aside for missionaries on furlough and the east gallery on the chairman's left for wives of official delegates (whether the same opportunity was extended to husbands of female delegates is not clear). These seats were allocated to those who had purchased tickets at the price of 7s. 6d. for missionaries, and 12s. 6d. for delegates' wives. The south gallery facing the platform, containing some 350 seats, was set aside for members of the public who were successful in obtaining day tickets; priority was given to those who had offered hospitality to delegates or assisted in some other way in the conference.[44] Competition for these ticketed seats was intense, and it was reported that throughout the ten days of the conference there was scarcely a vacant seat to be found anywhere in the Hall.[45] There was thus some strictly limited space for the general public, despite the fact that Edinburgh 1910 had been conceived by Mott and Oldham as primarily an event for officially appointed delegates.

The arrangement of the seating in the Assembly Hall made its own contribution to the degree of ecumenical interaction in the conference. It was not simply that the acoustics were described as excellent. W. H. Findlay, reflecting on the success of Edinburgh 1910, placed considerable emphasis on the benefits of the maximal eye contact between delegates which the Hall promoted:

> . . . it permitted the assembly to *look itself in the face.* Its seating was so arranged that almost every one present had before his eyes (or hers),

43. Gairdner, 'Edinburgh 1910', p. 65.

44. World Missionary Conference 1910, *Monthly News Sheet* 7 (April 1910), p. 146; *World Missionary Conference 1910, Edinburgh, June 14-23 [Official Handbook]*, p. 25; World Missionary Conference 1910, *Conference Daily Paper* 1 (14 June 1910), p. 1.

45. Smellie, *At the World Missionary Conference*, p. 9.

not, as in most halls, rows of backs of heads, with beyond them, the visages of a small platform group, but hundred of the faces of fellow-delegates and visitors. And as the days passed one realized how powerfully this providential arrangement contributed to the highest ends of the Conference, and in particular to its realization of fellowship.[46]

The Conference Programme

Beginning on Wednesday, 15 June, the conference followed a set daily pattern of meetings, which was followed without variation to its end, apart from on Sunday 19 June, when an evening meeting only was held. On the Sunday morning a communion service was held in St Giles' Cathedral, which was attended by members of 'many denominations and nationalities', though the Anglicans held their own eucharistic celebration in the church of St John the Evangelist: Edinburgh 1910 did not anticipate Kikuyu 1913 in promoting common eucharistic celebration between Anglicans and Protestants. Most of the pulpits of Edinburgh were also occupied both morning and evening by delegates to the conference.[47] Each of the eight days of normal conference business adhered, with only minor departures on timings, to the pattern proposed by the central advisory committee at its York meeting in December 1908.[48] The day began with fifteen minutes of devotions at 9.45 a.m., led by a different delegate each morning. After any conference business was speedily dispatched, the Commission report of the day was presented and discussed from 10 a.m. to 12.30 p.m. From 12.30 to 1.00 p.m. (and latterly at varying times during the morning) the conference devoted itself to united intercessory prayer. A light lunch was provided in the Rainy Hall, though delegates desiring a more substantial meal were advised to make their own arrangements in nearby hotels and restaurants.[49] The afternoon session, which always began with the singing of a hymn, took place from 2.30 to 4.30 p.m. and was devoted to further discussion of the Commission report. The evening meetings at 8.00 p.m. were intended to be of wider public interest, and two or three addresses were delivered each evening on a variety of mission themes.

---

46. W. H. Findlay, 'Sight, sound, and silence in Edinburgh', *London Quarterly Review* 114 (1910), p. 233.

47. *History and Records of the Conference*, p. 31.

48. See Chapter 2 above.

49. *World Missionary Conference 1910, Edinburgh, June 14-23 [Official Handbook]*, p. 27.

The Conduct of Debate

It was proposed at the meeting of the executive committee on 29 January 1910, and confirmed by the international committee on 1 April, that in its consideration of the Commission reports the conference should be deemed to be 'in Committee of the whole House', that there should be one chairman for all of these sessions, and that John R. Mott should be this chairman.[50] Mott was already an accomplished chairman before Edinburgh 1910, with wide experience in chairing meetings of the YMCA and WSCF. Nevertheless, he prepared himself with great seriousness for his forthcoming role at Edinburgh, studying manuals of procedure for public meetings and consulting widely with parliamentarians and other public figures on both sides of the Atlantic.[51] He seems, however, to have paid most attention to the methods that had been tried and tested at Edinburgh's ecumenical predecessors at Madras in 1902 and Shanghai in 1907. Mott's industry and attention to the minutiae of conference procedure paid dividends: the Edinburgh conference presents a model of how to manage large public assemblies. Each Commission was permitted no more than forty-five minutes to summarize and present its report: the remainder of the time was reserved for contributions by delegates who were not members of that Commission.[52] Following the procedure employed at the Madras conference of 1902 and again at the Shanghai conference in 1907,[53] delegates who wished to speak were required to obtain a printed card from an usher and complete it, giving details of their name, mission field of interest, and the aspect of the topic they wished to address. These cards were then passed to Mott as chairman, who continually sifted and re-classified the cards passed to him as the debate took its course and then called on those he wished to speak at a particular moment. To avoid delay Mott summoned two speakers together, with the second being ready to commence speaking as soon as the first had finished.[54] A

50. ECG, World Missionary Conference (1910), minutes of executive committee, 1 April 1910, p. 71, approval of minutes of international committee held on 29 Jan. 1910.

51. W. Richey Hogg, *Ecumenical Foundations: a history of the International Missionary Council and its nineteenth-century background* (New York: Harper & Bros, 1952), p. 122; Basil Mathews, *John R. Mott: world citizen* (New York and London: Harper Bros., 1934), pp. 318-19.

52. *History and Records of the Conference,* p. 73.

53. *Report of the Fourth Decennial Indian Missionary Conference Held in Madras December 11th-18th, 1902* (London and Madras: Christian Literature Society, n.d.), p. 16; *Records: China Centenary Missionary Conference Held at Shanghai, April 25 to May 8, 1907* (Shanghai: Centenary Conference Committee, 1907), p. xix.

54. Smellie, *At the World Missionary Conference,* pp. 9-10; Mathews, *John R. Mott,* p. 320.

rigid limit of seven minutes was placed on each speaker, no matter how eminent they might be: this rule again exactly duplicated that applied to the
Shanghai conference of 1907; at Madras in 1902 the limit had been only three
minutes.[55] A principal task of John H. Ritson as one of the two recording
clerks was surreptitiously to press the concealed button of the electric bell
which first sounded after six minutes and then again with uncompromising finality once seven minutes were up. He accomplished this task so inconspicu-
ously that even his fellow-Methodist, W. H. Findlay, a member of the British
executive committee, seemed unaware of precisely who had control of the bell;
and some have erroneously supposed that it was Mott's finger which pressed
the button.[56] Mott chaired the conference in a style which one observer described as 'formidable and Napoleonic'.[57] He would allow no-one to exceed
their allotted seven minutes, and wielded a benevolent dictatorship over the
conference that attracted general admiration but occasional hostility: 'Dr Mott
deals even-handed justice all round, and no speaker anxious to get in one more
telling illustration or appeal can hope to withstand the suave but ruthless bow
from the chair that dismisses him to his seat'.[58] One of those so dismissed, early
in the conference, was Bishop Gore, who was allegedly in the midst of a speech
explaining the basis on which the Anglo-Catholic representatives had consented to take part in the conference: that so eminent a personage should be
thus dealt with, and meekly accept his discipline, made a profound impression.[59] Mott was, however, scrupulously fair to the Anglo-Catholic minority,
giving their representatives ample opportunity to speak, as Bishop Montgomery gratefully acknowledged.[60]

By dint of Mott's draconian methods of time management, every Commission report received the attention of at least thirty separate speeches, and

55. *Records: China Centenary Missionary Conference Held at Shanghai*, p. xix; *Report of
the Fourth Decennial Indian Missionary Conference Held in Madras*, p. 16.

56. John H. Ritson, *The World is Our Parish* (London: Hodder & Stoughton, 1939),
p. 279; *Methodist Recorder*, 14 July 1910, p. 4, cited in Mathews, *John R. Mott*, pp. 321-2. Cf.
C. Howard Hopkins, *John R. Mott 1865-1955: a biography* (Grand Rapids: Eerdmans, 1979),
pp. 355, 732n. The bell was supplied by the conference treasurer, Harry Smith, who later re-
furbished it and offered it for use at the Jerusalem conference of 1928.

57. *Missionary Record of the United Free Church of Scotland* 116 (Aug. 1910), p. 343.

58. *Ibid.*, p. 344. The occasional hostility towards Mott as chairman is alluded to by Stephen Neill, *Men of Unity* (London: SCM Press, 1960), p. 15.

59. J. H. Oldham, 'Reflections on Edinburgh, 1910', *Religion and Life* 29:3 (Summer
1960), pp. 333-4. Oldham's recollection that this episode took place during the first morning session (15th) is not supported by the minutes. Gore did, however, speak in the morning session on the 16th.

60. Mathews, *John R. Mott*, pp. 319-20.

in the course of the conference as a whole, over 300 speeches were delivered. The seven-minute limit also had the virtue of giving what R. E. Speer called 'a spice of pungency' to the debates, in comparison with which the longer addresses delivered in the evening sessions seemed to several observers prolix and lacklustre.[61] As one delegate wryly commented, 'You can stand any kind of bore if you know he is to be extinguished in seven minutes.'[62] The American speakers tended to be noticeably more direct and concise than the British ones, who too often took precious seconds or even more in pleading how difficult it was to say all they had to say in the time allowed.[63] There were always, however, far more cards on the chairman's table than he could possibly call. In view of the number of those signalling a desire to speak during the sessions held during the first few days, the business committee proposed on Saturday the 18th that the time allotment should be reduced to five minutes. This motion was strongly supported, but did not obtain the two-thirds majority necessary to secure a modification of the conference standing orders. On the final day, however, the business committee unilaterally reduced the time limit for speeches to five minutes, with the result that nearly fifty delegates spoke in the debate on the Commission VI report.[64]

It should also be noted that Mott did not hesitate to use his role as chairman to exercise positive discrimination in favour of both the Asian Christians and women speakers. Chapter 5 will discuss the encouragement which he gave to the Asian delegates to contribute. There is also evidence that Mott at an early point drew the conference's attention to the paucity of women offering to speak; he complained that on this occasion he had received only one card from a woman desiring to speak, compared with seventy or eighty from men.[65] The gender inbalance improved a little as the conference proceeded, and women's voices came briefly into their own on the penultimate morning, devoted to the discussion of the Commission V report on The Preparation of Missionaries, when six women addressed the conference in succession, out of a total of fifteen speakers from the floor.[66]

---

61. Robert E. Speer, 'The Edinburgh Missionary Conference — II', *The East and the West* 8:32 (Oct. 1910), pp. 372-3; see also *Church Missionary Review* 61:735 (July 1910), p. 408; *Record of Christian Work* 29:8 (Aug. 1910), p. 498.

62. *Missionary Herald* (Boston) 106 (1910), p. 353.

63. *Missionary Herald of the Presbyterian Church of Ireland* (1 Aug. 1910), pp. 194-5; cf. Oldham, 'Reflections on Edinburgh, 1910', p. 334.

64. World Missionary Conference 1910, *Conference Daily Paper* 6 (20 June 1910). Gairdner, 'Edinburgh 1910', p. 62, incorrectly dates this vote to the second day of the conference.

65. Hanna, *Some Impressions of the World Missionary Conference*, p. 26.

66. *History and Records of the Conference*, pp. 99-100.

The Spirituality of the Conference

Edinburgh 1910 was a conference of eager Christian activists, presided over by a man who was evangelical activism embodied: Mott, as Oldham freely acknowledged in retrospect, was 'not seriously interested in ideas. He was entirely unversed in theology or philosophy'.[67] The theological foundations of the passion for world evangelism displayed at Edinburgh may appear rather slender: as Bishop Brent pointed out, the conference was firmly Christocentric but rarely Trinitarian in its utterances — 'the main thought of God was as Jesus Christ' and 'there was little mention of the Holy Spirit'.[68] It would be a mistake, however, to conclude that the conference was spiritually shallow. Temple Gairdner regarded Edinburgh as the exception to the normal rule that 'the spirituality of a conference is very often in inverse proportion to its size'.[69] The most frequently sung hymns from the conference hymnal were not specifically missionary hymns of activism that focussed on the plight of the 'heathen' world but classic hymns of Christian devotion, such as 'Jesu, Thou joy of loving hearts', 'Crown Him with many crowns', or 'When I survey the wondrous cross'.[70]

The ethos of the conference was shaped by the spirituality of the Student Volunteer Movement, which combined zeal for world mission with a consistent emphasis on both private and corporate prayer. The Movement did not simply bind its members to play their part in discharging the famous and much-debated Watchword — 'the evangelization of the world in this generation' — it also committed them to a rigorous observance of the Morning Watch, an extended period of private daily prayer and Bible study, when student volunteers would plead in secret with 'the Lord of the Harvest' on behalf of the world. The practice of the Morning Watch was formalized in Cambridge in the 1880s, commended to Mott by Handley Moule, then principal of Ridley Hall, when he visited Cambridge in 1894, and then disseminated in the student movement across the Atlantic by Mott. The Watch and the Watchword were symbiotic.[71] In January 1910 J. H. Oldham was profoundly impressed by reading the book on intercessory prayer published in 1885 by the

---

67. J. H. Oldham, 'John R. Mott', *Ecumenical Review* 7:3 (April 1955), p. 259.

68. C. H. Brent, 'The World Missionary Conference — an interpretation', *The East and the West* 8:32 (Oct. 1910), p. 365.

69. Gairdner, *'Edinburgh 1910'*, p. 66.

70. Findlay, 'Sight, sound, and silence in Edinburgh', p. 237.

71. See my article, "Hunting for souls": the missionary pilgrimage of George Sherwood Eddy', in Pieter N. Holtrop and Hugh McLeod (eds.), *Missions and Missionaries*, Studies in Church History Subsidia 13 (Woodbridge: Boydell Press, 2000), pp. 128-9.

South African holiness leader, Andrew Murray, *With Christ in the School of Prayer; thoughts on our training for the ministry of intercession;* he commended the book to his colleagues on the SVMU executive as 'a very rich education in the school of prayer'.[72] Murray had also published a book following the New York Ecumenical Conference of 1900, at which he was a speaker, urging that 'the key to the missionary problem' was the power of prayer.[73] Throughout his life Oldham practised the discipline of breakfast-table prayers. Among his own publications the most widely used was probably his prayer manual, *Devotional Diary,* published in 1925.[74] The Student Christian Movement which did so much to prepare the way for Edinburgh 1910 was marked by a continual emphasis on the importance of both private and corporate prayer.[75]

It was thus not accidental that the Edinburgh conference placed considerable importance on the observance of daily prayer, most notably in the half-hour of intercessions, originally scheduled for 12.30 each day. The *Official Handbook* of the conference informed delegates that 'the central act of each day's proceedings will be the mid-day half-hour devoted to intercession' and that those responsible for the programme (particularly Oldham, one may surmise) believed that through this meeting for united prayer the conference could render greater service to the cause of world mission 'than in any other way'.[76] A number of commentators testified that the half-hour of daily intercession was indeed for them, 'the crown of each day's proceedings'.[77] However, by Friday, 18 June the business committee had decided that in future the chairman should be given discretion to call for the half-hour's intercession whenever he saw fit during the morning session, as the experience of the first three days was that too many delegates took the opportunity at 12.30 to slip away for an early lunch; for the remainder of the conference the intercessions took place mid-way through the morning session.[78] They were led by a great

72. UBL, SCM Archives, box A16, circular letter from J. H. Oldham to SVMU Executive, 13 Jan. 1910.

73. Andrew Murray, *The Key to the Missionary Problem,* 3rd edn. (London: James Nisbet & Co., 1902).

74. Keith Clements, *Faith on the Frontier: a life of J. H. Oldham* (Edinburgh and Geneva: T&T Clark and WCC Publications, 1999), pp. 35, 208-10.

75. Tissington Tatlow, *The Story of the Student Christian Movement of Great Britain and Ireland* (London: SCM Press, 1933), p. 461.

76. *World Missionary Conference 1910, Edinburgh, June 14-23 [Official Handbook],* p. 30.

77. Smellie, *At the World Missionary Conference,* p. 11. See also W. B. Sloan and J. Campbell Gibson in *Presbyterian Messenger* (Sept. 1910), p. 329 and (Oct. 1910), pp. 362, 365.

78. Hanna, *Some Impressions of the World Missionary Conference,* pp. 30-1: *History and Records of the Conference,* pp. 87, 88, 92, 95, 99-100, 104; Gairdner, 'Edinburgh 1910', pp. 66-7; World Missionary Conference 1910, *Conference Daily Paper* 6 (20 June 1910), p. 93.

variety of Christian leaders, ranging from J. O. F. Murray, the High Church master of Selwyn College, Cambridge, to the Quaker, Dr Henry T. Hodgkin of the Friends' Foreign Mission Association, and D. E. Hoste of the China Inland Mission. The prayers led by W. H. Findlay of the WMMS (on Wednesday the 15th) and Bishop Handley Moule of Durham (on Thursday the 16th) attracted particularly appreciative comment.[79]

In the prayers of intercession, as in the debates themselves, the theme of the unity of the Church in mission continually surfaced: R. K. Hanna, a delegate of the Presbyterian Church of Ireland, noted that in this, 'the great central act of the Conference', the 'ever-recurring refrain' was 'that they may be one, that the world may believe'.[80] Regular use was made both in the mid-day intercessions and in the other devotions at the start of each session of periods of silent prayer, with or without specific direction by the worship leader. One delegate commented that 'the silences of the Conference were more to me than any of its speeches'; another, a renowned New Testament scholar, identified 'the devotional use of silence in the Conference as a contribution of the first order to the Church's resources for united worship and united intercession.' The creative use of silent corporate devotion at Edinburgh owed much to experience gained in SCM conferences (perhaps through the input of Quakers such as H. T. Hodgkin), and was one of the features of the conference that left an indelible impression on W. H. Findlay, as on many others.[81] The conference heard and pondered a great many words, but, to a much larger extent than might be imagined for an overwhelmingly evangelical gathering, drew many of its spiritual resources from silent prayer and meditation. Despite the professed intention to restrict the conference to what *Life and Work* termed 'the cold carefulness of the laboratory method' of dissecting 'the facts of the entire world with regard to religion', many delegates confessed to having coming away from Edinburgh profoundly moved in spirit: 'I do not ever remember', wrote R. K. Hanna, 'to have been more conscious of the presence of God than in Edinburgh.'[82]

---

79. Smellie, *At the World Missionary Conference*, p. 12; *Presbyterian Messenger* (Aug. 1910), p. 293.

80. Hanna, *Some Impressions of the World Missionary Conference*, p. 18.

81. Findlay, 'Sight, sound and silence in Edinburgh', pp. 241-5.

82. *Life and Work: the Church of Scotland Magazine and Mission Record* 32:8 (Aug. 1910), p. 246; Hanna, *Some Impressions of the World Missionary Conference*, p. 27.

CHAPTER 5

'Give Us Friends!'
The Voice of the 'Younger' Churches

The Non-Western Presence at Edinburgh

There were, according to the published records, 1,215 official delegates at the World Missionary Conference. However, nineteen at the most of these came from what would now be called the majority or non-western world. The main list of official delegates contains the names of eighteen Christian converts of the missionary enterprise who were in practice, though not in strict theory, representatives of the so-called 'younger' churches:[1]

Professor L. T. Ah Sou	Revd Dr Ibuka Kajinosuke
Revd Johannes Awetaranian	Revd Shivram Masoji
Revd V. S. Azariah	Revd John Rangiah
Revd Dr K. C. Chatterjee	Mr R. K. Sorabji
Mr Cheng Jingyi	Revd Thang Khan Sangma
Revd Chiba Yugoro	Mr Tsang Ding Tong [T. Y. Chang][2]
Revd J. R. Chitambar	Professor Tong Ching-en
Revd S. A. C. Ghose	[Tong Tsing-en or Dong Jingan]
Revd Dr Harada Tasuku	The Hon. Yun Ch'iho
Bishop Honda Yoitsu	

1. *History and Records of the Conference*, pp. 39-71. The names as printed do not always follow accepted modern orthography, and in some cases are differently spelt: Chitambar appears as Chitamber; Rangiah as Rungiah; Chatterjee appears in some other sources as Chatterji. W. R. Hogg, *Ecumenical Foundations: a history of the International Missionary Council and its nineteenth-century background* (New York: Harper & Bros, 1952), p. 396, lists 17 Asian delegates, but not J. Awetaranian. For the nineteenth name, M. C. Hayford, see below, pp. 97-8.

2. Hogg, *Ecumenical Foundations,* p. 396, appears to be correct in his surmise that Pro-

Of these eighteen, eight were Indians, four were Japanese, three were Chinese, one was Korean, one Burmese (Ah Sou), and one was of Turkish origin. Johannes Awetaranian (or Avetaranian) (1861-1919) was a former Muslim mullah and member of the Bektashi dervish sect from Erzerum in Anatolia. He was born as Muhammed Schükri Efendi, but, remarkably for a Turk, adopted the Armenian name of Awetaranian — 'son of the gospel' — following his conversion and adherence to an Armenian evangelical church. Awetarianian testified that his conversion to Christianity occurred independently of direct contact with Christians, but 'solely through the reading of the Gospel without any Christian preaching or Christian instruction whatsoever'.[3] He had worked as an evangelist in present-day Armenia, Georgia, and Azerbaijan, then at Kashgar in Chinese Turkestan, and finally among Muslims in Bulgaria as a missionary of Johannes Lepsius' Deutsche Orient-Mission, whose delegate he was at Edinburgh. However, his name does not appear in the list of registered addresses of delegates, so it is conceivable that, despite being listed as an official delegate, he may have been a late withdrawal. Even if he was present, his official status at the conference was not as a representative convert from Islam but as a missionary to that part of Europe included in the scope of the conference (the Ottoman empire and south-eastern Europe). W. Richey Hogg is therefore technically, though perhaps not substantially, correct to state that the continental European missions brought no representative of the 'younger churches' to Edinburgh.[4] There may have been one other indigenous Christian present from West Asia: one source re-

---

fessor T. Y. Chang of Beijing (or possibly Shanghai), who spoke in the Commission I debate, is the same person as Tsang Ding Tong (or Yung). See *Report of Commission I*, p. 410; Gairdner, *'Edinburgh 1910'*, p. 77; *History and Records of the Conference*, pp. 58-9; *Chinese Recorder*, Sept. 1910, p. 605; UTS, MRL 12, WMC papers, series 1, box 24, folder 5, item 532, 'List of Addresses Registered by Delegates During the Conference', pp. 52, 58.

3. AUL, MS 3291, Commission IV replies, 347, pp. 5, 8. This is a collective testimony produced by Aweteranian and two fellow converts, Scheich Ahmed Keschaf and Müderris Nessimi Efendi.

4. UTS, MRL 12, WMC papers, series 1, box 24, folder 5, item 532, 'List of Addresses Registered by Delegates During the Conference'. Hogg, *Ecumenical Foundations*, p. 125; idem, 'Edinburgh, 1910 — ecumenical keystone', *Religion and Life* 29: 3 (Summer 1960), p. 347. Awetaranian's autobiography, *Geschichte eines Muhammedaners der Christ wurde* (1905), was republished in an expanded edition by Richard Schäfer in Potsdam in 1930, and has now been published in English: *A Muslim who Became a Christian: the story of John Avetaranian (born Muhammed Schükri Efendi)*, transl. John Bechard (Hertford: AuthorsOnLine, 2002). Awetaranian makes no mention of the Edinburgh conference in his autobiography. The inclusion of the Ottoman empire and south-eastern Europe in the terms of the conference followed from the decision taken by Commission I in September 1908 about the statistical basis of the conference; see Chapter 3, p. 50.

fers to 'a bewhiskered delegate from Persia, whose sombrero had artistic curves unknown to Roosevelt, and whose long shapely coat was the envy of the women delegates'.[5]

Eleven of the eighteen names listed above attended as representatives of American mission boards, three as representatives of British missionary societies, one (Awetaranian) as a representative of a German mission, two (Bishop Honda Yoitsu and Yun Ch'iho) were guests invited specially by the American executive committee, and one (V. S. Azariah) by the British executive committee. In addition to the three Chinese listed as official delegates, two other Chinese Christians are recorded as participating in the conference in some capacity. Dr C. C. Wang, from the LMS church in Shanghai, a former student of the Imperial Medical College in Tianjin, who was pursuing further medical studies in Edinburgh, attended at least one session and made a forthright speech in the debate on the Commission VII report, criticising China missions' resort to the judicial and military aid of the western powers, but he does not appear in most lists of official delegates.[6] As part of the Synod Hall parallel conference programme, Dr Ida Kahn, a Chinese woman doctor working at Kiukiang in Jiangxi province, addressed an afternoon women's meeting, held in St George's United Free Church on Monday 20 June, on the topic 'present-day needs of Chinese Women', but she too was not an official delegate.[7]

The seventeen official delegates from East and South Asia formed an extremely well educated and distinguished international group. At least twelve were ordained in their respective communions.[8] Three had in recent years been elected as the heads of their respective national denominations. K. C. Chatterjee from the Punjab was moderator of the General Assembly of the Presbyterian

5. *Life and Work* 32:8 (Aug. 1910), p. 246. I have not been able to identify this delegate, who does not sound like a western missionary.

6. Hogg, *Ecumenical Foundations*, p. 396; *Report of Commission VII*, pp. 154-6; but see *Conference Daily Paper* 8 (22 June 1910), p. 143. Gairdner, *'Edinburgh 1910'*, pp. 164-5, confuses C. C. Wang with Chengting T. Wang, later general secretary of the YMCA in China, who was not present at Edinburgh. R. K. Hanna, *Some Impressions of the World Missionary Conference* (Belfast: Carswell & Son, 1910), pp. 15-16 calls Wang 'Dr Whan'.

7. *History and Records of the Conference*, p. 124; World Missionary Conference, *Conference Daily Paper* 6 (20 June 1910), p. 105. W. W. Lockwood, 'China's part in the Edinburgh conference', *Chinese Recorder*, Sept. 1910, p. 605. On Kahn, who was affiliated to the American Methodist Episcopal Mission, see Kathleen Lodwick (comp.), *The Chinese Recorder Index: a guide to Christian missions in Asia, 1867-1941*, 2 vols. (Wilmington, DE: Scholarly Resources Inc., 1986), I, p. 251.

8. Ah Sou, who taught at Rangoon Baptist College, may have been an ordained Baptist minister.

Church in India; Ibuka Kajinosuke was moderator of the United Church of Christ in Japan; and Honda Yoitsu had been elected in 1907 as the first bishop of the United Japan Methodist Church.[9] One of the seventeen — Yun Ch'iho — had held senior government office. Seven were professors or heads of institutions of higher or theological education.[10] As noted in Chapter 4, two of the seventeen — Chatterjee and Harada Tasuku — were among the fourteen leaders of the conference upon whom honorary degrees were conferred by the University of Edinburgh on the eve of the conference: Chatterjee was awarded a D.D. and Harada an LL.D.[11] Harada also had an earned doctorate from Yale. At least eight of the others had studied to a lower level in either the United States or Britain.[12] One of these, the Revd Thang Khan Sangma, a Baptist evangelist from Tura in the remote Garo Hills of Assam in north-east India, who had studied at the Newton Theological Institution (now Andover Newton Seminary) in Massachusetts, must have been one of the very first Assamese to have followed a course of higher education outside India.

These seventeen Asian Christians were accorded a place in the conference programme and in its discussions which the Presbyterian mission leader Robert E. Speer described as being 'out of proportion to their numbers but it was desired to exalt in them the Churches from which they came'.[13] Mott's biographer confirms that the prominence of the Asians was no accident: 'As Chairman, Mott recognized the few Orientals for whose presence he had labored, perhaps disproportionately.'[14] As observed in Chapter 4, Mott undoubtedly exercised positive discrimination as chairman in calling on the Asian delegates, and the East Asians in particular, to speak in the main conference sessions: each East Asian was given at least one opportunity to participate in the

---

9. On Chatterjee see *BDCM*, p. 127; J. C. R. Ewing, *A Prince of the Church in India: being a record of the life of the Rev. Kali Charan Chatterjee, D.D., for forty-eight years a missionary at Hoshyarpur, Punjab, India* (New York: Fleming H. Revell, 1918); J. C. B. Webster, *The Christian Community and Change in Nineteenth-Century North India* (Delhi: Macmillan, 1976). On Honda see below, pp. 114-15.

10. L. T. Ah Sou, T. Y. Chang, Chiba Yugoro, Harada Tasuku, Ibuka Kajinosuke, R. K. Sorabji, and Tong Ching-en.

11. Hopkins, *John R. Mott*, p. 352; Gairdner, *'Edinburgh 1910'*, p. 58; World Missionary Conference, *Conference Daily Paper* 1 (14 June 1910), p. 4.

12. Ah Sou (Moody Bible Institute); Cheng Jingyi (Bible Training Institute, Glasgow); Chiba (Colby College and Rochester Theological Seminary); Honda (Drew Theological Seminary); Ibuka (Union Theological Seminary, New York); Sorabji (Balliol College, Oxford); Thang Khan (Newton Theological Institution, Massachusetts); Yun Ch'iho (Emory College [now University] and Vanderbilt University).

13. *The East and the West* 8:32 (Oct. 1910), p. 376.

14. Hopkins, *John R. Mott*, p. 357.

debates, whereas only four of the nine South Asians did so. Twelve of these seventeen Asian delegates spoke to the conference, either by giving invited main addresses, or by being chosen to contribute to the debates, or in both capacities: six addressed the conference on more than one occasion.[15] K. C. Chatterjee, in addition to being called on to speak in the debate on Commission IV, was given the particular honour of leading the conference in its morning devotions on 21 June.[16] Two of the Asian contributions — by Cheng Jingyi and V. S. Azariah — are well known, and will be discussed later in this chapter. But they were not exceptional in being prepared to speak their minds. Thang Khan, for example, made a brief but bold speech in halting English in the debate on the 'Missions and Governments' report, protesting against the report's characterization of the stance of the British Government in India's stance as being one of 'religious neutrality'. The prohibition of the teaching of the Bible in government schools in his view betokened not neutrality but hostility. By its exclusion of Bible teaching from schools, the government was depriving itself of the only force capable of shaping good character and hence of 'turning into good subjects all the people of British India.'[17]

It is tempting to conclude, therefore, as a number of contemporary accounts did, that the voice of the 'younger' churches was heard at Edinburgh. However, it might be more accurate to state that certain voices from some of the 'younger' churches spoke. Whether what they said was truly heard is more open to question. Some sources assure us 'how very interested the Conference was in what they had to say, and there was none more heartily welcomed to the platform'.[18] However, some delegates, despite the fact that so many had themselves worked as missionaries in non-western cultural contexts, appear to have been attracted mainly by the 'picturesque' sartorial appearance of some of the Asians.[19] One who receives regular mention in contemporary accounts is the professor from Shanghai Baptist Theological Seminary, Tong Ching-en, the only Chinese to appear in national dress, resplendent in his skull-cap and

15. Those who addressed the conference in some capacity were: V. S. Azariah (twice), T. Y. Chang, K. C. Chatterjee (twice), Cheng Jingyi (twice), Chiba Yugoro, J. R. Chitambar, Harada Tasuku (three times), Honda Yoitsu, Ibuka Kajinosuke (twice), Thang Khan Sangma, Tong Ching-en, Yun Ch'iho (twice).

16. *History and Records of the Conference*, p. 94; *Report of Commission IV*, pp. 314-16.

17. *Report of Commission VII*, p. 176; see pp. 24-5 for the section on 'The policy of religious neutrality.'

18. R. K. Hanna, in *The Missionary Herald of the Presbyterian Church of Ireland*, 1 Aug. 1910, p. 195; see also *Chinese Recorder*, Sept. 1910, p. 606.

19. *Life and Work: the Church of Scotland Magazine and Mission Record* 32:8 (Aug. 1910), p. 251.

pigtail, flowing grey skirt, and 'stuffed, quilted jacket of richest peacock-blue silk'. Tong Ching-en, born in 1872, was one of three founding members of faculty of the Shanghai seminary from its inception in 1906 to 1919 (and was its vice-president from 1915); the seminary eventually evolved into the University of Shanghai for Science and Technology. Although the seminary was predominantly a Southern Baptist institution, Tong attended Edinburgh 1910 as a delegate of the American Baptist Foreign Missionary Society.[20] Tong is almost certainly the 'Chinese pastor in his quaint native costume' who is described by one female observer as having presided 'with much dignity and most acceptably' at one of the half-hour mid-day prayer meetings in the parallel conference for home supporters of missions held in the Synod Hall.[21] Also frequently singled out for his 'patriarchal' features is K. C. Chatterjee, 'with a beard like John Knox's', a 'venerable, one might say high-priestly figure, a pure Brahman by descent', of 'aristocratic, gentle features, and mild Indian voice.'[22] Whether delegates' orientalist fascination with the exotic hindered or assisted their attentiveness to what the Asians had to say is a moot point, but there is some evidence in favour of the latter interpretation. The colourful descriptions of Tong Ching-en by Temple Gairdner and Nelson Bitton (in the *Chinese Recorder*) are coupled with commendatory references to his speech in the Commission IV debate appealing for Christian education in China to engage in deeper study of the Confucian classics.[23] Similarly, Chatterjee is singled out not simply for his venerable appearance but also for the deep impression made by his contribution to the same debate, in which Chatterjee, describing himself as the only Hindu convert among the delegates, explained from his own experience how hard it was for a Hindu to accept a vicarious understanding of the atonement.[24] *The Missionary Review of the World* in its summary of the conference

---

20. I owe information on Tong to Dr Thomas G. Oey. Tong's colleagues as the first faculty members of the seminary were R. T. Bryan (a Southern Baptist) and F. J. White (a Northern Baptist).

21. *Women's Missionary Magazine of the United Presbyterian Church* 24:2 (Sept. 1910), p. 43.

22. *Missionary Record of the United Free Church of Scotland* 116 (Aug. 1910), pp. 342, 350; Gairdner, 'Edinburgh 1910', pp. 57-8; *Chinese Recorder*, Aug. 1910, pp. 530, 538; Alexander Smellie, *At the World Missionary Conference: a little narrative for friends who were not there* (Dundee: James P. Mathew & Co., 1910), p. 10.

23. Gairdner, 'Edinburgh 1910', p. 57; *Chinese Recorder*, Aug. 1910, p. 538; see *Report of Commission IV*, pp. 301-2.

24. *Missionary Record of the United Free Church of Scotland* 116 (Aug. 1910), p. 350; *Chinese Recorder*, Aug. 1910, p. 539; see *Report of Commission IV*, pp. 314-16. The other delegates from a Hindu background — Azariah, Chitambar, Ghose, and Rangiah — were all second-generation Christians.

proceedings gave particular prominence to choice quotations from the Asian Christian speakers.[25] A postcolonial perspective, with its vision so sharply focused to identify the slightest evidence of orientalist construction, might perhaps be inclined to read too much into the descriptions of the physical appearance of the Asian delegates. Contemporary accounts of the conference were just as intrigued by the 'strange medieval apparition' of F. J. Western of the Cambridge Delhi Brotherhood in his brown habit, sandals, and huge silver crucifix, as by the appearance in Edinburgh of anything indigenous to Asia.[26] The conference was endeavouring to span a cultural gulf between evangelical Protestantism and Catholic forms of Christianity that was almost as wide as that between European and Asian expressions of the faith.

A second question raised by the indigenous Christian presence at the conference is how representative these highly educated, socially superior, and primarily urban Asian Christians were of the ordinary membership of the wider churches from which they came. A third is why it was that the African continent was so grossly underrepresented at the conference — an omission that requires some extended comment.

The Virtual Absence of Africa

As mentioned in Chapter 1, the church in Africa was scarcely represented at the World Missionary Conference, except by expatriate missionaries. No indigenous black African Christian was originally deemed worthy of an invitation to Edinburgh. However, the ninth and final number of the *Conference Daily Paper* — that for 23 June — informed delegates of the presence of 'an additional African delegate': the Revd M. C. Hayford, D.D. The fact that his name does not appear in any of the official lists of delegates suggests that Hayford received his invitation at the last minute, and I have not seen reference to his presence in any other primary source.[27] His attendance at the conference, is however, confirmed, by G. M. Haliburton's study of Hayford's somewhat chequered career.[28] Mark Christian Hayford came from a distin-

25. *Missionary Review of the World*, Aug. 1910, pp. 652-63.
26. *Missionary Record of the United Free Church of Scotland* 116 (Aug. 1910), p. 350; *Life and Work* 32:8 (Aug. 1910), pp. 246, 251; Smellie, *At the World Missionary Conference*, p. 17.
27. *Conference Daily Paper* 9 (23 June 1910), p. 171. Hayford was not a delegate of the BMS, as his name is missing from the list of delegates in the BMS general committee minutes for 24 May 1910.
28. G. M. Haliburton, 'Mark Christian Hayford: a non-success story', *Journal of Religion in Africa* 12:1 (1981), p. 27.

guished Fante Euro-African family on the Gold Coast. His father, Joseph de Graft Hayford, was a leading Wesleyan Methodist minister. His mother, Mary Brew, was descended on her father's side from a family of Irish merchants. Joseph de Graft Hayford and Mary Brew had several sons, of whom by far the most famous was Joseph Ephraim Casely Hayford (1866-1930), author of the political novel *Ethiopia Unbound* (1911) and one of the founders in 1920 of the National Congress of British West Africa. Mark Christian Hayford is not so well known as his brother, but is still a figure of some interest. In 1898 he forsook the Methodist family tradition to be baptized as an adult believer by Dr Mojola Agbebi, founder of the Native Baptist Church in Lagos. Later he became secretary of the Native Baptist Union of West Africa, of which Agbebi was the president. From July 1899 to June 1902 he spent time in England and the United States, lecturing and fund-raising for a building for his church, the Baptist Church Mission and Christian Army of the Gold Coast. While in America, he gave a lecture at the Rochester Theological Seminary on 28 September 1900, which he later expanded into a publication, *West Africa and Christianity*, arguing that native churches of the kind established by Agbebi or the Delta Native Pastorate 'will be the crowning glory of Christianity in Modern Africa, as in other lands.'[29]

Hayford's presence at the conference was exceptional and has gone generally unnoticed by historians (including this author, until the final stage of the preparation of this book). He was an uncharacteristically westernized African, 'an inhabitant of two cultures' with European friends and patrons, and what Haliburton describes as 'a tragic succession of European wives'. He lived in Liverpool for two years after the conference, and did not return to West Africa until 1913.[30] The absence of other African representatives demands explanation. The Protestant church in most parts of Africa was still very young, but the same was true of many of the churches in Japan or Korea. In contrast to East Asia, however, Africa in 1910 generally lacked the advanced educational and primarily urban institutions with which the majority of the Asian delegates were associated, either as members of staff or as former students. Nevertheless, the standard of education provided by such African institutions as Fourah Bay College or Lovedale was such that broader explanations for the

---

29. Mark C. Hayford, *West Africa and Christianity* (London: Baptist Tract and Book Society, n.d. [1903]), pp. 60-1. Hayford dedicated his book to the Baptist stockbroker and treasurer of the Baptist Union, Herbert Marnham, in acknowledgement of 'his liberal spirit and Christian generosity by which the cause of Christ in Africa has been materially served.' Generally, however, Hayford's fund-raising efforts met with a disappointing response: see Haliburton, 'Mark Christian Hayford', pp. 25-6.

30. Haliburton, 'Mark Christian Hayford', pp. 22, 27.

general exclusion of African voices from Edinburgh must be sought. If the African churches were deemed to be insufficiently 'advanced' to merit their own representatives, it was not simply because these churches were young in years, but also because their members were thought to be starting from much further back in the process of human development than were Christian converts in Asia. The inhabitants of the African continent were still in 1910 regarded as primitive, childlike, and at the bottom of the evolutionary hierarchy, relatively unimportant for the future of the world church.

The sources suggest that nobody passed critical comment on the fact that there were virtually no Africans present. Indeed, nobody seemed even to notice. On the contrary, numerous contemporary accounts of the conference (among them the reference in the *Conference Daily Paper* to Hayford as an '*additional* African delegate') implied that *several* Africans were in attendance. W. H. Findlay, for example, writing in the English Methodist periodical, the *London Quarterly Review*, commented that 'The Orientals and the Africans took a day or two — as well they might — to learn to treat as a matter of course the status of intimate brotherhood to which they were welcomed.'[31] The Boston *Missionary Herald*, organ of the American Baptists, similarly observed that 'Europeans, Americans, Asiatics, and Africans rubbed elbows, and with their various and often picturesque garbs made a scene never to be forgotten.'[32] Temple Gairdner's officially authorised record of the conference declared that 'possibly the most interesting, certainly by far the most significant figures of all, were those of the Oriental and African delegates, yellow, brown, or black in race.'[33] One may well ask how such apparently well-informed commentators managed to invent a cohort of African delegates when in reality there was only one. The answer lies in the fact that African Americans were, as late as 1910, still widely regarded as Africans living in America rather than as true Americans. There were at least six and possibly eight or more African American delegates: two or possibly three from the Foreign Mission Board of the National Baptist Convention; at least two from the Foreign Missionary Society of the African Methodist Episcopal Zion Church (one of whom was a woman); while two formed part of the larger delegation from the Board of Foreign Missions of the Methodist Episcopal Church — the Revd Dr W. H. Brooks of New York and the Revd Dr Alexander Camphor (1865-1919), who originally came from Louisiana and had served as a mission-

---

31. W. H. Findlay, 'Sight, sound, and silence in Edinburgh', *London Quarterly Review* 114 (1910), p. 232.

32. *Missionary Herald* (Boston) 106 (1910), p. 351.

33. Gairdner, *'Edinburgh 1910'*, p. 56.

ary in Liberia.[34] Camphor was described by Temple Gairdner as being 'a negro of immense size and glorying in his African race'.[35] Brooks, together with one of the National Baptist Convention delegates, the Revd Dr L. G. Jordan of Louisville, organised an unofficial meeting for all coloured delegates at 5 p.m. on Saturday the 18th in the Mission Hall of the Tolbooth Church, which was advertised in the *Conference Daily Paper* for that morning; how many turned up, and whether any of the Indian delegates attended, are not known.[36] At least seven sons or daughters of Africa were, therefore, present at Edinburgh; the fact that only one of them had been born on African soil simply did not register in white consciousness.

It should also be noted that Camphor was not the only non-white missionary to Africa among the delegates. The Revd John Rangiah (sometimes called Rungiah in the records) from south India was one of five Asian delegates of the American Baptist Foreign Missionary Society. Rangiah was not simply the first missionary sent (in 1903) by the Telegu Baptist Home Missionary Society to the Telegu-speaking workers of the sugar plantations in Natal, but also the first overseas missionary sent out by any of the mission churches of the American Baptists. He is an early example of what would now be called 'south-to-south' mission. By 1910 he had been instrumental in planting ten Baptist churches in the Durban and Pietermaritzburg areas, which remain the basis of the Indian Baptist community in Natal to this day.[37] Rangiah did not make any public contribution to the conference.

34. *History and Records of the Conference*, pp. 52 (W. W. Brown and L. G. [mis-spelt as J. G.] Jordan); 56 (Brooks and Camphor); 58 (Miss H. Quinn Brown and J. W. Rankin). On Camphor see *BDCM*, p. 112. The conference handbook, *World Missionary Conference 1910* (Edinburgh: World Missionary Conference Office, n.d. [1910]), gives some different names as delegates: Rev. Dr C. H. Parrish of Louisville instead of W. W. Brown; and Rev. W. W. Beckett of New York and Bishop C. T. Shaffer of Chicago instead of Miss H. Quinn Brown and Rev. J. W. Rankin. The printed 'List of Addresses Registered by Delegates During the Conference' (in UTS, MRL 12, WMC papers, series 1, box 24, folder 5, item 532) includes W. W. Brown and H. Quinn Brown, but also Beckett, Parrish, and Shaffer, though not Rankin. It is also conceivable that there were African American members of other American delegations. It seems probable that the 'List of Addresses Registered by Delegates During the Conference' is the most accurate record, and that yields a minimum of eight African American delegates.

35. Gairdner, *'Edinburgh 1910'*, p. 58. Hogg, *Ecumenical Foundations*, p. 396.

36. World Missionary Conference 1910, *Conference Daily Paper* 5 (18 June 1910), p. 86.

37. On Rangiah (d. 1915) see J. B. Brain, *Christian Indians in Natal 1860-1911: an historical and statistical study* (Cape Town: OUP, 1983), pp. 222-4; A. W. Wardin (ed.), *Baptists around the World: a comprehensive handbook* (Nashville, TN: Broadman & Holman, 1995), p. 57; S. Hudson-Reed (ed.), *Together for a Century: the history of the Baptist Union of South Africa 1877-1977* (Pietermaritzburg: South African Baptist Historical Society, n.d. [1977]), p. 86.

Although it is true that Christian education in Africa in 1910 was much less advanced than in parts of Asia, there were a few African Christian indigenous leaders in 1910 who undoubtedly had sufficient education to have participated meaningfully in the conference. The Anglican communion at the time included such figures as Archdeacon Dandeson Crowther, son of the famous bishop on the Niger, Samuel Adjai Crowther, or Bishop James Johnson, the Sierra Leonean who in 1900 had been consecrated assistant bishop of Western Equatorial Africa. Methodism had John Tengo Jabavu, a newspaper editor, educationalist, and champion of black African rights from the Eastern Cape: indeed in 1909 he had travelled to London in a vain attempt to fight the inclusion of the colour bar in the constitution of the new Union of South Africa.[38] Also of the Wesleyan Methodist tradition was another educationalist, James E. K. Aggrey from the Gold Coast.[39] Aggrey was probably the most highly educated black African of his day. In 1898 he had come to the United States to study at the African Methodist Episcopal Zion Church's Livingstone College and the associated Hood Theological Seminary in Salisbury, North Carolina. His academic career there was distinguished, and by 1910 he was already a professor. In 1912 he would be awarded the degrees of M.A. and D.D. But by severing his ties with the Wesleyan Methodist Missionary Society and becoming in 1903 an elder in the African Methodist Episcopal Zion Church, Aggrey had in effect ruled himself out from participation at Edinburgh. The missionary society of the African Methodist Episcopal Zion Church was still relatively small and poor: its income entitled it only to the two delegates already mentioned. Aggrey, Jabavu, Johnson, and Dandeson Crowther were all conspicuous by their absence from Edinburgh 1910.

If the conference had taken place twenty-five years earlier, one may speculate that Bishop Samuel Crowther or James Johnson might have been invited. Bishop Crowther had, after all, received an invitation, as was his indubitable right as an Anglican diocesan bishop, to the first two Lambeth Conferences in 1867 and 1878, and was actually present at the third Conference in 1888. 'Holy Johnson', as James Johnson was known, had been a notable speaker at the great Pan-Anglican Congress in London as recently as 1908. But the last years of Crowther's episcopate on the Niger were marked by bitter controversy, and most white missionary opinion deduced from the sorry episode that blacks were not yet fit to exercise major ecclesiastical responsibility. As for Johnson,

38. On Jabavu (1859-1921) see *BDCM*, p. 325; Davidson D. T. Jabavu, *The Life of John Tengo Jabavu: editor of Imvo Zabantsundu, 1880-1921* (Lovedale: Lovedale Institution Press, 1922).

39. On Aggrey (1875-1927) see *BDCM*, p. 7; Edwin Smith, *Aggrey of Africa: a study in black and white* (London: SCM Press, 1929).

by 1910 he was voicing publicly his 'deep disappointment' at the failure of both Lambeth Palace and the Church Missionary Society to redeem their commitments to implement a West Africa Native Bishoprics scheme that would have placed African bishops in charge of autonomous Anglican dioceses in West Africa.[40] African Christian leadership had fallen into grave disrepute in the aftermath of the Niger controversy and in the face of the growth of Ethiopianism in South Africa, and the shadow of disapproval extended even to Edinburgh.

The Missionary Societies and
Indigenous Representation at Edinburgh

The international committee responsible for preparations for the conference had suggested as early as July 1908 that missionary societies should be asked to include in their delegations 'if practicable, one or two natives from mission lands'.[41] Most missions, however, failed to fulfil even this modest injunction. The case of one of the largest British societies, the London Missionary Society (LMS), is instructive in illuminating the decision-making processes that lay behind this failure. In January 1910 one of its leading China missionaries, W. Nelson Bitton, wrote to J. H. Oldham from Shanghai, alerting him to the concern felt by some of his missionary colleagues in China, in view of the rising tide of anti-foreign sentiment in the Orient, about the inadequate provision made to include indigenous Christians in the conference delegations. Bitton calculated, on the basis of the information then available to him, that only 3% of the expected delegates would represent the 'native Christian churches', compared with 60% from those involved in the home branches of foreign missions and 37% from those currently active as foreign missionaries.[42] Oldham acted promptly, forwarding Bitton's letter to John Mott, together with a letter from Dr Arthur Judson Brown, of the Presbyterian Board of Foreign Missions in New York, which appears to have made a similar criticism.[43] Oldham also sent a copy

40. E. A. Ayandele, *Holy Johnson: pioneer of African nationalism, 1836-1917* (London: Frank Cass, 1970), p. 333.

41. ECG, Third Ecumenical Missionary Conference (June 1910), minutes of international committee, 14-20 July 1908, p. 9.

42. YDS, RG45, Mott papers, box 63, folder 1169, copy of Bitton to Oldham, 12 Jan. 1910. The actual percentage of delegates from the indigenous churches was only 1.56% (19 out of 1,215).

43. YDS, RG45, box 63, folder 1169, copies of Oldham to Mott, 2 Feb. 1910, and Oldham to Brown, 2 Feb. 1910. Brown's letter appears not to have been preserved.

of Bitton's letter to Ralph Wardlaw Thompson, the venerable (and exceedingly powerful) foreign secretary of the LMS, who had occupied that pre-eminent office in the life of the society since 1881: Thompson's nickname among his staff was 'the Chief'.[44] The LMS, however, was in dire financial straits in 1910, needing to reduce its expenditure by about £10,000 a year. Thompson's reply to Oldham pointed out that every Asian delegate would cost the society an additional £100, and informed him merely that he had written to China inviting the society's churches to send one or two representatives *at their own expense.*[45] The LMS Board agreed in February 1910 that four of its thirty-eight allocated places should be reserved for native delegates, two from China and two from India, but that their expenses should be met entirely from local funds.[46]

The LMS Indian churches, being substantially poorer even than their Chinese counterparts, had no realistic prospect of raising the funds to send any representatives to Edinburgh. The financial crisis facing the LMS in 1910 was real enough, but the society never considered reducing its conference expenditure by forgoing some of its thirty-eight places in order to make it possible for national Christians to attend. What proved decisive was Thompson's conviction that the 'younger' churches were not yet ready to take their place in such exalted company: 'I do not think the time is ripe for the inclusion of delegates appointed by the Churches in non-Christian lands in any great Conference such as ours. Ten years hence I hope there may be such a development of independent Church life as will make it necessary to have representation from various parts of the world.'[47]

Two names of national delegates were subsequently put forward to the LMS by the Chinese churches. The first was Cheng Jingyi (Ch'eng Ching-yi, 1881-1939), who will be discussed in the following section. The second nominee was Moses Chiu, who was currently studying for a doctor of philosophy degree in the University of Berlin. In the event, Chiu was unable to attend the conference owing to a clash of dates with his doctoral examination.[48]

44. Basil Mathews, *Dr Ralph Wardlaw Thompson* (London: RTS, 1917), p. 161.

45. SOAS, CWMA, box 2, LMS Home Office Outward Letters, Thompson to Oldham, 7 Feb. 1910.

46. SOAS, CWMA, box 53, LMS Board Minutes, 15 Feb. 1910. Only ten places were allocated to serving missionaries.

47. SOAS, CWMA, box 2, LMS Home Office Outward Letters, Thompson to Oldham, 7 Feb. 1910.

48. SOAS, CWMA, box 2, LMS Home Office Outward Letters, Thompson to K. Maclennan, 12 May 1910; Thompson to E. Curwen, 17 May 1910; and Thompson to M. Chiu, 18 May 1910. On Dr, later Prof. Moses Chiu see Kathleen Lodwick, (comp.), *The Chinese Recorder Index: a guide to Christian missions in Asia, 1867-1941*, 2 vols. (Wilmington, DE: Scholarly Resources Inc., 1986), I, p. 86.

One of Nelson Bitton's travelling companions from Mukden in Manchuria all the way by rail across Siberia and Europe to Edinburgh had been the Manchu, Cheng Jingyi, an experience which left an enduring imprint on Bitton, and not purely on account of the scenery.[49] Bitton felt keenly that more should have been done to include Asian representatives. He wrote an article in the September 1910 issue of the LMS magazine, the *Chronicle*, regretting the lack of opportunity given at Edinburgh for the expression of indigenous Christian viewpoints; one suspects that the criticism was aimed in part at his own society.[50] Bitton also wrote the main report on the conference for the *Chinese Recorder,* and again observed that 'it was felt by many that more good might have been accomplished had it been possible to find room for more representatives of the indigenous mission church in certain of the more advanced fields' (even Bitton appears not to have thought Africans ready for inclusion).[51] Bitton's commitment to Asian representation was shared by both Mott and Oldham. Oldham later testified that 'it was Mott above all others who insisted in the face of a good deal of conservative opposition that the younger Churches should be represented at the Edinburgh Conference in 1910'.[52] It seems likely that Mott and Oldham were disappointed that relatively few such representatives actually attended the conference. As late as April 1910, the *Monthly News Sheet* published by the conference office was expressing the confident expectation that 'the number of delegates from non-Christian countries will be considerably larger' than the twelve names that had been notified to date.[53]

The lukewarm attitude of the LMS to securing indigenous representation at the conference is illustrative of an assumption shared by many, though not all, of those involved in Edinburgh 1910. The conference was a gathering of mission executives and missionaries; indigenous Christians were a dubious and expensive luxury whose presence was not integral to the character of the event, though there is indirect evidence that most, if not all, of the other fifteen indigenous representatives of mission boards or committees, unlike Cheng, had their travelling expenses paid by their missionary societies.[54]

The other major British societies did no better than the LMS. The Wesleyan Methodist Missionary Society, the Baptist Missionary Society, and the

---

49. Nelson Bitton, 'Cheng Ching-Yi: a Christian statesman', *IRM* 30 (1941), pp. 515-16.

50. *The Chronicle of the London Missionary Society* 75 (1910), pp. 165-6.

51. *Chinese Recorder,* Aug. 1910, p. 530.

52. J. H. Oldham, 'John R. Mott', *Ecumenical Review* 7 (1955), p. 258; cited in Hopkins, *John R. Mott,* p. 348.

53. World Missionary Conference 1910, *Monthly News Sheet* 7 (April 1910), p. 142.

54. *The East and the West* 8:32 (Oct. 1910), p. 376.

Foreign Mission Committees of the Church of Scotland and United Free Church of Scotland were in fact unable or unwilling to muster a single non-western Christian between them. The Church Missionary Society included in its vast delegation of eighty-nine persons (the largest of any mission body) just one Asian, Richard K. Sorabji, a prominent Oxford-educated barrister who had been appointed acting principal of the University School of Law, Allahabad, on its creation in 1907. Sorabji's late father was a prominent CMS convert and clergyman from the wealthy Parsi community in western India. His sister, Cornelia, also educated at Oxford, became well known in India and England as a lawyer. Although Richard Sorabji had spoken at the CMS anniversary meetings in 1907,[55] he was not an entirely safe choice for the society. As recently as January 1910 the secretary of the Allahabad corresponding committee of the CMS, E. H. M. Waller, had blocked his appointment to the committee on the grounds that Sorabji was of 'peculiar temperament', an outspoken person of 'rather strong feelings', and had failed fully to identify himself with CMS work in Allahabad.[56] There is no direct evidence, however, that Sorabji held radical political views. The one Asian representative of the Society for the Propagation of the Gospel was a more controversial figure. The Revd Samuel Abinash Chunder Ghose was the first Indian priest to be ordained in the Cambridge Mission to Delhi and a professor at St Stephen's College, Delhi. Ghose, a Bengali, was a close friend of C. F. Andrews, and had earned a reputation in the Lahore diocese as a maverick who insisted on equal treatment with his European missionary colleagues. At Andrews' request he had written a forthright paper for The Student Movement in 1907 criticizing young missionaries in India for imbibing 'a vast heritage of accumulated prejudice against the Indian as such.'[57] Ghose was involved, with other Delhi nationalists, in the swadeshi movement, and had known sympathies with the Arya Samaj. In 1912 he had his licence withdrawn by Bishop Lefroy on account of alleged unorthodoxy.[58] In view of his controversial standing in the

55. On R. K. Sorabji and his family see Ivor Elliott (ed.), The Balliol College Register Second Edition 1833-1933 (Oxford: OUP, 1934), p. 197; E. Stock, The History of the Church Missionary Society, 4 vols. (London: 1899-1916), IV, p. 217; Church Missionary Society, Register of Missionaries and Native Clergy from 1804 to 1904 (CMS, n.p., n.d.), p. 336; Cornelia Sorabji, India Calling: the memories of Cornelia Sorabji (London: Nisbet, 1934).

56. UBL, CMS archives, G2 I 7/o, 30, E. H. M. Waller to G. B. Durrant, 6 Jan. 1910. See also items 46 and 50 in the same letter book: by 2 Feb. Waller and the other [European] members of the corresponding committee had withdrawn their objection to Sorabji on the grounds that he had 'sobered down lately'.

57. S. A. C. Ghose, 'The Indian nation and Christianity', The Student Movement 9:8 (May 1907), p. 173.

58. On Ghose see D. O'Connor, Three Centuries of Mission: the United Society for the

Lahore diocese, it is perhaps surprising that the SPG was prepared to include him in its delegation, though not surprising that Mott did not call on him to speak.

Although the American Baptist Foreign Mission Society distinguished itself by including five Asians in its delegation of forty-three (a higher proportion than any other mission),[59] and the Board of Foreign Missions of the Presbyterian Church in the USA had four out of fifty-five,[60] the other American mission boards did no better than their British counterparts. The mission boards of the Protestant Episcopal Church, the Disciples of Christ, the Southern Baptist Convention, and the Methodist Episcopal Church, South, had no indigenous Christian delegates, even though the Southern Methodists owed the foundation of their Korean mission to Yun Ch'iho, who was brought to Edinburgh independently as the guest of the American executive committee (see below). The American Board of Commissioners for Foreign Missions and the Board of Foreign Missions of the Methodist Episcopal Church could each manage only one representative of national churches as part of their large delegations of forty-two and fifty-eight persons respectively. The American Board delegation included Harada Tasuku from Japan (see below). The one Asian selected by the American Methodists was a young and emerging Christian leader, the Revd Jashwant Rao Chitambar (1879-1940) of Lucknow. Chitambar was the son of a Maratha Brahman convert. He had received his call to the ministry in February 1896 during student meetings led by Mott in Lahore,[61] and was one of the founders, with V. S. Azariah, L. T. Ah Sou, and others, of the National Missionary Society in 1905. A graduate of Lucknow Christian College and the Methodist Theological Seminary at Bareilly, Chitambar participated in the debate on the Commission II report, warning against the divisive effect of missionary societies employing national workers who had received a university education as 'missionaries', while leaving those with lesser qualifications in the employ of native church councils or conferences. He later became the first Indian prin-

---

Propagation of the Gospel, 1701-2000 (London and New York: Continuum, 2000), p. 93; idem, *A Clear Star: C. F. Andrews and India 1904-1914* (New Delhi: Chronicle Books, 2005), pp. 34, 61, 99, 227, 234; Hugh Tinker, *The Ordeal of Love: C. F. Andrews and India* (Delhi: OUP, 1979), pp. 32-3, 38, 51 n. 2, 63-4, 111; *Delhi Mission News,* July 1910, p. 32, Oct. 1910, pp. 41, 49-50, Jan. 1911, pp. 57-8. I owe these references to Dr Dan O'Connor.

59. Ah Sou, Chiba, Thang Khan Sangma, Rangiah, Tong Ching-en. On the five Baptists as a group see *Missions* 1 (1910), pp. 189-90; World Missionary Conference 1910, *Monthly News Sheet* 7 (April 1910), p. 142.

60. Chatterjee, Ibuka, Masoji, and T. Y. Chang (Tsang Ding Tong).

61. Hopkins, *John R. Mott,* pp. 149-50.

cipal of Lucknow Christian College and in 1931 the first Indian bishop of the Methodist Episcopal Church of South East Asia. He was also a delegate at Jerusalem in 1928.[62]

Cheng Jingyi and the Call for a United Church in China

Unlike Moses Chiu, Cheng Jingyi did attend the Edinburgh conference, financed by the LMS churches in China, which was no mean feat. Cheng was the twenty-eight-year-old assistant pastor of the Mi-shih Hutung church in Beijing.[63] This was a newly formed church, associated with the LMS but moving towards independence, that had attracted a number of Chinese professionals and academics to its membership. Cheng had been converted at the age of seventeen during a revival meeting in Tianjin.[64] He was first invited to Britain in 1903 to assist the LMS missionary, George Owen (from 1908 to 1913 professor of Chinese at King's College, London), in revising the Union version of the Mandarin New Testament for the British and Foreign Bible Society.[65] From February 1906 to June 1908 Cheng studied at one of the first British Bible colleges, the Bible Training Institute in Glasgow (founded on the initiative of D. L. Moody in 1892) which had close connections with missions in China.[66] Having spent several years in Britain, Cheng possessed unusually

62. *Report of Commission II*, pp. 362-3; Gairdner, *'Edinburgh 1910'*, p. 109. See Chapter 4, p. 141. On Chitambar see *BDCM*, p. 132; Susan B. Harper, *In the Shadow of the Mahatma: Bishop V. S. Azariah and the travails of Christianity in British India* (Grand Rapids, MI, and Richmond, Surrey: Eerdmans and Curzon Press, 2000), p. 84n. Brenton T. Badley, *The Making of a Bishop: the lifestory of Bishop Jashwant Rao Chitambar, bishop of the Methodist church* (Lucknow: Lucknow Publishing House, 1949); J. N. Hollister, *The Centenary of the Methodist Church in Southern Asia* (Lucknow: Lucknow Publishing House, 1956), pp. 255-6.

63. On Cheng Jingyi see H. L. Boorman and R. C. Howard (eds.), *Biographical Dictionary of Republican China*, 5 vols. (New York & London: Columbia UP, 1967-79), I, pp. 284-6; Lodwick (comp.), *Chinese Recorder Index*, I, pp. 83-4; C. Boynton, 'Dr Cheng Ching-Yi', *Chinese Recorder* 70 (1939), pp. 689-98; N. Bitton, 'Cheng Ching-yi: a Christian statesman', *IRM* 30 (1941), pp. 513-20.

64. Glasgow, International Christian College, Bible Training Institute student record register, vol. 4 (1904-10).

65. Jost O. Zetzsche, *The Bible in China: the history of the Union Version or the culmination of Protestant missionary Bible translation in China* (Nettetal: Monumenta Serica Institute & Steyler Verlag, 1999), pp. 268-9.

66. Of the 775 students who had studied at the Institute by 1909, 83 had gone to work in China, 3 of whom (including Cheng) were native Chinese. This compares with 45 in India, and 49 in Africa. Cheng's fees were paid by Dr Elliot Curwen of the LMS (Glasgow, In-

fluent English for a Chinese at that time. In the light of his identity as a Manchu, who might have been deemed to represent the ruling Qing dynasty, it is significant that the LMS churches selected him as one of their two delegates. He may in fact have been the youngest delegate at Edinburgh; his official status in the LMS was still only that of assistant pastor of the Mi-shih Hutung church, serving under the LMS missionary, Dr William Hopkyn Rees (who had other duties at the Union Theological College and Language School for Missionaries). Cheng was not ordained to the pastorate until his return to Beijing after the conference.

This young Chinese made a profound and even disturbing impact at Edinburgh through two speeches. He spoke first on the morning of Thursday 16 June in the debate of the report of Commission II on 'The Church in the Mission Field', urging the conference not to be afraid to allow the Chinese church to assume the challenge of sustaining and managing its own life. Self-support should be viewed as a joy, not a burden. The controlling power over the Chinese churches had in the past been in missionary hands, and appropriately so, but the time had now come for every Chinese Christian to assume responsibility for their own church and the propagation of the faith.[67] But it was Cheng's second contribution, to the debate of the report of Commission VIII on 'Co-operation and the Promotion of Unity' on the morning of Tuesday 21 June, that made the more lasting impression on his hearers and is far more widely cited in both contemporary and retrospective accounts: the Boston *Missionary Herald* judged it 'without question the best speech' made at Edinburgh.[68] In his allotted seven minutes (in fact one report suggests that Mott quite exceptionally permitted him an extra thirty seconds before being halted by Ritson's bell),[69] Cheng referred to the modest progress the Protestant churches in China had already made towards a federal structure, and went on to say that

> Speaking plainly we hope to see, in the near future, a united Christian Church without any denominational distinctions. This may seem somewhat peculiar to you, but, friends, do not forget to view us from *our* standpoint, and if you fail to do that, the Chinese will remain always as a mysterious people to you![70]

---

ternational Christian College, *Bible Training Institute Annual Report* for 1908-09, p. 7; and Bible Training Institute student fees register, 1905-14, p. 7.

67. *Report of Commission II*, pp. 352-3.
68. *Missionary Herald* (Boston) 106 (1910), p. 354.
69. *Missionary Record of the United Free Church of Scotland*, Aug. 1910, p. 352.
70. *Report of Commission VIII*, p. 196.

Cheng endeavoured to convince his audience of how urgent a priority the formation of a united Protestant church was for Chinese Christian leaders. He observed that 'denominationalism has never interested the Chinese mind. He finds no delight in it, but sometimes he suffers for it!' The only conceivable obstacles to the formation of a united church in China would be 'due to our Western friends and not ourselves.' Cheng reminded the conference of the theological truth that 'The Church of Christ is universal, not only irrespective of denominations, but also irrespective of nationalities', and cited the famous motto of the Keswick holiness conventions — 'All one in Christ Jesus'.[71] Temple Gairdner, who described the speech as 'another vivid insight into the Oriental point of view', felt it sufficiently important to reproduce it in its entirety in his published account of the conference, the only address to which he gave that privilege. Yet Gairdner also cited Cheng's contribution as evidence of 'how completely unaware of the real difficulties and essentialities' of the question of church unity Chinese Christians were.[72] What Gairdner euphemistically termed Cheng's 'artlessness' — by implication, his theological naivety — had to his mind amply proved the validity of Bishop Charles Gore's earlier warning in the debate on the Commission II report that questions of fundamental ecclesiology must not be swept aside in the haste for functional unity:

> if we, as foreign missionaries, are to hand over Christianity to the Church of China, and Japan, and India with a good courage, then we must have done more than at the present moment we seem . . . inclined to do, to contribute to a definition of what the Church is, the definitions of its essentials or real Catholic features.[73]

Despite such theological anxieties voiced by some Anglicans, it is clear that Cheng's forthrightness and perspicacity had immediately established his credentials with Mott and Oldham. Nelson Bitton wrote many years later that 'In those seven minutes he had found his place in the leadership of the Christian missionary enterprise in China.'[74] When, on the following afternoon, the recommendations of the business committee were read out for membership

---

71. *Ibid.*, pp. 196-7. It is also worth remembering that Cheng had studied in an interdenominational Bible college: the Bible Training Institute had received students from 19 different denominations up to 1909 (Glasgow, International Christian College, *Bible Training Institute Annual Report* for 1908-09, p. 7).

72. Gairdner, *'Edinburgh 1910'*, pp. 184-6.

73. *Report of Commission II*, p. 355.

74. Bitton, 'Ch'eng Ching-yi', p. 516.

of the Continuation Committee to carry forward the spirit of co-operation in the work of mission, Cheng was chosen as the one representative from China among the thirty-five members; Japan and India were also given one member each (Honda Yoitsu and K. C. Chatterjee respectively).[75] The Continuation Committee would eventually, in 1921, evolve into the International Missionary Council (IMC), one of the foremost bodies in twentieth-century ecumenism. In China itself, steps were taken in 1912-13 to establish a national branch of the Continuation Committee; and somewhat similar bodies were formed in Korea and Japan. With a missionary colleague, Cheng was appointed the first joint secretary of the China Continuation Committee. His selection for such a post was noteworthy, in view of the fact that Cheng was a Manchu, and the Republican Revolution of 1911-12 had overthrown the centuries-old Manchu domination of the Chinese empire. Cheng held this office until 1922, when he presided over the inaugural conference in Shanghai of the successor to the China Continuation Committee — the National Christian Council of China. From 1924 to 1933 he served as the Council's general secretary. In 1927, the vision outlined in his second Edinburgh speech was partly realized through the formation of the Church of Christ in China, which united sixteen different Presbyterian, Congregational, and Baptist church bodies; Cheng was appointed as its first moderator (and later general secretary, a position he held until his death in 1939). He attended the Jerusalem conference of the International Missionary Council in 1928, and was elected as vice-chairman of the conference. He was appointed a member of the IMC executive committee, and served in that capacity until the Tambaram meeting of the IMC in 1938.

After the Communist revolution of 1949 all denominational distinctions were compulsorily expunged from Chinese Christianity, other than the fundamental division between Catholic and Protestant. Although the church in China remains divided between Catholic and Protestant, and unhappily also between the officially recognized Three-Self Patriotic Movement Church and the so-called 'underground' congregations, something of Cheng's vision from 1910 has come to fruition. Cheng became one of the major figures in early twentieth-century ecumenism (he was the only Chinese to be present at Edinburgh 1910, Jerusalem 1928, and Tambaram 1938),[76] yet he never lost his original evangelical faith nor his passion for evangelism: he taught Chinese Christians to pray a prayer which became well known internationally: 'O Lord, revive Thy Church, beginning with me'. He visited the United States on

75. *History and Records of the Conference*, p. 102.
76. Boynton, 'Dr Cheng Ching-Yi', p. 693.

several occasions, and was awarded honorary doctorates from Knox College, Toronto, St John's University, Shanghai, and the College of Wooster in Ohio.[77]

Christianity and the National Spirit: Four Voices from Japan — Harada Tasuku, Honda Yoitsu, Ibuka Kajinosuke, and Chiba Yugoro

The Japanese, perhaps more forcibly than any other group of Asian delegates, brought home to at least some of those who attended the conference the salience of growing national sentiment in the life of the Asian churches. One Scottish delegate recorded for publication his very clear impression that

> The spirit of nationalism, so deeply stirring in all lands, found utterance again and again at the Conference. It is not English speech and English thought on which the new churches in the Mission-field are to be formed: else they would be foreign churches. China, Japan, India must bring their own traditions and their own passion of patriotism into a Church of Christ, truly become also the Church of China, Japan, India. Missions exist to make missions unnecessary.[78]

'The demand for greater autonomy,' noted another delegate, 'came especially from Japan'.[79] Protestant Christianity in Japan in 1910 was still numerically small, with some 80,000 adherents out of a population of 52 million,[80] and as recently as the 1890s had been politically vulnerable to the charge that it represented a treasonous departure from Japanese national identity. However, it now exercised a social influence out of all proportion to its numbers, partly because its leaders came almost without exception from strata that had fulfilled leadership roles in feudal Japan and had not easily abandoned those roles in the changed political circumstances created by the Meiji restoration of 1868. Those leaders were also able to achieve a synthesis between the values of American liberal Protestantism in the social gospel era and the aspirations of Meiji Japan for enhanced national influence through social reform and modernization. The four representatives of those leaders who attended the Edinburgh conference were thus able to paint a somewhat rosy picture of a

---

77. *Ibid.*, pp. 693-4; Bitton, 'Ch'eng Ching-yi', pp. 516-17.
78. *Life and Work* 32:8 (Aug. 1910), p. 244.
79. Hanna, *Some Impressions of the World Missionary Conference*, p. 9.
80. Figures cited by Chiba Yugoro in his contribution to the discussion of the Commission I Report; see *Report of Commission I*, p. 408.

Christian-inspired national, social, and ethical renaissance in Japan that was eagerly hailed by the delegates as a beacon that pointed the way to the rest of Asia. In their different ways, each proclaimed the possibility that an indigenized form of Christianity offered the only assured route to national modernization, not simply in Japan, but more broadly in Asia as a whole.

The sole Asian Christian whom the American Board of Commissioners for Foreign Missions included in its delegation was one of these leading figures in Japanese Protestantism, and possibly the most highly educated Asian Christian of his day. The Revd Dr Harada Tasuku (1863-1940), like most of Japan's first generation of Protestant leaders, came from the samurai class that found the basis of its historic dominance challenged as a result of the Meiji restoration. As a young man, Harada had been a member of the Kumamoto 'band' of Christians led by Neesima Jo (1843-90), the founder of the Board's Doshisha College (later University).[81] Harada had gone on to study at the University of Chicago and Yale Divinity School, where he received his doctorate, and later in England and Germany. He returned to Japan in 1896, and in 1907 was appointed president of the Doshisha institution, described by Gairdner as 'the most famous Christian College in Japan'.[82] Harada held this office until 1919. From 1921 to 1932 he was a professor of Japanese history, literature, and language, and dean of the new department of Asian studies, at the University of Hawaii.[83]

Harada spoke on three occasions to the Edinburgh conference — the only Asian delegate to do so. All three of his contributions revealed his indebtedness to contemporary idealist emphases in western Protestant theology for his advocacy of uniquely Asian expressions of Christianity. First, he participated in the debate on the Commission II report, warning against the inflexible application to eastern churches of doctrinal statements formulated in the West; rather, a church's expressions of faith should grow naturally out of the distinctive Christian life and spiritual experience of its adherents. Harada urged that all Christians should 'teach the Bible without too much of our interpretation, and then be patient as well as watchful to await the outcome of the Christian life in non-Christian lands'.[84] Second, Harada spoke in the debate on 'The Missionary Message in Relation to Other Religions', emphasizing the appeal of the 'courage, manliness, sympathy, serenity, and self-

81. *BDCM*, p. 279. On the 'bands' in early Meiji Protestantism see R. H. Drummond, *A History of Christianity in Japan* (Grand Rapids, MI: Eerdmans, 1971), pp. 166-72.

82. Gairdner, '*Edinburgh 1910*', p. 57.

83. http://www2.hawaii.edu/~georgeo/ipr/HARADA.htm (accessed 01/06/04). On Harada see also Lodwick (comp.), *Chinese Recorder Index*, I, p. 196.

84. *Report of Commission II*, pp. 372-3.

sacrifice' of Jesus Christ to the Japanese national character and love of hero-worship. Young Japanese of the student class would be repelled by anything in Christianity which hurt their sense of loyalty to the nation and the emperor, but any presentation of the gospel which majored on the love of God and the character of Jesus would receive a ready hearing.[85] The loving and manly Christ of liberal Protestantism seemed tailor-made for the Japanese context.

Harada also delivered an evening address in the Assembly Hall on the evening of Sunday, 19 June on the topic 'The Contribution of Non-Christian Races to the Body of Christ' — a title that typifies the Christendom assumptions shared by so many at the conference, including some, if not all, of the Asian Christians. The 'European race' could simply be denominated 'Christian', but its understanding of the Christian faith was partial, needing to be supplemented and enriched by the distinctive insights of other 'races' that were as yet 'un-Christian'. The heart of Harada's paper was an exposition from an organic liberal Protestant perspective of the essential spiritual qualities that each of three Asian nations could offer to the body of Christ. The 'Indian race' possessed 'a deep religious consciousness' and 'a reflective spirit'[86] that had already made its mark on Christian spirituality through the devoted lives of such Christian leaders as Professor Samuel Satthianadan of Madras or Father Nehemiah Goreh.[87] Chinese Christians were distinguished by the Confucian ethic of obedience to superiors — a virtue enshrined in the Fifth Commandment — and by patience under suffering, as exemplified during the Boxer rising. Japanese spirituality was characterized by an intense loyalty rooted in patriotism and the cult of the emperor but capable also of being fused with the Christian faith. Harada told how his mentor Neesima used to tell his 'boys' in the Kumamoto Christian 'band': 'We want you to be men willing to live and die for the sake of *your country.*' It also displayed pronounced veneration for the ancestors and great men of all nations. This feature Harada personally endorsed (though he repudiated ancestor *worship*), and illustrated by the memorial services recently held in Tokyo, Kobe, and

---

85. *Report of Commission IV,* p. 305.

86. Harada drew these phrases more or less directly from T. E. Slater, *The Higher Hinduism in Relation to Christianity,* 2nd edn. (London: Elliott Stock, 1903), pp. 4-5. For Slater's influence on the fulfilment theology of J. N. Farquhar see Eric J. Sharpe, *Not to Destroy but to Fulfil: the contribution of J. N. Farquhar to Protestant missionary thought in India before 1914* (Uppsala: Gleerup, 1965), pp. 94-105.

87. On Samuel Satthianadan (1861-1906), professor of mental and moral philosophy at Presidency College, Madras, and a leading figure in the Indian YMCA, see Stock, *History of the CMS,* III, pp. 757, 767, and IV, pp. 198, 239; and Harper, *In the Shadow of the Mahatma,* p. 84n. On Father Nehemiah Nilankanth Goreh (1825-95) see *BDCM,* p. 252.

other Japanese cities for the late 'august and beloved' King Edward VII. At the service held in the largest Buddhist temple in Tokyo, a tablet for the late king had been placed on the altar and 'worshipped', leading Harada to describe Edward VII, without apparent irony, as 'the first Christian saint ever worshipped in a Buddhist temple'. Harada apologized that time prevented him from saying something about 'the Koreans and the Africans, and the people of Polynesia', but he was 'sure they will all contribute something to the glory of Christ.' Harada, who had earlier in his address cited the LMS missionary T. E. Slater's *The Higher Hinduism in Relation to Christianity* on the theme of Indian religiosity, concluded by quoting Slater again, on the need for West to learn from the East, and the East from the West, so that each could benefit from the best insights of the other. Just as early Christianity triumphed over the religion of Rome not by destroying, but by absorption of what was valuable in the older faith, so 'the appropriation of all that the ancient culture of the Orient can contribute will be for the Glory of God, our Father, and of our common Lord and Saviour, Jesus Christ.'[88]

The second Japanese delegate at Edinburgh, Bishop Honda Yoitsu (or Honda Yoichi; 1848-1912), came, like Harada, from a samurai family, in this case of a very high rank. Whereas Harada's Christian faith had been nurtured in the second Japanese Christian 'band' at Kumamoto, Honda had been a member of the very first 'band' which gathered at Yokohama from 1872 under the leadership of Samuel R. Brown and James Ballagh of the Reformed Church in America. He had thus begun his Christian life as a Presbyterian. He became a Methodist as a result of contact with an American Methodist missionary, John Ing, who was en route with his wife to China, but was persuaded by Honda to accompany him to Hirosaki, where Honda needed a teacher of English for the clan school for sons of samurai, of which he was principal. Honda and Ing soon gathered around them a group of some fifteen students who desired baptism. From that nucleus developed one of the most influential churches in Japanese Protestant history, sending more than 200 people into Christian ministry over the next century. The church became affiliated with the American Methodist Episcopal Church, into which Honda was ordained. Following study at Drew Theological Seminary in New Jersey, Honda returned to Japan in 1890 to become president of the Methodist boys' school in Tokyo, Aoyama Gakuin. He was instrumental in uniting the three

88. *History and Records of the Conference*, pp. 283-8. The quotation is from Slater, *Higher Hinduism*, p. 291. For fuller expositions of Harada's view of the relationship of Christianity to Japanese tradition see his 'The present position and problems of Christianity in Japan', *IRM* 1 (1912), pp. 79-97 and his *The Faith of Japan* (New York: Macmillan, 1914).

Japanese Methodist bodies in 1907 to form the United Japan Methodist Church, of which he was elected the first bishop. As someone whose own personal Christian history transcended denominational barriers, Honda was strongly committed to ecumenical relationships: he was chairman of the Japanese YMCA from 1903 to 1909 and a vice-chairman of the World's Student Christian Federation from 1900 to 1909.[89]

It is worthy of note that Bishop Honda, probably the most distinguished Asian Methodist minister of the day, was invited to Edinburgh, not by the Board of Foreign Missions of the church into which he was ordained, the Methodist Episcopal Church, but by the American executive committee. Known personally to Mott from as early as 1901 through the YMCA and World's Student Christian Federation, he was someone whose presence at Edinburgh Mott was determined to secure.[90]

Honda was not an invited speaker at the conference, but participated in the debate on the report of Commission II. He was the only Asian speaker to elect to address the conference in his native vernacular (with interpretation by Galen M. Fisher of the YMCA in Tokyo). Honda's choice to speak in Japanese was presumably the result of deliberate cultural preference, rather than linguistic necessity; he had, after all, spent two years of advanced study in the USA. It was certainly an appropriate medium to signal the radical content of his message, whose burden was that missions should not be afraid to allow the Asian churches to express 'the national spirit'. The Great Commission of Christ in Matthew 28:19 was evidence that 'our Master and Lord recognised nationality.' Moreover, in 'this age of strong nationality' any mission work that did not 'recognise the national spirit and the spirit of independence will make weak-kneed and dependent Christians' and was courting disaster in the shape of persecution. The Presbyterian, Congregational, Episcopal, and Methodist Churches of Japan were all 'practically independent and self-governing', and supplied evidence that a 'nationalised Church' could still find a legitimate place for foreign missionaries.[91]

The third Japanese to be present at Edinburgh, Revd Dr Ibuka Kajinosuke

89. On Honda see *BDCM*, p. 302; Lodwick (comp.), *Chinese Recorder Index*, I, p. 219; Drummond, *Christianity in Japan*, pp. 166-7, 172; Y. Aizan, *Essays on the Modern Japanese Church: Christianity in Meiji Japan* (Ann Arbor, MI: Center for Japanese Studies, University of Michigan, 1999), pp. 65-7; John F. Howes, 'Japanese Christians and American missionaries', in Marius B. Jansen (ed.), *Changing Japanese Attitudes Toward Modernization* (Princeton: Princeton UP, 1965), pp. 337-68.

90. Hopkins, *John R. Mott*, pp. 255, 266. See YDS, RG45, Mott papers, box 42, folder 764, Honda to Mott, 26 May 1909.

91. *Report of Commission II*, pp. 349-50. See Chapter 6, p. 143.

(1854-1940), was a long-standing friend of Honda and member of the Yokohama 'band'. Again from a high-ranking samurai family that had lost its former pre-eminence founded on landed wealth, Ibuka sought new influence through western education, and in finding that, found Christ. R. K. Hanna, a delegate of the Foreign Mission Committee of the Presbyterian Church in Ireland, remarked with ironic overstatement in his published reflections on the conference, 'Many a Japanese was first attracted towards the new faith, not because he had any leaning towards the new religion, but because he wanted a good English accent, and he could learn that only from the missionary.'[92] After pursuing theological studies at the Union Theological School in Tokyo and then church history at Union Theological Seminary in New York, Ibuka became in 1891 the first Japanese chancellor of Meiji Gakuin Christian College.[93] As with Honda, Mott had made his acquaintance through YMCA and World's Student Christian Federation networks.[94]

Ibuka was the sole non-western member of the conference business committee, and as such had the privilege of a seat at the clerks' table, just below the chairman. He addressed the conference on two occasions. He spoke first in the debate on the report of Commission III on education, urging that more needed to be done to strengthen Christian schools and colleges in Japan, and recommending in particular the foundation of a Christian university that could do for Japan what Oxford, Cambridge, Edinburgh, Yale, or Princeton had done for the west. This was, Ibuka admitted, an exalted ambition, but he asked, evoking William Carey's famous phrase, 'may we not expect great things of God?'[95] His second speech was the second of three major programmed addresses (the other two being by Bishop Logan Roots of the Hankow mission of the Protestant Episcopal Church and V. S. Azariah) in the evening session on Monday, 20 June, supposedly on the theme of 'The Problem of Co-operation between Foreign and Native Workers.' In point of fact Ibuka's address was more concerned with theological and constitutional issues in church-mission relationships. He made extensive reference to the formation in 1877 by eight different Presbyterian or Reformed churches of the *Nihon Kirisuto Itchi Kyokai* (United Church of Christ in Japan), of which he was in 1910 the moderator. The missionaries involved had insisted that the

92. Hanna, *Some Impressions of The World Missionary Conference*, p. 9.
93. On Ibuka Kajinosuke see *BDCM*, pp. 315-16; Lodwick (comp.), *Chinese Recorder Index*, I, p. 234; Scott Sunquist (ed.), *A Dictionary of Asian Christianity* (Grand Rapids: Eerdmans, 2001), pp. 358-9.
94. Hopkins, *John R. Mott*, pp. 199, 208, 255, 266. See YDS, RG45, Mott papers, box 43, folder 798.
95. *Report of Commission III*, pp. 437-8; Gairdner, 'Edinburgh 1910', p. 127.

doctrinal standards of the new church should be those of the European Reformed tradition: the Westminster Confession, the Canons of the Synod of Dort, and the Shorter and Heidelberg Catechisms. Ibuka referred modestly to himself as one of the Japanese Christians who had argued instead for a simple indigenous confession of faith, but had eventually deferred to the missionaries' wishes. He then went on to describe the progress of the church towards the adoption in 1890 of its own confession of faith, which, placed as a preamble to the Apostles' Creed, superceded the European credal statements. In this process he himself had played a major role.[96] The second half of Ibuka's paper was devoted to a defence of what were known as agreements of 'co-operation' between the United Church and each of the various missions which had originally planted its constituent churches: 'co-operation' implied an equal share between church and foreign mission in the administration of all strategic evangelistic work, and hence an equal voice in the distribution of foreign funds. By 1910 three of the six foreign missions involved had signed such an agreement; the other three had accepted a less radical relationship between church and mission, known as a 'plan of affiliation.'[97] In comparison with the address by V. S. Azariah that immediately followed, Ibuka's paper appears to have aroused very little reaction.

The final Japanese delegate was less well known than the other three outside his own Baptist denomination, though in later years he acquired wider renown. The Revd Chiba Yugoro was born in Sendai and adopted into a family of 'high rank'. He was converted in about 1887 as a result of attending evening classes run by American Baptist missionaries. After graduating from the Methodist Aoyama Gakuin school in Tokyo, Chiba went to the USA, to study first at Colby College in Maine from 1893 to 1895, and then from 1895 to 1898 at Rochester Theological Seminary. In 1910 he was president of the Southern Baptist Theological Seminary at Fukuoka, Japan, and dean-elect of the new Japan Baptist Seminary in Tokyo, a co-operative venture between American Baptists and Southern Baptists.[98] At Edinburgh he participated in the debate on the Commission I report, pointing out that the Japanese church was still largely an urban phenomenon, with very little work having been done among

96. A. J. Brown, *The Mastery of the Far East: the story of Korea's transformation and Japan's rise to supremacy in the Orient* (London: G. Bell & Sons, 1919), p. 643; Drummond, *Christianity in Japan*, p. 177. For the confession see *Report of Commission II*, p. 294.

97. *History and Records of the Conference*, pp. 294-305. For 'co-operation' in Japan see *Report of Commission II*, pp. 36-8, 350-1.

98. On Chiba see *Missions* 1 (1910), p. 190; F. C. Parker, *The Southern Baptist Mission in Japan, 1889-1989* (Lanham, MD: University Press of America, 1991), pp. 19, 64, 72, 78-80, 155-6, 169; Lodwick (comp.), *Chinese Recorder Index*, I, p. 85.

farmers and the labouring classes.[99] Chiba later became chairman of the National Christian Council of Japan, and the most prominent leader in twentieth-century Japanese Baptist life.

Yun Ch'iho and Christian Nationalism in Korea

Korea had become a Japanese protectorate in November 1905 and was fully annexed by Japan just two months after the Edinburgh conference, on 22 August 1910. In this context the strengthening forces of Asian nationalism took a form that could more easily be harmonized with Christian commitment and a pro-western modernizing alignment than was the case in India, China, or even Japan. The harmonious union of Protestant Christianity and Korean nationalism was symbolized in the person of the Honourable Yun Ch'iho (1865-1945). Yun is without doubt the most politically significant of the Asian delegates, and remains a major figure in Korean modern history, despite the bad odour in which his name is now held on account of the pro-Japanese stance he adopted later in life. He was, for example, the author of the words of the South Korean national anthem.[100] It is also claimed that he was responsible for introducing the bicycle from the USA to Korea.[101]

As his title suggests, Yun Ch'iho was a member of the Korean aristocracy, belonging to the old and prestigious Haep'yong clan. His father was one of the earliest members of the pro-Japanese Reform Party. As a youth, Yun was sent to Japan for language study, where his linguistic ability so impressed the first American emissary to Korea that he was brought back to Korea at the age of eighteen to work as an interpreter at the American legation. He has been described as the first Korean to master the English language with flu-

---

99. *Report of Commission I*, p. 408.

100. On Ch'iho see *BDCM*, pp. 757-8; Sunquist (ed.), *Dictionary of Asian Christianity*, p. 929; Hopkins, *John R. Mott*, pp. 307-8, 316, 382, 606, 648-9; Koen de Ceuster, *From Modernization to Collaboration, the Dilemma of Korean Cultural Nationalism: the case of Yun Ch'i-ho*, 2 vols. (Leuven: Katholieke Universiteit Leuven, 1994); Hyung-chan Kim, 'Portrait of a troubled Korean patriot: Yun Ch'i-ho's views of the March First Independence Movement and World War II', *Korean Studies* 13 (1989), pp. 76-91; Vladimir Tikhonov, 'Social Darwinism in Korea and its influence on early modern Korean Buddhism', *International Journal of Korean History* 2 (Aug. 2002), pp. 65-97; Elizabeth Underwood, *Challenged Identities: North American missionaries in Korea, 1884-1934* (Seoul: Royal Asiatic Society, Korea Branch, 2003), pp. 254-6; Kenneth M. Wells, *New God, New Nation: Protestants and self-reconstruction nationalism in Korea, 1896-1937* (Honolulu: University of Hawaii Press, 1990), pp. 39-40, 47-70, and *passim*.

101. See http://www.ccrc.or.kr/english_chanwon/korea_cycle.jsp (accessed 08.03.2007)

ency.[102] When Yun was wrongly suspected of involvement in the abortive Korean reform coup in December 1884, he left for Shanghai, where he enrolled in the Anglo-Chinese College established by Young J. Allen of the American Southern Methodist mission. Here he became a Christian, being baptized in April 1887. Young J. Allen's conviction that spiritual reformation was the key to national renaissance made a lasting impact on Yun.[103] His Methodist connections gave him the opportunity, very rare for a Korean at that time, to study in the USA, first at Vanderbilt University, then at Emory College (Emory University from 1915). At Vanderbilt, Yun imbibed from his teachers the principles of social Darwinism. Although he struggled with the apparent incompatibility between a Christian doctrine of providence and the merciless nature of social Darwinist racial theory, Yun reached the conclusion that Korea would be fitted for national survival neither through 'degenerate' Confucianism nor through 'abstract' and 'abstruse' Buddhism, but only by adopting the progressive and morally vibrant faith of Christianity. At Emory Yun accordingly persuaded President Warren A. Candler to use his influence with the Foreign Mission Board of the Methodist Episcopal Church, South, to induce the Board to commence operations in Korea.

In October 1893 Yun returned to teach at the college in Shanghai, before returning to Korea in February 1895 in response to an invitation from the Korean government to serve as vice-minister of education. In collaboration with another returned Korean American, Philip Jaisohn, Yun began publication of the first Korean newspaper to be printed entirely in the Korean phonetic script, the *Tongnip Sinmun* ('The Independent'), which advocated an openly reformist and pro-Christian stance. When the newspaper was shut down for overly aggressive political tactics, Yun withdrew for a while to the provinces. He was recalled to government service as vice-minister of foreign affairs (and later acting foreign minister) in 1904, but resigned following the declaration of the Japanese protectorate in November. He withdrew once again from political life and concentrated on the empowerment of his people through the Christian education of young people. He was the founder and first principal of the Anglo-Korean College (later Songdo High School), for which he secured Southern Methodist funding, and was a founding member of the Seoul YMCA. He became known to Mott as his interpreter during his first visit to Korea in February 1907, and again in April that year as one of the speakers at the Tokyo international conference of the World's Student Christian Federation. Although he may have been considered as too controversial a political

---

102. Tikhonov, 'Social Darwinism in Korea'.
103. De Ceuster, *From Modernization to Collaboration,* vol. II, pp. 633-4.

figure for the Southern Methodists to invite to represent them at the conference, he was, like Honda Yoitsu, high on Mott's 'wanted' list for Edinburgh, and was thus invited as a guest of the American executive committee. Yun had already travelled to the USA in January 1910 as a guest of the Board of Missions of the Methodist Episcopal Church, South, and it was on arriving in February at the Nashville home of Dr W. R. Lambuth, long-serving secretary of the Board, that Yun received Mott's pressing invitation to attend 'the great World Missionary Conference in Edinburgh next June': 'You', wrote Mott, 'are pre-eminently the man to represent your important and beloved country. In view of God's mighty work it is most desirable that you be present at Edinburgh.'[104]

Yun's first public contribution at Edinburgh was in relation to Commission I (of which he was also a correspondent). He referred to the remarkably rapid expansion of the Korean Protestant churches, growing in the space of twenty-five years to a membership of nearly 200,000 Christians. But he also warned of the consequent danger of shallow doctrinal understanding, combined with the revival of both Buddhism and Confucianism, and the growing influence of western materialist philosophies.[105] It should be remembered that Yun had become a Christian before he arrived at a social Darwinist understanding of Korean nationalism; for Yun, as also for the four Japanese delegates, Christianity was always more than a means to a nationalist end. Yun also spoke in the debate on the Commission II report, gently challenging the almost universally accepted principle that money contributed by western Christians should be under their control, and urging that national leaders be taken fully into consultation in the allocation of funds.[106]

Yun made an impression at Edinburgh more by who he was — the most prominent Christian advocate of national reform and independence in Korea — than by what he said. Contemporary accounts of the conference speak of him reverentially as a figure who commanded great respect.[107] Yun kept a diary (now published in eleven volumes), but unfortunately no diaries are extant for the period from July 1906 to December 1915.[108] Yun's later recollec-

104. YDS, RG45, Mott papers, box 101, folder 1782, Mott to Yun Ch'iho, 1 Feb. 1910, and Yun Ch'iho to Mott, 11 Feb. 1910. On Lambuth see *BDCM*, p. 382.

105. *Report of Commission I*, pp. 410-11; Gairdner, '*Edinburgh 1910*', pp. 79, 98.

106. *Report of Commission II*, pp. 358-9; Gairdner, '*Edinburgh 1910*', p. 106.

107. Gairdner, '*Edinburgh 1910*', p. 57; Smellie, *At the World Missionary Conference*, p. 10;

108. The first seven volumes were published as *Yun Ch'iho Ilgi* (Diary of Yun Ch'iho), 7 vols. (Seoul: Kuksa p'yonch'an wiwonhoe, 1971-1986). The remaining volumes have been privately printed and distributed to interested libraries; see de Ceuster, *From Modernization to Collaboration*, vol. I, pp. 14-15.

tions of the conference appear not to be particularly favourable: what stood out in his mind thirty years later was the Anglo-Saxon arrogance displayed by some speakers.[109] Within a year of the conference, Yun was under investigation by the Japanese, accused of involvement in a conspiracy to assassinate the Japanese governor-general of Korea, Terauchi Masatake. Of the 124 so accused, 98 were Christians. In June 1912 105 of the accused, including Yun, were sentenced to terms of imprisonment of between five and ten years. The second meeting of the Edinburgh Continuation Committee, which took place at Lake Mohonk, New York, from 26 September to 2 October 1912, sent a letter of protest to the Japanese ambassador in Washington. The case went to appeal, and a new trial was ordered, which resulted in March 1913 in the acquittal of all except six of the defendants, who were sentenced to six years in prison: one of the six was Yun. Although many Japanese, and most foreign opinion, had already concluded that the evidence against the 'conspirators' had been fabricated by the police, the six remained in custody until February 1915, when all were released as a gesture of clemency on the coronation of the new emperor.[110] On his release from prison, Yun became actively involved in the quest for financial autonomy of the Korean churches, and of the Korean Methodist church in particular.[111]

V. S. Azariah and the Challenge of Inter-Cultural Friendship

We have noted that both Oldham and Mott were personally strongly committed to securing the presence of national Christians at the conference. One of the ways in which Oldham responded to Nelson Bitton's letter in January 1910 appears to have been to issue, on behalf of the British executive committee, a special invitation to his former colleague in the Indian YMCA, Vedanayagam Samuel Azariah (1874-1945), an Anglican clergyman from Tirunelveli in south India. Oldham was acting on a strong recommendation from Henry Whitehead, the Anglo-Catholic bishop of Madras, who had suggested Azariah as a suitable speaker for one of the evening meetings.[112]

109. Diary of Yun Ch'iho, 5 Nov. 1940. I owe this reference to Dr Shin Ahn, formerly of the University of Edinburgh.

110. On the 'Korean Conspiracy case' see Brown, *The Mastery of the Far East,* pp. 571-3; idem, *The Korean Conspiracy Case* (Northfield, MA: Northfield Press, 1912); James Huntley Grayson, *Korea — A Religious History,* revised edn. (London: RoutledgeCurzon, 2002), p. 160; Hopkins, *John R. Mott,* p. 382; Hogg, *Ecumenical Foundations,* p. 150.

111. De Ceuster, *From Modernization to Collaboration,* vol. II, p. 644.

112. LP, Davidson papers, vol. 269, fol. 28, Oldham to Randall Davidson, 9 July 1909. The

Like the great majority of those who have become Christian in south India over the last century or so, Azariah came, not from the high castes whom many European missionaries as late as 1910 still believed to be the key to India's conversion, but from a group towards the bottom of India's caste hierarchy: he was a Nadar, a caste that was not strictly one of the so-called 'untouchables', 'depressed classes', or 'scheduled castes', those now known as Dalits (the 'crushed or broken ones'), but one that still shared many of the exclusions and disadvantages experienced by the scheduled castes. In addition to a prominent role in the Indian YMCA, Azariah had been the prime mover in setting up the first two missionary societies established and run entirely by Indians, the Indian Missionary Society of Tirunelveli in 1903 and the National Missionary Society two years later: he was thus the pioneer of a trend — the growth of missions from non-western countries such as India or Korea — which has contributed very significantly to the transformation of the face of Christian world mission.

By 1910 Azariah had proved himself to be a totally dedicated evangelist or missionary (the tendency to reserve that word for whites should be resisted) in the area of Dornakal, where some 2,000-3,000 converts a year were joining the Anglican church. Outside of south India, however, he was virtually unknown. Though he had been ordained priest only a few months previously on 5 December 1909, he was already being groomed by Bishop Whitehead for the post of assistant bishop in the diocese of Madras. He was on the fast track for ecclesiastical promotion, and he was one of only six Indians selected as correspondents for Mott's Commission I questionnaire. His answer to question IX which inquired in patronising terms about the efficiency of the native church in evangelism was an eloquent rebuttal of European scepticism about the capacity of 'native Christian workers' to work independently of European supervision: where Indian evangelists were regarded as mere machines in the employment of European missionary agencies in which they had no voice, it was not surprising, Azariah pointed out, that there were problems; genuinely Indian missions such as the Indian Missionary Society, on the other hand, showed the discipline and efficiency of Indian evangelists to be quite comparable with that of European missionaries.[113]

Azariah travelled to Edinburgh all the way from south India in the domi-

connection with Bitton's letter is also made by Kathleen Bliss in NCE, Oldham papers, box 22, folder 2, unpublished manuscript on Oldham, pp. 74-5.

113. UTS, MRL 12, WMC papers, series 1, box 3, folder 2. The question implied that 'at first' native agency would 'prove slower and less efficient than that of the foreign missionary'; see UTS, MRL 12, WMC papers, series 1, box 7, folder 9.

neering company of the bishop's wife, Mrs Isabel Whitehead, who, almost certainly, was responsible for sowing in her husband's mind the thought that Azariah could be elevated to the episcopate, but, also less happily, for the absurd attempt to make this young south Indian conform to western preconceptions of the Orient by dressing him up in a turban at every conceivable opportunity. On disembarking from the steamer at Naples, Mrs Whitehead was installed into an expensive hotel, while her Indian protegé had to make do with a pension ten minutes' walk away. Travelling onwards by rail, the bishop's wife showed appropriate humility by travelling second-class. However, we should not be too impressed with the fact that she chose not to travel first-class, for Azariah had to be content with roughing it in third-class, that is, in a wholly separate and inferior railway carriage. By the time they reached Edinburgh, Azariah's exasperation had led him close to the point of abandoning the Whiteheads' patronage and their exalted plans for him. The stifling experience of being chaperoned by Mrs Whitehead forms an indispensable part of the background to what Azariah had to say at Edinburgh.[114]

Azariah's qualities had become known not only to Oldham, but also to Mott. In July 1909 Mott had tried without success to secure Azariah's presence in Britain, at the Oxford conference of the World's Student Christian Federation, and it is probable that Mott had a hand in securing Azariah's invitation to Edinburgh also.[115] In the Mott papers at Yale Divinity School, there is preserved a small yellowing postcard written by Mott to his wife, Leila, on 7 May 1910 from the small rural village of Goathland in north Yorkshire. Mott, Oldham, his wife, Mary, and some of the key figures involved in the organization of the conference had gathered in this remote spot for a spiritual retreat in preparation for the conference. The postcard reveals that one of the eight persons who gathered for that retreat was Azariah. The formidable Mrs Isabel Whitehead was not invited to join the party. This young, newly ordained, and still largely unknown Indian priest thus formed one of the select few who were invited to set the spiritual tone of the conference by prayer and silent reflection amidst the beauty of the Yorkshire Moors.[116]

To those assembled at Edinburgh 1910, Azariah was still an unknown

---

114. Harper, *In the Shadow of the Mahatma*, pp. 121-2, 139-47.

115. YDS, RG 45, Mott papers, box 4, folder 61, Azariah to Mott, 25 May 1909.

116. YDS, RG45, Mott papers, box 107, folder 1835, Postcard from John R. Mott to Leila Mott, 7 May 1910. The others present at Goathland included Kenneth Maclennan (assistant conference secretary), George Robson (chairman of the business committee), the Methodist, W. H. Findlay (a member of the international committee), and Mrs Alexander Whyte of Edinburgh. On Azariah and Mrs Whitehead see Harper, *In the Shadow of the Mahatma*, pp. 121-2, 139-47.

name. He spoke twice at the conference. His first speech, in the Commission I debate on 15 June, was an impassioned plea that, relative to its vast population, India — even though it had far more western missionaries than anywhere else — was the real neglected continent of the missionary enterprise (rather than Latin America, which, because of its exclusion from the agenda, was regarded by many evangelicals at Edinburgh as the neglected continent). He argued that there were 100 million Indians beyond the reach of any missionary agency, presented 'an appalling list of states and districts in India which had no missionary', and claimed that there were 50 million of 'the masses of the people of India' (by which he meant the untouchables) 'who are ready to hear the Gospel and join the Church'.[117] His address was well received but nobody remembers that speech today. Azariah's second contribution, by contrast, is the one speech delivered at Edinburgh that is still regularly cited by historians and theologians. It was made, not in the main business sessions of the conference, but to one of the evening meetings (on Monday 20 June), which were designed to have a more devotional and uplifting tone, and where speakers were allowed up to forty minutes. Azariah followed immediately after Dr Ibuka Kajinosuke in tackling one of the most sensitive topics on the conference agenda, 'The Problem of Co-operation between Foreign and Native Workers.' In contrast to Ibuka, his approach was unflinchingly personal.

Azariah's address began with the statement that 'The problem of race relationships is one of the most serious problems confronting the Church today'. It went on to complain of 'a certain aloofness, a lack of mutual understanding and openness, a great lack of frank intercourse and friendliness' between European missionaries and national Christians, citing examples of experienced Indian national missionaries who had never once been invited to share a meal with any of their European brethren, and conversely of European missionaries who had never dreamt of visiting the homes of their Indian missionary colleagues. He pointed out that 'Friendship is more than condescending love' and urged that, on the basis of his own experience, friendship between two very different races was possible. According to one of the stewards, H. F. Houlder, Azariah remarked that 'Too often you promise us thrones in heaven, but will not offer us chairs in your drawing rooms.'[118] Perhaps significantly, that observation did not find its way into the official conference record of the address.

---

117. *Report of Commission I*, pp. 411-12; *Church Missionary Review* 61:735 (July 1910), p. 407.

118. UBL, CMS Archives, Acc215 Z1, H. F. Houlder, ' "Edinburgh 1910": reminiscences of the World Missionary Conference held in Edinburgh in June 1910', p. 3.

The problem Azariah had identified was related to the financial structures of the mission movement. Most Indian Christian leaders were employed and supported not by their own national church but by foreign missionary agencies. 'The missionary', Azariah pointed out, 'is the paymaster, the worker his servant. As long as this relationship exists, we must admit that no sense of self-respect and individuality can grow in the Indian Church'. That was an admission which most missionaries were, at least in theory, quite prepared to make. His pleas for the devolution of responsibility and financial control from missionaries to national church leaders were in conformity with what progressive missionary strategists were already saying, even if hardly any missions had yet put these principles into practice. But what made Azariah's audience so desperately uncomfortable was his assertion that the real problem lay with a failure of basic Christian spirituality. Such failures of friendship, he argued, were impoverishing the church's theology and spiritual life. At the climax of his address Azariah used two portions of Pauline language, drawn first from Ephesians 3:18-19, and then from the celebrated 'hymn to love' in 1 Corinthians 13, to drive his point home:

> The exceeding riches of the glory of Christ can be fully realised not by the Englishman, the American, and the Continental alone, nor by the Japanese, the Chinese, and the Indians by themselves — but by all working together, worshipping together, and learning together the Perfect Image of our Lord and Christ. It is only 'with all the Saints' that we can 'comprehend the love of Christ which passeth knowledge, that we might be filled with all the fullness of God.' This will be possible only from spiritual friendships between the two races. We ought to be willing to learn from one another and to help one another.
>
> Through all the ages to come the Indian Church will rise up in gratitude to attest the heroism and self-denying labours of the missionary body. You have given your goods to feed the poor. You have given your bodies to be burned. We also ask for *love*. Give us FRIENDS![119]

Azariah was insisting that the riches of the glory of God in Christ will be appropriated by the Church only if *all* the saints inter-relate in Christian fellowship. No one ethnic group acting in isolation from other Christians can discover the full riches of Christ. If the church is not multi-racial, its Christology will actually be distorted.

---

119. The fullest record of the address is in *History and Records of the Conference*, pp. 306-15.

This prophetic word was received in what Temple Gairdner described as 'an electric silence, broken now by a sort of subterraneous rumbling of dissent' and some applause when Azariah conceded that the failing he was alluding to was not typical. But he immediately qualified the concession by an impromptu 'At the same time it would be a mistake to think it was exceptional!', and there was some nervous laughter and further applause. Gairdner comments that 'Possibly some of the men — Indian missionaries they were — whose dissent, and even more than dissent, boiled every now and then to the surface, did not quite understand what the speaker was intending.'[120] One missionary journal also notes that 'there were a few cries of dissent' in response to Azariah's accusations of failures of missionary hospitality, but that 'the Indian was heard through, and was applauded.'[121]

The chairman of the meeting was one of the vice-presidents of the conference, Lord Reay, a former British governor of Bombay, and under-secretary of state for India in W. E. Gladstone's last ministry in 1894-5. Evidently conscious that it was his duty to say something to reduce the tension, Reay responded to Azariah's address by assuring the conference that 'some of his best friends' were Indians. Perhaps they were, but the scholars and Indian princes whom he had welcomed to the governor's palatial residence at Bombay were not the same sort of Indians of whose treatment at the hands of missionaries Azariah was complaining. Indeed, according to one source, what Reay said was that during his governorship of Bombay 'he had no more trusted friend than one of the Brahmins of the city'.[122] Reay asked Azariah to take back to his church the assurance that this conference of Christians was prepared 'at all times to shake the hand of fellowship with them' ('Hear, hear!').[123]

Whether anyone present actually shook Azariah's hand at the end of the meeting is not known. What we do know is that Isabel Whitehead later wrote to Azariah's wife, Anbu, back in India, reporting that the speech had struck the company 'like a bomb', with half of the audience being delighted 'and the other half very angry'. Mrs Whitehead counted herself in the former camp, 'little realizing that she was part of the problem'.[124] Azariah's indictment of missionaries as being deficient in the essential Christian motivation of fraternal love had caused such a sensation that an informal meeting was called to discuss what should be done. Some pressed for 'something in the nature of a public protest' or, at least an explanation that would reassure the

120. Gairdner, 'Edinburgh 1910', pp. 109-10.
121. Missionary Herald of the Presbyterian Church of Ireland, 1 Aug. 1910, p. 195.
122. Smellie, At the World Missionary Conference, p. 17.
123. The Scotsman, 21 June 1910, p. 10.
124. Harper, In the Shadow of the Mahatma, p. 148.

faithful that reality on the mission field was not as this unknown Indian had suggested. In the end, it was agreed simply that George Sherwood Eddy, the American Congregationalist and YMCA evangelist who was Azariah's closest confidant, would administer a 'fatherly admonition'.[125] In fact it is possible that Eddy had helped him write the speech in the first place.[126] Whether Eddy himself really believed that an admonition was necessary is not known. There is evidence, almost certainly autobiographical in nature, that Azariah had been diffident about speaking so frankly, but had been urged by John Mott, as the chairman of the conference, to 'tell out freely what lay on his heart'. We may speculate that Azariah felt that his initial doubts had been amply vindicated. In later years he told J. Z. Hodge, his biographer and the secretary (under Azariah's chairmanship) of the National Christian Council of India, Burma, and Ceylon, that he had spoken 'under a severe nervous strain, and, while he did not regret having entered his remonstrance, he mentioned that were he called to take similar action again he would do it more circumspectly'.[127]

Most of the Christian press either ignored his address or took exception to it. According to *The Harvest Field,* the main interdenominational journal concerned with India missions, Azariah's address was 'unfortunate, most unfair.' 'It is difficult to know exactly what Mr Azariah wants': the journal's editorial pointed out the 'practical difficulty' of Europeans entertaining Indians, because of the difference in social customs.

> We have had Indian brethren at our table who have been most uncomfortable. They knew not how to use the implements Europeans are accustomed to, and some of the food was of a kind that nature's tools could not well bring to one's mouth. We have tried various plans. We have treated them as ourselves and supplied them at table with knife, fork and spoon; we have put them with a leaf plate on the floor, where they are more at home. We doubt much whether the workers have been brought closer together in this way than by a quiet talk and prayer together in the study. There is the danger of accustoming poorly-paid workers to a European style of living.[128]

125. J. Z. Hodge, *Bishop Azariah of Dornakal* (Madras: Christian Literature Society for India, 1946), p. 4.

126. Rick L. Nutt, *The Whole Gospel for the Whole World: Sherwood Eddy and the American Protestant mission* (Macon, Ga: Mercer University Press, 1997), p. 72.

127. Hodge, *Bishop Azariah*, pp. 3, 6.

128. *The Harvest Field* 30:9 (Sept. 1910), p. 345; 30:12 (Dec. 1910), pp. 442-4.

Confronted with the challenge of trying to bridge the gap in cultural norms of eating, drinking, and hospitality, it would appear that this missionary, like the many others to whom Azariah was referring, had eventually given up the struggle and retreated into European social isolation, justifying his withdrawal from social intimacy with Indian Christian workers by the need not to give them a taste for a style of living which the Indian church could not possibly afford to sustain. When, two years later, Azariah was consecrated bishop of Dornakal, the first Indian to be made an Anglican bishop, there was much shaking of missionary heads.

If Azariah's speech was an accurate identification of the heart of 'The Problem of Co-operation between Foreign and Native Workers', as surely it was, hardly anyone in the western churches in 1910 seemed ready to listen. Only in retrospect, from the standpoint of the 1940s, during the turbulent years of the end of the British Raj in India, did some of those who had listened as young people to Azariah in 1910, recognize that he had then spoken a word of prophecy that western Christians desperately needed to hear. Even those missionary reactions to the speech which were essentially sympathetic strike the modern ear as either patronising or wilfully blind. In the former category belongs Azariah's later friend and colleague, J. Z. Hodge, then a missionary in Bihar with the Regions Beyond Missionary Union, a British evangelical 'faith mission'. At the time, Hodge found Azariah's statements incredible: 'It had never occurred to me that a mission station could exist where the missionary and the resident pastor were not on social visiting terms'. In retrospect, in 1946, the speech stood out in Hodge's mind as 'the outstanding memory' of Edinburgh 1910 and as perhaps 'the first shot in the campaign against "missionary imperialism"'. Yet its value, according to Hodge, was in its Dickensian use of over-statement, painting 'in too sombre colours' in order to drive home the point.[129] In the second category belongs Temple Gairdner, whose official account of the conference devotes two pages to the subject, commending Azariah for courage, delicacy, humour, and sincerity. Yet his closing comment cannot resist repudiating the accuracy of Azariah's charge even as he urges missionaries to take note of it. In his comment Gairdner mis-quotes Robert Burns' famous poem, 'To a Louse' (1786) in which the poet describes an incident in which he saw a woman in church proudly sporting a new hat. Unknown to her, there was a louse visible crawling all over the feathers on the hat, subjecting her to the ridicule of her neighbours:

129. Hodge, *Bishop Azariah*, pp. 3-6.

It could after all do one no harm to be reminded of the difficult ideal of inter-racial friendship. And as for the criticism, what does it matter even if criticism passed on us is false? The point is, that in *that* we see the impression we have made on those who pass the criticism; that thus and not otherwise they feel about us. The old couplet — 'Oh wad some fay the giftie gie us to see ourselves as ithers see us', loses no particle of its point if the vision of those others is most unaccountably mistaken.[130]

Hodge described Azariah's address as 'the first shot in the campaign against "missionary imperialism"', and in a profound sense that was what it was. But it would be a mistake to range Azariah alongside those who since the 1960s have attacked the western missionary enterprise (and indeed Christian mission itself) as essentially and irredeemably imperialistic. Azariah remained for the rest of his life unflinching in his commitment to the necessity of calling Hindus to conversion to Jesus Christ, and believed that European missionaries still had a part to play in that endeavour. As such, he, along with some leading Indian missionaries, famously clashed in February 1937 at a meeting with the champion of Indian nationalism, Mohandas K. Gandhi. Gandhi had become increasingly anxious about the number of members of the 'scheduled castes' who were converting to Christianity, and had therefore called on all Christian missions to confine themselves to humanitarian work and eschew any attempt at religious conversion. As one who had himself found in the Christian gospel dignity and liberation from the social oppression and exclusion experienced by his own caste, Azariah was not going to deny that same opportunity to others. Gandhi privately considered him to be his 'Enemy Number One' on account of his lifelong commitment to the evangelization of the depressed classes.[131]

Azariah's second Edinburgh address was a plea for a visible demonstration to a society fragmented by caste and structural injustice that the Christian vision of the kingdom of God really is different, just as Cheng Jingyi had pleaded that in the Chinese context a Christianity fractured by denominational argument or national allegiances would never commend itself with apostolic missionary power. India needed to see that the church was held together across the dividing lines of caste, ethnicity, culture, and empire by a unique quality of friendship that derived from the knowledge of what Azariah, following the letter to the Ephesians, called 'the exceeding riches of

---

130. Gairdner, *'Edinburgh 1910'*, p. 111. Burns's couplet in fact reads 'O wad some Power the *giftie gie* us, To see oursels as ithers see us!'

131. Harper, *In the Shadow of the Mahatma*, p. 7.

the glory of Christ'. What is more, Azariah had argued that such genuine Christian fellowship across racial fault-lines also *contributed to* knowledge of the riches of the glory of Christ. In other words, Christ would be more fully and more profoundly known as Christians allowed themselves to be changed by real, intimate, brotherly and sisterly fellowship with believers from other cultures. In the language of the New Testament, the richer their experience of the *body* of Christ, the richer would be their knowledge of Christ *himself.* By identifying failures in human relationship as the most fundamental of all missionary failures, he had touched a raw nerve in the western Christian conscience.

Pleas for an Asian Theology

Robert E. Speer, reflecting in print on the contributions made by the Asian delegates, reached conclusions that suggest that, in his case at least, true listening to their message had been, at best, partial:

> By what they were and what they said they illustrated the fallacy of the idea that the Oriental consciousness is radically different from the Occidental consciousness; and also the distance of the day when we may hope to receive from Asia any substantial modification of our interpretation of Christianity. It is probably inevitable and desirable that the new Churches should be closely similar to the older Churches which established them, but the prospect seems more distant than we have desired of the contribution by the great Asiatic races to our apprehension of that revelation of God in Christ which is richer than any one people's confessions or any one race's experience. For the present, if there are any grounds for anxiety, it is not because the native Churches are making innovations, for all of their innovations of doctrine or of polity are reproductions of incidents in the Church history of the West, but because they have as yet contributed nothing new to our understanding of the truth of God in Christ. It is evident that to such an end Christianity must lay deeper and wider hold upon the national and racial life of Asia. The mind of the Conference, holding firmly to the sufficiency and finality of Christ, was entirely open to whatever such a future expansion may bring.[132]

132. *The East and the West* 8:32 (Oct. 1910), p. 376.

Speer was representative of the leaders of the conference in his apparently progressive enthusiasm to see the western churches receive from 'the great Asiatic races' 'a substantial modification of our interpretation of Christianity', but, like others (such as John Campbell Gibson in his Commission II report),[133] expressed profound disappointment that no distinctive Asian contribution to theology or church polity had as yet been forthcoming. But Speer, along with everyone else, had heard Cheng Ji appealing for a church in China that would be entirely free of western denominational divisions. He had heard Harada Tasuku urging that missions should 'teach the Bible without too much of our interpretation, and then be patient as well as watchful to await the outcome of the Christian life in non-Christian lands'. He had heard Ibuka Kajinosuke's account of the adoption by the *Nihon Kirisuto Itchi Kyokai* of its own confession of faith in place of the doctrinal formulae of the western Reformed tradition. And he had heard Azariah's insistence that what Speer termed 'our understanding of the truth of God in Christ' (to which Asians had as yet supposedly contributed 'nothing new') would find its needed enrichment only through the slow, painful discipline of developing intercultural friendships. From the perspective of a century later, it is hard to identify what more the Asians could have done to convince western Protestant missionary strategists that the Asian interpretations of Christianity which they professed so much to desire were in fact already emerging before their eyes.

133. *Report of Commission II*, pp. 12, 258; see Chapter 6 below, pp. 135, 160.

The Church of the Three Selves

A Church-Centric Conference

The emphasis that the formation, growth, and nurture of the national church must be the central goal of all foreign missionary activity is more usually associated with the Jerusalem meeting of the International Missionary Council in 1928 than with the Edinburgh conference. But the 'church-centric' focus of Jerusalem 1928 was substantially anticipated in 1910 through the report of Commission II on 'The Church in the Mission Field', which will form the subject matter of this chapter. The report began by recalling in somewhat caricatured fashion the time

> when the work of foreign missions was commonly regarded by Christian people as the sending of a small forlorn hope into the midst of great masses of darkness and superstition, from which very little could be looked for in return. The missionaries' work was conceived to be a continual struggle with heathenism, and at the best the converts gained were thought of as little groups of unimportant people, whose conversion was gratifying for the sake of the individuals gained, but who had no important share in the missionary enterprise as a whole.[1]

'The most important general conclusion' the Commission believed it could draw from the replies submitted by the 217 serving missionaries, mission executives, and national church leaders who responded to its question-

1. *Report of Commission II*, p. 2.

naire was that this individualistic view of the missionary task must now be 'entirely abandoned'. The church on the mission field could no longer be regarded as a mere by-product of mission work, but rather as what the report termed 'the most efficient element in the Christian propaganda'. Albeit in non-theological language, the report was half-way towards enunciating the principle that was to become so axiomatic for Protestant missionary theory in the inter-war period, namely, that the church was not simply the goal but also the instrument of mission.[2]

The preface to the report went on to affirm that

> the Church on which we report presents itself no longer as an inspiring but distant ideal, nor even as a tender plant or a young child, appealing to our compassion and nurturing care. We see it now an actual Church in being, strongly rooted, and fruitful in many lands. The child has, in many places, reached, and in others is fast reaching, maturity; and is now both fitted and willing, perhaps in a few cases too eager, to take upon itself its full burden of responsibility and service.[3]

The assertion that in many lands the objective of a genuinely independent 'three-self' church was now within reach was perhaps the central claim of the report, and the discussion of the evidence on which this claim was based will form the first and longest section of this chapter.

The Three-Self Principle: Rhetoric and Reality

The chairman of Commission II, and also the person responsible for drafting its report,[4] was the Revd Dr J. Campbell Gibson (1849-1919), an eminent missionary of the Presbyterian Church of England from Lingtung, south China. The stamp of Gibson's progressive ideas and sanguine personality on the report are evident, although the absence of any surviving records of the Commission's deliberations makes it impossible to identify the particular contributions that other members of the Commission, some of them people of more conservative inclination than Gibson, may have made to its text. It is, for example, worthy of note that one member was the Revd Frederick Baylis,

2. *Ibid.*, p. 2. See T. E. Yates, *Christian Mission in the Twentieth Century* (Cambridge: CUP, 1994), pp. 60-2, 120-1, 127-8.

3. *Report of Commission II*, p. 3. For a reiteration of the point see p. 38.

4. P. J. Maclagan, *J. Campbell Gibson, D.D. Missionary of the Presbyterian Church of England: a biographical sketch* (London: Religious Tract Society, n.d. [1922]), p. 28.

Africa secretary (and later Far East secretary) of the CMS, and that Appendix K of the report reproduced the 'Memorandum on Development of Church Organisation in the Mission Field', adopted by the CMS in 1909, which Baylis wrote.[5] Baylis has been characterised as a cautious and pragmatic thinker who steered the CMS away from its earlier commitment to make rapid progress towards the appointment of native bishops; his Memorandum was sadly remarkable for its advocacy of distinct mission structures in India rather than immediate progress towards synodical government, and for its total silence on the subject of an indigenous episcopate.[6] Nevertheless, it is clear that the Commission was particularly anxious for the respondents to its questionnaire to supply evidence of the extent of their progress towards a three-self church: number 4 of the very long list of questions on the questionnaire requested respondents to describe the working of their church organisation in regard to self-government, self-support, and self-propagation.[7] Edinburgh 1910 thus gives no reinforcement to the supposition that the commitment of leading missionary strategists to the *principle* of the three-self formula had weakened by the Edwardian period. It may, however, strengthen the case that commitment in principle was one thing, and the will to achieve practical implementation quite another.

There is little doubt that Gibson was chosen as chairman of the Commission on the basis of his leading role at the China Centenary Missionary Conference held in Shanghai from 25 April to 8 May 1907.[8] Gibson was one of the two vice-chairmen of that conference, and in particular chaired its committee on the Chinese church. The sentiments and in places even the phraseology of the Commission II report in 1910 correspond closely to the precedent set three years earlier at Shanghai. Thus the claim of the report that a mature church with its own independent life and institutions 'presented itself no longer as an inspiring but distant ideal' echoed Gibson's report on the Chinese church to the Shanghai conference which had concluded that self-support was 'no longer an ideal for a distant future, but a practical object to be imme-

5. *Report of Commission II*, pp. 317-20.

6. On Baylis see C. Peter Williams, *The Ideal of the Self-Governing Church: a study in Victorian missionary strategy* (Leiden: E. J. Brill, 1990), pp. 202-3, 213, 230-51; K. J. T. Farrimond, 'The policy of the Church Missionary Society concerning the development of self-governing indigenous churches 1900-1942' (Ph.D. thesis, University of Leeds, 2004), pp. 79, 100-111.

7. *Report of Commission II*, p. 277.

8. Maclagan, *J. Campbell Gibson*, p. 28; George Hood, *Mission Accomplished? The English Presbyterian Mission in Lingtung, South China: a study of the interplay between mission methods and their historical context* (Frankfurt: Verlag Peter Lang, 1986), p. 153.

diately worked for and speedily realized. . . . we have already in China a Church which in a substantial degree is already [*sic*], and which is perfectly able soon to be entirely, self-governing, self-supporting, and self-propagating.'[9] The Edinburgh report also included repeated quotations on a number of topics from the records of the Shanghai conference, and printed all of its resolutions as Appendix M.[10] The Commission followed the Shanghai conference in exuding Gibson's optimism that a three-self church could be achieved within the foreseeable future. However, this confidence was tempered by three concerns which are given more or less emphasis in the report.

Church Organization and the 'Native Mind'

The first was the fact that the patterns of constitutional development of the indigenous church described in the questionnaire replies appeared to conform so closely to the models familiar from western denominational tradition. The report observed with evident disappointment the complete absence of what it termed 'an Indian system, a Chinese method, or an African type of church organisation.' Instead, the denominational affiliation of the sending mission defined the ideal and method of the emerging local church organization with depressing predictability. What would be regarded from an early twenty-first-century perspective as a failure in inculturation or contextual sensitivity was interpreted in 1910 as an inability to treat the distinctive characteristics of different races as a fruitful resource for the development of authentic church life:

> Much has been written, both in missionary and other literature, about racial temperaments and endowments, and high hopes have been formed as to how these varieties of gift should enrich and deepen Christian thought and religious experience. It is, we think, disappointing that the native mind in the countries concerned has not made a deeper mark on Church organisation.[11]

As if to underline the regrettable dominance of western ecclesiological traditions, the bulk of the first chapter of the report, on the 'constitution and

9. *Records: China Centenary Missionary Conference Held at Shanghai, April 25 to May 8, 1907* (Shanghai: Methodist Publishing House for the Centenary Conference Committee, 1907) [hereafter cited as *Records*], pp. 12, 18.

10. *Report of Commission II,* Appendix M, pp. 328-36, and Index, pp. 375 and 379.

11. *Ibid.,* p. 12.

organisation of the Church', was devoted to a rather laborious discussion of how each of nine different models of western Protestant church polity was handling the issue of church-mission relationships: Congregational polity; the polity of 'Continental' [mainly Lutheran] churches; Moravian polity; Anglican polity; Presbyterian polity; Methodist polity; the polity of the Society of Friends' missions; the polity of the Reformed Church of France (the missions of the Paris Evangelical Society); and the polity of interdenominational missions.[12]

In point of fact, it is arguable that the Commission overlooked the substantial evidence that was available in the questionnaire replies of considerable modification of western denominational polities. In response to the pressures of a missionary context, Anglicans were developing synodical structures with a guaranteed voice for the laity; Baptists and Congregationalists were radically compromising pure independency through the overtly episcopal role of their missionaries and the institution of regional church meetings or church unions which exercised control over individual congregations; interdenominational missions such as the China Inland Mission were constructing church bodies that married elements of Congregationalism and Presbyterianism; while Reformed and Presbyterian churches in China and Japan planted by several different missions had joined national federations in a way that had no parallel in western ecclesiastical experience at that time.[13] It may be objected that such trends represented no more than the addition of new minor variations to essentially European ecclesiastical melodies. But it could equally well be argued that the inevitable resort to combinations of western denominational labels to describe the hybridised forms of church life that were emerging disguised the true extent of the innovations being made. There was a measure of romanticism in the Commission's wistful longing for distinctively 'native' church forms that would somehow be essentially 'Indian', 'Chinese', or 'African', and a reluctance to acknowledge that ecclesiastical models that drew any features from the west could be fully authentic.

12. *Ibid.,* pp. 14-30.

13. UTS, MRL 12, WMC papers, series 1, boxes 11-13. See, for example, the responses by Ibuka (12/5/17), Gibson (13/1/98a), Lutley (13/2/139), Sparham (13/4/180), Hacker (11/8/270), Whitehead, (12/3/375), Tucker (11/3/464), Stephens (11/4/558). For a fuller exposition of this theme see Brian Stanley, 'The re-shaping of Christian tradition: western denominational identity in a non-western context', in R. N. Swanson (ed.), *Unity and Diversity in the Church* (Studies in Church History, vol. 32, Oxford: Blackwell, 1996), pp. 399-426.

The Remuneration of National Workers

A second concern of the Commission was that the level of remuneration being offered to church workers in Asia and Africa was alarmingly and consistently low.[14] The Commission II questionnaire asked questions about the salaries currently being paid to ordained clergy, preachers and catechists, male and female schoolteachers, and Bible women, and how these compared to wage levels outside the church. The majority of respondents had reported that all these categories of church workers were receiving considerably less than they could have earned in secular employment.[15] A few examples will have to suffice:

William Campbell of the English Presbyterian mission in Formosa reported that 'the salaries paid to Church employees are small, very small compared with the earnings of men following other occupations, and with the average standard of living in society'. Pastors received a basic wage of 16 dollars a month, plus a children's allowance of a dollar a child, and an additional dollar for living in a market town. Preachers were paid 8 dollars a month if single, and 10 if married, plus the same additional allowances as applied to pastors. Those who were ranked as second-grade, being deemed 'less efficient', received even less. If these church workers had joined the postal, telegraph, railway, or customs services in Formosa, Campbell observed, they could easily have obtained 15 to 40 dollars a month.[16] From Rajpur in the United Provinces in India, Canon S. Nihal Singh of the CMS mission replied that salaries of catechists and teachers were less than half of what those of similar competence earned in secular employment, and in some cases as little as one-quarter. Rates for catechists and male teachers began at only 10 rupees a month and rose to a maximum of 30 for senior catechists and 20 for higher grade teachers; Bible women and women teachers started on just 8 rupees, rising to a maximum of 12 for Bible women and 10 for teachers. Church pay compared 'very unfavourably' with average wage levels.[17] The situation was no better, sometimes worse, in most African churches. At Ngombe Lutete (Wathen), the principal British Baptist station in the lower Congo, there were as yet no African pastors, but evangelists were paid the equivalent of 6 shillings a month if single or 9 shillings and 3 pence if married. The BMS missionary, J. R. M. Stephens, estimated that these rates were no more than one-fifth of what the men could have

14. *Report of Commission II*, p. 202.

15. For a rare exception see R. H. Glover of the Christian and Missionary Alliance in China: UTS, MRL 12, WMC papers, series 1, box 13, folder 1, item 100, pp. 23-4.

16. UTS, MRL 12, WMC papers, series 1, box 12, folder 5, item 72, pp. 24-5.

17. UTS, MRL 12, WMC papers, series 1, box 12, folder 1, item 312, pp. 20-1.

earned as railway or traders' clerks.[18] In the Free Church of Scotland's Livingstonia Mission in Nyasaland, evangelists' wages were between a quarter and three-quarters of equivalent secular rates.[19] In the Church of Scotland's Blantyre Mission, African clergy earned only about half of what they could have earned in secular callings, and teachers less by an unspecified amount; evangelists, however, were, according to Alexander Hetherwick, paid 'about the same as they would get in secular employment.'[20]

The general picture painted by these figures will not surprise anyone familiar with mission history, or, for that matter, with scales of remuneration in Christian ministry and institutions in many countries today. There have been, and continue to be, widely varying views among Christians as to whether those employed by the church ought to be paid a salary commensurate with secular norms, or merely a basic stipend sufficient to meet what are deemed to be basic everyday needs. What is of interest in this evidence supplied to the Edinburgh conference is not so much the fact of the low levels of church workers' remuneration as the source of the remuneration and the interpretation placed on the evidence by the Commission.

The great majority of the church workers reported on in the questionnaire replies were still supported in large part, if not in their entirety, from mission funds. In China, Korea, and Japan, and in some places in India and Africa, ordained national pastors — who even in Asia were still very few in number in 1910 — were now generally regarded as the financial responsibility of the church, even if evangelists and teachers were supported by the missionary society. Indeed, the Commission's report explicitly commended the principle advocated by some respondents that ordination to the pastoral ministry should be made dependent on the existence of financial guarantees of support from the congregation or group of congregations that would benefit from the prospective pastor's ministry.[21] Evangelists and schoolteachers, on the other hand, were in most cases still a charge on mission funds. Both the Livingstonia Mission and the BMS lower Congo mission were noteworthy partial exceptions, with all evangelists' salaries being entirely supported by the indigenous church. Even in such cases, however, the level of their salaries still tended to be fixed, either directly or indirectly, by the mission. From Livingstonia W. A. Elmslie replied that 'The Livingstonia Mission Council, as having at first paid all workers fixed the

18. UTS, MRL 12, WMC papers, series 1, box 11, folder 4, item 558, p. 25.

19. UTS, MRL 12, WMC papers, series 1, box 11, folder 2, item 412, pp. 16-17. Response of W. A. Elmslie.

20. UTS, MRL 12, WMC papers, series 1, box 11, folder 2, item 424, pp. 17-18.

21. *Report of Commission II,* p. 201. See, for example, James D. Taylor from the ABCFM mission in Natal in UTS, MRL 12, WMC papers, series 1, box 11, folder 3, item 462, p. 3.

salaries. Since congregations support their evangelists and preachers they have accepted the rates fixed.'[22] Stephens reported that at Ngombe Lutete 'the Church *with the advice of the missionary* fixes the amount of pay.'[23]

The report drew the general conclusion from the evidence submitted to it that the prevailing rates of payment to all classes of national workers were usually too low. It then proceeded to suggest that 'the time has clearly come for considering whether grave injustice is not being done to native workers in many mission fields, — an injustice which must unavoidably have a most injurious effect upon the character of the work that is done by their means.'[24] The suggestion that an injustice was being committed was clearly premised on the fact that in most cases it was the mission, not the church, that was the paymaster. For the report warned that

> Anything that gives apparent ground for suspicion that the missionary or the mission is making unfair use of the services of native workers, and taking advantage of their inability or unwillingness to seek more profitable employment elsewhere, and on that account giving them less than fair payment for the services which they render, must have a disastrous effect upon the future relations between the growing Church and the missions which have planted it. We must beware of the tendency, which has undoubtedly sometimes existed, to make the control of the purse the basis of authority exercised by missions over the local Church and its workers.[25]

Thus far the logic of the Commission's argument might appear to lead to the conclusion that missions ought to take steps to reduce the yawning gap that invariably existed between the stipends of European missionaries and those paid to national workers.[26] In fact, however, the report then pursued its argument in precisely the opposite direction by warning missions against taking any action to remedy the problem of underpayment from their own resources:

> While it may be recognised that, generally speaking, the salaries of native workers in the mission field are lower than they ought to be, it

22. UTS, MRL 12, WMC papers, series 1, box 11, folder 2, item 412, p. 16.
23. UTS, MRL 12, WMC papers, series 1, box 11, folder 4, item 558, p. 25. My italics.
24. *Report of Commission II*, pp. 202-3.
25. *Ibid.*, p. 203.
26. For example, in the Norwegian Zulu mission, where missionary stipends were up to five times those of ordained African ministers; UTS, MRL 12, WMC papers, series 1, box 11, folder 1, item 395, p. 16 (Bishop Nils Astrup).

does not follow that the deficiency ought to be made good from foreign funds. It should everywhere be impressed upon the members of the Church in the mission field that the remedy lies with themselves. They should be taught to regard the contributions of the foreign Church as a temporary aid, cheerfully given during infancy, but not as the main or permanent basis of support. If the subject is patiently and persistently treated in a Christian spirit, it will be found that the cases are very rare in which a growing Christian community is not able to give adequate support to the ministrations by which it is spiritually nourished.[27]

If in 1910, as many of the questionnaire replies suggested, the second leg in the stool of the self-governing, self-supporting, and self-propagating church was still looking decidedly wobbly (which usually meant that the first leg was wobbly also), the principal fault and hence also the remedy was said to lie, not with the foreign mission boards, but with the national Christians on the mission field. Almost in the same breath the report had said that missions were doing the indigenous church a repeated injustice, and then that the solution to that injustice lay with the injured party rather than the perpetrator of the injustice. The inconsistency is blatant to the modern ear, but appears not to have been noticed by the conference delegates. The point was not specifically taken up in the discussion of the report at the conference session on 16 June. The speakers who came closest to the issue were, not surprisingly, the Asian representatives of the national churches, who, in different ways, all emphasized the inescapable connections between self-support and self-government. Bishop Honda Yoitsu of the Methodist Church of Japan, speaking through a translator, warned that missionary work 'which does not recognise the national spirit and the spirit of independence will make weak-kneed and dependent Christians, and it will give rise to persecution.'[28] From China, Cheng Jingyi, youthful and inexperienced though he was, acknowledged that the Chinese church was weak and poor, but insisted that 'experience shows that out of deep poverty Christian liberality may abound.' Self-support and self-government, urged Cheng, were to be regarded as a privilege and a joy, not a burden.[29] From Korea, Yun Ch'iho questioned the widespread assumption that all work carried on by foreign

27. *Report of Commission II*, pp. 204-5.
28. *Ibid.*, p. 349. See Chapter 5, p. 115.
29. *Ibid.*, p. 352. On Cheng and his two speeches at Edinburgh see Chapter 5, pp. 107-11.

money must be under foreign control, and urged that national leaders be consulted in the distribution of mission funds.[30] One of the Indian delegates, the Revd J. R. Chitambar, from the American Methodist Episcopal Church in Lucknow, addressed the issue of support of national workers, but was more concerned to rebut as unwise and divisive the suggestion that the best educated among them should be given the title of 'missionaries' and employed by the mission boards, leaving the inferior grade of national workers to be supported by their churches.[31]

Just how concerned the Commission really was about the chronic under-payment of the main body of national Christians in mission or church employment is debatable. The issue received no more than a passing mention in the summative chapter VIII of the report, and then only as one of the reasons for the dearth of candidates for higher level theological training. The report regarded the lack of clergy trained to a high level as a grave deficiency in 'the great civilised countries, such as India, China, and Japan', for here the Christian message was being challenged by alternative philosophies, especially those fashioned in the west.[32] The chapter accordingly gave particular emphasis to the need for wealthy western friends of missions to endow teaching posts and scholarships in non-western theological institutions, since it was unrealistic to expect young and poor churches 'struggling with the initial problems of self-support' to make such provision a priority.[33] The likelihood of such institutions aggravating those problems was not contemplated. The logic of the questionnaire replies received by the Commission in fact suggested that even if such higher-grade institutions were more widely established on the basis of foreign funding, their graduates would in many cases prove beyond the limited financial capacity of the indigenous church to support. The Commission had in effect concluded that national workers were ill-paid because they were insufficiently educated to merit being well-paid.

Failures in Self-Support

The third and most serious concern to surface here and there in the Commission's report was the evident inability or unwillingness of some churches to

30. *Report of Commission II*, pp. 358-9. On Yun Ch'iho see Chapter 5, pp. 118-21.
31. *Ibid.*, pp. 362-3. See Gairdner, *"Edinburgh 1910"*, p. 109, and Chapter 5, p. 106.
32. *Report of Commission II*, p. 197. The report here was influenced by the Shanghai conference; see *Records*, pp. 450-1.
33. *Report of Commission II*, pp. 271-2.

match the vigour and enthusiasm for self-support which Gibson had observed in south China. The report of the committee on the Chinese church submitted to the Shanghai conference in 1907 had made extensive reference to Gibson's own mission in Swatow, where by 1905 80 per cent of the costs of supporting the entire staff of Chinese clergy, preachers, and teachers were being met by Chinese contributions.[34] In point of fact the majority of churches even in China were less far advanced towards self-support than was the Swatow church, and Gibson's wording of a resolution on the Chinese ministry was amended by the Shanghai conference on the grounds that it was too optimistic: the words 'This Conference rejoices that the Chinese Church already supports its own ministry entirely in many cases, and partially in nearly all . . .' was amended to read 'and partially in others.'[35] The conference also recommended that 'every effort be made by Missions and Chinese Churches, to place the salaries of Chinese brethren engaged in church work on a scale adequate to the requirements of their position.'[36]

Hence at Shanghai in 1907, Gibson's statements on self-support had had to be toned down as being too optimistic to describe the reality of the Chinese church as a whole. Nevertheless, at Edinburgh sufficient evidence was submitted from various respondents in China, Formosa, Japan, and Korea to the Commission II questionnaire to give substantiation to Gibson's confidence that the day of the self-supporting church was indeed at hand. Albert Lutley, reporting on the China Inland Mission churches in Shanxi province, recorded that the churches were governed by an annual provincial conference, in which Chinese outnumbered missionaries by two to one, and with two elected chairmen, one being Chinese. Each country or village church was, according to Lutley, 'practically self-supporting', and the church also supported some village school teachers and a few evangelists. Lutley attributed the prominent role of Chinese in the government of the Shanxi churches to the example and influence of the remarkable late Pastor Hsi (Hsi Shengmo), though he also observed that there were as yet no signs among church leaders of a desire for a rapid transfer of full authority.[37] William Campbell supplied evidence from Formosa that, despite the admittedly low level of salaries, the Presbyterian Church still received nearly twice as much for general church

34. *Records*, pp. 12, 32-3.

35. *Ibid.*, pp. 469-70. See Hood, *Mission Accomplished*, pp. 146, 149.

36. *Records*, p. 441.

37. UTS, MRL 12, WMC papers, series 1, box 13, folder 2, item 139, pp. 1-2, 4-5, 21-2. On Pastor Hsi see Mrs Howard Taylor, *Pastor Hsi (of North China): one of China's Christians* (London: Morgan & Scott, n.d. [1904]) and Alvyn Austin, *China's Millions: the China Inland Mission 1832-1905 and Late Qing Society* (Grand Rapids and Cambridge, 2007).

work from national contributions as it did from foreign mission funds.[38] From Japan, Dr Ibuka Kajinosuke reported that the *Nihon Kirisuto Itchi Kyokai,* the (Presbyterian) United Church of Christ in Japan, now had some ninety congregations formally constituted as financially independent churches, supporting their own pastors; any church which failed to maintain its financial independence would automatically lose its voting rights in the presbytery.[39] Self-support was well advanced in the Japanese Protestant churches, the majority of whose leaders, as well as many of the members, were from the traditionally dominant samurai class. Most Japanese Christians were urban and middle-class. The resulting spirit of self-reliance was particularly strong in the United Church of Christ in Japan.[40] Similarly, the young Presbyterian Church in Korea, constituted on a national basis as recently as 1907, had been reared on the principles of self-support: the church already had more Korean ministers than missionaries in the presbytery, all of whom were fully supported by church contributions, despite the fact that all church members were, in the words of Revd J. E. Adams from Taiku, 'about equally poor'. Other workers, known as 'helpers', were supported in some cases by the church and in others from mission funds. It is worthy of note that Adams recorded that the salary rates for the former were 'rather higher' than for the latter.[41]

Prominent churches in East Asia, particularly those of Gibson's own Presbyterian polity, thus supplied corroboration for what he already believed to be the case on the basis of his own experience in Swatow: namely, that the attainment of full self-support was within the grasp of the indigenous church. From parts of the African church similarly encouraging reports were forthcoming. One of the pioneers of West African independency, Pastor Mojola Agbebi, founder of the Native Baptist Church of Lagos and president of the Native Baptist Union of West Africa, was able to describe his churches as being self-governing, self-supporting, and self-propagating, for he had agreed to link his network of independent churches with the Southern Baptist Convention's Foreign Mission Board only on condition that African leadership

38. UTS, MRL 12, WMC papers, series 1, box 12, folder 5, item 72, p. 4.

39. UTS, MRL 12, WMC papers, series 1, box 12, folder 5, item 17, pp. 1-2. On Dr Ibuka Kajinosuke see above, Chapter 5.

40. R. H. Drummond, *A History of Christianity in Japan* (Grand Rapids, MI: Eerdmans, 1971), pp. 169, 180; Arthur Judson Brown, *The Mastery of the Far East: the story of Korea's transformation and Japan's rise to supremacy in the Orient* (London: G. Bell & Sons, 1919), p. 647.

41. UTS, MRL 12, WMC papers, series 1, box 12, folder 5, item 1, pp. 1-3, 13-14, 16; see Brown, *The Mastery of the Far East,* pp. 521-2.

was maintained.[42] A correspondent from the Basel Mission church on the Gold Coast reported that the church's two synods had recently more than doubled the set rate of communicants' contributions to church funds, and was confident that within a few years the church would be 'entirely self-supporting'.[43] From Uganda, Bishop Alfred Tucker reported that self-support (as well as self-government and self-propagation) in the Anglican Church was already 'fully secured': the thirty indigenous clergy, plus all 2,000 lay readers and teachers, were entirely supported from native sources. Although stipends were low, all clergy, lay readers, and teachers were also given a house, a garden for cultivation and grazing, and had their hut tax paid by the church.[44] In the American Board mission in Natal, all foreign funding for the support of native pastors had been discontinued in about 1894; all churches with ordained pastors, and some with lay pastors, were now self-supporting.[45]

These examples were, however, probably unrepresentative of Africa as a whole. More typical was Livingstonia, where only the oldest church at Bandawe was fully self-supporting, and there were as yet no African pastors,[46] or the Baptist churches of the Ngombe Lutete district, which remained firmly under missionary control, even though the churches now supported between 55 and 67 of the 155 Bakongo teachers (the remainder being voluntary).[47] At Rustenberg in the Transvaal the Revd W. Behrens, of the Hermannsburg Mission, claimed that members of the native congregations were 'being educated up to Self-Support' through a per capita levy of five shillings per annum, and insisted that self-government and self-support must be 'the eventual goal'. Yet

42. UTS, MRL 12, WMC papers, series 1, box 11, folder 2, item 434, p. 1. See Hazel King, 'Co-operation in contextualization: two visionaries of the African Church — Mojola Agbebi and William Hughes of the African Institute, Colwyn Bay', *Journal of Religion in Africa* 16 (1986), pp. 2-21; also E. A. Ayandele, *A Visionary of the African Church: Mojola Agbebi, 1860-1917* (Nairobi: East African Publishing House, 1971).

43. UTS, MRL 12, WMC papers, series 1, box 11, folder 1, item 422, pp. 1-2 (Rev. B. Groh).

44. UTS, MRL 12, WMC papers, series 1, box 11, folder 3, item 464, pp. 2, 4, 6, 22-23.

45. UTS, MRL 12, WMC papers, series 1, box 11, folder 3, item 462, p. 3 (Rev. James Dexter Taylor).

46. UTS, MRL 12, WMC papers, series 1, box 11, folder 1, item 412, p. 1 (Rev. W. A. Elmslie). The first pastors were ordained in 1914; see John McCracken, *Politics and Christianity in Malawi 1875-1940: the impact of the Livingstonia Mission in the Northern Province* (Cambridge: Cambridge UP, 1977), p. 244.

47. UTS, MRL 12, WMC papers, series 1, box 11, folder 4, item 468, p. 2, and item 558, pp. 2-3, 5. The two respondents from Ngombe Lutete gave differing figures: John Weeks (468) reported that 55 out of 153 teachers were supported; J. R. M. Stephens (558) said 67 out of 155.

Behrens warned that 'we foreign Missionaries', in contrast to some 'unruly but educationally advanced natives' who had imbibed 'Ethiopianism', 'fear that this is a long way off still with the South Africa natives, who had no culture worth speaking of, until the white man came to this country.'[48] Nonetheless, there was enough evidence of a contrary kind in the Africa replies to persuade the members of Commission II that what worked in East Asia could work in Africa also, given the right determination of mind on the part of both missionaries and national Christians.

In East Asia, and even in parts of Africa, the gap between Gibson's own experience in Swatow and that of many mission churches seemed to be bridgeable. The Commission's deepest underlying concern was that in much of India this was not the case. The BMS Indian secretary, Herbert Anderson, recorded that his society employed some 500-600 Indians as evangelists, teachers, 'assistant missionaries', and 'missionaries' serving a total of 200 churches, all of whose salaries were fixed and paid by the London committee, and cited only one church, in Cuttack in Orissa, as being wholly self-governing, self-supporting, and self-propagating. Anderson's claim that, in accordance with Baptist ecclesiological principle, the society possessed 'no authority' over local churches and that therefore no transfer of power was necessary, disguised the extraordinary influence which the power of the purse still exercised.[49] In the CMS Punjab mission 80 per cent of the central fund from which church salaries were paid still came from London, and no congregation as yet supported its own pastor.[50] Also in the Punjab, in the American Presbyterian church at Hoshiarpur, though the ideal of self-support had been taught from the inception of the mission in 1875, monthly subscriptions from communicants (many of them from the depressed classes) were still inadequate to support the pastor without foreign aid.[51] In the SPG church in Delhi, according to Sushil K. Rudra, the notable Bengali principal of St Stephen's College, 'self support — in the real sense of the word does not exist, and for a long time cannot exist'. Nine-tenths of the congregation came from the depressed classes, being menial servants or from the humblest class of wage

48. UTS, MRL 12, WMC papers, series 1, box 11, folder 1, item 399, pp. 1, 3.

49. UTS, MRL 12, WMC papers, series 1, box 11, folder 6, item 214, pp. 1, 4, 5, 7, 22-3. It should, however, be noted that by 1913 47 Indian pastors and 30 evangelists were supported by the churches associated with the BMS; see Brian Stanley, *The History of the Baptist Missionary Society 1792-1992* (Edinburgh: T&T Clark, 1992), p. 155.

50. UTS, MRL 12, WMC papers, series 1, box 12, folder 1, item 362, p. 6 (E. F. E. Wigram); see also box 11, folder 6, item 213, pp. 1, 15 (Rev. J. Ali Baksh).

51. UTS, MRL 12, WMC papers, series 1, box 11, folder 7, item 233, pp. 1, 4 (Rev. K. C. Chatterjee).

earners.[52] The Methodist Episcopal mission, located mainly in western and central India, had encouraged tithing and other means of systematic proportionate giving, but had to report that amongst a poor and illiterate membership repeated famines and epidemics 'have interfered sadly with the development of self-support'.[53]

The situation was a little better in the stronger Christian Tamil communities in the south. There were a few instances where mature congregations had become self-supporting. In the CMS Tirunelveli mission, two of the fourteen 'Circles' of village pastorates were fully self-supporting, and one was nearly so.[54] In the LMS mission in south Travancore, founded by W. Ringeltaube as early as 1809, there were now seventeen self-supporting and self-governing pastorates, comprising some sixty-nine congregations.[55] The Wesleyan Methodist Tamil church at Royapettah in Madras had for the past ten years been independent of all financial help from the mission.[56] Bishop Alfred Whitehead of Madras pointed out in his response that self-support was further advanced among the long-established urban Tamil congregations, which contained numbers of educated and well-to-do members, than among the recently planted rural Telegu congregations, where the Christians were very poor and from the depressed classes. In the SPG mission 12,000 baptised Tamil Christians contributed 15,000 rupees a year towards their pastoral work, while 13,000 baptised Telegu Christians contributed only 5,200 rupees a year. The CMS was rather more successful than the SPG in developing self-support among the Telegu Christians, with 25,000 baptised Christians contributing 12,000 rupees annually. Whitehead attributed the noticeable but not large difference in per capita giving partly to the greater poverty and susceptibility to famine of the SPG districts, but also to the greater progress made by the CMS in giving Indians a share in church government through a system of District Church Councils.[57] In the Lutheran church in Madras, where more than two-thirds of the 1,009 members were 'cooly earning poor people' [sic], one-third

52. UTS, MRL 12, WMC papers, series 1, box 12, folder 2, item 329, p. 2. On Rudra see D. O'Connor, *A Clear Star: C. F. Andrews and India 1904-1914* (New Delhi: Chronicle Books, 2005), *passim*.

53. UTS, MRL 12, WMC papers, series 1, box 12, folder 1, item 325, 'Constitution and Organisation', p. 1 (Bishop J. E. Robinson).

54. UTS, MRL 12, WMC papers, series 1, box 11, folder 6, item 228, pp. 3-4 (Rev. E. S. Carr).

55. UTS, MRL 12, WMC papers, series 1, box 11, folder 8, item 270, pp. 6-7 (Rev. I. H. Hacker).

56. UTS, MRL 12, WMC papers, series 1, box 12, folder 1, item 322, p. 1 (Mr Krishna Ram).

57. UTS, MRL 12, WMC papers, series 1, box 12, folder 3, item 375, pp. 5-9.

of the salary of the pastor, N. Devasahayam, was still paid by the Leipzig Mission. Only a few of the Mission's churches had risen to the duty of supporting their pastors, 'and that not fully as yet'. 'The duty of selfsupport', reflected Devasahayam ruefully, 'was not impressed upon the converts from the *beginning*.'[58] Similarly, in the American Baptist Telegu mission, self-support was making 'very slow progress in most places', although the churches had organised a Home Missionary Society, which had several missionaries at work among the hill tribes, and one operating overseas, namely, John Rangiah, working among the Telegu sugar workers in Natal, who was present at the Edinburgh conference and was discussed in the previous chapter.[59]

It was the preponderance of Indian examples of the continuing dependence of churches on foreign funds that led Commission II to warn against the dangers of increasing foreign support as a solution to the underpayment of national church workers, even though the members of the Commission, as representatives of the western missionary agencies that employed the bulk of those workers, felt morally responsible for the problem. Having witnessed the development of a successful system of self-support among a rural Christian population in south China, and learnt of similar achievements in Japan and Korea, Gibson evidently found the far slower progress of the Indian churches in this respect perplexing. His sixty-three-page response to his own questionnaire included a lengthy extract from his report to the Shanghai Centenary Conference, concluding with the claim that 'There is more money among our people than we sometimes suppose . . . we have now reached a stage where there should be no long delay in the complete attainment of self-support.'[60] Gibson's questionnaire response went on to attribute the energy of the Swatow church in propagating itself to 'The conditions of social life, the entire absence of caste divisions, and perhaps the national temperament of the people.'[61] It thus comes as no surprise to find that the only attempt at a systematic explanation of the Indian Christian failure in the Commission II report is in a passage headed 'Racial Characteristics':

> . . . In India it is found that the Hindus as a race have marked religious tendencies, and are not slow to respond to religious teaching, but the features of the social organisation greatly hinder personal liberty. The

58. UTS, MRL 12, WMC papers, series 1, box 11, folder 7, item 250, pp. 1-2, 12.

59. UTS, MRL 12, WMC papers, series 1, box 11, folder 6, item 261, p. 2 (Rev. W. L. Fergusson). See Chapter 5 above.

60. UTS, MRL 12, WMC papers, series 1, box 13, folder 1, item 98a, p. 15, citing *Records*, pp. 15-16.

61. UTS, MRL 12, WMC papers, series 1, box 13, folder 1, item 98a, p. 16.

individual is not the unit of life, he is a mere fraction of an overgrown family, whom custom constrains in all things to act together. On the other hand, the village system in India is on the whole favourable to the spread and growth of Christianity, though being a compact organism, it tends to resist the profession of Christian faith on the part of its members as a disintegrating force threatening its own existence. Personal independence is, moreover, checked by the gentle and submissive nature of the Hindu temperament. It has, therefore, been difficult in India to raise up strong, independent, self-supporting Churches, and the tendency of Hindu Christians to rely upon the guidance and control of their foreign Mission is only too apparent.

The report argued that in China on the other hand, both 'racial characteristics' and 'the fabric of social observances' were more favourable to mission work. In the absence of the caste system, there was greater scope for individual will and action, and hence it had proved easier to 'lead the Chinese Church to take upon its own shoulders its own burdens without leaning upon foreign help than it has been in India.'[62] The section of the report devoted to 'support of workers' accordingly began by arguing that the view taken of these matters by the national church depended, not simply on the teaching of the early missionaries, but also on 'the characteristics of the race of people among whom the Church is being formed.'[63] The same report which castigated national churches for failing to reflect their own racial characteristics in their patterns of organisation thus resorted, in the case of the largest single Protestant mission field — India — to blaming racial characteristics for the financially dependent condition of the Indian church.

Modern commentators would no doubt accuse the report of falling back on a crude form of racial essentialism in an attempt to excuse a lamentable failure of missionary policy. However, if, as Devasahayam's response suggested, missions in India (to a much greater extent than missions in China) had omitted from the beginning to insist on the priority of self-support, that omission is to be understood as a failure of collective nerve in a context shaped, first by the uniquely inhibiting constraints of caste solidarity, and later by the irruption into the church of large numbers of the depressed classes (Dalits), whose poverty in relative if not absolute terms was unusual, even for Asia. Dependency has thus been a feature of modern Indian Christianity to an extent not matched elsewhere in Asia or in Africa. Nonetheless, it

62. *Report of Commission II*, pp. 91-2.
63. *Ibid.* p. 199.

should be remembered that the confidence expressed by the 1910 report that Chinese Christianity was about to achieve complete financial and administrative independence was somewhat misplaced. The fact that the 'Christian Manifesto' of 1950 was able to throw the slogan of the three-selves back in the face of the missions as an objective that had, at best, achieved only 'a measure of success' is evidence that in the four decades after the Edinburgh conference relatively little progress was made in extending self-support from the pastoral ministry to the full range of Christian agency and institutions in China.[64] The conference's insistence that 'the remedy lies with themselves' did nothing to open the eyes of missions to their own role after 1910 in continuing to aggravate the problem by insisting that the Chinese church could not expect to function adequately without a panoply of complex and expensive institutions.

Issues of Christian Nurture and Discipleship

Chapter II of the Commission II report was devoted to the topic of 'Conditions of Membership,' and Chapter III to 'Church Discipline'. Because of their focus on the criteria determining admission to, and exclusion from the Christian community, these are the sections of the Edinburgh documents which come closest to an analysis of the intensifying cultural and ethical problems confronting the missionary movement as processes of conversion to Christianity began to acquire an independent and accelerating momentum that had been absent for most of the nineteenth century. However, the degree of emphasis and amount of space given to church discipline — a theme which Gibson reiterated strongly in introducing the report to the conference — tended in practice to overshadow the commitment of the Commission to the goal of building a three-self church.[65]

In terms of the attitudes prevalent in foreign missions at that time, the theological presuppositions evident in these chapters were, nonetheless, decidedly progressive (Gibson's own stance was towards the liberal end of the evangelical spectrum).[66] The report urged missionaries to be positive rather than negative in their responses to the 'false systems' they encountered, aided in their perspective by 'the modern science of comparative religion, and by the more careful

---

64. V. E. W. Hayward, *Christians and China* (Belfast: Christian Journals Ltd., 1974), p. 50.

65. *Report of Commission II*, pp. 343-4.

66. Maclagan, *J. Campbell Gibson*, pp. 5-6.

canons of criticism in modern times'. In the light of the incarnational emphasis of modern theology, they should look for 'fragments of Truth' among all peoples, and aim to 'build up rather than to break down, to fulfil rather than to destroy.'[67] In formulating their policies of Christian nurture and church discipline, therefore, the aim of missionaries should be to sensitise the moral conscience of the young church. Precisely how that task would be discharged depended, as liberal race theory of the day taught, on 'the ethical stage already attained by the people or race in question'. Among 'the more educated and cultured classes of pagan communities' it was said to be imperative to rebut the accusation that 'the Christian religion ignores social customs and thought, tends towards denationalisation, and is essentially a religion peculiar to the West.'[68] The report accordingly adopted a moderately liberal attitude to the vexed issue of ancestor veneration in east Asia. It commended a paper on the subject given at the Shanghai conference, which argued that the greater challenge for the church in China in the future would not be the superstitious ancestral worship of the masses, but the increasing materialism and atheism of the educated.[69] The resolutions of the Shanghai conference, urging a repudiation of ancestral 'worship' but a more earnest cultivation of filial piety by Chinese Christians — on whom the ultimate responsibility for judging the issue must rest — were also printed in an appendix.[70]

The more 'primitive' a people, on the other hand, the greater the need for the firm hand of missionary control, shaping and enforcing the law codes of the infant Christian community: 'In childhood law plays — and ought to play — a far larger part than in manhood. This is true no less of the nation and of the Church than of the individual.'[71] The challenge and irony was, that by 1910 it was the 'primitive' peoples of the depressed classes of India and of Africa who were responding most eagerly to the Christian message. With regard to such peoples, the report spoke in much less ambiguous terms than it did about the 'higher' populations of Asia. What was alleged to be needed in the former case was not so much the cultural flexibility deriving from an incarnational theology as carefully constructed structures of probation and a clear framework of moral discipline to curb the baser instincts of the African race. Thus James Dexter Taylor of the American Board mission in Natal, responding to the questionnaire's invitation to comment on the

---

67. *Report of Commission II*, pp. 113-14.
68. *Ibid.*, p. 111.
69. *Ibid.*, p. 114; see *Records*, pp. 215-46.
70. *Report of Commission II*, pp. 328-9.
71. *Ibid.*, pp. 111-12.

bearing of 'Racial Characteristics' on matters of Christian nurture and spirituality, replied that

> The power of the fleshly instincts and passions in the African races makes necessary great strictness of discipline and close supervision over the lives of members. . . . The incapacity of the African for abstract thinking is a further reason for giving concreteness to the ethical teachings of the gospel by the insistence on rules of life.[72]

Chapter II opened with the wry and almost certainly accurate observation that much more missionary time and effort were apparently being spent in 'anxiously keeping people out of the Church, than in gathering them into it,'[73] a point which some modern historical writing, with its persistent tendency to explain conversion in terms of the power of the missionary, would do well to heed. The questionnaire had included detailed questions about the tests or conditions required of applicants for baptism and the catechumenate, and also for admission to full communicant membership. In summarising the replies received, the Commission urged the wisdom of steering a middle course between too eager a desire for numerical growth — which would result in the church being 'swamped in a flood of baptized heathenism' — and undue severity — which could 'discourage and exclude many who might have been led by more gentle handling to a sincere and fruitful Christian life.'[74] Most converts, the report noted, were initially drawn to Christian faith, not by individual conviction of sin, which was normally a product of the first stages of Christian discipleship, but by a range of other aspirations or circumstances. The 'careful missionary', therefore, animated by a desire to build a truly 'spiritual' church, was repeatedly confronted with converts impelled by a variety of motives and whose moral standards were, from a Christian perspective, of decidedly mixed quality.[75]

Those who supplied evidence to the Commission on these topics were in many instances responding to movements of religious conversion that were substantially independent of missionary direction and frequently subversive of western Protestant notions of the essentially individual and cognitive nature of religious belief. This was most obviously true of the so-called 'mass' or 'people' movements in India, but applied also to processes of group conver-

---

72. UTS, MRL 12, WMC papers, series 1, box 11, folder 3, item 462, pp. 13-14.
73. *Report of Commission II*, p. 40.
74. *Ibid.*, p. 41.
75. *Ibid.*, p. 42.

sion in China, Korea, and some parts of Africa. Immediately following the questions about admission to baptism, communion, and the catechumenate, respondents were asked about their experience and personal evaluation of 'mass movements', which were allocated a section of their own in the chapter.[76] The heavy emphasis placed on 'probation' by the report and the questionnaire replies on which it was based was consistent with a long-established Protestant missionary tradition of concern to test the spiritual authenticity of conversion, but it also needs to be understood against the background of the emergence since the 1880s of such movements in India and elsewhere.

Applicants for baptism or confirmation (and sometimes even those seeking admission to catechetical classes) were almost invariably described both by questionnaire respondents and by the report as 'candidates'. The process of assessment of whether a convert possessed sufficient knowledge and understanding to be admitted to baptism or communion was habitually termed an 'examination', often with certain set texts being prescribed for individual and class study. Such language was to an extent conventional in European church life, but in a context where the implantation of a body of Christian knowledge to those deemed to be wholly ignorant was at a premium, conventional linguistic usage acquired new connotations that encouraged an overestimation of intellectual and cultural as opposed to ethical criteria for the determination of spiritual maturity. This tendency was always latent in Protestantism, especially in those traditions which placed pre-eminent value on a learned ministry, but became most visible where the mission concerned was operating among supposedly 'primitive' people, such as in Africa.

Thus Alexander Hetherwick described the two-stage process of probation practised in the Blantyre Mission, where converts had to spend at least six months in the hearers' class, followed by two years in the catechumens' class before being admitted to baptism. To pass from the first to the second stage, candidates had to pass an examination on the Creed, the Ten Commandments, the Lord's Prayer, and a small catechism. In the second stage, they would receive further instruction in the above, be taught 'the main facts of Old Testament History', the doctrine of the sacraments, and the Larger Catechism, and be examined by both the minister (i.e. a missionary) and elders, before being recommended to the session of African elders for admission to baptism.[77] In the Livingstonia Mission also, where the Tonga had been flocking to the church in vast numbers since the mid-1890s, missionaries had instituted a two-stage process of probation which lasted for a minimum of three years be-

76. *Ibid.*, pp. 85-91, 278.
77. UTS, MRL 12, WMC papers, series 1, box 11, folder 1, item 424, p. 5.

fore baptism — 'a very long period of probation', commented the report, 'which may perhaps be justified, or even necessary, where a hitherto untaught and barbarous race is being dealt with.'[78] Even missions from denominations that placed less emphasis on a learned ministry, such as the British Baptists, tended to adhere in the African context to a minimum period of probation, although this was shorter than in the Presbyterian missions. BMS missionaries in the Congo required their converts to spend between six and twelve months (or even longer) on probation before baptism. At Yakusu on the Upper Congo they were required to enrol for at least six months as members of a 'Christian Endeavour Society' before passing an oral examination.[79] Some missions, such as the CMS, made ability to read a virtual or even absolute pre-condition for baptism, and catechumens became widely known as 'Gospel Readers' or in Kikuyu *'athomi'* (readers), an emerging literate elite among their societies. With 'numbers pressing forward towards Christianity', observed Bishop Tucker, this policy had the advantage of lengthening the probationary period between confession of faith and baptism, and had ensured that the majority of the 70,000 communicants in the Church of Uganda were able to read the Bible in the vernacular.[80] In the Livingstonia Mission, even admission to the catechumens' class was from 1906 made conditional on literacy.[81]

The trend was not confined to Africa. In the Punjab, similarly, in a context where many Chuhras, a scavenger and sweeper caste, were moving towards Christian faith,[82] probation in the CMS mission usually lasted at least a year and often much longer. E. F. E. Wigram, secretary of the CMS India committee, noted with approval that one of his best Indian clergy had begun to insist on converts learning to read during the period of their catechumenate, 'partly

78. *Report of Commission II,* pp. 45-6; see McCracken, *Politics and Christianity in Malawi,* pp. 186-7.

79. *Report of Commission II,* p. 52, citing William Millman, UTS, MRL 12, WMC papers, series 1, box 11, folder 2, item 439, p. 5. See also box 11, folder 4, item 468, p. 5 (J. H. Weeks), and box 11, folder 2, item 590, p. 3 (Kenred Smith).

80. UTS, MRL 12, WMC papers, series 1, box 11, folder 3, item 464, section II, pp. 1-2. The Luganda Bible was completed in 1896. On the *athomi* see John Karanja, 'The role of Kikuyu Christians in developing a self-consciously African Anglicanism', in Kevin Ward and Brian Stanley (eds.), *The Church Mission Society and World Christianity, 1799-1999* (Grand Rapids and Richmond, Surrey: Eerdmans and Curzon Press, 2000), p. 264.

81. McCracken, *Politics and Christianity in Malawi,* p. 188.

82. See Jeffrey Cox, *Imperial Fault-Lines: Christianity and Colonialism in the Punjab* (Stanford, CA: Stanford UP, 2001), pp. 116-30; Kenneth W. Jones, *Arya Dharm: Hindu consciousness in 19th-century Punjab* (Berkeley: University of California Press, 1976), pp. 10-12; J. C. B. Webster, *A History of the Dalit Christians in India* (San Francisco: Mellen Research University Press, 1992), pp. 44-9.

as a test of sincerity, partly that they may afterwards be able to read their own Bibles in their frequent terrible isolation from the means of grace'. A regular condition of baptism in the Punjab (as in other parts of India) was also that converts should renounce the habit of eating carrion, as a visible sign of their 'uplift' from their depressed class status. Among educated Muslims or Hindus, on the other hand, the CMS was prepared to administer baptism as soon as possible after the genuineness of an enquirer's conversion and basic understanding of the faith had been established.[83] For the educated and socially respectable convert, it seemed rather easier to convince missionaries of the genuineness of one's regeneration than it was for the barbarous or the outcaste — there was less need for the rigours of law which the report commended as so much more necessary for races still in 'childhood'.

The cumulative frustration which missions caused to converts by impeding or delaying their baptism was already leading to secessions to independent church movements in some contexts, such as Malawi.[84] In the Transvaal similarly, W. Behrens noted that Ethiopian churches were baptizing those who had 'learned nothing and lacked all necessary instruction', while many persons had left the Hermannsburg Mission church 'saying that our baptismal classes lasted too long'. Yet in Behrens' view, 'This only shows that we are trying to do our work thoroughly which is the best policy in the long run'.[85] The Commission, which had very few members with recent field experience (and none with recent experience of Africa)[86] made no reference to such dangers, but did warn that probation should not be extended to such a point that 'baptism should be made to seem the goal, rather than the starting-point of the visible Christian life.' It also cited Gustav Warneck's insistence that as communication of knowledge is not the main object of the missionary, so the possession of it ought never to be the main test for admission to baptism, and referred to a response from A. T. Howard, a United Brethren Christ missionary in Japan, who reported that candidates there had come to regard baptism as a 'graduating' service after which the baptised Christian saw no need of further teaching.[87]

83. UTS, MRL 12, WMC papers, series 1, box 12, folder 1, item 362, p. 15 (E. F. E. Wigram); Cox, *Imperial Fault-Lines*, p. 129. For other examples of depressed-class converts being required to abandon carrion-eating see Webster, *A History of the Dalit Christians*, pp. 42, 54, 183n.

84. McCracken, *Politics and Christianity in Malawi*, pp. 189-90.

85. UTS, MRL 12, WMC papers, series 1, box 11, folder 1, item 399, pp. 5-6.

86. Apart from Bishop John E. Hine of Zanzibar who served briefly as a member of Commission II before resigning in June 1909; *Report of Commission II*, p. vii.

87. *Report of Commission II*, p. 48 and p. 50; UTS, MRL 12, WMC papers, series 1, box 12, folder 5, item 46, p. 6.

Among the responses a few stood out as valuing education less highly than evidence of inner regeneration. In Shanxi, for example, Albert Lutley reported that the CIM required of candidates only 'evidence of repentance, faith in Christ, and of being born again' before baptism. There was no time limit, or knowledge test. There was still some testing of basic Christian knowledge, but of an essentially informal kind: 'all except the very aged are expected to answer questions on the main facts and truths of the Gospel, and if they cannot do this, it is regarded as a proof of lack of real love and earnestness for the truth.'[88]

The section of the report concerned specifically with mass movements noted that there was 'some divergence of opinion among our correspondents', ranging from those who deeply suspected any movement of conversion that was not made up of individual decisions to those such as the bishop of Madras, whose enthusiastic and lengthy response to the question on mass movements urged that 'A mass movement is an open door, and the church should press through it with all her might.' Whitehead believed mass movements to be motivated by 'a genuine desire for a better life' on the part of victims of tyranny and oppression; they were a profound challenge to missions to develop more efficient strategies of discipleship and instruction in the principles of self-support and self-government.[89] Confronted with such diversity of assessment, the Commission took a cautiously welcoming line, recommending that missionaries should deal charitably with converts whose motives were palpably of a material kind, in view of the fact that 'God uses the lower elements and movements of human life as a means of ascent into the higher, and the unrest which sometimes strongly arises in the general mind of a degraded community while seeking mainly social and material improvement, may well be a divine unrest through which God is leading them to a nobler life.'[90]

Uncertainty on how to respond mass movements was not restricted to European missionaries, but was equally reflected among the small number of Indian Christians included in the respondents. Being themselves from a high-caste Hindu (or occasionally Muslim) background and members of the Indian Christian elite, they tended to regard depressed class converts with a disdain or even contempt that foreign missionary invective could not match. The Brahman convert, K. C. Chatterjee, commenting on the movement

88. *Report of Commission II*, p. 54, citing UTS, MRL 12, WMC papers, series 1, box 13, folder 2, item 139, p. 8.

89. *Report of Commission II*, pp. 85, 90; UTS, MRL 12, WMC papers, series 1, box 12, folder 3, item 375, pp. 12-33.

90. *Report of Commission II*, p. 86.

among the Chuhras in the Punjab, described the Chuhras as illiterate, sunk in vice, dull of understanding, and almost entirely lacking in moral sensitivity. Yet Chatterjee was in no doubt that a genuine 'work of the Spirit' was under way among them. All inquirers should be received and instructed en masse, but not baptised: baptism should be administered only when an individual was ready to make an intelligent confession of faith. Although initially the admission of the Chuhras into the church had lowered its social standing, Chatterjee observed that after a while Hindu reforming movements such as the Sanatana Dharma Sabha or the Arya Samaj had felt compelled to follow the Christian example and admit Chuhras into the Hindu community by ceremonies of reconversion through ritual purification *(shuddhi)*.[91]

The Revd. J. Ali Bakhsh, also from the Punjab and a convert from Islam, was still more blunt than Chatterjee in his low estimation of the Chuhra community. Like Chatterjee, he held that they had 'no religion or their own', adopting Hindu practices among Hindus and Muslim customs among Muslims; but they were also 'hereditary criminals' with 'no idea of sin'. The mass movements, in Bakhsh's view, were due, not to mission preaching (this was largely true), but to 'worldly motives', such as the desire to be exempt from 'Begar', the obligation on the depressed classes to provide forced labour to civil or police officers, which could usually be avoided after Christian baptism. Bakhsh agreed with Chatterjee that missions were far too ready to baptize depressed class people, 'not that they are fit for baptism, or they have any intelligent hold on the faith, but simply to catch hold of their children and hope to see them christians sometime.' Unlike Chatterjee, however, he saw little evidence of the Spirit at work amongst such human dross. These adherents had had no cross to bear as a result of 'conversion', and consequently little fruit could be expected from them. Whereas converts from higher caste backgrounds were generally well spoken of by outsiders, the products of mass movements were widely despised.[92]

If in Asia mass movements constituted the most important issue of Christian nurture and discipline on which the Commission sought respondents' views, in Africa it was their policy on the admission of polygamists to

91. UTS, MRL 12, WMC papers, series 1, box 11, folder 5, item 233, pp. 10-14. See Charles H. Heimsath, *Indian Nationalism and Hindu Social Reform* (Princeton: Princeton UP, 1964), pp. 276, 301-5, 318; Jones, *Arya Dharm*, pp. 202-3.

92. UTS, MRL 12, WMC papers, series 1, box 11, folder 6, item 213, pp. 5-7. On Revd (later Canon) John Ali Bakhsh see Church Missionary Society, *Register of Missionaries . . . and Native Clergy, from 1804 to 1904* (Privately printed, CMS, n.d. [1904]), p. 479, no. 498, Eugene Stock, *The History of the Church Missionary Society*, 4 vols. (London: CMS, 1899-1916), IV, pp. 118, 187, 198, 206-7, 245.

baptism and church membership. The report devoted eleven pages to the topic of 'bigamy and polygamy', and printed as an appendix the resolutions of various church and mission bodies on the subject, including the 1888 Lambeth Conference.[93] The general problem for the Commission was that its inclination to seek fragments of spiritual light among all peoples ran up against the 'great difficulty . . . that in most non-Christian lands the practice of polygamy is not contrary to the natural and unenlightened conscience.' The difficulty was less acute in China, where there were limited forms of polygamy that co-existed with 'a really high ideal of family life and of conjugal rights and obligations', and also in India, where polygamy was comparatively rare, except among certain depressed classes in the south. The Commission recorded the considerable range of missionary practice on the question in China and India, noting in particular, though without explicit endorsement, the view of 'some thoughtful missionaries' in China who advocated a lenient policy towards the baptism of those who had before their conversion taken a second or third wife under pressure from the dominating ideals of filial piety and ancestor veneration.[94] In Africa, on the other hand, polygamy took a form that the Commission thought no Christian could tolerate, with women treated virtually as slaves and a companionate ideal of marriage almost non-existent.[95] Bishop Tucker's verdict was baldly stated, but probably not unrepresentative of a naïve belief among foreign missionaries in Africa that Christianity was not simply reforming family life, but introducing it for the first time:

> Through the influence and power of the Gospel *Family Life* is now coming into existence in Uganda. In the old days it was unknown. Parents never trained their children. Wives were never companions to their husbands. Now, however, parental responsibility with regard to the education and training of children is being realised. And it is no uncommon thing to see parents and children sitting together, eating together, and walking together. The institution of family prayer has had largely to do with this changed condition of things.[96]

J. J. Willis, Tucker's colleague in the Uganda mission and later his successor as bishop of Uganda, gave an identical verdict: 'The system of purely [*sic*]

93. *Report of Commission II*, pp. 64-74, 321-7.
94. *Ibid.*, pp. 66-7, 73.
95. *Ibid.*, pp. 64-5.
96. UTS, MRL 12, WMC papers, series 1, box 11, folder 3, item 464, pp. 24-5.

family life is itself a product of Christianity. The new life does not so much improve as create family life, as we understand it.'[97] Similar statements were made by missionaries in other parts of the continent. 'It will take many years', commented W. Behrens from the Transvaal, 'before family life attains the standard it has with us.'[98] The responses the Commission received from African correspondents contained little or no trace of the incarnational theological principle of identifying partial spiritual truth in indigenous systems of value. 'With them', commented the report, 'there can be no "question" of polygamy. It is simply one of the gross evils of heathen society which, like habitual murder or slavery, must at all costs be ended.'[99] The report implied that among Africa missionaries diversity existed only on the secondary question of whether a polygamous wife could be baptised; in relation to the polygamist himself there was 'almost complete unanimity of opinion: Every Mission within our review refuses admission to the Church in Africa to any man who is actually living with more than one wife.'[100]

This judgment was broadly, but not entirely, accurate. It ignored the blatant exception of Mojola Agbebi's Native Baptist Church in Lagos, where converted polygamists were admitted to church membership on the sole condition 'that they will not increase their number of wives', and were even permitted to hold church office 'in temporal matters' and 'in the absence of monogamists.'[101] It also misrepresented the current policy of the BMS Lower Congo mission. Initially the BMS, in common with the other Protestant missions working in the region, had baptised anyone whose confession of faith seemed genuine, irrespective of their marital status. This policy had proved unproblematic in the early days of Protestant work in the Congo, when most converts were single young men, often 'house-boys' of the missionaries. It had become untenable as the rate of conversion increased, leading both the American Baptist Missionary Union and the Svenska Missionsförbundet to require converted polygamists to put away all but the first wife prior to baptism. A young missionary at Ngombe Lutete, George Cameron, had tried in 1898 to persuade the BMS to take the same line, but had met stalwart opposition from older missionaries. Faced with an irreconcilable diversity of view, the BMS in 1900 ruled that each Congolese church 'in conference with' its

97. UTS, MRL 12, WMC papers, series 1, box 11, folder 4, item 472, p. 24.

98. UTS, MRL 12, WMC papers, series 1, box 11, folder 1, item 399, p. 20. For a similar emphasis on Christianity as the creator of family life see B. Groh from the Gold Coast in box 11, folder 1, item 422, p. 14.

99. *Report of Commission II*, pp. 65-6.

100. *Ibid.*, pp. 70-1.

101. UTS, MRL 12, WMC papers, series 1, box 11, folder 2, item 434, pp. 4-5.

missionaries must decide its own policy on the question. At some stations, such as Ngombe Lutete, even this proved difficult.[102] By 1909, when the Commission's questionnaire reached the station, an elaborate compromise had been agreed. It was decided that no missionary should baptise and receive a polygamist residing within his church district, on the case being first brought to his notice, but should endeavour to persuade the man to put away his extra wives honourably, and with regard to their future maintenance. If persuasion failed, the missionary was to leave the matter for six months until he visited the district again. In the meantime he would have explained all the circumstances to his colleagues of the station, and have their views submitted to him, but when the missionary went out again to the district, he was to have liberty (subject to the agreement of the local church) to baptise and receive the polygamist into fellowship. At least in theory, therefore, the BMS policy on the lower Congo was more flexible than the report's generalisation implied. However, the Ngombe Lutete church had also adopted the general rule that those married 'country fashion' (that is, by African custom) must also engage in 'holy matrimony' (that is, a church wedding) or a State marriage before being admitted to the church.[103] In practice, as elsewhere in Africa, the equation between a church wedding and Christian marriage was rapidly being established, thus making it more and more difficult to accommodate with generous sympathy the exceptional cases of polygamous converts that the older generation of missionaries had argued for. Reality on the African continent was in fact conforming increasingly closely to the simple picture painted by the report of a unified missionary stance against any compromise with the sin of polygamy.

Theology and Spiritual Life

The report's disappointment that 'the native mind . . . has not made a deeper mark on Church organisation' in the mission fields[104] was symptomatic of a broader and more fundamental regret that there was as yet so little sign of the 'younger' churches developing their own forms and patterns of theological thinking. The report discussed this theme twice, first in relation to theological training in Chapter V on 'Training and Employment of Workers', and then

102. For a fuller account see Stanley, *History of the BMS*, pp. 128-30.
103. UTS, MRL 12, WMC papers, series 1, box 11, folder 4, items 558, pp. 13-14 (Stephens) and 468, p. 12 (Weeks).
104. See above, n. 11.

more fully in Chapter VII on 'Christian Literature and Theology.' The Commission's questionnaire had inquired hopefully whether there were 'any indications of original and formative native thought in Theology'; but the replies, lamented Chapter V, were 'with noticeable unanimity, in the negative.'[105] It was true that the Christian gospel itself was universal, but mere regurgitation of the theological formulations of the West was never going to meet the needs of 'the oriental races' for an expression of Christianity that could be authentically their own:

> We advocate no new Gospel, and our chief concern is with the permanent and fundamental elements of theology. These are neither oriental nor occidental, but in order to build up the Church on these lasting foundations Christian theology must be written afresh for every fresh race to whom it comes, so that it may justify itself to all as the abiding wisdom that cometh from above, every quick and powerful, and not be misrepresented as if it were no more than a precipitation from the antiquated text-books of the West.[106]

The Commission diagnosed the problem with regard to theological training as two-fold. First, missions had in their institutions for training national clergy and church leaders relied almost entirely on translations or adaptations of western text-books, with the result that 'theology, instead of wearing its true aspect of a search for the many-sided truth which is vital to spiritual life, appears rather as a *hortus siccus* which has exhausted, and contains, in improved and final form, all that is found in the Bible.' Second, theological students had either slavishly adhered to the thought-forms and even verbal expressions of their teachers, or, in reaction against such undue dependence, had manifested 'a spirit of revolt', a politicised form of theological expression that by silent implication the report appeared to regard as illegitimate. What was conspicuously lacking, in the Commission's view, was a 'living form of Christian knowledge', nurtured by fresh indigenous reflection on the Bible rather than by western types of thought.[107]

Chapter VII delivered an equally depressing verdict in a section headed 'Lack of Independent Thought among Native Christians': the church in the mission field showed, with only a few exceptions, 'very little sign of literary power, and still less of any original and formative thought on the great ques-

---

105. *Report of Commission II*, p. 283.
106. *Ibid.*, p. 191.
107. *Ibid.*, pp. 190-1.

tions of the Divine revelation and of spiritual life.'[108] The Commission cited various respondents, mainly from India, in support of this judgement. One leading India missionary commented: 'I have hardly known one Indian Christian thinker whose theology has revealed definite constructive thought, who has been able to shake himself away from the trammels of the West.'[109] From Delhi, Sushil K. Rudra identified the problem as being the paucity of Christians among 'the better classes' who could act as thinkers and leaders of the community, and hinted that the low rates of pay attached to mission employment were partly to blame:

> But in the present state of western dominance and supremacy they cannot do so. They have enough to do to seek an honourable livelihood in the world and maintain their position in Indian society generally. . . . The number from this class engaging in Mission service is small on account of the present conditions attaching to such service. Thinkers and leaders can come only from this class at present where they are highly educated.[110]

The report also cited an unnamed foreign missionary who was more explicit than Rudra in asserting that intellectual dependence was inevitably linked to financial dependence: 'The hand of the foreign padris who hold the purse strings is too heavy for anything like original and formative thought, or any other sort of real originality in India. . . . Till Indians get loose from the bondage to foreign money, it is useless to expect much or any really inspired general literature.'[111]

The report was not afraid to print and endorse these accusations that the dominance of the western missionary lay at the root of the matter, but this theme was expounded in a fashion that used racial stereotyping to throw at least some of the collective blame back onto Asian shoulders:

> When we realise for how many centuries the vigorous, progressive races of the West were under the domination of the Latin Fathers, in their doctrine of the inspiration of Scripture, their canons of interpretation, and their whole system of theological thought and statement, and how slowly, partially, and with what mental and spiritual conflict they have

108. *Ibid.*, p. 258.
109. *Report of Commission II*, p. 259.
110. UTS, MRL 12, WMC papers, series 1, box 12, folder 2, item 329, p. 18, cited in part in *Report of Commission II*, p. 260.
111. *Report of Commission II*, pp. 260-1.

striven to attain to independence of thought and interpretation, it cannot be surprising that those who have received their knowledge of Christianity through the English language and from the vigorous, dogmatic teaching of the European races, should be for a long time in bondage to European statements of Christian doctrine and forms of Christian organisation.[112]

The report thus implied that the underlying reason that missionaries were so dominant was that they came from the 'vigorous' and 'progressive' European races, full of 'bustling activity'. Conversely, oriental (and especially Indian) Christians possessed a more contemplative and mystical spirituality which was apt to be dismissed by westerners as 'inert and idle'.[113] The impression had thus been given that 'the masterful leadership of the European nature is an effectual barrier to any free expression of opinions which may not be in complete harmony with the missionary teaching.'[114] The Commission was in no doubt that the stultifying tradition of foreign missionary dominance must be eroded and that a more sympathetic appreciation of the distinctive features of eastern spirituality was required, but the resort to inherent racial characteristics in analysis of the problem implied a protracted time scale. Though self-support might be just round the corner, it would be 'a long time' before Asian Christians — let alone African ones, who scarcely receive a mention in these sections of the report — would be emancipated from western forms of theology and ecclesiology.

The report passed with astonishing rapidity over the practical reality that, far more than any supposed set of racial characteristics, stood in the way of the growth of non-western theology. Chapter VII emphasised momentarily that 'a very large proportion of the converts in every field are illiterate', yet proceeded immediately thereafter to expound what forms of apologetic and devotional literature were most needed on the mission field, as if such provision in itself could provide the answer to the educational needs of the emerging national churches.[115] Even in China, where the literary class possessed such status, some 90 per cent of the population were estimated to be illiterate. Yet nowhere did the report make any mention of the need to develop programmes in popular literacy as an appropriate priority in mission education. There could hardly be a clearer indication of the assumptions that gov-

112. *Report of Commission II*, p. 262.

113. *Ibid.*, p. 210. The report here is dependent on Herbert Anderson's reply in UTS, MRL 12, WMC papers, series 1, box 11, folder 6, item 214, p. 24.

114. *Report of Commission II*, p. 260.

115. *Ibid.*, pp. 238-9.

erned the thinking of Commission II, as of the other Commissions: the spiritual nurture of the 'younger' churches was to be led by the literate few, not built upon the foundations of a basic education for the many.

So far as India was concerned, the report's pessimistic assessment of the underdeveloped state of indigenous Christian theology was an accurate enough reflection of the views of foreign missionaries as represented by the questionnaire replies. Even those who had wide responsibility for their mission's work in the subcontinent could offer no reassurance. Herbert Anderson, the BMS India secretary (and from 1914 the first secretary of the National Missionary Council of India), was not only sceptical about the capacity of the Baptist community in Bengal to produce 'indigenous and original literature', but was unable to identify 'any indications of any original or formulative theological work' in the Baptist communities throughout north India.[116] In south India, however, where the Christian community was larger, better educated, and exposed to a wider range of intellectual influences, there were at least some voices suggesting that the current barrenness of Indian theology was unlikely to last for long. I. H. Hacker of the LMS, though of the opinion that 'the time had not yet come for much formative native thought in theology', assured the Commission that he and his colleagues in the Travancore mission were praying for the emergence of Indian Christians who would 'interpret Christ from their own standpoints in sweet, winning and noble forms', and expressed the hope that the time for this was hastening.[117] The Revd N. Devasahayam, writing from Madras, where 'Hixley [*sic*] and Heckel [*sic*] and Schopenhauer are read by intelligent people', predicted rather more bluntly that

> A vigorous form of 'Theology', quite of native originality is likely to arise. Many thinking natives are of opinion that Theology ought to be reconstructed on its simple scriptural basis. India need not borrow the numerous controversies which shaped European theology.[118]

Whereas in relation to self-support the Commission drew a clear distinction between the progress made by the East Asian churches and the tardiness of the churches in India, in the realm of theology the contrast was much less stark. The theological development of Chinese Christianity was being ham-

---

116. UTS, MRL 12, WMC papers, series 1, box 11, folder 6, item 214, p. 29.

117. UTS, MRL 12, WMC papers, series 1, box 11, folder 8, item 270, p. 45.

118. UTS, MRL 12, WMC papers, series 1, box 11, folder 7, item 250, pp. 15-16, cited in part in *Report of Commission II*, p. 197.

pered by the Confucian habit of mind, which led to 'unquestioning acceptance of the thoughts and precepts of the mighty past.' Even in Japan, where
the church showed greater signs of intellectual activity, this did not yet extend
to the strictly theological sphere: the Commission claimed that it could not
discover 'much sign yet of any independent treatment of the great themes of
the Christian revelation.'[119]

The missionary evidence submitted to the Commission in fact suggested
the existence of rather more independence of mind in the Chinese and Japanese churches than the report's dismissive generalisations implied. The Revd
S. George Tope, a Wesleyan missionary in Canton, submitted a supplementary
letter alongside his questionnaire replies that was unusually forthright in its
warnings of the extent to which the nationalistic maxim of 'China for the Chinese' had penetrated the Chinese Christian community, so that missions 'were
now in actual danger of alienation from Chinese Christians themselves'. Tope
believed it was therefore imperative that independent Chinese churches be set
up with a legal status quite autonomous of the foreign missions, and that priority be given in the formulation of evangelistic strategy to the viewpoint of
Chinese Christians, who included 'many persons of intelligence and sound
judgment'. The churches of Europe and America should be prepared to give
their missions 'full authority' to modify western forms of church organization,
and even to combine in promoting 'a great united Church for China'.[120]

Tope did not point to any evidence of a distinctively Chinese theology in
the sense that the Commission was impatient to see, and his letter was not referred to in the report. Yet the inescapably political variety of independence
of thought which he described was both more challenging in the present and
closer to the forms of Chinese Christianity that began to emerge during the
1920s than was the brand of highly civilised, literary, indigenized Chinese theology that the Commission envisaged. The uncomfortable reality was that the
theological and political agendas could not be neatly separated in the way
that the Commission appeared to believe. One of the few respondents who
gave a resounding 'yes' to the question about 'original and formative native
thought in Theology', was R. E. McAlpine, an American Presbyterian missionary in Japan:

> Yes indeed, there are emphatic indications of native thought in Theol-
> ogy. One might also be tempted to say there is too much such evidence,

119. *Report of Commission II*, p. 259.
120. UTS, MRL 12, WMC papers, series 1, box 13, folder 4, appendix to item 184, pp. 1-7,
11.

but for the comforting indications now visible that the effervescence of first energy is toning down and turning into right channels. For a full decade there has been a persistent tendency to reject 'the worn out theology of the West, throw off the domination of foreign thought and elaborate a Japanese theology which will be in harmony with our institutions and include all the truth in our previous religions.' Naturally then, the Deity of our Lord, His atoning work and all kindred 'effete doctrines' were whistled down the wind and the newest of New Theology was eagerly sought after; and any missionary or pastor who refused to fall in with the movement was sneered at, the one as a 'moss back' and the other as an 'hireling of foreigners'.

McAlpine referred to the Congregational pastor and theologian, Ebina Danjo (1856-1937), as the leading representative of this form of new theology. He was confident that the movement had reached its peak and was beginning to ebb.[121] Danjo's undogmatic and syncretistic form of Japanese Christian theology (which was in fact highly indebted to western liberal theology as well as Confucian concepts) had indeed been most influential during the 1890s, but there was more of an indigenous character to Japanese Protestantism in 1910 than the report conceded. The marked congruence that existed between the pronounced socio-ethical emphases of the American missions and the enthusiasm of Christian former samurai such as Honda Yoitsu and Ibuka Kajinosuke for Christianity as a moral force for regenerating the Japanese nation made it more difficult for the Commission to perceive the reality that the dominant cultural motifs of Japanese Protestantism were not simply an aping of missionary teaching.[122]

What should be underlined in conclusion is the general absence in the questionnaire replies of foreign missionary dissent from the unspoken premise of the Commission's question, namely the assumption that 'original and formative native thought in Theology' was in principle desirable. The Commission had unambiguously endorsed the goal of a three-self church, but had to concede that in India at least, the goal was some way from realisation. Similarly, the Commission (to an extent that may now seem surprising) was strongly committed to the achievement of what current missiological theory sometimes terms the 'fourth self', namely, 'self-theologising.' However, it was compelled to report that this objective still looked frustratingly distant, in-

---

121. UTS, MRL 12, WMC papers, series 1, box 12, folder 6, item 27, pp. 20-1. On Danjo see Drummond, *History of Christianity in Japan*, p. 218.

122. See Drummond, *History of Christianity in Japan*, p. 190.

deed considerably more distant than the goal of autonomy in finance and governance, about whose achievement the report, as has been seen, was so generally, if unrealistically, sanguine. It is hard to escape the conclusion that, in this respect also, the report was faithfully reflecting Gibson's own experience in Swatow. It is also clear that, if the report seriously underestimated the obstacles that still lay in the path of the achievement of self-support for most younger churches, it equally overestimated the permanence of the obstacles which in 1910 appeared to prevent those churches from speaking with their own distinctive voice, in tones that would soon prove to be political as well as theological.

1. Randall Davidson, Archbishop of Canterbury

G. K. A. Bell, *Randall Davidson: Archbishop of Canterbury* (OUP 1938),
photograph by A. A. Campbell-Swinton, 1916, courtesy of Oxford University Press

2. John R. Mott, chairman of the World Missionary Conference

3. J. H. Oldham, secretary of the World Missionary Conference

A. W. Schreiber (ed.) *Die Edinburger Welt-Missions-Konferenz* (Verlag der Basler Missionsbuchhandlung 1910), courtesy of Mission-21, Basel

4. The conference in session in the Assembly Hall of the United Free Church of Scotland

CMS archives, University of Birmingham Special Collections, courtesy of the Church Mission Society

5. The S.S. *Kroonland* of the Red Star Line, which transported many of the American delegates across the Atlantic
Courtesy of www.norway.heritage.com

6. Dr K. C. Chatterjee of the Presbyterian Church in India, wearing the robes of his honorary D.D. bestowed by the University of Edinburgh on the eve of the conference

J. C. R. Ewing, *A Prince of the Church In India* (Fleming H. Revell 1918), courtesy of Princeton Theological Seminary Libraries

7. Lord Balfour of Burleigh,
president of the conference

A. W. Schreiber (ed.) *Die Edinburger
Welt-Missions-Konferenz* (Verlag der Basler
Missionsbuchhandlung 1910),
courtesy of Mission-21, Basel

8. J. H. Ritson, Bible Society secretary,
clerk to the conference, and member of
Commission VIII

John H. Ritson, *The World is Our Parish*
(Hodder & Stoughton, 1939),
photograph by Lafayette Ltd.

9. John Rangiah, delegate of the
American Baptist Foreign
Missionary Society

Baptist Association of South Africa,
courtesy of the Revd Rodney Tagwan

10. Cheng Jingyi, delegate of the London Missionary Society

U. W. Schreiber (ed.) *Die Edinburger Welt-Missions-Konferenz* (Verlag der Basler Missionsbuchhandlung 1910), courtesy of Mission-21, Basel

11. Bishop Honda Yoitsu, invited by the American executive committee

Burke Library, Union Theological Seminary, New York

12. The Honourable Yun Ch'iho, invited by the American executive committee

Burke Library, Union Theological Seminary, New York

13. Tarada Hasuku, Thang Khan Sangma, V. S. Azariah, and Tong Ching-en, at the entrance to the United Free Church Women's Missionary Institute (St Colm's)

Archives, St Colm's International Centre, 23 Inverleith Terrace, Edinburgh

14. Sir Michael Sadler, member of Commission III

Photograph by George Charles Beresford, 1914. National Portrait Gallery, London

15. Professor Ernest DeWitt Burton, member of Commission III

University of Chicago Library, Special Collections Research Center

**16. Professor David S. Cairns,
chairman of Commission IV**

D. M. Baillie (ed.), *David Cairns:
an autobiography* (SCM Press 1950)

**17. W. H. Temple Gairdner,
respondent to Commission IV**

Constance E. Padwick,
Temple Gairdner of Cairo
(SPCK 1929)

The Aims of Mission Education:
Cultural 'Accommodation' and the Catholicity of Christianity

The Brief, Composition, and
Mode of Operation of Commission III

Commission III of the World Missionary Conference was charged with the task of investigating the work of 'Education in relation to the Christianisation of national life'. The very title of the Commission thus defined the place of education in the missionary enterprise in a broad sense which implied that mission education was integral to the task of creating new Christian identities for nations in the non-western world. The brief given to the Commission by the meeting of the International Committee at Oxford in July 1908 suggested that its attention should not be focused solely on the education of the young of the Christian community nor on the formation and training of its church leadership: rather its horizons were to extend to the permeation of the entire fabric of national life in the mission lands by Christian ideals. Whether such an expansive vision was in fact the most appropriate goal for mission education was, however, a subject of lively debate in Protestant missionary circles, and had been so for some time. Indeed, the over two hundred questionnaire replies received by the Commission reveal just how complex and contested an issue this was, and the report which the Commission produced on the basis of these replies ultimately placed its most pronounced emphasis on a definition of the function of Christian education which was noticeably more church-centric than the title of the Commission implied.

In view of the broad brief given to the Commission by the conference organizers, it may not be wholly coincidental that Commission III was perhaps the most conspicuously Anglican in composition of all the eight Commissions. Of the twenty members of the Commission, no fewer than eleven were members of the Anglican communion, five of whom were Anglican clergy.[1] Of the clerics, only H. G. Grey, education secretary of the CMS, had missionary experience (in north India; in addition to having served for two periods as principal of Wycliffe Hall in Oxford).[2] Three of the Commission's British members — Professor M. E. Sadler of the University of Manchester, Miss Anne Richardson, a Quaker on the staff of Westfield College in Hampstead, and Miss Jane Leeke Latham, principal of St Mary's College, Paddington, from 1903 to 1908 — could be described as professional educators, all people of considerable distinction and expertise in their field but with only limited experience of the non-western world. However, Latham visited India for six months in 1908-9 at the request of Commission V in order to prepare a report on the training of women missionaries, and later in 1910 herself became a missionary with the SPG at Ahmednagar in western India.[3] She appears to have been responsible for preparing at least two sections of the report: the brief section that dealt with the training of women teachers in India, and, more important, the 'General Conclusions' to Chapter VII on 'The relating of Christian truth to indigenous thought and feeling'.[4] The Commission's one

1. Charles Gore (bishop of Birmingham), Rev. A. R. Buckland (secretary of the Religious Tract Society), Rev. Lord William Gascoyne-Cecil, Rev. H. G. Grey, Rev. M. W. Myres. The lay Anglicans were Miss Jane Latham; R. Maconachie, a former member of the Indian Civil Service, and friend and biographer of Rowland Bateman of the CMS Punjab mission; Dr George R. Parkin; Professor M. E. Sadler; the distinguished East Asian diplomat, Sir Ernest Satow; and the American Episcopalian, George Wharton Pepper. There was one representative of Scottish missions, Dr John Morrison, formerly principal of the Church of Scotland College in Calcutta. Rev. William Bolton (1846-1921), of Acton, was a Congregational minister who had taken part in deputations sent by the LMS to China in 1903-4 and India in 1906 to investigate the educational work of the society; see Norman Goodall, *A History of the London Missionary Society 1895-1945* (London: OUP, 1954), pp. 167, 460, 462; *Congregational Year Book*, 1922, p. 100.

2. Grey served as education secretary of the CMS from 1909 to 1910; see Eugene Stock, *The History of the Church Missionary Society*, 4 vols. (London: Church Missionary Society, 1899, 1916), IV, p. 527.

3. On Sadler (1861-1943) see *ODNB* and L. Grier, *Achievement in Education: the work of Michael Ernest Sadler, 1885-1935* (London: Constable, 1952). On Richardson (1859-1942), classics lecturer and later acting principal of Westfield College in Hampstead, see Janet Sondheimer, *Castle Adamant in Hampstead: a history of Westfield College, 1882-1982* (London: Westfield College, 1983), pp. 30, 178-9. Westfield College was founded in part with a view to training women missionaries. On Latham (1867-1938) see *ODNB* and H. P. Thompson, *Into all Lands: the history of the Society for the Propagation of the Gospel in Foreign Parts 1701-1950* (London: SPCK, 1951), pp. 623, 625; see also *Report of Commission V,* pp. 317-18.

4. *Report of Commission III*, pp. 311-12. See UCL, Ernest deWitt Burton papers, box 27,

Canadian member, Dr George R. Parkin, the former headmaster of Upper Canada College in Toronto and self-styled 'wandering Evangelist of Empire', had travelled extensively, but his experience was principally, if not exclusively, in the white dominions and settler colonies.[5]

The great lengths to which J. H. Oldham went during the early months of 1909 to prevent the threatened resignations from the Commission of its chairman, Charles Gore, bishop of Birmingham, and of distinguished Anglican educational experts such as Parkin and Sadler suggests that he attached particular importance to their participation in the Commission.[6] In the bishop's case, no doubt, this was primarily because of Gore's crucial representative significance as the acknowledged leader of the Anglo-Catholic party. Nevertheless, irrespective of party considerations, Oldham seems to have been genuinely anxious to retain the presence on the Commission of those whose perspective on education was shaped by the distinctive Anglican vision of the potential of church schools to impart a Christian character to the values of national life. The provision of Anglican elementary education by means of the National Society was in fact one of only two philanthropic causes during the nineteenth century (the other being church building) whose scale exceeded the dimensions of Anglican giving to the missionary enterprise. Sadler played a key part in the Commission's deliberations, acting as convenor of the sub-committee given responsibility for preparing the section of the report which dealt with Africa, and also drafting chapter X of the report, on Christian literature.[7] Other sections were deputed to various British members of the Commission for drafting.

The American Reception of the British Drafts of the Commission III Report

The broad outline and initial drafts of the Commission III report were agreed at a six-day residential meeting of the English members of the Commission held at Bible House in London in the first week of November 1909.[8] At the

---

folder 8, World Missionary Conference, 1910, minutes of the American section of Commission III, 8-9-10-11 Feb. 1910, p. 15.

5. On Parkin (1846-1922) see *ODNB*.

6. See Chapter 3 above, pp. 55-6.

7. UCL, Ernest deWitt Burton papers, box 27, 'Commission III . . . Africa. Digest of Replies by Professor M. E. Sadler'; and 'Commission III. IX. The Problem of Christian Literature. Digest of Replies by Professor M. E. Sadler'.

8. The duration of the meeting is mentioned in UTS, MRL 12, WMC papers, series 1, box 23, folder 15, A. H. L. Fraser to Silas McBee, 29 Oct. 1909.

meeting the British members of the Commission agreed that questions I, II, III, IV, VI, VII, IX, X, XII(b), (c), and (d), and XIV of the questionnaire (see Appendix to this chapter pp. 202-4) should be dealt with in a series of regional chapters. The remaining questions — V, VIII, XI, XII(a), and XIII — were isolated for individual thematic treatment. This resulted in a structure of the report in which, after an introductory chapter, chapters II to VI focused respectively on India, China, Japan, Africa, and 'Mohammedan Lands in the Near East'; there then followed the four thematic chapters (VII to X) devoted to 'The Relating of Christian Truth to Indigenous Thought and Feeling', 'Industrial Training', 'The Training of Teachers', 'Literature', and finally a chapter of 'Conclusions'. The structure chosen for the report thus highlighted four areas of mission policy which the Commission wished to commend to the conference for particular reflection and action. It also had the virtue of facilitating some focused discussion of the current challenges facing mission educators in India, China, Japan, Africa, and the Middle East. What it tended to conceal, however, was the pattern of regional diversity between the answers supplied by missionaries from different geographical contexts to the first group of questions. This was particularly so in relation to the foundational questions I and II on the purposes and results of mission education, and to question III on the impact on mission education of recent movements of intellectual and national 'awakening'. Moreover, it appears that the first drafts of the Commission report struck the North American side of the Commission as being deficient in certain major respects, particularly in their coverage of Christian higher education in East Asia, a sphere of work which the Americans regarded with some justification as their peculiar territory. Documents surviving in Chicago make it clear that as a result the work of Commission III came perilously close to disaster.

Of the seven North American members of Commission III, six were professors or senior managers of universities or colleges. The vice-chairman of the Commission was a Presbyterian theologian, the Revd Professor Edward Caldwell Moore of Harvard University, who believed that the Christianization of the world would come by a long slow process of mutual religious assimilation.[9] Moore visited Britain for ten days in September 1909 to confer with Oldham and British members of the Commission; he unsuccessfully tried to persuade Oldham that the entire conference would have to be post-

9. Moore (1857-1943) gave the Dale Lectures in Oxford in 1913 on a missionary theme: see Edward Caldwell Moore, *West and East: the expansion of Christendom and the naturalization of Christianity in the Orient in the XIXth century, being the Dale lectures, Oxford, 1913* (London: Duckworth, 1920), pp. 312-23.

poned by one year to allow Commission III sufficient time for the accumula-
tion and scholarly analysis of questionnaire replies and other data.[10] The secretary of the American section was also a university theologian: Professor
Ernest DeWitt Burton, a Baptist professor at the (then primarily Baptist)
University of Chicago, had made a tour of Asian educational institutions in
1909 and would later (in 1921-2) lead a major American commission of inquiry into Christian education in China.[11] The other two North Americans
with educational expertise were Miss Grace Hoadley Dodge (1856-1914), a
wealthy New York philanthropist and a trustee of the Teachers' College at Columbia University; and Professor R. A. Falconer of the University of Toronto.
Only two of the seven American members — William Chamberlain and John
Goucher — had significant overseas missionary experience.[12]

The drafts produced by the London meeting were sent to North America for comment and were exhaustively considered at a series of lengthy
meetings held in the New York home of Grace Dodge from 8 to 11 February
1910.[13] Although some drafts, such as Sadler's on Africa, emerged relatively
unscathed from the American scrutiny, others received a very unfavourable
response. Objection was made to the repeated British use of the terms 'heathen' and 'heathenism'.[14] In particular, the section on Japan, prepared by Sir
Ernest Satow, was regarded as 'inadequate in the last degree'.[15] Satow, concluded Professor Moore, 'has had no time to do the thing as it needs to be

10. YDS, RG45, Mott papers, box 63, folder 1168, Oldham to Mott, 23 Sept. 1909.

11. Ernest DeWitt Burton (1856-1925) was professor of theology at the University of
Chicago. See *Christian Education in China: a study made by an educational commission rep-
resenting the mission boards and societies conducting work in China* (New York: Committee
of Reference and Counsel of the Foreign Missions Conference of North America, 1922);
Peter Tze Ming Ng, *Changing Paradigms of Christian Higher Education in China, 1888-1950*
(Lewiston, Queenston, and Lampeter: Edwin Mellen Press, 2002), pp. 7, 60-1 and *passim*.
The seventh North American member was George Wharton Pepper (1867-1961), a Phila-
delphia lawyer, Episcopalian, and Republican member of the US Senate from 1922 to 1927.
Neither Falconer nor Pepper played any significant role in the business of the American
section of Commission III.

12. The Revd Professor William I. Chamberlain (Rutgers College) had served at Vellore
in South India. The Revd John H. Goucher (1845-1922; Goucher College, Baltimore) had
been a founding member of West China Union University, Chengdu.

13. UCL, Ernest deWitt Burton papers, box 27, folder 8, World Missionary Conference,
1910, minutes of the American section of Commission III, 8-9-10-11 Feb. 1910.

14. UCL, Ernest deWitt Burton papers, box 27, folder 8, World Missionary Conference,
1910, minutes of the American section of Commission III, Education in Relation to the
Christianisation of National Life. 8-9-10-11 Feb. 1910, p. 3.

15. UTS, MRL 12, WMC papers, series 1, box 14, folder 1, copy of Edward C. Moore to
Edward Warren Capen, 12 Feb. 1910.

done'.[16] Oldham had already offered the services of the Commission secretary, the Revd M. W. Myres, chaplain of Magdalen College, Oxford, to recast Satow's manifestly deficient material, but the Americans rejected the offer: 'Mr Myres', wrote Moore, 'has no technical or expert knowledge whatsoever; there is no paragraph in the report concerning which we could so ill afford a failure as in the paragraph on Japan'.[17] Japan was an American rather than a British Protestant field, and the Americans insisted on commissioning their own Japan section, written by Dr Edward Capen of the American Board of Commissioners for Foreign Missions. With minor amendments, this was to form the basis of the report's chapter on Japan, replacing Satow's draft.[18]

The American section of the Commission also submitted radically revised drafts on those parts of the report dealing with India, China, Korea, and 'The Relationship of Christian Truth to Indigenous Thought and Feeling' (a chapter which Bishop Gore had drafted). Gore's draft conclusion to the report was also dismissed as 'wholly inadequate and incapable of correction.'[19] The British had invited the Americans to respond with written comments to their drafts, which would have left the British side of the Commission with entire discretion to deal with American objections as they wished. The New York meeting in February 1910 regarded this manner of proceeding as wholly unacceptable. Some issues of fundamental principle, particularly in the treatment given to East Asia, were at stake on which the Americans felt themselves 'bound to stand'. The minutes of the meeting record that:

> In event [sic] that the British section cannot assent to these, we ask in accordance with Secretary Oldham's own suggestion, that they be placed in an appendix to be attached to each section. In event [sic] that our views cannot be met in this way or in some other way which shall approve itself to our representative, we ask him to withhold our signatures and indicate that we respectfully withdraw from the Commission.[20]

16. UTS, MRL 12, WMC papers, series 1, box 14, folder 1, copy of Edward C. Moore to Edward Warren Capen, 19 Feb. 1910.

17. UTS, MRL 12, WMC papers, series 1, box 14, folder 1, copy of Edward C. Moore to Edward Warren Capen, 12 Feb. 1910.

18. See UTS, MRL 12, WMC papers, series 1, box 14, folder 1, copies of letters in Case Memorial Library, Hartford Seminary Foundation, note on p. 10.

19. UCL, Ernest deWitt Burton papers, box 27, folder 8, World Missionary Conference, 1910, minutes of the American section of Commission III. Education in Relation to the Christianisation of National Life. 8-9-10-11 Feb. 1910, p. 18.

20. Ibid., p. 19.

Moore was adamant that he would not sign the report in anything like the form prepared by the British, and Ernest Burton was dispatched in person to London (a journey paid for by Grace Dodge's munificence) to present the American revised drafts to the British side of the Commission.[21]

Burton attended the meeting of the Commission held in London on 22 April 1910, when the revised text of the report was agreed.[22] Although no minutes of the meeting survive, it is clear that Burton's mission was very largely successful and that the American text of the sections in dispute was generally accepted. He returned to the USA before the conference itself, but Edward Moore was present at Edinburgh as a guest of the American executive committee, along with John Goucher and Grace Dodge. When Moore spoke in the debate on the Commission, he expressed his gratitude for the kindness and courtesy extended to the North American members by the British side of the Commission — which was a coded acknowledgement of just how much had been conceded to the American perspective on Christian education in East Asia; he spoke specifically about Christian education in China and Japan, commending the latter in particular as a model of 'a Christian system from top to bottom' which commanded the respect of the nation.[23] Moore wrote jubilantly from Edinburgh to Burton, informing him that the Commission's report had met with 'a glorious reception', and assuring him that 'our success is really very largely due to you.'[24] For Commission III, scarcely less than Commission I, the boundary between success and failure had proved to be extraordinarily fragile.

An Anglophone Perspective

The Commission III report was the product of a process of negotiation between British and American educationalists and ecclesiastics. There were no continental European members of the Commission. It is also striking that the missionary respondents to the Commission III questionnaire were overwhelmingly Anglophones and the majority were operating in British imperial contexts. The only non-Anglophone missionary respondents comprised: seven Dutchmen and one German (Johannes Warneck) working in the Dutch

---

21. UCL, Ernest deWitt Burton papers, box 27, folder 8, Edward C. Moore to Ernest de Witt Burton, 14 Feb. 1910.

22. *Report of Commission III*, pp. 3-4.

23. *Report of Commission III*, pp. 425-7.

24. UCL, Ernest deWitt Burton papers, box 28, folder 2, Edward C. Moore to Ernest de Witt Burton, 20 June 1910.

East Indies, whose collective evidence was strangely not incorporated in the main report but relegated to a separate appendix; two distinguished representatives of Francophone missions (Jean Bianquis of the Paris Evangelical Society and Henri Junod of the Swiss Mission Romande in Mozambique); two Swedish missionaries (Miss V. Rinman from Chindwara, India, and K. Hallendorf from Natal); and Bishop La Trobe from the Moravian mission headquarters in Herrnhut. The report was honest enough to concede that its evidence was 'almost limited to the missions conducted by English-speaking missionaries'.[25] It also acknowledged that it had been unable (for some unexplained reason) to consider other regions in which educational missionaries were active: three appendices were therefore added, giving brief surveys of Korea, the Dutch East Indies, and missions among 'Indians' in North America.[26] There were in addition nine indigenous respondents. India was represented by J. R. Banerjea from the college branch of the YMCA and the Scottish mission in Calcutta, S. V. Karmakar from the American Board's Marathi mission in Bombay,[27] A. Perianayakam from the CMS Tirunelveli mission, and S. K. Rudra, principal of St Stephen's College in Delhi. There was just one Chinese respondent, Chung Wan Man from the Southern Baptist mission at Shiuhing in Guangdong province. There were four Japanese correspondents: Kajinosuke Ibuka; Sennosuke Ogata, a Methodist minister from the Aoyama Gakuin College in Tokyo; Miss Umé Tsuda, a leading educator from Tokyo; and Professor S. Uchigasaki of Waseda University, Tokyo. Some of their replies — notably those by Chung Wan Man and Umé Tsuda — were extensively quoted in the report. On the whole, however, the report paid relatively little attention to these nine indigenous voices: four of the nine (Banerjea, Perianayakam, Ogata, and Uchigasaki) were not cited at all in the text.

Given the Anglophone predominance on Commission III, it is not surprising that the questionnaire which the Commission issued made assumptions which were manifestly not applicable to all mission contexts. Most notably, question VI asked 'Do you advocate the use of English (a) as a branch of study, (b) as the medium of instruction, as being helpful to the Christianising influence of education? What limits would you place to the use

25. *Report of Commission III*, p. 5.

26. *Report of Commission III*, pp. 5, 385-400. It is unclear why the Dutch East Indies were treated in this fashion, when there were eight questionnaire respondents from the field. In the cases of Korea and the native American missions, the Commission relied on three eleventh-hour commissioned papers (one on Korea, one on native Americans in Canada, and one on native Americans in America).

27. The typescript of Karmakar's questionnaire response gives his initials as S. V., but in the report they are given as S. K.

of English?' Missionaries working in the Dutch East Indies had to point out in their replies that 'the native population has no notion of the existence of the English language' and did their best to apply the question to assessing what place the Dutch language should occupy in mission education; Johannes Warneck, for example, emphasized that in Sumatra Dutch was never employed as a medium of teaching, in accordance with the universal principle of German missions to base education on local vernaculars.[28] The appendix to the report which dealt with the Dutch East Indies accordingly included a brief section on the use of the Dutch language.[29] Henri Junod from Ricatla in Mozambique, on the other hand, chose to broaden the scope of his answer to Question VI by referring to the practice of the Mission Romande in neighbouring South Africa in using the vernacular as a medium of instruction whilst encouraging the teaching of English as a subject which would 'broaden the mind' of pupils and enhance their prospects in life.[30] Jean Bianquis, writing from the headquarters of the Paris Evangelical Mission, offered some general reflections about the relationship of the vernacular with French in Francophone contexts in Senegal, Madagascar, and New Caledonia.[31]

The remainder of this chapter will concentrate on the foundational topics addressed most directly by questions I, II, III and V: that is, respectively, the purposes, results, political context, and cultural relevance of mission education. In addition to the text of the report itself, use will be made of a sample of the questionnaire responses drawn from different regions. The purposes and results of mission education (questions I and II respectively) will be treated as a single subject, for both questionnaire replies and the report itself migrated frequently from purposes to results and back again: Protestant missions were a highly instrumental activity in which what could be shown to have worked in the past tended to shape definitions of purpose for the future. Each of the three principal statements of rationale for mission education given in the report on the basis of the replies given to questions I and II will be discussed in turn. The chapter will then examine Charles Gore's central argument as chairman of the Commission that Christian education was integral to the missionary task of achieving a true catholicity which combined a shared doctrinal foundation with a great variety of cultural and structural expression. The conclusion to the chapter will assess how far the recommendations made

28. ECG, Commission III replies from N. Adriani, vol. 5, pp. 385-6 and J. Warneck, vol. 5, p. 457.

29. *Report of Commission III*, p. 394.

30. ECG, Commission III replies, vol. 6, pp. 220-1. See *Report of Commission III*, p. 205.

31. ECG, Commission III replies, vol. 6, pp. 50-3. See *Report of Commission III*, p. 208.

by Commission III influenced the course of educational policy in Protestant missions in the years following the Edinburgh conference.

Defining the Purposes of Mission Education

The majority of respondents to the Commission III questionnaire tended to identify three main purposes of mission education, although they varied considerably in the relative importance they attached to each.[32] The first line of response evident in the questionnaire replies was unashamedly to defend missionary involvement in education (and in most cases primary education was meant) as an instrument of direct evangelism, usually of the pupils themselves but sometimes also of their parents and relatives. A second category of response was to emphasize the indispensable role of education in developing and training leaders for the indigenous church; most weight here tended to be given to the role of secondary and higher education, though industrial and agricultural education for rural communities, especially in Africa, was strongly advocated as a strategy designed to achieve the goal of a self-supporting church. A third line of response most closely reflected the full title of the Commission by envisaging Christian schools and colleges as a means of diffusing Christian ideals and influence through society at large, and especially its leaders, even if such diffusion did not result in conversion and adherence to the institutional church. These defences of missionary involvement in education as integral to the evangelistic and church-planting task were not new, but stood in a tradition of apologetic that stretched back through the utterances of educational missionaries such as William Miller of Madras to the Liverpool missionary conference of 1860, if not to Alexander Duff himself.[33] These three aims of mission education were denominated in the conclusions to the report as, respectively, the *evangelistic,* the *edificatory,* and the *leavening.*[34]

The report also listed a fourth motive of missionary education, which it described as 'the philanthropic desire to promote the general welfare of the

32. For a summary of the report's discussion of these three purposes see J. C. Ingleby, *Missionaries, Education and India: issues in Protestant missionary education in the long nineteenth century* (Delhi: ISPCK, 2000), pp. 341-4.

33. *Conference on Missions Held in 1860 at Liverpool* (London: James Nisbet, 1860), pp. 111-27, 150-1; see also [A. D. Lindsay (chairman)], *Report of the Commission on Christian Higher Education in India: an enquiry into the place of the Christian College in modern India* (London: OUP, 1931), pp. 22-23; and Jessie G. Lutz, *China and the Christian Colleges 1850-1950* (Ithaca and London: Cornell University Press, 1971), p. 17.

34. *Report of Commission III,* p. 369.

people'. Here the Commission was taking note of the emphatically liberal views of some of its American members, especially Professor Ernest Burton, who believed that there were certain contexts, both at home and overseas, such as China, where the 'wisest thing that the Christian church can do is neither to seek converts nor to propagate by voice or pen the ideas for which the church stands', but simply 'to extend the hand of relief to help those who are in distress'. Burton's response to the invitation from Professor Edward Moore to join Commission III stated his belief, not simply that in India, China, and Japan 'the time for the treatment of education as a mere adjunct to evangelization is past', but more fundamentally that at least in China any direct pursuit of the goal of widespread conversion to Christianity was no longer appropriate.[35] Such a position was rare in Protestant missionary circles in 1910, though not so eccentric as to disqualify him from appointment as the secretary of the American section of the Commission. However, only occasionally do the questionnaire responses from working missionaries defend mission education as a disinterested act of philanthropic service. The report defended the philanthropic motive of Christian education as a supplementary motive, and one that stood in conformity to the spirit of Jesus, who responded to pressing human need. This emphasis was said to express the mind of the majority of the Commission, but the report noted that a minority of the members of the Commission were 'unwilling to include among the objects of missionary education the general philanthropic aim', fearing that such an inclusion would weaken 'the definite Christian motive' of missionary involvement in education.[36] Earlier the report itself had in fact declared that 'We of this Commission are concerned with education considered only as a means, direct or indirect', towards the end of making Christian disciples.'[37] The notion that to extend to people the benefits of education purely for its own sake, as a means of enriching the quality of human life, might itself form a legitimate part of Christian mission had not yet established itself as a missiological orthodoxy. What is most striking to the present-day reader is the regularity with which arguments for education as a means of proselytism were combined with those that identified education as the key to the problem of establishing churches which would be autonomous of European control: the modern tendency to reject the former as unethical but to affirm the latter as sound policy found very few echoes in 1910.

35. UTS, MRL 12, WMC papers, series 1, box 14, folder 2, Ernest de Witt Burton to Edward C. Moore, 14 Sept. 1909, pp. 5, 7.
36. *Report of Commission III*, pp. 370-1.
37. *Report of Commission III*, p. 16.

Education as a Form of Evangelism

Those respondents who saw education as a directly evangelistic instrument tended to be working in Africa or in certain types of rural context in South Asia (in China and Japan, on the other hand, where advanced national systems of government education existed, few missions attempted to compete at elementary level). Perhaps the most telling evidence of the evangelistic potential of mission education was supplied by H. W. Weatherhead, a CMS missionary of broad theological sympathies who was headmaster of the prestigious King's School at Budo in Buganda, in a context where to be a 'reader' was virtually synonymous with being a professed Christian.[38] Primary education, declared Weatherhead in a passage which the report partially cited,

> has been the backbone of mission work in Uganda. Everything of the Faith is learnt through learning to read, unless the candidate is too old. The motives for coming to learn are doubtless always mixed, and often not the best, but many a man as he stumbles through the reading 'spells his way to conviction'.[39]

Testimony from elsewhere in Africa was virtually identical, even though few if any locations could match Buganda's record of apparently successful Christianisation: elementary schools staffed by teacher-catechists had proven the most effective means of growing the Christian community.[40] That fact in itself seemed to afford clinching evidence that missions should continue to invest in elementary education as a directly evangelistic strategy. From the Livingstonia Mission in Malawi Robert Laws reported that primary education had been responsible for bringing in perhaps half of the church membership and had raised living and ethical standards both among Christians and more generally.[41] Missionaries in Africa saw education as intrinsic to the wider 'civilizing' task of 'weaning' the people from their 'ignorance' and 'bar-

---

38. For the accusations of unsound theological views made against Weatherhead in 1911-12 see Gordon Hewitt, *The Problems of Success: a history of the Church Missionary Society 1910-1942*, 2 vols. (London: SCM Press, 1971), I, pp. 222-4.

39. ECG, Commission III replies, vol. 6, p. 353; see *Report of Commission III*, p. 188.

40. For a discussion of the Commission III report's treatment of Africa see Ogbu Kalu, 'To hang a ladder in the air: talking about African education in Edinburgh in 1910', in Chima J. Korieh and Raphael Chijoke Njoku (eds.), *Missions, States and European Expansion in Africa* (New York and London: Routledge, 2007), pp. 101-26.

41. ECG, Commission III replies, vol. 6, pp. 246, 248; cited in *Report of Commission III*, pp. 185-6.

barism'; Jean Bianquis, reflecting on the Paris Mission's experience in Basutoland and Barotseland, affirmed that schooling 'causes sorcerers to lose the credit they have enjoyed among the heathen, and opens up the way for hygiene and rational education'.[42] Africans who encountered the missionary message rarely made any separation between what missionaries would have termed the conversion of the spirit and an option to pursue western learning. Among the Thonga of southern Mozambique, as among the Baganda, a decision to become a Christian was signalled by a declaration 'I want to learn' *(dondja)*. Missionaries did not necessarily approve of what from an Enlightenment perspective appeared to be a dangerous confusion of spiritual and intellectual categories, in which mere knowledge was regarded as tantamount to belief, but did little to resist a trend that yielded such apparently encouraging results. 'Though in itself wrong', commented Henri Junod, 'the impression of the heathen must be respected, and it is our duty, we, who are above all missionaries of the Cross, to provide also for their education. The school all over the country goes hand in hand with the preaching of the Gospel.'[43] Or, as Janet Beck, a Church of Scotland missionary from Blantyre, put it, one of the chief purposes of elementary education was 'to fill their minds with the true knowledge of God and His Will towards men, that the truth may drive out the belief in native customs and superstitions by what is living and real'.[44] Knowledge was the missionary's chief weapon against 'heathen superstition'. The report universalized these conclusions with reference to the whole African continent: 'That education is an indispensable factor in the spread of Christianity is a point in regard to which the answers received from South, Central, West, and East Africa are in complete agreement.'[45]

Similar verdicts on the efficacy of village primary schools were supplied from some Asian respondents. A. G. Fraser reported from Ceylon that 'by far the majority' of the converts in the CMS mission and over 60 per cent of those in the Methodist mission were the result of village schools.[46] Dr J. E. Cummings, an American Baptist missionary among the Karen people in Burma, was in no doubt that primary schools in which the teacher was also the local preacher and conductor of Sunday services were responsible for most Karen conversions to Christianity.[47] A parallel report issued from the SPG mission in Trichonopoly in south India, where small mission schools

---

42. ECG, Commission III replies, vol. 6, p. 43; cited in *Report of Commission III*, p. 184.
43. ECG, Commission III replies, vol. 6, pp. 213-14; see *Report of Commission III*, p. 173.
44. ECG, Commission III replies, vol. 6, p. 31.
45. *Report of Commission III*, p. 172.
46. ECG, Commission III replies, vol. 1, pp. 165-6; see *Report of Commission III*, p. 24.
47. ECG, Commission III replies, vol. 1, p. 72; see *Report of Commission III*, p. 24.

had been the means of converting many Hindu children and in some cases even of entire villages.[48] Perhaps more surprising was the fact that the principal of the China Inland Mission Bible Training Institute at Hangzhou in Zhejiang province, W. J. Doherty, was no less enthusiastic about primary schools as 'our only means of reaching certain classes of the community'.[49] Theological standpoint apparently made little difference to the generally favourable assessment of the evangelistic potential of Christian elementary education. The report also cited statistics supplied in 1909 at the celebration of fiftieth anniversary of Protestant missions in Japan to the effect that of the 6,000 students in the schools affiliated to the prestigious Dōshisha institution in Kyōto, 2,000 had been baptised.[50]

Schools were not, however, an invariably effective means of evangelisation. If they had been, many of the deliberations of the Commission and indeed of the conference as a whole would have been simply unnecessary. Even some Africa respondents conceded that the enormous missionary investment in education had not always paid the expected dividends. W. T. Balmer, a Methodist from Sierra Leone, observed that a missionary who had served for any length of time on the west coast of Africa 'has to think twice before he remembers the distinction between the educational missionary and the purely preaching missionary', yet admitted that in retrospect the results of such a conflation of roles were disappointing: mission-educated West Africans had acquired a form of verbal knowledge by rote learning, but it had failed to produce a transformation of moral ideals and practice. Balmer regretted that the educated West African community had yet to 'evolve any original thinker, or [show] any signs of permanent constructive ability'.[51] The report deployed such essentialised criticisms of 'African character' as those made by Balmer to conclude that 'The difficulties of African native education are great, and in no sense would it appear to be a waste to send the best educators to these uncivilised tribes'[52] — which was clearly a plea to mission boards to reconsider their general if not formally defined policy of sending their best university graduates to educational institutions in India or China, leaving Africa to receive missionaries who possessed zeal but limited intellectual ability. Ogbu Kalu, who delivers a generally severe

48. ECG, Commission III replies, vol. 2, p. 188 (J. A. Sharrock).

49. ECG, Commission III replies, vol. 3, p. 226.

50. *Report of Commission III*, p. 133. In 1912 the Doshisha gained recognition as the first Christian university in Japan.

51. ECG, Commission III replies, vol. 6, pp. 2, 4-7; cited in *Report of Commission III*, pp. 190-2. The printed report (p. 192) has 'or to show any signs of pre-eminent constructive ability' rather than the typed response's 'or any signs of permanent constructive ability'.

52. *Report of Commission III*, pp. 316-17.

verdict on the Commission III report for its viewing of Africans through distorting European lenses, is nevertheless impressed by the World Missionary Conference's 'astonishing level of self-criticism' exemplified by the report.[53]

The Achilles heel of reliance on education as an evangelistic strategy was so often the difficulty of finding teachers who combined pedagogical competence with Christian conviction. Where, as in much of sub-Saharan Africa, the village evangelist or catechist was also the school-teacher, primary schools generally reaped a harvest of converts, even if their standards of education and Christian understanding were pitifully low: 'the great drawback in education, has been, and now is', wrote Janet Beck from the Blantyre mission, 'the lack of thoroughly trained teachers'.[54] But where, as in most locations in India, the churches were simply not producing sufficient indigenous Christian workers of the right calibre to staff such a system, the failure of schools to deliver on their Christian objectives was of a more absolute kind. Probably the most damning of the questionnaire replies received on this subject (and one which significantly received no mention whatsoever in the report) came from A. Perianayakam, a schoolmaster in the CMS Tirunelveli mission. Perianayakam employed language about his fellow-countrymen's lack of moral fibre which if it had been uttered by a European missionary would now be castigated as racist:

> Our schools have produced clever men, but alas! have completely failed in producing clever men of character. This is the one thing needful, but that is the one thing absent. I cannot say conscientiously that more than 10% of the vast army of mission workers possess any character. Character is not a thing they care for, and we need not feel surprised if this be rare. The ever expanding work in mission fields requires new hands, and in a hurry no selection is made. A single pastor or teacher in whom missionary enthusiasm burns can do more work than half-a-dozen unworthy men. The central African savage has been well known to tell the bare truth. The European monks are supposed not to have been licentious even during their worst days. I wish I could say this of more than 25% of my countrymen. The modern missionary is partly responsible for this state of things — in being satisfied with a low ideal and in too many cases by being drawn by the reaction of surroundings down to a low level.[55]

53. Kalu, 'To hang a ladder in the air', p. 109.
54. ECG, Commission III replies, vol. 6, p. 36; cited in *Report of Commission III*, p. 316.
55. ECG, Commission III replies, vol. 2, p. 99.

Although the report noted at the outset of its section on 'The Training of Teachers' that the problem of finding Christian teachers of competence and character was a continual obstacle to the goal of Christianising national life,[56] the section which followed treated the problem almost entirely as one of adopting the right methods for training teachers, rather than as a question of what strategies needed to be adopted in the indigenous churches if candidates appropriate for training for any form of leadership were to be found. Hence little attempt was made to relate the discussion of teacher training in India to the underlying problems of the social constituency, impoverishment, and dependent condition of most Indian churches. The report commented that in India 'the greatest obstacle everywhere to the advance of true education is the lack of enough competent teachers', but offered few suggestions as to how such persons were to be found, other than noting the problem that rates of pay for village teachers of only 8 to 10 rupees a month narrowed the field to those who were willing to live at this level.[57] In this respect in particular, the Commission's lack of experience of the realities of Asian or African contexts proved a serious hindrance. No amount of professional academic expertise in teacher training in a British or North American context could compensate for this weakness in the Commission's membership and hence in its perception.

Education as a Strategy for a Three-Self Church

A second defence of mission education offered by the questionnaire respondents, often advanced in parallel to the evangelistic arguments considered in the previous section, though sometimes as a preferred alternative to them, was to present education as an indispensable means to the end of establishing churches that would be self-governing, self-supporting, and self-propagating. Such apologias were most frequently put forward with reference to the role of higher education. Some of the most powerful of these were to be found in the replies from missionaries in China. In a context where most elementary education was in the hands of the state and where government educational institutions now required their teachers and students to participate in regular acts of corporate veneration of Confucius, the foundation of independent mission colleges at secondary or tertiary level became the principal focus of Christian educational strategy: the aggregate number of students in all Protestant colleges in China grew from only 164 in 1900 to 898 in 1910; by 1925

56. *Report of Commission III*, p. 303.
57. *Ibid.*, pp. 309-10.

the total would be 3,500.[58] The decision of the imperial government in September 1905 to abolish the traditional examination system and introduce a western pattern of public education stimulated a considerable expansion in mission educational institutions,[59] but some missionaries believed that the reforms had eroded the distinctiveness of lower level mission schools, and warned that the controlling hands behind the new system were still Confucianist. In this environment, pronounced Timothy Richard somewhat dismissively, elementary education was 'of little help to the missionary enterprise as a whole.' High-level Christian institutions where learned and virtuous missionary sages could impart Christian wisdom were the only way forward.[60] A supplementary strategy which commanded wide support among China missions by this date was to employ the YMCA, introduced to China in 1895, as a means of propagating Christian influence in government colleges, a policy which circumvented the dilemma of whether or not missionaries should require their staff and pupils to pay possibly idolatrous homage to the tablet of Confucius.[61]

The first national secretary of the Chinese YMCA, Fletcher Brockman, was in no doubt in his reply to question I that 'the primary function of the Missionary College is to furnish an educated ministry. . . . It is the most economical way of evangelising or Christianising the Empire — much more so than sending out new evangelistic missionaries'.[62] Educated church leaders would enable the Chinese church to be both self-governing and self-supporting, hence the heavy expenditure that mission colleges required would in the long term prove a sound investment, supplying high-quality pastors for the churches. This was a claim that within twelve years of 1910 two separate reports would regard with considerable scepticism, for the numbers of college graduates who entered the Christian ministry proved disappointing in comparison with the resources expended.[63] For Brockman and others of the Edinburgh respondents, however, this argument seemed a compelling

---

58. Lutz, *China and the Christian Colleges*, p. 161.

59. *Ibid.*, pp. 97-8.

60. ECG, Commission III replies, vol. 4, pp. 265, 268-9; see *Report of Commission III*, pp. 73, 83-4, and Lutz, *China and the Christian Colleges*, p. 19.

61. ECG, Commission III replies, vol. 4, pp. 290-1 (reply from Dr D. Z. Sheffield). See Shirley S. Garrett, *Social Reformers in Urban China: the Chinese Y.M.C.A., 1895-1926* (Cambridge, Mass.: Harvard University Press, 1970).

62. ECG, Commission III replies, vol. 4, p. 150; see also *Report of Commission III*, p. 68.

63. For the criticisms made by both *The Christian Occupation of China* report (1922) and the *Christian Education in China* report (1922) see Ng, *Changing Paradigms of Christian Higher Education*, pp. 60-1 and Lutz, *China and the Christian Colleges*, pp. 233-5.

one. It gained added force from the recent growth of a more militant Chinese national spirit and the fact that Christians no longer had a monopoly on the dissemination of western learning in China, which placed a further premium on the development of an educated Christian leadership:

> The ignorant Church is condemned to foreign leadership. The dominance of the foreigner in Chinese Christianity is to-day the greatest incubus which the Church has to carry. The Chinese speak ordinarily of 'the Chinese people and the church members'. To their minds the Christians are apart from the people — aliens, traitors. When one considers the strained political conditions which have existed in the Far East during the past few decades, the constant fear which still haunts China, that the country is to be divided up among foreign powers, it is not strange that an organisation which allies itself so closely with the representatives of these foreign powers should be looked upon as a political party. The only cure for this state of things is Chinese leadership. There cannot be leadership without leaders, and the most fruitful source for leaders is the missionary college.[64]

Similar apologetic rationales for Christian higher education in China as a bulwark against the current inroads of materialistic western philosophy were supplied by Dr F. L. Hawks Pott, the president of St John's University, Shanghai,[65] and by the only indigenous Chinese respondent — Chung Wan Man from Shiuhing. 'Those who read the works of Harnack and Darwin', commented Chung, 'hate the Church and despise to have all foreigners expelled from China.' Hence 'preachers who do not read works on history, science and the like will be unable to gain a hearing from scholars in general. Therefore let the Church speedily establish Colleges where men of virtue and ability may be trained.'[66] An autonomous Chinese church, for Chung as for Brockman, meant a church that was not immediately and fatally identified with foreign influence or control. As the Quaker missionary educationalist, Dr Henry T. Hodgkin, put it, 'for the development of a strong self-reliant and safe Christian Church a strong educational policy is a sine qua non.' The great weakness

---

64. ECG, Commission III replies, vol. 4, pp. 157-8; the first two sentences of this passage were cited in *Report of Commission III*, p. 66.

65. ECG, Commission III replies, vol. 4, p. 186. St John's College, Shanghai, was founded by the American Episcopal Mission in 1879, and acquired university status in 1905. See Ng, *Changing Paradigms of Christian Higher Education*, p. 48.

66. ECG, Commission III replies, vol. 3, pp. 176-7; see also his remarks cited in *Report of Commission III*, pp. 355-6.

of many Chinese adherents to the churches was 'a wheedling fawning attitude': only those who had received a mission education demonstrated a proper self-reliance and could now be trusted to take the lead.[67]

Arguments for education as a necessary means towards the end of an autonomous and genuinely indigenous church were not, however, confined to the China respondents. The India section of the report observed 'a significant growth of opinion towards giving the place of first importance to the training of Christians, whether young converts or children of Christian parents, with a special emphasis on the importance of providing the Indian Church with teachers and leaders'. The report cited various respondents — among them G. Hibbert Ware of the SPG Dornakal mission and A. G. Fraser, principal of Trinity College, Kandy — who were unambiguous in their verdict that the main focus of mission education should be on the Christian community rather than on non-Christians.[68] They were not, however, agreed on whether elementary or more advanced education should receive the greater emphasis. Hibbert Ware saw the priority as 'primary education for every Christian child',[69] whereas Fraser, despite his recognition of the evangelistic fruits of elementary education in Ceylon, was in no doubt that the production of church leaders, chiefly through higher education, was 'by far the most important purpose in educational work, and the one which justifies its greater cost.'[70]

Questions of cost in relation to the demonstrable returns of mission educational institutions in India had become an urgent preoccupation for many mission agencies since the late 1880s, notably in Scotland but also more generally. No longer was the famous Alexander Duff argument that Anglophone Christian education was a slow-burning mine laid under the foundations of Hinduism unchallenged.[71] Strategies that prioritized village evangelistic work and low-level vernacular schools were increasingly favoured.[72] Some of the India respondents to Commission III bore the bruises of encounters with mission superiors who had begun to lose faith in the efficacy of large educa-

67. ECG, Commission III replies, vol. 3, pp. 388, 392. Hodgkin served at West China Union University at Chengdu from 1905 to January 1910 and then returned to England to become the secretary of the Friends' Foreign Missionary Association. See H. G. Wood, *Henry T. Hodgkin: a memoir* (London: SCM Press, 1937).

68. *Report of Commission III*, pp. 17-18.

69. ECG, Commission III replies, vol. 1, p. 224.

70. ECG, Commission III replies, vol. 1, p. 164.

71. For Duff's analogy see George Smith, *The Life of Alexander Duff, D.D., LL.D.*, 2 vols. (London: Hodder & Stoughton, 1879), I, pp. 108-9.

72. See Andrew Porter, 'Scottish missions and education in nineteenth-century India: the changing face of "trusteeship"', *Journal of Imperial and Commonwealth History* 16:3 (May 1988), pp. 35-57.

tional institutions. One such was the Revd John A. Sharrock, formerly principal, first of Caldwell College at Tuticorin and then of Bishop Heber College at Trichinopoly and superintending missionary of the SPG Trichinopoly district. Acutely conscious of the low levels of literacy and social status of the Christian population of Madras Presidency, Sharrock argued that Christian colleges offered the only hope of raising educational standards in the Christian community to a level sufficient to supply the teachers and pastors which the churches needed and also challenge the dominant position of the Brahmans in the public life of the Presidency (he noted that five-sixths of the graduates of the University of Madras were Brahmans). Caldwell College had educated every Christian professor in the Trichinopoly college, and every Church of England high school headmaster, except one, in the Madras diocese. During his fourteen years as principal, Sharrock had endeavoured to maintain the strongly Christian character of Caldwell College, but the result was a small student enrolment, which had led the SPG committee in Madras, 'egged on by some adverse critics', to close the college on economic grounds. This experience led him to reflect in his questionnaire response on the fundamental dilemma of Christian colleges in India: for a college to succeed in its essential purpose and pay its way, it had to attract a considerable number of Brahman students, a task which was well-nigh impossible if the staff were known to be all Christians.[73]

Hence in India, as in China, the argument that Christian colleges were essential to the staffing of an autonomous church, though impressively sound in theory, often proved fragile in practice. The Commission seems to have taken no notice of Sharrock's perceptive analysis of the inherent problems of the Christian college in India: his reply is not mentioned in the report. Indeed in the conference debate at Edinburgh on 17 June he complained that the report had 'ignored so many of the problems with which we have to deal in our great colleges'. Any attempt to justify Christian colleges as the purveyor of 'a Christian atmosphere' in Indian society failed in Sharrock's mind to take account of the basic incompatibility between such ideals and stark economic logic.[74]

Education as the Diffusion of Christian Influence

Question II of the Commission's questionnaire defined the desired results of mission education as two-fold: first, the raising up of 'men and women who

---

73. ECG, Commission III replies, vol. 2, pp. 186-91.
74. *Report of Commission III*, pp. 417-18.

are at once Christian in conviction and indigenous in thought, feeling, and outlook upon life'; and, second, the 'diffusing, through the direct and indirect influences of the schools, a higher ideal of life among the non-Christian community'. There was thus a close relationship in the mind of the Commission between the twin goals of raising up Christian leaders who were not exotic to their own cultures and the diffusion of Christian moral principles throughout society. However, the precise relationship between the two varied greatly, according to the context which the Commission had in mind. When commenting on Africa, the report placed predictably scant emphasis on the desirability of developing Christian leaders rooted in indigenous culture, and much greater stress on the function of education in diffusing Christian moral principles that would subvert the structures of 'heathenism'. This was particularly the case in relation to the need to free uneducated African women from their supposed 'ignorance' and 'degradation'; girls' education ought therefore to be designed to fit young women for the twin goals of 'marriage and motherhood' and to inculcate skills in domestic science and craftwork.[75] Question V, on the other hand, invited respondents to expand on the first of the two goals by considering to what extent, and with what degree of success, efforts had been made 'to relate the subject-matter and methods of Christian education to the thought, traditions, and literature of the indigenous population'. This version of diffusion was an ideal which appealed to theologically progressive missionaries working in higher educational institutions in India, Japan, or China. For example, George Howells, principal of Serampore College, thought that the history of Serampore College since its foundation in 1818 as a Christian university for India provided 'the most conspicuous example' in the history of Indian missions of what Question V had in mind.[76] Missionaries in Africa, by contrast, could see little relevance in this question: 'I do not quite understand', confessed H. W. Weatherhead, 'how far the question applies to Uganda. There is no indigenous literature.'[77] W. T. Balmer from Sierra Leone gave a similar verdict: 'Work of this kind on the West Coast has been very meagre, so much so indeed as practically to amount to nothing. The attitude seems to have been that the degradation of heathenism is so great that the only way to cure it is to leave it out of account, to ignore it.' Although Balmer conceded that 'even heathen do not live by bread alone', he felt that

75. *Ibid.*, pp. 210-11. On this theme see Deborah Gaitskell, 'Power in prayer and service: women's Christian organizations', in Richard Elphick and Rodney Davenport (eds.), *Christianity in South Africa: a political, social and cultural history* (Oxford and Cape Town: James Currey and David Philip, 1997), p. 255.

76. ECG, Commission III replies, vol. 1, p. 317.

77. ECG, Commission III replies, vol. 6, p. 360.

'the lack of a national history and any account of realized ideals' left missionaries without any point of contact in the life of the people, and hence with no alternative to 'beginning at the bottom', seeking to construct a Christian culture from the foundations.[78]

Other respondents answered Question V in ways that the Commission neither anticipated nor intended. In his answer to Question V, the leading Calcutta Presbyterian educationalist, J. R. Banerjea, judged missions to have had only 'very limited success' in relating the subject-matter and methods of Christian education to the thought of the indigenous population, an answer which, though disappointing to the Commission, was at least capable of an interpretation that conformed to the intention of the question.[79] However, in a subsequently written covering letter to the secretary of Commission III, Banerjea expressed his confidence that 'the subject matter and methods of Christian education cannot but go a long way towards demolishing indigenous thoughts about caste system [sic] and idolatry'. Christian education had exerted a positive influence on Hindu thinking as a whole, eroding 'idolatry' and stimulating monotheistic reform movements such as the Brahmo Samaj. 'Evidences are abundant', he noted, 'of Hindus speaking like Christians about God.'[80] Rather than viewing mission education as an opportunity to synthesize Christian truth with indigenous cultural traditions (as the Commission clearly intended), Banerjea's conclusion revealed that the intellectual legacy of Alexander Duff retained its hold on Presbyterian circles in Calcutta:

> so much are the non-Christian people here trying to buttress up their rotten faiths by assimilating Christian elements, that the observer of religious changes in India is bound to feel that if Christians gird up their loins and address themselves manfully to their work, the citadels of non-Christian faiths will surely one day be blown up and Jesus shall reign supreme in the heart of India, and fulfil His purpose by cleansing and regenerating her by His Spirit.[81]

78. ECG, Commission III replies, vol. 6, pp. 12-13.

79. ECG, Commission III replies, vol. 1, p. 4. Banerjea (or Banerjee) was an elder in the Scottish mission church and vice-principal of the Metropolitan Institution, Calcutta (founded in 1872), known from 1917 as Vidyasagar College. He was also involved in the College branch of the Calcutta YMCA, and by 1918 was a member of the Senate of Serampore College.

80. ECG, Commission III replies, vol. 1, pp. 9-10 (letter from Banerjea to M. W. Myres, 26 Aug. 1909). Banerjea admits in his letter that he cannot remember what answer he had given to Question V.

81. ECG, Commission III replies, vol. 1, p. 10.

Even among some Indian Christian leaders in 1909-10, a diffusionist rationale for mission education could thus still co-exist comfortably with a traditional approach to confrontation with Hindu 'idolatry'. Perhaps not surprisingly, Banerjea's remarks were ignored by the Commission report.

The central conviction of those who took a diffusionist line on mission education was, as Kajinosuke Ibuka memorably put it in his response, 'education is yeast, and Christian education is Christian yeast.' At a time when Japan was espousing many more material aspects of western civilization, it would, reflected Ibuka, 'make a vast difference to the future of Japan if now, in this crisis of its history, large numbers of young men and young women have lodged in their minds the Christian world-view and the foundation truths of historical Christianity.' Although emphatic that Christian education was essential to the creation of a competent Christian ministry, Ibuka was in no doubt that the potential impact of Christian education was not limited to those who would 'accept Christianity as the rule of their lives'; it was equally strategic in relation to those who might 'yield to it only the assent of their minds'.[82] His travels to North America (on three occasions) and Europe (once) had impressed on him how many Japanese diplomats and business-men owed their education to mission schools, and their alumni were also to be found among the editors of the leading secular newspapers in Japan. Ibuka was equally emphatic that the national mood of Japan made it imperative that Christian educational institutions should increasingly be administered by Japanese Christians rather than by missionaries: half of the members of the board of trustees of the Meiji Gakuin institution were, he reported, Japanese, and the proportion would be sure to rise rapidly.[83]

Somewhat similar views to Ibuka's on the timeliness of a strategy to diffuse Christian ideals were expressed by leading China missionaries, with frequent reference to the implications of the abolition of the traditional Chinese examination system in 1905. F. L. Hawks Pott, the American Episcopalian president of St John's University, Shanghai, compared the potential of the new system of education in China to what the Renaissance did in Europe, freeing the mind from the fetters of traditional authority, in this case that of the Chinese classics.[84] The Welsh Baptist missionary, Timothy Richard, placed a still more pronounced emphasis on the crucial significance of the abolition of the examination system. The decision of the Chinese government

---

82. ECG, Commission III replies, vol. 5, pp. 138-9, cited in *Report of Commission III*, p. 127.

83. ECG, Commission III replies, vol. 5, pp. 142-4.

84. ECG, Commission III replies, vol. 4, pp. 185-6.

to pursue western patterns of education, he wrote in his answer to Question III with characteristic hyperbole, 'was a gigantic revolution incomparable in magnitude in the history of the human race and a long stride onwards.' Educational missionaries had not yet realised that what was needed in response was a corresponding revolutionary re-adjustment in their methods: a world civilization (Richard even used the term 'a world Empire') was being born, and it was the responsibility of Christian missions to infuse the emerging new order with principles of divine wisdom.[85] Richard's call for a 'higher type of missionary' who could fulfil the role of a Confucian sage and advise the rulers of the land on what would make for the good of the nation was a distinctive and rather eccentric variant of the Commission's theme of the role of education in the Christianisation of national life.[86] His confidence in the attractive power of Christian morality was wholly characteristic of the liberal end of the missionary movement at the time, but in Richard's quaint prose this vision assumed the form of a peculiar brand of Christian scientism:

> Obsolete creeds and Western religious ceremonies are as repellent to the average Chinaman as the Eastern obsolete creeds and religious ceremonies are repellent to us. But when he learns that we follow Christ to serve God and love our fellow men in deed as well as in word, and that when earnestly practised, this Christian life becomes an electro magnet which inevitably attracts every soul. Many theories of religion act like non-conductors and prevent the flow of the Divine current. But when the flow is uninterrupted the action is irresistible and it is also like gravitation always exerting its binding influence over the hearts of all men.[87]

Advocates of Christian education as diffusion thus included some notable voices from East Asia, but India was the field where such views had for long wielded the greatest influence. The most sustained exposition of the diffusionist view of mission education in the questionnaire replies came from the pen of the venerable Scottish missionary, William Miller, former principal of Madras Christian College. Miller affirmed that 'the great central purpose of mission education is to influence the general life and thought of the community, and thereby to lay a greatly needed foundation for all forms of Christian work.' In India Christian education was the chief means whereby the

85. ECG, Commission III replies, vol. 4, pp. 268-9.

86. ECG, Commission III replies, vol. 4, pp 268-9; see *Report of Commission III*, pp. 83-4.

87. ECG, Commission III replies, vol. 4, p. 270.

Holy Spirit would ultimately effect his appointed work of convicting humanity of sin, righteousness, and judgment.[88] So far as Miller was concerned, educational work was the only option on the Indian table. The all-pervasive influence of 'a hoary civilization' and the power of 'inveterate' caste prejudice meant that 'the real Hindu and Mohammedan population' (a loose phrase which the report rendered still more loosely as 'the real people of India'),[89] who together accounted for some five-sixths of the populace, were 'practically inaccessible to the simple proclamation of Christian truth'. Christian education, however, 'has been found to be a solvent of prejudice and a preparation for higher things of which the value cannot be over-estimated'. Although he conceded that relatively few former pupils of mission institutions had become formal church members, Miller believed that educated south Indians now displayed 'an amount of friendliness in the community towards missionaries, and of loyalty to Christian educational institutions, which would have been absolutely incredible 30 or 40 years ago'. The crucial factor contributing to this significant change in intellectual climate he identified as the personal influence of missionary educators, whose devotion and Christian character were remembered with deep gratitude by their former pupils. Unlike Duff and his generation, Miller placed his confidence for the future regeneration of Hindu society less in the compelling logical authority of Christian reason than in the incarnational magnetism of personalities indwelt by the Spirit of Christ. Miller's conclusion, therefore, was that the current criticism of mission investment in educational strategies in India was wholly misconceived and must be resisted: 'I do not admit that in India, higher Christian education has been in any sense a failure. I am sure that it cannot be regarded as a failure by men who understand the whole position of the Indian castes and classes influenced by higher education, and who at the same time take the lessons of history into account.'[90]

Chapter Two of the report employed Miller's reply as a representative statement of the diffusionist view of the purpose of mission education in India, and endorsed his verdict that it would be irresponsible for missions to withdraw altogether from their educational efforts among the five-sixths majority of the population in favour of educating the young of the Christian community, however gratifying it might be that the gospel was being 'first accepted by the poor and ignoble' from the tribal and depressed caste communities.[91] Nev-

88. See John 16:8-11.
89. *Report of Commission III*, p. 22.
90. ECG, Commission III replies, vol. 2, pp. 38-46.
91. *Report of Commission III*, pp. 20-22.

ertheless, the Commission's deepest sympathies were not with Miller's side of the argument. Having summarized the three main rationales for mission education (evangelistic, edificatory, and leavening) the final chapter of the report pronounced that 'as a matter of general principle', a 'quite distinct priority' should be given to the first two functions, with pride of place being given to the building up of the native church wherever that was in existence. The Commission members believed that 'the primary purpose to be served by the educational work of missionaries is that of training the native Church to bear its own proper witness'. In the appointed task of Christianising national life, the most important goal to pursue was to train those destined to be the spiritual leaders and teachers of the nation — by which was meant the leaders of the indigenous church.[92]

This conclusion ran contrary to William Miller's deepest convictions. He was unable through blindness and fragile health to be present at the conference, but, along with a number of other leading correspondents of the Commission, he was invited to submit comments on the draft report. In response Miller sent a lengthy document roundly criticizing its conclusions. This was widely copied, circulated among delegates, and summarized by Gore from the chair.[93] Miller's statement was a trenchant defence of the diffusionist ideal of education as a Christian leaven in a Hindu society. Miller argued that as the vast bulk of the Indian church was drawn from outside 'the charmed circles of caste' and 'the social organisation of Hinduism', it was even more prone than were mission churches elsewhere to the besetting danger of bearing an exotic and alien character. The depressed classes constituted 'a kind of outside fringe on the entire Indian community' and hence were incapable of forming 'national religion in India'. A church made up of 'races which lie outside the pale of Hinduism' was doomed to be 'an alien Church in India'. Miller commented on the reference in the draft report to the conviction of 'the Anglican minority' (no doubt he had Henry Whitehead particularly in mind) that it should devote its educational energies entirely to the uplifting of the depressed classes. Such a policy, he contended, would be disastrous if adopted by all missions, for it would leave 'the real people of India, i.e. the Hindus and Mohammedans who form the overwhelming bulk of the population, not only untouched but almost unapproached by any Christian influence.' The most valuable function of Christian education was rather to instil broad Christian principles of racial harmony among the Hindu majority: the fact

92. *Ibid.*, pp. 371-2.

93. *Ibid.*, pp. 417-18. Miller's document is to be found in UTS, MRL 12, WMC papers, series 1, box 14, folder 2, alongside a number of other such responses to the draft report.

that the south of India had during the recent years of political turbulence shown 'greater calmness and loyalty to British rule' was due in no small measure, Miller believed, to the impact of Christian education. The logic of his remarks thus led to the conclusion that the primary aim of Christian missions in India should not be direct conversion but rather to permeate with principles of Christian morality the Hinduism which he regarded as the essence of Indian national identity. The premise of Miller's argument was that 'Indianness' was to be defined in essentially Hindu terms. The role of missions, therefore, was not to subvert Hindu identity but to perfect, even reinforce it by infusing Hindu consciousness with Christian ideals of inter-racial brotherhood.[94]

Education as the Key to Catholicity

Charles Gore's opening speech to the Commission III debate on the morning of Friday 17 June gave William Miller's statement sustained and respectful attention, but made it very clear that the views expressed therein did not command his personal support. The weight of evidence from India, as from elsewhere, Gore insisted, was that educational strategy should concentrate on the training of church leaders who could combine the spirit of Christ with the spirit of their own nation. The supreme task of earthing the Christian gospel in the national soil of different countries could only be accomplished by educated Christian nationals. At this point, Gore's perspective expressed a particular understanding of social Catholicism that may appear paradoxical, but was in fact becoming foundational to his conception of the global mission of the Church:

> . . . we recognise with assured conviction that that work of accommodation by which the catholic message is expressed in each national shape will be the work of the spirit of God through teachers belonging to the country and not through any efforts of accommodation made by foreigners.[95]

Catholicity was not to be equated with bland uniformity. Gore declared it to be 'shocking' that Indian pastors had been saddled with subscription to

---

94. *Report of Commission III*, pp. 407-8; UTS, MRL 12, WMC papers, series 1, box 14, folder 2, Comments and Criticisms of Proposed Report of Commission III by William Miller, pp. 2-3, 14-15, 23-24.
95. *Report of Commission III*, p. 409.

documents such as the Thirty-Nine Articles or the Westminster Confession which he deemed to be 'full of controversies', merely 'partial', and not of 'the universal substance of our religion'.[96] The report similarly commented that the training of native clergy in India had commonly been, 'even to a ludicrous extent, western in type.'[97] True catholicity depended instead on the interrelationship of innumerable processes of what Gore termed 'accommodation' which lay largely in the hands of indigenous Christians. The universality of the Christian religion depended not simply on the possession of a common apostolic message, as expressed in the Apostles' Creed and recorded in the Bible, but also on the fact that the common message should be severally understood by various peoples in such diverse ways that 'each in receiving the one message brings out some different or special aspect of the universal truth or character which lies in the common religion.' Only in this way could 'the glory and honour of all nations' be 'brought within the light and circle of the Holy City'.[98]

What were the origins of Gore's insistence at Edinburgh that catholicity demanded the inculturation of Christianity in Asian forms? One possible source is a collection of essays edited by Bishop Montgomery and published in 1907 under the title: *Mankind and the Church: being an attempt to estimate the contribution of great races to the fullness of the church of God.* Montgomery's central thesis was that 'while the Church must be Catholic it must also be racially and nationally expressed. . . . We shall never obtain the true contribution of any Church to the Body of Christ till the Church of that land is racy of the soil while it remains Catholic.' Like Gore, Montgomery found in the book of Revelation a vision of the final union of all races and, indeed, of the whole created order.[99] Montgomery, however, tended to see catholicity and the demands of racial authenticity to be two poles that needed to be kept in tension, whereas Gore's argument was that it was precisely the richness imparted by diverse racial characteristics that gave the notion of catholicity any

96. *Ibid.*, p. 407.

97. *Ibid.*, pp. 262-3.

98. Gairdner, 'Edinburgh 1910', p. 114, links Gore's phrase to Revelation 21:3, where the singular 'my people' of Zechariah 8:8 is significantly modified to the plural 'peoples' or 'nations'. Gore was in fact more directly dependent on Revelation 21:23-6.

99. H. H. Montgomery (ed.), *Mankind and the Church: being an attempt to estimate the contribution of great races to the fullness of the church of God* (London: Longmans, Green & Co., 1907), pp. xxx, xlvii. On Montgomery's racial theory see Steven Maughan, 'Imperial Christianity? Bishop Montgomery and the foreign missions of the Church of England, 1895-1915', in Andrew Porter (ed.), *The Imperial Horizons of British Protestant Missions, 1880-1914* (Grand Rapids and Cambridge: Eerdmans, 2003), pp. 32-57.

meaning deeper than that of mere uniformity. There is evidence that for some months Gore, doubtless stimulated by his work for Commission III, had been reflecting on this theme of the plurality of what he termed 'pagan' cultures as an indication of the manifold riches that would characterize the final consummation of the kingdom of God. He had written in January 1909 to his regular correspondent, Mrs Agnes Illingworth of Oxford, wife of J. R. Illingworth, assuring her of his confidence that '"the glory and honour of all nations" — their intellectual and artistic gifts, even if they have been executed in ignorance of God — are still God given gifts and are to be "brought within the holy City" at last.'[100] It was this powerful Christian vision of unity in cultural diversity which Gore laid before the Edinburgh conference. Despite being expressed in language that reflected the influence of dubious current theories of the supposedly distinctive religious proclivities of different 'races'[101] (or even, paradoxically, precisely *because* of the influence of such racial theories), Gore's vision anticipated the direction in which missionary theology would move over the remainder of the twentieth century:

> We look around, we see the profound and wonderful qualities of the Indian, and the Chinese, and the Japanese and the Africans, and we are sure that when the whole witness of Christianity is borne, when Christ is fulfilled in all men, each of these races and nations must have brought out into the world a Christianity with its own indigenous colour and character, and that the rising up of any really national Church will be to us, who remain, who were there before, life from the dead. We regard this question as central. We start from this. Are we, by means of education, training truly national Churches to stand each on its own basis, and bring out that aspect of Christian truth and grace which it is the special province of each separate race to bring out?[102]

A more frequently cited contribution of Charles Gore's to the Edinburgh conference is his solemn warning uttered in the Commission II debate that the challenge of 'handing over' Christianity to 'the Church of China, and Japan, and India with a good courage' presupposed a sharper and more confident

100. University of York, Borthwick Institute for Archives, Mirfield Deposit, Gore papers (5.6), Charles Gore to Mrs [Agnes] Illingworth, 28 Jan. 1909. John Richardson Illingworth was an Anglo-Catholic theologian, who, together with Gore, had been a member of the 'Holy Party' in Oxford and a contributor of two essays to *Lux Mundi* (1889).

101. See Colin Kidd, *The Forging of Races: race and scripture in the Protestant Atlantic world, 1600-2000* (Cambridge: CUP, 2006), chapter 6.

102. *Report of Commission III*, pp. 406-7.

definition of the invariable essence of the faith than currently commanded general assent in Protestant circles. Despite his typically Anglo-Catholic caution about 'the breaking down of what you may describe as denominational standards, barriers, and exclusiveness',[103] Gore's Commission III address, on the other hand, makes it plain that his commitment to the encouragement of autonomous non-western churches was unambiguous: genuine catholicity required both clear agreement on essentials and a diversity of forms of appropriation of the gospel.[104]

With the passing of the years, Gore's version of Anglo-Catholicism became increasingly non-sectarian in its insistence, as he would put it to Agnes Illingworth in 1923, that 'Catholic *principles* give one the right and duty to be truly broadminded.'[105] It has been suggested that by 1914 Gore and his fellow Anglo-Catholic leader, E. S. Talbot, had reached the revisionist position that English Nonconformist bodies could indeed be granted the title of 'churches' without injury to Catholic convictions.[106] Gore's contributions to the Edinburgh conference indicate that he may have been helped to reach this conclusion by the challenge of having to reflect on the questions raised for catholicity by the emergence of new churches on the Asian mission field. Moreover, the forthright interchanges between the British and American sections of Commission III appear to have played an important part in moving him in this direction.

Chapter VII of the report, entitled 'The relating of Christian truth to indigenous thought and feeling', began by expounding the catholicity of Christianity as a 'root principle' which, from New Testament times, had distinguished the Christian religion from its Jewish antecedents and Hellenistic competitors. The early church had pursued policies of 'accommodation' with the customary practices of 'pagan races', though (and here the imprint of Gore's Catholic convictions is clear), the apostolic age was said to be distinguished by 'a special inspiration of the Divine spirit . . . guiding the minds of the great apostolic teachers to present the apostolic message in the form best suited for catholic acceptance'. Thereafter, the report claimed, 'there was very little conscious accommodation of the original doctrine on the part of the

103. *Report of Commission II*, pp. 354-5; Gairdner, 'Edinburgh 1910', pp. 112-13.

104. See G. L. Prestige, *The Life of Charles Gore: a great Englishman* (London: Heinemann, 1935), p. 312.

105. University of York, Borthwick Institute for Archives, Mirfield Deposit, Gore papers (5.6), Charles Gore to Mrs [Agnes] Illingworth, 20 Nov. 1923.

106. See David M. Thompson, 'The unity of the Church in twentieth-century England: pleasing dream or common calling?', in R. N. Swanson (ed.), *Unity and Diversity in the Church*, Studies in Church History, vol. 32 (Oxford: Blackwell, 1996), p. 511.

evangelists of Europe'. The key to the successful indigenization of Christianity in Europe was rather the entrusting of the message to 'native teachers and rulers almost at once'.[107] Similarly it was the education of indigenous leaders that would provide the answer to the problem currently confronting the Asian churches of how to prevent Christianity appearing as an 'exotic' European implant while still maintaining the demands of catholicity:

> The ideal method of propagating Christianity is that the Gospel should be received by each race through the ministry of evangelists from nations already Christian, but that the Church should pass as rapidly as possible under the control of native pastors and teachers, so that while all Churches hold the same faith, use the same Scriptures, celebrate the same sacraments, and inhere in the same universal religion, each local Church should from the first have the opportunity of developing a local character and colour. It is also the ideal method that the Christian converts should, with their children, continue to share the education and social life of their own race and nation. In this way can 'the glory and honour of all nations' — that is, their own distinctive genius and its products — best be brought within the circle of the Holy City.[108]

The final section of Chapter VII presented a set of 'General Conclusions', in which the Commission reproduced almost verbatim a series of 'Judgments and Recommendations' apparently written by Jane Latham with the encouragement of the American members of the Commission.[109] These placed great emphasis on the need for missions to confine themselves to instilling 'the fundamental and vital truths of Christianity', leaving each people to develop their own national expression of the faith. The appropriate standard by which to measure the success of Christian missions in Asia (Africa, as so often, quietly dropped out of the picture) was whether they could be shown to have contributed to the 'development of an oriental type of Christianity, or as many oriental types as the varieties of national life and spirit shall demand'.[110] The vision (which by June 1910 Gore had made his own) of the development of a variety of indigenous types of catholic Christianity ensured

107. *Report of Commission III*, pp. 238-41.

108. *Ibid.*, p. 244.

109. UTS, MRL 12 WMC papers, series 1, box 14, folder 3 'Judgments and Recommendations' proposed by the American Section. For Latham's authorship see UCL, Ernest deWitt Burton papers, box 27, folder 8, World Missionary Conference, 1910, minutes of the American section of Commission III, 11 Feb. 1910, p. 15.

110. *Report of Commission III*, p. 264.

that the conclusion to the report, in its consideration of the answers to Question VI, came down firmly on the side of the use of the vernacular in the age-old missionary debate over the competing merits of English and vernacular languages in the impartation of religious teaching. The report asserted that 'a theology, which is really indigenous as well as truly and properly Christian and Biblical, must develop a native terminology, an end which is only likely to be attained where the vernacular is used for the expression of religious ideas'.[111] Nevertheless, what Gore and his colleagues singularly failed to do, either in the text of the report or in their contributions to the Commission III debate, was to grapple with the conundrum of what standard of 'accommodation', what 'distinctive genius' or 'oriental type', might be appropriate for the majority of Indian churches, composed of members from the *avarna* (polluting) or *adivasi* (tribal) sections of Indian society, that desired to be neither European nor Hindu in their cultural orientation. That remains possibly the most pressing dilemma of Indian Christianity today.

The Legacy of the Commission III Report

What difference, if any, did the Edinburgh conference make to educational strategy and practice in Protestant missions? The Commission report made seventeen specific recommendations for future mission policy. The most important, as we have seen, was that mission boards should give a higher priority to the evangelistic and edificatory functions of Christian education than to its 'leavening' function. Nevertheless, in 'countries at a low stage of civilisation' where the church was in its infancy, the report placed greatest stress on the provision of elementary village education, industrial education, and women's education. Western influence in Africa, it was asserted, had 'destroyed the whole social system of the tribes', rendering it necessary to develop 'a new social system adapted to backward races'. In such contexts, the crucial component of mission educational strategy was the training of village school teachers to provide effective Christian teaching in the vernacular.[112] Thus where Christianity and civilization were judged to be at an early stage of development, the Commission tended to revert to a diffusionist view that saw mission education as integral to the task of constructing a new Christian social and cultural fabric. On the other hand, in those countries (mainly Asian) where the Christian community had a longer history, the report urged that

111. *Ibid.*, p. 373.
112. *Ibid.*, pp. 376-8.

the primary purpose of education was to build up the native Church and train its spiritual leaders and teachers to 'bear its own proper witness'.[113]

In these respects, the Edinburgh conference simply confirmed the existing direction in which Protestant missionary education had been moving for some time: although mission schools continued to be viewed as essential instruments of evangelism in pioneering contexts, as in much of Africa, the accent of educational policy in Asia had moved from the diffusionist rationale of Duff or Miller towards a strategy of leadership training focused particularly on the development of advanced institutions of Christian higher education. It was this central emphasis of the report that led William Miller to write his dissenting letter which attracted considerable comment, mainly of a critical nature, in the debate on Commission III. By 1910 Miller's was a minority voice, and the trend which he deplored in vain at Edinburgh was to continue for the remainder of the western missionary era in Asia. By the Jerusalem conference of the International Missionary Council in 1928 a policy that had been defended in 1910 as essential to the construction of three-self indigenous churches was being radically questioned on the grounds that it had burdened the 'younger' churches with institutions (both educational and medical) of a size, character, and cost that were far beyond their capacity to support.[114] Three years later, the Lindsay Commission on Christian Higher Education in India, set up in 1929, reached a decidedly negative conclusion about the evangelistic efficacy of Christian colleges in India, whether understood in terms of direct conversions and baptisms or in terms of general leavening of Hindu society. Although the Commission strongly defended the colleges as a means of raising up Christian leadership for the church and nation, it reported that the colleges had become dangerously isolated from the life of both church and nation.[115]

Most of the other recommendations made by Commission III derived from the confidence it placed in advanced educational institutions as an appropriate strategy of Christian leadership training. A general appeal was made for 'far more abundant' provision of both men and money for the task of Christian education, though without any recommendation of the means by which how this expansive goal could be achieved.[116] Co-operation with

---

113. *Ibid.*, pp. 371-2.

114. *The Relations between the Younger and Older Churches: report of the Jerusalem meeting of the International Missionary Council March 24th-April 8th, 1928 Volume III* (London: OUP, 1928), pp. 18-22.

115. [Lindsay], *Report of the Commission on Christian Higher Education in India*, pp. 96-120. See Ingleby, *Missionaries, Education and India*, pp. 356-9.

116. *Report of Commission III*, p. 380.

government (which usually, of course, meant a British colonial government) in the provision of schools and colleges was enjoined as 'the manifest course of wisdom'.[117] The development of indigenous Christianity was, as we have noted, advocated as a consistent goal to ensure that the new leadership to be trained in such institutions should not be 'denationalised'.[118] More specifically, the report recommended as an 'essential' objective that first-rate Christian colleges or even Christian universities were to be established in 'the great strategic centres' in India, China, and Japan.[119]

In fact, very few new educational institutions were founded as a result of the Edinburgh conference. In China the only institution established as a direct consequence of the Commission's recommendation was Fukieh Christian College, opened by six collaborating missions in 1915; the college gained its university charter in 1918.[120] In Japan and India there appear to have been none such. The Lindsay Commission reported that the principals of existing Christian colleges were mostly strongly opposed to the foundation of a Christian university in India on the grounds that it would signal Christian approval of the religious communalism which had become such a marked and problematic feature of Indian society since 1910.[121] The Lindsay Report surveyed in detail all the Christian colleges of India but did not find it necessary to refer even once to the Edinburgh Commission. Rather than being able to comment on new institutions founded as a result of the call issued at Edinburgh, the Lindsay Report had to wrestle with the intensifying dilemma of Christian colleges which had been forced by lack of funds to depend more and more heavily on government grants and on fees paid by a student body that was overwhelmingly non-Christian: the Lindsay Commission found that 68 per cent of the income of Christian colleges in India came from grants from the government of India or from student fees, and only 32 per cent from overseas sources (income from the Indian church was presumably too small to warrant inclusion in these figures). As a result, the Christian character of many Christian colleges was in peril.[122] By 1931, many of the arguments advanced by Commission III were looking decidedly threadbare. For all of the theological creativity evinced by Moore, Burton, and Gore in ensuring that

117. *Ibid.*, p. 372.
118. *Ibid.*, p. 373.
119. *Ibid.*, pp. 372-3.
120. Lutz, *China and the Christian Colleges*, pp. 119-20. It is probably significant that this is the only mention of the Edinburgh conference in Lutz's major study.
121. [Lindsay], *Report of the Commission on Christian Higher Education in India*, pp. 23, 132.
122. *Ibid.*, pp. 15-16.

the Commission took proper note of the need for indigenous expressions of Christianity, the report of Commission III is likely to be dismissed by most readers today as a document which failed to grasp the necessity of developing strategies of education for the non-western churches that would not in the long run impair their future growth towards self-sustaining life.

The Commission III Questionnaire

I. What do you regard as the special purposes which educational missionary work should serve in reference to missionary enterprise as a whole? What relative importance do you attach to each of these purposes? (Kindly distinguish in your reply between elementary and higher education, and also between the education provided for those who are already members of the Christian community and the education offered as a means of attracting non-Christians within the sphere of Christian influence.)

II. What, in your judgment, have been the main results of the educational work of Christian Missions, with special reference to the outcome of —

(a) Primary education?
(b) Higher education?
(c) Industrial education?
(d) Professional training of teachers?

In summing up the main results, please state how far the courses of education provided by Christian Missions have been successful — (a) in raising up men and women who are at once Christian in conviction and indigenous in thought, feeling, and outlook upon life; and (b) in diffusing, through the direct and indirect influences of the schools, a higher ideal of life among the non-Christian community. In each case, state what seem to you the chief causes of success or failure.

III. In what respects has the missionary problem changed within recent years as a result of intellectual awakening, the growth of a national spirit, or of other causes? Do these changes call for any reconsideration of the educational policy of Missionary Societies?

IV. How far is the attainment of your educational missionary aim facilitated or made more difficult by the conditions imposed by the Government system of education? What do you think should be the policy of Missions in relation to the Government system of education in your part of the mission field? Have you had practical experience of the working of a "conscience clause" in mission schools? If so, state its terms and give your opinion as to its effects. In what way may Christian influences best be brought to bear on pupils of both sexes in Government institutions, including universities and training colleges, e.g. by means of hostels?

V. How far has an effort been made, and if so with what success, to relate the subject-matter and methods of Christian education to the thought, traditions, and literature of the indigenous population?

VI. Do you advocate the use of English (a) as a branch of study, (b) as the medium of instruction, as being helpful to the Christianising influence of education? What limits would you place to the use of English? In what cases would you recommend that the whole course of instruction should be given through the pupils' mother tongue?

VII. What, in your judgment, should be the aim of the education of girls and women in your part of the mission field, with special regard to the changes in the position of women which are resulting from the influence of Western ideas? Are any systematic efforts being made to train native women to hold responsible posts in educational work? If so, kindly describe what is being done.

VIII. Should more be done to develop industrial, including agricultural, training in the educational work of missions, with a view to (a) the formation of individual character, (b) the strengthening of the economic condition of the Christian community? Have any special difficulties, economic or educational, been experienced in the provision of such forms of industrial education?

IX. How far are systematic efforts made to exert continued influence upon students after they have ceased to attend school or college?

X. Are any systematic efforts being made to develop or improve the work of Sunday schools?

XI. What does your experience in the mission field lead you to regard as the most pressing needs in the provision of Christian literature, especially under the heads of (a) religious and devotional literature, (b) apologetic literature, (c) moral, scientific and general literature? In what respects do existing efforts for the preparation and supply of Christian literature seem to you inadequate, and in what directions do you think there is need for advance?

XII. Is further co-operation or federation desirable in the educational work of different Missionary Societies, e.g. in (a) the training of teachers, both men and women? (b) the appointment of educational advisers or inspectors for Christian schools? (c) medical training? (d) the establishment of universities, each Society maintaining its own hostel or hostels, but combining with other Societies in the provision of teaching and in the general university equipment and organisation? Have you had practical experience of any of these forms of co-operation? If so, please indicate causes of success or failure.

XIII. What do you regard as the most valuable kind of home training for a Missionary (man or woman) preparing himself or herself for educational work in your part of the mission field?

XIV. If it were found possible largely to increase the amount of money appropriated for educational work in your part of the mission field, on what purpose or purposes would you recommend that the additional funds should be expended?

CHAPTER 8

Fulfilment and Challenge: Christianity and the World Faiths

Previous Scholarship on Commission IV

Commission IV of the World Missionary Conference, entrusted with investigating 'The Christian Message in Relation to Non-Christian Religions', has received more intensive scholarly attention than any other. Contemporary ecumenical preoccupations with inter-faith relationships and the roots of a dialogical rather than confrontational Christian approach to other faiths (especially Hinduism) have drawn a considerable number of theologians and scholars of religions to study the Commission IV report, some of whom have taken the further step of reading the questionnaire responses on which it was based: this is the only Commission whose questionnaire responses have been analysed in published work, other than that undertaken by the present writer in preparation for this book. The late Eric J. Sharpe was the first scholar to do so, including in his *Not to Destroy but to Fulfil: the contribution of J. N. Farquhar to Protestant missionary thought in India before 1914* (1965), a brief summary of the replies from India.[1] In 1974 the Dutch scholar, J. J. E. van Lin, devoted the first chapter of his study of Protestant theology of religions from 1910 to 1938 to an analysis of the Commission IV replies: van Lin emphasised in particular the contrast between the responses from continental European missionaries, which tended to insist on the absolute superiority of the Christian revelation, and those from Anglo-American missionaries, which favoured a more liberal 'fulfilment' approach. Van Lin, however, reached the

---

1. Eric J. Sharpe, *Not to Destroy but to Fulfil: the contribution of J. N. Farquhar to Protestant missionary thought in India before 1914* (Uppsala: Gleerup, 1965), pp. 278-82.

rather tentative conclusion that the extant sources supplied 'only scanty information about the theological foundation for the missionary approach of other religions that was looked for. The exact differences of opinion cannot be ascertained.'[2] In 1977 James L. Cox included in his Aberdeen PhD thesis on the theology of A. G. Hogg (who was in 1910 the most penetrating contemporary critic of 'fulfilment theology') a detailed analysis of Hogg's contribution to the content of the Commission IV report, and noted the crucial significance of his relationship with the chairman of the Commission, Professor David S. Cairns. Cox also incorporated a brief discussion of the questionnaire replies from other missionaries working in Hindu contexts. Like van Lin, Cox emphasized that the continental European missionary respondents were less committed to the idea of 'fulfilment' than were the Anglo-Americans.[3]

Martin Maw surveyed the Indian responses to Commissions III and IV in his *Visions of India* (1990), but his analysis was limited by a predominant concern to label respondents according to a rather crude classification of their attitude to fulfilment theology.[4] The Sri Lankan Methodist ecumenist, Wesley Ariarajah, included a discussion of the report's treatment of Hinduism, and paid some attention to the questionnaire responses on Hinduism, in his *Hindus and Christians: a century of Protestant ecumenical thought* (1991).[5] More detailed and comprehensive surveys of the Commission IV responses have been undertaken by the British Methodist theologian Kenneth Cracknell in his *Justice, Courtesy and Love: theologians and missionaries encountering world religions, 1846-1914* (1995) and by Paul Hedges in his *Preparation and Fulfilment: a history and study of fulfilment theology in modern British thought in the Indian context* (2001). Cracknell's interest in the questionnaire replies lay in the wisdom they might offer to 'contemporary Christians locked in the same conflicts about the uniqueness, finality and insurpassability of Christian revelation'. He was consistently impressed (and evidently surprised) by the sympathetic and affirmative tone of the replies, and by the fact that the 'note of condemnation

---

2. J. J. E. van Lin, *Protestantse Theologie der Godsdiensten van Edinburgh naar Tambaram 1910-1938* (Assen: Van Gorcum and Comp., B.V., 1974), pp. 1-35, 374.

3. James L. Cox, 'The development of A. G. Hogg's theology in relation to non-Christian faith: its significance for the Tambaram meeting of the International Missionary Council, 1938' (University of Aberdeen PhD thesis, 1977), chapter III, and p. 103.

4. Martin Maw, *Visions of India: fulfilment theology, Aryan race theory, and the work of British Protestant missionaries in Victorian India* (Bern: Peter Lang, 1990), pp. 325-78, 390-3. Missionaries who showed 'sympathy for other faiths or a respect for "truth"' are thereby classified as 'partially in favour of fulfilment'. As a result, Hogg strangely emerges as 'partially in favour'.

5. S. Wesley Ariarajah, *Hindus and Christians: a century of Protestant ecumenical thought* (Amsterdam and Grand Rapids: Editions Rodopi and Eerdmans, 1991), pp. 17-31.

of superstition and idolatry' (widely, but incorrectly, assumed to be uniformly characteristic of the Protestant missionary movement in the high imperial period) was, so far as he could see, 'entirely missing'. In Cracknell's view, the Commission expounded 'an incipient theology of dialogue' that combined a belief in the finality of the Christian revelation with a generous and humble attitude to the insights of other religious traditions.[6] Hedges's treatment was more descriptive in nature, though he too paid sustained attention to A. G. Hogg, drawing on the prior work of James L. Cox.[7]

Cracknell's primary focus was on India missionaries who saw Hinduism as standing in either a preparatory or a dialectical relationship to Christianity. He paid little attention, for example, to the responses of missionaries from Africa, other than to acknowledge that 'Missionaries of this period were ill-equipped to do more than speak of African worship in terms of "Fetishism"'. They, and he conceded also, missionaries to Muslims, did not lend such ready support to his thesis that the respondents should be seen as pioneers of modern inter-faith dialogue.[8] An American Mennonite who has served as a missionary in West Africa, J. Stanley Friesen, worked approximately contemporaneously with Cracknell on a much smaller category of the Commission IV responses, namely those made by missionaries working among 'tribal' or 'primal' religionists or, to use the term current in 1910, 'animists'. Friesen was motivated by similar contemporary didactic concerns to Cracknell, and reached broadly similar conclusions in his book, *Missionary Responses to Tribal Religions at Edinburgh, 1910* (1996). Friesen asserted that 'the characterization that missionaries at Edinburgh regarded African religions as demonic and to be uprooted is a judgment which is not supported by the research'. On the contrary, missionaries in primal contexts, scarcely less than the India missionaries studied by Cracknell, were, in Friesen's view, engaged 'in a conversational process in the interreligious encounter and witness.'[9] Despite the manifest anachronism involved in the attribution of such quintessentially late twentieth-century views to missionaries in 1910, Friesen's book is valuable for the studies it contains of some of the most important respondents from primal contexts to the Commission IV questionnaire.

6. Kenneth Cracknell, *Justice, Courtesy and Love: theologians and missionaries encountering world religions, 1846-1914* (London: Epworth Press, 1995), pp. 194, 202, 259-60.

7. Paul Hedges, *Preparation and Fulfilment: a history and study of fulfilment theology in modern British thought in the Indian context* (Bern: Peter Lang, 2001), chapters 6 and 8, especially pp. 264-5.

8. Cracknell, *Justice, Courtesy and Love*, pp. 198, 376.

9. J. S. Friesen, *Missionary Responses to Tribal Religions at Edinburgh, 1910* (New York: Peter Lang, 1996), p. 141.

Another scholar who has examined the Commission IV responses, albeit more briefly than Cox, Maw, Cracknell, Hedges, or Friesen, is T. E. Yates, who published an article on the eve of the 1980 Melbourne conference of the Council for World Mission and Evangelism, the wing of the World Council of Churches that most directly traces its ancestry to the Edinburgh conference. Yates sought to recapture and assess the 'spirit of Edinburgh' in order to draw lessons which the Melbourne conference might profitably learn. To a greater extent than Cracknell, Yates took note of the replies from an Islamic context, and properly emphasized the considerable theological variety exhibited by the range of replies from both Islamic and Hindu fields.[10]

The Membership of Commission IV

The chairman and primary architect of Commission IV was the eminent Scottish theologian, David S. Cairns (1862-1946), professor of systematic theology in the United Free Church College (later known as Christ's College) in Aberdeen. Cairns had no personal experience of missionary work, and owed his role at the conference to his personal friendship with J. H. Oldham, with whom he had been a fellow student at New College, Edinburgh. The friendship became one of close spiritual affinity in the years from 1906 to 1910. Cairns's wife, Helen, whom he had married only in December 1901, was diagnosed with an incurable illness (presumably cancer) in September 1906, and she died on 4 May 1910. During this period in which Cairns had to combine his major responsibility for Commission IV with great personal stress, Oldham supplied his friend with regular spiritual support and guidance, assuring Cairns of his prayers and encouraging him to seek the help of a healer from the Christian Science movement. Donald Baillie in his memoir of David Cairns was referring to Oldham (and probably also to Hogg) when he noted that the same men who were closest to him in the work of Commission IV 'were also sharing most intimately in his domestic anxiety in a fellowship of importunate faith and prayer'. Baillie notes that in Cairns' mind the two preoccupations of Edinburgh 1910 and his wife's terminal illness converged, 'since both were essentially concerned with the victory of God over all evils'.[11]

10. T. E. Yates, 'Edinburgh revisited: Edinburgh 1910 to Melbourne 1980', *Churchman* 94:2 (1980), pp. 145-55.

11. David S. Cairns, *An Autobiography: some recollections of a long life, and selected letters, edited by his son and daughter, with a memoir by Professor D. M. Baillie* (London: SCM Press, 1950), p. 24. For Cairns' own reflections on 'the terrible strain' of his wife's terminal illness as the background to his work on Commission IV see AUL, D. S. Cairns papers, MS

Oldham himself wrote of the experience of fellowship with his friend in his time of personal trial as one which 'in a mysterious way' became 'the occasion through which God has opened up new truth', leading him to reflect on the abiding relevance of prayer in the healing of the sick and increasing his own sympathies with some aspects of Christian Science teaching.[12]

Of the twenty members of the Commission, it appears that only six had themselves been missionaries: in the appointment of members of this Commission, as of several others, experience of the mission field seems to have been regarded as a qualification of relatively low priority, a fact which attracted some criticism, notably from the Indian mission periodical, *The Harvest Field*.[13] George Owen (1843-1914) had for many years been an LMS missionary in Shanghai and Beijing; he was a leading figure in the translation of the New Testament into Mandarin in the Union Version, and since 1908 professor of Chinese at King's College, London. Despite the overwhelming weight that the report gave to Indian religions, only two members had in fact been missionaries in India — J. E. Padfield, a former CMS missionary with thirty years of experience among the Telegu people,[14] and the Indologist, Wilhelm Dilger of the University of Tübingen, who had served with the Basel Mission on the Malabar coast of India from 1880 to 1900, and again briefly from 1906 to 1907. Two members had experience of what is now Indonesia: both Gottfried Simon (1870-1951)[15] and Johannes Warneck (1867-1944; son of Professor Gustav Warneck of Halle)[16] had worked with the Rheinische Missionsgesellschaft among the Batak peoples of Sumatra. The only member who had worked in Africa was Charles H. Robinson (1861-1925), editorial secretary of the SPG, who was an expert on the Hausa of northern Nigeria. However, Robinson's interests were now focused more on Hinduism — he was made chairman of the Commission's sub-committee on Hinduism — and appears to have made no contribution to the Commission's discussion of Africa.

3384/1/6/1900-1912, Cairns to James Hewat Craw, 18 Feb. 1910; see also his remarks cited in Gwendoline Stephenson, *Edward Stuart Talbot 1844-1934* (London: SPCK, 1936), p. 189.

12. AUL, D. S. Cairns papers, MS 3384/1/4/1910, Oldham to Cairns, 20 Sept. 1906 and 26 April 1907.

13. Cox, 'The development of A. G. Hogg's theology', p. 87.

14. On Padfield see Church Missionary Society, *Register of Missionaries . . . from 1804 to 1904* (printed for private circulation, n.p., n.d.), p. 149, no. 711.

15. Simon served in the RMG field of Tapanuli from 1896 to 1907, doing pioneer work among the Simalungun Batak. From 1910 to 1915 he was a teacher at the Theological Seminary at Bethel in Wuppertal. See Gustav Menzel, *Die Rheinische Mission: aus 150 Jahren Missionsgeschichte* (Wuppertal: Verlag der Vereinigten Evangelische Mission, 1978), p. 440, n. 743. I owe this reference to Dr Thomas van der End.

16. On Johannes Warneck see *BDCM*.

Other members of the Commission had travelled more or less widely in their capacity as missionary society executives or Board members, but had not faced the challenge of long-term exposure to another religion. J. W. Gunning (1862-1923) had been director of the Nederlandsche Zendelingenootschap since 1897, and had visited the Dutch East Indies in 1900-1, but had no long-term mission field experience.[17] Johannes Lepsius (1858-1926), founder of the Deutsche Orient Mission, had served as assistant pastor to the German Protestant congregation in Jerusalem from 1884 to 1886, and had travelled widely in the Near East, but had never been a missionary as such. Robert E. Speer (1867-1947), secretary of the Board of Foreign Missions of the Presbyterian Church of the USA since 1891, had toured Asia and Persia in 1896-7.[18] Adna B. Leonard (1837-1916) was a long-serving corresponding secretary of the Board of Foreign Missions of the Methodist Episcopal Church, and by 1910 had visited some twenty-five countries.[19] Richard Glover (1837-1919), a distinguished Baptist minister from Bristol and a senior member of the BMS general committee, had led the Society's first deputation to its China field in 1890-1, and as a young man had travelled to South Africa, Russia, and the South Seas.[20] Henry Chapman (1844-1919) was missionary secretary of the United Methodist Church and president of the United Methodist Conference for 1910, but had no overseas experience, other than possible deputation tours.[21] Others, such as A. E. Garvie, principal of the Congregational New College, London, or C. F. D'Arcy (1859-1937), the Anglican bishop of the Irish see of Ossory, or W. P. Paterson (1860-1939), professor of divinity at Edinburgh since 1907, had theological expertise of a purely academic kind to offer. There were only five North American members: Speer, who was vice-chairman; Leonard; Robert Mackenzie, secretary of the College Board of the Presbyterian Church in

17. On Gunning see *BDCM*. He had previously been a pastor for ten years in the village of Eerbeek in the central Netherlands. As director of the NZG, he initiated a centripetal movement in Dutch Protestant missions, after more than half a century of rifts and schisms. He also reorganised and professionalised the mission in the Netherlands Indies. I owe this information to Dr Thomas van der End.

18. John F. Piper, *Robert E. Speer: prophet of the American church* (Louisville: Geneva Press, 2000), pp. 168-9, 462.

19. Cracknell, *Justice, Courtesy and Love*, p. 370.

20. See David Roberts, 'Mission: home and overseas. Richard Glover of Bristol', *Baptist Quarterly* 35:3 (July 1993), 108-20. Roberts notes (110-11) that as early as 1883 Glover expressed the view that all heathen religions should be seen as preparing the way for Christ.

21. Oliver A. Beckerlegge (comp.), *United Methodist Ministers and their Circuits* (London: Epworth Press, 1968), p. 43. Cracknell, *Justice, Courtesy and Love*, p. 189, appears to be incorrect in describing Chapman as a former missionary in China. I am grateful to the Rev Dr Albert W. Mosley for information on Chapman.

the USA; E. Y. Mullins (1860-1928), president of the Southern Baptist Seminary in Louisville, Kentucky; and a veteran Lutheran pastor from New York, Junius B. Remensnyder (b. 1843), who had published a number of books on theological themes.[22]

Virtually no documentation of the proceedings of the Commission or its British executive committee survives, but it seems likely that the contribution of the five Americans was relatively slight, except perhaps for Speer, whose correspondence with Cairns appears to have been regular enough to have formed the basis of a continuing friendship.[23] The draft text of each of the five principal sections of the report was the product of deliberations by a sub-committee involving British and European members only, and written by the chairman of the sub-committee, who was in every case British: Paterson for 'animistic religions'; Owen for Chinese religions; D'Arcy for the religions of Japan (much to his embarrassment, he found he was the sole member of the sub-committee, despite never having visited Japan); Garvie for Islam; and Robinson for Hinduism.[24] There was one female member of the Commission, Mrs Ethel Romanes (d. 1927), a prominent Anglo-Catholic churchwoman and widow of the physiologist and evolutionary theorist, Professor G. J. Romanes; along with Dilger and Padfield, she was appointed to the sub-committee on Hinduism, even though she had never been to India and had no specialist knowledge of Indian religions.[25]

The Theology and Religious Perspective of Commission IV

Although the five main sections of the report were drafted by the chairmen of the sub-committees, Cairns shaped the conclusions to each section and himself wrote the lengthy final chapter of the report, giving its 'General Conclusions'. He also appears to have been responsible for the text of the question-

---

22. See http://www.ccel.org/s/schaff/encyc/encyc09/htm/iv.vii.cxlvii.htm (accessed 18.12.2007).

23. Piper, *Robert E. Speer*, p. 203. Speer, however, seems to have had no hand in writing the report; see Sharpe, *Not to destroy*, p. 276n.

24. *Report of Commission IV*, p. 4. For fuller biographical details of the members of Commission IV see Cracknell, *Justice, Courtesy and Love*, pp. 189-90, 369-73. On D'Arcy's predicament see his *The Adventures of a Bishop* (London: Hodder & Stoughton, 1934), p. 170, cited in Cracknell, *Justice, Courtesy and Love*, p. 372.

25. See Ethel Romanes, *The Story of an English Sister* (London: Longmans, Green & Co., 1918), p. 166n. for Mrs Romanes' attendance at Edinburgh and comments on the disapproving stance towards the conference of her fellow 'Catholics'.

naire.[26] He expressed the hope that his report would be used to lead men to 'very different conclusions about God and His heart to men, and the possibilities of human life'.[27] Cairns' reading of F. D. Maurice and John MacLeod Campbell, and the impact of a summer spent as a student in Marburg at the feet of the Ritschlian theologian, Wilhelm Herrmann, had led him to forsake the orthodox Calvinism of his Presbyterian upbringing for an immanentist theology of the universal fatherhood of God; he had come to believe that the kingdom of God was embryonically present in all humanity, but completely expressed only in the life and teachings of the perfect Son, Jesus. Applied to the theology of religions, this perspective seemed to imply that signs of God's presence could be found in all human religiosity, albeit intermingled with inevitable error and corruption. The task of the missionary, therefore, was in a sympathetic spirit of humble enquiry to identify such 'points of contact' in non-Christian religions and then use them to draw adherents of other faiths towards the full revelation of truth found in the Christ who was the perfect manifestation of the fatherhood of God.[28] Question 6 of the questionnaire accordingly invited missionaries to identify those elements in the religions they had encountered which 'present points of contact with Christianity and may be regarded as a preparation for it.' Such points of contact might include: a recognition of the existence of a Supreme Being; an awareness of personal immortality; or any religious practices which expressed a genuine search for truth or holiness and afforded the adherent observable spiritual sustenance. Question 2 of the questionnaire thus asked respondents to distinguish those religious observances which were 'mainly traditional and formal from others which are taken in earnest and are genuinely prized as a religious help and consolation'. Question 8 inquired whether the people among whom the missionary worked displayed 'a practical belief in immortality and in the existence of a Supreme God'. Cairns' personal theological interests are surely also evident in Question 9, which asked whether questions of higher criticism and other 'developments of modern thought' had exerted an influence on the respondent's part of the mission field, and what effect they had on missionary work.[29]

The questionnaire thus presupposed an understanding of religion as

26. Cairns, *Autobiography*, p. 16; Cox, 'The development of the theology of A. G. Hogg', p. 99, n. 90.

27. AUL, D. S. Cairns papers, MS 3384/1/6/1900-1912, Cairns to James Hewat Craw, 18 Feb. 1910.

28. Cracknell, *Justice, Courtesy and Love*, pp. 186-9; Cairns, *Autobiography*, pp. 11, 51, 85, 122, 132-5, 151, 167-8.

29. *Report of Commission IV*, p. 2.

made up of two layers: first, the 'traditional and formal' body of inherited custom and unquestioned communal practice; and, second, the deeper level of personal devotion and belief. It further implied that the second level was essential if true religion were to be present: unless customary ritual observances and 'doctrines' were demonstrably and earnestly espoused by individuals, and unless they were 'genuinely prized' as sources of spiritual strength and comfort, it was doubtful whether such observances or beliefs merited the label of 'religion' at all. This, of course, was a characteristically Protestant, evangelical, and modern way of approaching the subject of human religiosity. What communities do because they have always done it that way (or incorrectly assume that they have always done it that way) was not to be dignified with the title 'religion' unless it was infused and renewed by the element of personal 'faith'.

Nevertheless, it should be noted that the questionnaire encouraged its respondents to identify analogies and correspondences with a western Christian understanding of religious faith. Points of difference were of lesser interest than points of similarity, for it was the latter that could be utilised as bridges for apologetic evangelism. Question 6 was an invitation to missionaries to isolate particular features of religious belief and practice, and give them the most favourable Christian gloss possible, even if the identification of such 'points of contact' distorted the meaning of such features in their original setting.

The arrangement of the report in five sections (plus Introduction and Conclusion), beginning with animistic religions, followed in turn by Chinese religions, Japanese religions, Islam, and culminating in Hinduism, was surely not coincidental, but implicitly expressed an assumed hierarchy of sophistication and value. Such, at least, was Temple Gairdner's interpretation of the report: 'the interest, great throughout, rises steadily, reaching the highest point in the last division on Hinduism.'[30] This chapter will follow the reverse order in its discussion of the report. It should also be noted that the report tended simply to equate the religions of the Indian subcontinent with 'Hinduism', and in practice concentrated on the so-called 'higher' Hinduism of the Vedanta tradition. Sikhism received only one brief mention,[31] while Jainism or the Zoroastrianism of the Parsis of western India was not referred to at all. The Baha'i faith received a few references, but none in relation to India.[32] Most serious of all, Buddhism was dealt with solely in relation to the Mahayana traditions of China and Japan, and was not granted the dignity of

30. Gairdner, *'Edinburgh 1910'*, p. 135.
31. *Report of Commission IV*, p. 184.
32. *Ibid.*, pp. 123-4, 131, 143, 239, 288.

a chapter of its own: it was subsumed under the chapter headings 'Chinese Religions' and 'The Religions of Japan'. Only four responses were received from missionaries operating in predominantly Buddhist environments, and they were all listed under other headings in the 'List of Correspondents': those of A. G. Fraser (CMS, Ceylon), and R. S. Fyffe and George Whitehead (both SPG, Burma) appeared under 'Hinduism' and that of William Harris (Presbyterian Church in the USA, Siam) under 'Chinese religions'.[33] The report thus managed to ignore entirely the older Hinayaya (or Theravada) traditions of South and South-East Asia. One of the great religions of Asia was thus marginalised at Edinburgh.

In response to criticisms received at the conference that South Asian Buddhism had been neglected, a 'Concluding Note' and Appendix on Burma, Siam, and Ceylon were subsequently added to the report. The Concluding Note admitted that 'by some oversight' only four responses had been received from missionaries working among Buddhists in South Asia, and explained that the Commission had originally judged such a sample too small to form the basis of satisfactory induction. The Appendix sought to rectify the omission by summarising the four responses received from Buddhist South Asia.[34] A brief apologetic paragraph was also inserted in the General Conclusions to the report admitting that the report was defective in taking 'only incidental' account of Buddhism, and expressing the hope that future enquiries would remedy the defect.[35]

The Relation of Hinduism to Christianity

Of the 187 missionaries who responded to the Commission IV questionnaire, about sixty (almost exactly one-third) were working in predominantly Hindu contexts.[36] They included virtually all the names of missionaries who have at-

33. *Ibid.*, pp. xiii, xviii, and xx. Fraser's pupils at Trinity College, Kandy did include Hindus as well as Buddhists.

34. *Ibid.*, pp. 275, 281-7; see Gairdner, *'Edinburgh 1910'*, p. 149.

35. *Report of Commission IV*, p. 236.

36. *Ibid.*, pp. xvii-xx. The figure is 65 minus A. G. Fraser, R. S. Fyffe, and G. Whitehead, who were working in a mainly Buddhist environment, and possibly a few others. A number of those who responded from N. W. India worked with Muslims as well as Hindus. More or less complete copies of the replies to Commission IV may be found in several locations, but with some variation in the number and labelling of volumes into which the set has been bound. ECG has six bound volumes: two on Hinduism, one on Islam, one on Chinese religions, one on Japanese, and one on animistic religions. These are available on microfiche from IDC Publishers of Leiden. AUL, MS 3291, has five volumes: three volumes

tracted subsequent scholarly attention as among the first architects of a dialogical mode of relationship between Christianity and Hinduism: T. E. Slater, Bernard Lucas, and J. N. Farquhar of the LMS, A. G. Hogg and Nicol Macnicol of the United Free Church of Scotland, Robert A. Hume of the ABCFM, George Howells of the BMS, and C. F. Andrews of the Cambridge Mission to Delhi. There were also a number of leading Indian Christian leaders, such as J. R. Banerjea (or Banerjee) of Calcutta and Pandita Ramabai of Poona.

Although the section on Hinduism began by emphasizing that 'the word Hinduism covers a number of religions which are apparently inconsistent with and contradictory to each other', it went on to argue, citing the response of James Mathers, an LMS missionary in Bangalore, that 'all the religions that are termed Hindu are unified consciously in the thought of the thinking classes, and semi-consciously or implicitly in the faith and worship of the common people, by that form of highly speculative and mystical religion which has been termed the Higher Hinduism.'[37] The Brahmanical Vedantism of the 'twice-born' or 'educated' classes was thus assumed to constitute the essence of the religion, whilst the beliefs and practices of the common people were regarded as a debased and imperfect reflection of the 'true' Hinduism, and hence of only secondary interest in the quest to relate the Christian message to other religious systems. This was an assumption with a long history in Protestant missionary interpretations of Hinduism, going back to William Ward's famous published account of the 'religion of the Hindoos' in the early nineteenth century.[38] However, some of those who responded to the questionnaire — including those who were advocates of fulfilment theology — gave rather

---

of India responses, one of responses from the Islamic world; and one of China responses — Japanese and animistic religions are missing. UTS has a complete set, bound in five volumes: one on Africa, Japan, Burma, Siam, and Ceylon; one on Chinese religions; two on Indian religions; and one on Mohammedanism. The set was donated to UTS Library by the vice-chairman, R. E. Speer (UTS, MRL 12, WMC papers, series 1, box 15, folder 1, R. E. Speer to William Adams Brown, 26 Sept. 1912). YDS has two boxes of loose-leaf copies of the replies for Commissions IV and I. The Henry Martyn Centre, Westminster College, Cambridge, has loose photocopies of almost all the Commissions IV responses, made by Kenneth Cracknell. There is also an incomplete set of Commission replies at the Centre for the Study of Christianity in the non-Western World, New College, University of Edinburgh.

37. *Report of Commission IV*, pp. 156-7, citing Commission IV replies, 203, p. 2. Cracknell, *Justice, Courtesy and Love*, p. 223, identifies Mathers as a disciple of T. E. Slater.

38. See Geoffrey A. Oddie, *Imagined Hinduism: British Protestant missionary constructions of Hinduism, 1793-1900* (New Delhi, Thousand Oaks, and London: Sage, 2006), pp. 173-4.

more weight to the plurality of popular religion than did the report itself. For instance, George Howells, the Baptist principal of Serampore College, had insisted that 'Hinduism is a vast conglomeration of religious beliefs and non-beliefs, ranging from unadulterated pantheism to blank atheism, from the purest ethics to the grossest immorality.' Precisely because of this immense diversity, however, the liberal Protestant search for 'points of contact' was sure eventually to find its target: 'I do not know', affirmed Howells, 'of a single doctrine or precept of Christianity for which a parallel cannot be found somewhere in the writings of Hinduism, often hidden away, no doubt, in a heap of rubbish. Arguments of the most cogent character can be adduced in support of distinctively Christian doctrines from great Hindu Theologians and reformers.'[39] Although Howells commended a missionary approach which identified commonalities between the *Bhagavad Gita* and the New Testament in their doctrine of God, and believed that the Hindu scriptures contained 'large elements of truth as helpful and as noble as anything in the Old Testament', he could dismiss 'the evils and follies of popular Hinduism' as 'so great and many' and the teachings of philosophic Hinduism as 'vague, intangible and unsatisfying.'[40] In the final analysis, Howells believed that the most fruitful missionary approach to the Hindu lay not in any comparison of theological systems, but simply in the commendation of the person of Christ.[41]

In the discussion of the report in the conference, some speakers felt that the report had placed Hinduism in an unduly optimistic light, complaining, as C. H. Robinson noted in his response on behalf of the Commission, that 'the Hinduism which we describe is not the Hinduism of India'.[42] In introducing the report to the conference, Cairns conceded the substantial accuracy of the objection that 'we have said very little about the popular religion of India, that we have confined ourselves in the main to dealing with Vedantism', though he disagreed with the implication that 'Vedantism is the theory of a very small proportion of the population of India.'[43]

39. Commission IV replies, 179, p. 3.

40. *Ibid.*, pp. 5-6.

41. *Ibid.*, pp. 7-8, 11-12 (the latter section is cited anonymously in the *Report of Commission IV*, pp. 206-7). See Cracknell, *Justice, Courtesy and Love*, pp. 225, 252. For Howells' *The Soul of India* (1913), which expounded his fulfilment theology, see Brian Stanley, *The History of the Baptist Missionary Society 1792-1992* (Edinburgh: T&T Clark, 1992), pp. 279-80.

42. *Report of Commission IV*, p. 320. However, of the contributions to the debate printed in the report, only that of G. T. Manley of the CMS (pp. 316-17) seems to correspond to Robinson's description of the criticism. Not all that was said in debate was printed (see p. 291 of the report).

43. *Ibid.*, p. 293.

Cairns was deeply impressed by the reflective quality of the Indian responses, and commented to Hogg in July 1909 that they alone had amply justified the work of the Commission.[44] The section devoted to Hinduism in Cairns's final chapter began revealingly by describing the field of 'Indian religions' as being 'by far the richest of all in suggestion'. It is clear that the insights offered by missionaries on the relation of Christianity to Hinduism at a time of both religious and national resurgence in India were for him, as for present-day commentators, the most intellectually fertile aspect of the work of the Commission. Cairns wrote that the contact between 'the minds of the missionaries' (the encounter was seen as essentially an intellectual one) and Hinduism 'with its three thousand years of history has come at a moment in the course of theology when Christian intelligence has been deeply stirred by the problems raised by science and historical criticism and the rise of Comparative Religion'. India was a vast laboratory of experimental religious science in which new and exciting theories of the 'modern' theology of religion were being both concocted and empirically tested. Cairns saw 'at every turn' 'very remarkable' parallels between the current encounter of Christianity with India's 'strange blend of a crude, popular polytheism' and 'a deep and subtle esoteric philosophy' and the second-century encounter between Christianity and Hellenism that stimulated the rich theological writings of the Alexandrian Fathers.[45] India, above all, seemed to offer best scope for the attractive thesis that the work of the Christian missionary, in Robinson's words to the conference, 'must be constructive, not destructive. Christ is the Sun of Righteousness we believe, but in order to prepare for His complete manifestation we have not got to extinguish the stars which have helped to illumine the darkness of the non-Christian world but to guide seekers after the truth in their search for God.'[46]

In this broad sense it is true, as Cracknell claims, that the dominant motif of the India responses was that of fulfilment.[47] As Godfrey Phillips of the LMS Madras mission said to the conference, 'I firmly believe that we can

---

44. Hogg collection, Cairns to Hogg, 7 July 1909, cited in Cox, 'The development of A. G. Hogg's theology', p. 100, n. 91. The Hogg collection was in the possession of the late Professor Eric Sharpe, and is still in the possession of his widow, Mrs Birgitta Sharpe of Sydney. I am grateful to Mrs Sharpe, Dr James L. Cox of the University of Edinburgh, and Dr Carole Cusack of the University of Sydney for assistance in locating this collection. At the time of going to press, however, Mrs Sharpe has been unable to locate any correspondence between Cairns and Hogg between 23 March and 12 Sept. 1910.

45. *Report of Commission IV*, pp. 244, 245.

46. *Ibid.*, p. 320.

47. Cracknell, *Justice, Courtesy and Love*, pp. 219-27.

present Jesus Christ to-day with wonderful force in India as the fulfiller of all that is best in the past of India and I heartily agree with all that has been said in the Report on that head.'[48] The chapter on Hinduism in the report gave prominence to the arguments of a series of questionnaire respondents, among them C. F. Andrews, Nicol Macnicol, T. E. Slater, and Wilhelm Dilger, who identified either the tradition of *bhakti* personal devotion represented above all by the *Bhagavad Gita,* or the Hindu doctrine of liberation *(mokshi),* as providentially intended to prepare Hindus for the reception of the Christian gospel.[49] There was considerable variation, however, in the use which respondents made of the idea of 'points of contact': Dilger, for example, argued that the value of *mokshi* for Christian apologetic was that it was 'a means of elucidation by contrast': the understanding of *mokshi* as annihilation was, Dilger pointed out, 'exactly the opposite of what the gospel of Jesus Christ offers to the believer.' The report carefully distinguished between Dilger's understanding of 'points of contact' and a fulfilment view.[50]

A few correspondents were even prepared to extend the principle of fulfilment from the realm of religious ideas to that of social organisation. C. F. Andrews, for example, thought that even caste, 'with all its radical evils,'

> has been and will be a *praeparatio evangelica.* The very fact, that we have taken over the caste words panchayat and biraderi [*sic*] ('council' and 'brotherhood') in almost every Christian community and find acts of Christian discipline comparatively easy, on account of caste training in our people, shows that the heritage of caste has an important part to play in the future Indian Church, however great the safeguards that are clearly needed to prevent the *evil* caste-spirit from entering during the process.[51]

Early twentieth-century fulfilment ideology should not, however, be presented as if it were essentially analogous to the attitudes of mutual openness that are now enjoined as indispensable to the conduct of inter-faith dialogue. Although Robinson's chapter on Hinduism declared that the essential task of the missionary was not to supplant, but 'rather to transfigure the religion of a

48. *Report of Commission IV,* p. 312.

49. Ibid., pp. 159-61, 178-80. See Commission IV replies, 123, pp. 1-2 (Andrews); 147, pp. 6-7 (Dilger); 198, pp. 16-17 (Macnicol); 229, p. 12 (Slater). See also Dilger's contribution to the debate of the Commission IV report (pp. 317-18). Dilger was a retired Basel missionary who had served in Malabar from 1880 to 1900, and from 1906 to 1907.

50. *Report of Commission IV,* pp. 180-1, 318.

51. Commission IV replies, 123, p. 13.

non-Christian people' and underlined the necessity of doing the fullest justice to the religions of India, it spoke also of 'conserving the supreme place of Christianity as that which absolutely supersedes Hinduism by absolutely fulfilling all that is noblest in the ancient faiths'.[52] More bluntly, Cairns's conclusion pronounced, in a passage that Temple Gairdner quoted with enthusiasm, that 'The spectacle of the advance of the Christian Church along many lines of action to the conquest of the five great religions of the modern world is one of singular interest and grandeur.'[53] Sentiments that were regarded as 'liberal' in 1910 would occupy a very different position on the theological spectrum of today. George Sherwood Eddy, YMCA secretary in Madras, was emphatic that the correct missionary approach to Hindus and Buddhists was 'to build upon the measure of truth which they already possess' but also that the unmistakable evidence of divine activity in these faiths was precisely that 'Hinduism is decaying', while Buddhism (in Ceylon and Burma) was 'trying, ineffectually, to hold its own on the defensive' against the irresistible advance of Christianity.[54] Cracknell concedes that the most celebrated expositor of fulfilment theology, J. N. Farquhar, was even more explicit in his response that, though fulfilment dictated sympathy and reverence as the only 'way of wisdom' for the missionary to the Hindu, it also spelt ultimate extinction for all religions other than Christianity:

> . . . while all religions are human, there is only one which satisfies all the religious instincts and yet can be held by modern thinking man. Every religion except Christianity is incredible, either on account of crude metaphysics, or a wild theology or a low ethical system. Clearly Christianity will yet be the one religion of man, or else there will be no religion.
>
> But, if all religions are human, and yet men can in the long run hold only Christianity, clearly it must be, in some sense, the climax of the religious development of the world, the end and culmination of all religions. If all the great religious instincts, which have created the other faiths, find ultimate satisfaction in Christianity, then Christianity stands in a very definite relation to every other religion. It is the fulfilment and crown of each; and it is our privilege and duty to trace the lines of connection and lead the peoples up to the Christ.[55]

52. *Report of Commission IV*, pp. 174, 176.
53. *Ibid.*, p. 273; cited in Gairdner, *'Edinburgh 1910'*, p. 135.
54. Commission IV replies, 153, pp. 2 and 5.
55. Commission IV replies, 154, pp. 13-14, 17; see Cracknell, *Justice, Courtesy and Love*, pp. 171-2.

T. E. Slater and the Case for Concentration on 'Higher Hinduism'

By far the longest of all the responses received by Commission IV was that from T. E. Slater (1840-1912), LMS missionary in Calcutta, Madras, and Bangalore from 1866 to 1905. Slater, rather than the better-known J. N. Farquhar, deserves to be remembered as the most important pioneer of the theology of fulfilment.[56] His questionnaire response extends to over 122 pages, and was quoted nine times by C. H. Robinson in the Hinduism section of the report, more frequently than any other respondent. It began with an apologia for the view that the educated classes should form the principal object of missionary endeavour in India. Slater, and in its turn the Commission IV report, cited the claim made at the Centenary Missionary Conference in London in 1888 (by the same J. E. Padfield who was a member of Commission IV) that 'when you have converted thousands upon thousands' of the lower castes or outcastes, 'you may not have touched *Hinduism* one bit'. In contrast, a strategy aimed at the educated (and largely Brahmanical) elite, held out the promise that 'some great apostle and leader, an Origen or an Augustine, may any day be raised up who would far outpay all our efforts'. Though for a time the Indian church would be built upon the poor and the depressed classes, 'the time must come when the intellectual power, and meditative spirit, and mystical genius of the Brahman will be required for the development and enrichment of the Church.'[57] The report employed Slater's quotation of Padfield as part of its armoury to defend the traditional concentration of missions in India on educational work in schools and colleges against the widespread criticism that this strategy had yielded only meagre results in terms of conversions. It commented that its respondents were 'practically unanimous' in urging that this emphasis should be retained.[58] This was true enough, but the great majority of the India respondents were, or had been, engaged in this work, and were its natural defenders.

The premise that it was the 'higher' Vedic Hinduism of the educated that should be the chief concern of missionary theology was foundational to Slater's argument in two respects. First, it provided the only credible basis for his philosophy of fulfilment. The 'highest thought of India', representing 'probably the high-water mark of non-Christian religious thought', was a refined form of religious monism that maintained the illusory nature of all matter

---

56. See Cracknell, *Justice, Courtesy and Love*, pp. 108-19; Sharpe, *Not to Destroy*, pp. 94-107, 208, 330.

57. Commission IV replies, 229, pp. 3-4; *Report of Commission IV*, p. 157; James Johnston (ed.), *Report of the Centenary Conference on the Protestant Missions of the World* 2 vols. (London: James Nisbet, 1888), II, p. 246.

58. *Report of Commission IV*, p. 158.

other than the supreme reality of God. However 'erroneous and degraded' some of the 'lower forms' of Hinduism might be, union with this supreme divine reality or Brahman represented 'the best and deepest passion of the Hindu soul.' Despite the manifestly unchristian nature of the claim that all material things constituted illusion, Slater regarded the aspiration of the Vedic tradition towards union with the divine as 'the *truest possible preparation* for the complete response of Christianity' which proclaimed the union of the eternal Logos with the highest of creation in the person of Jesus of Nazareth.[59]

Second, Slater advanced the pragmatic argument that the only form of Christianity that 'progressive India' would accept was a 'healthy, broad, undogmatic, ethical presentation' shorn of its foreignness and all that went with it. Since '*organised Western Christianity,* a schedule of Church doctrine, a "body of divinity"', were all foreign to Hindu thought and did not appeal to the Indian elite, it was essential for missionaries to confine their efforts to the presentation of Christ himself, leaving all doctrinal or theological system till later. In his quest for the undogmatic Christ, Slater thus conveniently ignored the essential contradiction between Hindu and Christian ethics posed by the relegation to a status beyond the ranks of full humanity of all *avarna* ('colourless', meaning the Dalit peoples outside of the fourfold colour-coded structure of the Hindu caste system) and *adivasi* (aboriginal or tribal) peoples.

The task of mission, in Slater's view, was simply to bring India to Christ, leaving Indians in their own way to systematize what they saw in Christ according to the fabric of eastern thought. This approach was said to imply, for example, that the central Christian doctrine of the incarnation of God in Christ was to be presented, not as 'an isolated historical fact' — which was unacceptable to the Hindu passion for unity, but as the natural culmination of God as the Logos 'working Himself into our humanity as an eternal process, till He becomes its final revelation.'[60] Slater was not indifferent to the charge that he was diluting the uniqueness of Christianity, and even warned that 'there can be on our part no Hinduising of Christianity'. All that was distinctive and unique in the Christian message must be preserved, but there was a happy spiritual affinity between 'exactly those elements in the Christian Gospel and life which are most distinctive, and all that was 'best and highest' in the Hindu religious nature. There was a blessed, indeed providential convergence between the higher Hinduism and the essential Christianity: what was 'distinctive' in Christianity was, according to Slater, not distinctive after all.[61] The

---

59. Commission IV replies, 229, pp. 70-6.
60. Commission IV replies, 229, continuation papers, pp. 4-6, 21-2.
61. Commission IV replies, 229, continuation papers, pp. 6-7.

world had been governed providentially with the goal that all religions should develop towards their completion in Christianity. Even Slater, for all his theological liberalism, held that 'apart from Christ, these old religions are fragmentary and decaying systems, and this is their weakness and their sadness; their capacity of union with Him is their strength and justification.'[62]

The Influence of Alfred George Hogg

Adherence to fulfilment theology did not imply any diminution in belief in the impending universal triumph of Christianity: it had merely (though radically) re-conceived the process which would effect that triumph of displacement. Neither, conversely, did openness to new theological influences from Germany lead necessarily to an endorsement of the idea that Christian truth could simply be presented as the fulfilment of the highest aspirations of Hindu devotion. Arguably the most creative theologian represented in the Commission IV replies was Alfred George Hogg, a lay missionary of the United Free Church of Scotland and professor of mental and moral science at Madras Christian College. Hogg had been deeply influenced as a theological student by the writings of the German Protestant theologians Albrecht Ritschl, William Herrmann, and Julius Kaftan on the Kingdom of God and the atonement. He was a close friend of David Cairns, and in addition to submitting a sixty-six-page response to the Commission IV questionnaire, sent Cairns his recently published *Karma and Redemption: an essay toward the interpretation of Hinduism and the re-statement of Christianity* (1909).[63] Cairns was lavish in his praise for Hogg's response, and was so impressed with *Karma and Redemption* that he ordered copies for all members of the Commission, together, very probably, with two articles written by Hogg for the *Madras Christian College Magazine* on 'Christianity as emancipation from this world'. The two men were also in regular correspondence from June 1909 until the conference assembled in June 1910 — in other words, during the very period when Cairns was putting the Commission IV report into its final form.[64]

62. Commission IV replies, 229, p. 59, cited in Cracknell, *Justice, Courtesy and Love*, p. 119.

63. A. G. Hogg, *Karma and Redemption: an essay toward the interpretation of Hinduism and the re-statement of Christianity* (Madras: Christian Literature Society, 1909).

64. Cox, 'The development of A. G. Hogg's theology', pp. 42, 109-110, 113, 115-16; Eric J. Sharpe, *Alfred George Hogg* (Chennai: Christian Literature Society, 1999), p. 94; idem, *Not to Destroy*, pp. 288-9, 293-5. The Hogg-Cairns correspondence forms part of the Hogg collection (see footnote 44 above). Cox, p. 458, lists eight letters exchanged between Hogg and

Hogg's lengthy questionnaire response included a summary dismissal both of the conservative theological position which held that all non-Christians were destined for hell and of a traditional style of missionary apologetic that presented Christianity as an intellectually demonstrable and supremely rational system of ideas. He also had little time for what he termed the presumptuous claim that the missionary could present himself as one who had found what India through the ages had been seeking: the history of Indian religion, Hogg protested, had been one of 'finding as well as a seeking'.[65] Hogg went on to repudiate the view that Christianity could be presented as the fulfilment of Hinduism, and gently criticised Cairns's question 6 for presupposing an acceptance of the fulfilment theory.[66] Hogg suggested that a more fruitful question would have been to ask 'where one can most readily create in the Hindu consciousness points of contact with the Christian consciousness, and thereby prepare the way for the emergence of an Indian type of Christianity?'[67] Although fulfilment theory had the merit of conceding that there had been 'partial finding' in Hinduism, it was founded on a fundamental misconception:

> Christian doctrines are not the fulfilment of Hindu doctrines, nor Christian rites of Hindu rites. Christian ideals of practice do not uniformly commend themselves to Hindus as better than their own, and if it be alleged that the Christian's experience of Christian religious fruition is a deeper satisfaction of his religious yearning than the Hindu finds in his own experience of Hindu religious fruition, the assertion is one incapable of proof or disproof.[68]

According to Hogg, Christian belief fulfilled the yearning only of a Hindu consciousness that had been thrown out of equilibrium by the weight of Christian influence in India; 'Christianity is the solution of a religious problem which the typical Hindu does not feel but which, under favourable conditions, he can be made to feel.' If Christianity was beginning to look like the fulfilment of Hinduism, it had done so, at least partially, by destroying the stability of the previous religion.[69]

Cairns in the period from June 1909 to June 1910, though Mrs Sharpe has been unable to locate any correspondence between Cairns and Hogg between 23 March and 12 Sept. 1910.

65. Commission IV replies, 176, pp. 11-13.

66. *Ibid.*, p. 25.

67. Commission IV replies, 176, pp. 30-1; cited in *Report of Commission IV*, p. 185.

68. *Ibid.*, 13-14, cited in Cracknell, *Justice, Courtesy, and Love*, p. 240.

69. Commission IV replies, 176, pp. 14-15.

Hogg's response then proceeded to expound what he felt to be the only way to achieve the goal of 'not simply Christianity in India but an Indian Christianity'. Rather than concluding, as Slater and Howells among other respondents did, that this called for a theologically minimalist Christianity that confined itself to telling the story of Jesus, Hogg insisted that the gospel always interpreted history, that Jesus could not be described without also proclaiming him as Christ. Although initially this compelled the missionary to employ western theological categories, in time these would be modified by growing contact with Indian religious ideas. However, rather than seeking any form of convergence, the missionary should seek out points of religious difference, deliberately aiming to upset the equilibrium of Hindu consciousness at the very points at which spiritual dissatisfaction would arise for a Christian if he were compelled to accept the truth of Hindu ideas. At the same time the missionary should 'seek to work out such a reformulation of his own Christian beliefs as will enable him most strikingly and persuasively to exhibit Christ as the Satisfier of the new sense of need which his work is awakening.'[70] This dialectical approach, which Hogg himself was later to describe as 'challenging relevancy',[71] was in fact deeply subversive of the doctrinal minimalism which Hogg had imbibed from German sources as a student in Scotland. In his response he described how he had accepted a Ritschlian theological framework that had evacuated the doctrines of the divinity of Christ and the atonement of any specific content other than the role they played in the consciousness of the believer. He had arrived in India with 'a very slender equipment of crystallised doctrinal belief', supposing that the historical basis of Christian doctrine could be minimised and subsumed within a monistic religious philosophy. India, however, had effected a 'radical change' in his thinking, forcing him to assert two fundamentals unique to Christianity: the affirmation that God was active Will, self-expressed in history, and culminating in the fact of the coming of Jesus Christ; and the principle of divine grace, always treating humans better than they deserve, a principle that stood in sharp contrast to the Hindu doctrine of Karma, and one that Hogg now declared to be 'the essential message of Christianity.'[72]

Hogg's encounter with Hindus had impelled him towards a reaffirmation of the distinctiveness of Christian doctrine and the enunciation of a Christian apologetic towards Hinduism that, while recognizing the real-

---

70. *Ibid.*, pp. 20-22.

71. Eric J. Sharpe, *From Faith to Faith: some Christian attitudes to Hinduism in the nineteenth and twentieth centuries* (London: SCM Press, 1977), p. 40.

72. Commission IV replies, 176, pp. 59-61.

ity and value of Hindu spiritual experience, emphasized the discontinuity and contrast between Hindu and Christian beliefs. He achieved this balance between spiritual continuity and theological discontinuity by means of a distinction, characteristic of Ritschlian theology, between *faith* and *faiths* (or doctrines). Hogg, like most of the advocates of fulfilment theology, believed that Hindus could exhibit a saving faith in response to the imperfect divine revelation they had received; much more emphatically than them, however, he stressed the radical distinctiveness of the Christian belief in the unique self-manifestation of God in Christ as the supreme revelation which must be proclaimed to Hindus, in order to awaken that sense of religious need which would impel them to discover the only form of faith that would prove enduring in a changing world.[73]

James Cox and Eric Sharpe have demonstrated that Hogg's influence lay behind the bold contention in Cairns's 'General Conclusions' to the Commission IV report that the redemption from the world effected by the Kingdom of God was of a totality in scope, embracing even the suffering embedded in the natural order, that Hinduism, for all of its challenge to the naturalism of the degenerate Christian West, could not match.[74] It was an argument that Cairns found immensely helpful as he wrestled with the personal trauma of his wife's terminal illness; the 'General Conclusions' faithfully reproduced Hogg's insistence that 'primitive Christianity was supernaturalist through and through'.[75] Hogg's thesis, replicated in the report, was that Hinduism pointed naturalized modern Christianity in the right direction by its emphasis on redemption from the world by union with the Supreme Being. Hindus could help Christians to rediscover the early Christian teaching that the Kingdom of God was not merely about inward deliverance from the power of sin, but 'ultimate deliverance from everything that cripples and depresses the entire life of man'. The Kingdom would indeed be realized in the world by the union of humans with God, but this was a union that would be effected, not, as in Vedanta, by abstraction from the body, but only by personal faith in Christ.[76]

Hogg's position represented a substantial modification of the presumption shared by so many of his Indian colleagues, and which Cairns's question

73. Cox, 'The development of A. G. Hogg's theology', pp. 438-40.

74. *Ibid.*, pp. 110-19, 122-3; Sharpe, *Not to Destroy*, pp. 291-6, cf. *Report of Commission IV*, pp. 249-53. Hogg's theology of 'redemption from the world' was drawn, with modifications, from Julius Kaftan.

75. Cox, 'The development of A. G. Hogg's theology', p. 109; *Report of Commission IV*, p. 251.

76. *Report of Commission IV*, pp. 249-50, 257-9.

6 had actively encouraged, that the 'correct' missionary approach in any context was to uncover those points of similarity between Christianity and non-Christian religions in order to employ them as 'preparation' for a fuller acceptance of Christian truth. The 'General Conclusions' to the report retained the idea of Christ as the one who fulfils 'the elemental needs of the human soul' as disclosed in other religions, and in one crucial passage affirmed Slater's contention that the missionary should 'seek for the nobler elements in the non-Christian religions and use them as steps to higher things'. However, Cairns immediately qualified this statement with an explicit assertion of the 'absoluteness and finality of Christ':

> . . . Nowhere [in the questionnaire responses] is the slightest support found for the idea that Christianity is only one religion among others, or that all religions are simply different ways of seeking the one Father, and therefore equally pleasing in His sight. One massive conviction animates the whole evidence that Jesus Christ fulfils and supersedes all other religions, and that the day is approaching when to Him every knee shall bow and every tongue confess that He is Lord to the glory of God the Father.[77]

The Commission IV report thus expounded a highly qualified version of fulfilment theology. Chapter VI of the report, devoted to Hinduism, drafted by Robinson, came closest to an unambiguous endorsement of fulfilment theory through its sustained commendatory references to the replies of T. E. Slater, C. F. Andrews, Bernard Lucas, J. N. Farquhar, and other advocates of fulfilment theology. Cairns's 'General Conclusions', on the other hand, were heavily indebted to Hogg's theological arguments which undermined the desire of Slater and his ilk to present a doctrinally minimalist Christianity. The passage cited above (which does not form part of the section which Cox attributes to Hogg's collaboration with Cairns)[78] is in fact the only place in the 'General Conclusions' in which explicit reference is made to ideas of fulfilment. Cairns devoted far more space to an extended exposition of Hogg's 'supernaturalist' theology of the transforming power of the Spirit, appropriated through faith in Christ. Cairns wished that he could have affirmed Hogg's views even more openly than he did: he confessed both to Hogg and to his own brother-in-law that he had not been able to say in the report nearly

---

77. *Ibid.*, pp. 267-8.
78. Cox, 'The development of A. G. Hogg's theology', p. 110, identifies pp. 246-67 as the section which reflects Hogg's collaboration with Cairns.

all that he would have liked, but was constrained by the need to carry all members of the Commission with him.[79] In reality the gap between Slater or Farquhar and Hogg was not as large as might be supposed: all affirmed the finality of Christ, and all advocated a form of missionary apologetic which affirmed both continuities and discontinuities between Hinduism and Christianity. Even Hogg, despite his insistence that missionaries to Hindus should first identify points of religious difference rather than similarity, depended on a prior (and, it must be said, strained) analogy between Hindu and Christian doctrines of redemption from the world for his claim that the uniqueness of Christianity lay in the response of faith to the self-revelation of God in Christ.[80]

The Relation of Islam to Christianity

David Cairns confessed to his brother-in-law that Alfred Garvie, who was responsible for the section on Islam in the report, was 'one of the men of whom I was most doubtful' with regard to how they would respond to the argument of the report as a whole. This was despite the fact that Garvie was the first British theologian to expound Ritschl's theology sympathetically.[81] In fact, to Cairns' relief, Garvie cordially welcomed the draft of the report when it appeared in February 1910.[82] Nevertheless, Garvie's section frankly acknowledged the extreme difficulty of assimilating Islam to a philosophy of fulfilment. Islam, wrote Garvie,

> cannot be regarded as anticipation, however defective, of the Christian Gospel, a promise to which Christ gives fulfilment. It is not only later in point of time, but it has also borrowed from Christianity as well as from Judaism, degrading what it has borrowed, and it claims the right in virtue of its superiority to supersede and supplant Christianity.[83]

79. Hogg collection, Cairns to Hogg, 19 March 1910, cited in Sharpe, *Not to Destroy*, p. 295 and Cox, 'The development of A. G. Hogg's theology', pp. 116-17; AUL, D. S. Cairns papers, MS 3384/1/6/1900-1912, Cairns to James Hewat Craw, 18 Feb. 1910.

80. Hedges, *Preparation and Fulfilment*, pp. 358-60, also concludes that in some respects Hogg was closer to the fulfilment theologians he criticised than some commentators have implied.

81. Cox, 'The development of A. G. Hogg's theology', p. 41, n. 43.

82. AUL, D. S. Cairns papers, MS 3384/1/6/1900-1912, David S. Cairns to James Hewat Craw, 18 Feb. 1910.

83. *Report of Commission IV*, p. 140.

Garvie went on to quote from Temple Gairdner's recently published *The Reproach of Islam* which avowed that 'it is more difficult to concede to it [Islam] what is gladly conceded to other religions that appeared before Christ, that they in some part [Gairdner's original has 'sort'] prepared and prepare the way for Him.'[84] In his questionnaire response, Gairdner, whose contributions to the Pan-Anglican Congress of 1908 had established his reputation as the leading Anglican expert on Islam, made the same point in language too blunt to be reproduced in the report, asserting that it was 'so transparently absurd to take this attitude towards a faith which explicitly says it came to *supersede* the *original* revelation of Jesus and to *destroy* the *current* religion of Jesus.' The only sense in which Gairdner, from the perspective of his own missionary experience in Cairo, saw some validity in the approach commended by question 6 was in his acceptance that to agree with a Muslim on 'some common doctrine or some O.T. story' 'puts him in a good humour and makes him willing to consider the next thing you say': it was a 'somewhat more *external matter*' than the advocates of fulfilment had in mind, more an evangelistic method than a theological principle.[85] At this stage in his theological pilgrimage, Gairdner evinced scant sympathy for the Commission's evident enthusiasm for the discovery of an 'Eastern Christ' as opposed to the 'Western Christ' allegedly proclaimed by missions:

> This distinction hails from India; and whatever meaning they attach to it there, (and I am not convinced it has any very deep meaning), it has none in our part of the East I am glad to say. . . . The Christ of the Gospel is so clearly a fellow-countryman (if I may say so) to the Egyptian and Palestinian of today, that he figures Him without effort as what He indeed was. Moreover our people grasp that the Son of Man is neither Eastern nor Western, but universal; more particularly since after breaking through the barrier of His earth-born flesh and putting on a heavenly body, He broke down the race-barriers down [*sic*] here also and made us all one in Him. The preaching of the Missionaries as far as I can make out, is not in the least felt to be tinctured by any Western dye, whether in content or presentation.[86]

Gairdner should not be misunderstood as suggesting that the Islamic context should have no effect at all on Christian proclamation. On the contrary,

---

84. *Ibid.*, p. 141, citing W. H. T. Gairdner, *The Reproach of Islam* (London: CMS, 1909), p. 311.
85. Commission IV replies, 263, pp. 5-7.
86. *Ibid.*, pp. 13-14.

his answer to question 10 ('Has your experience in missionary labour altered either in form or in substance your impression as to what constitute the most important and vital elements in the Christian Gospel?') explained how his presentation of the Trinity had been modified by his exposure to Muslims away from the fine metaphysical distinctions of European theology towards a more practical emphasis that the Holy Spirit was always the Spirit of the Incarnate One, the Spirit of Jesus.[87] Gairdner was far from an arch-conservative, and Garvie quoted him liberally and approvingly in the report. Gairdner's published account of Edinburgh 1910 hailed the Commission IV report as a masterpiece and 'perhaps the most remarkable, of a great series'. Yet it is noticeable that his chapter on Commission IV strangely devotes least attention to the sections of the report on Islam and Hinduism, even though they are said to be of 'greater intrinsic interest'.[88] That may have been Gairdner's way of quietly suppressing the discomforting tension between the report's predominant emphasis on the need for a sympathetic evaluation of non-Christian religions as a *praeparatio evangelica,* an emphasis which in general he warmly endorsed, and his continuing grave reservations about the applicability of such an approach to Islam, which he still saw as 'the great antagonist' of Christianity. Michael Shelley has observed the rapidity with which Gairdner's attitude to Islam developed in the months after the Edinburgh conference, as he pursued a year of study leave from his work with the CMS in Cairo, sitting at the feet of such notable Islamic scholars as Duncan Black Macdonald in Hartford, Connecticut, and Ignaz Goldziher in Budapest. Shelley concludes, however, that, whilst the work of Commission IV made a deep impression on Gairdner, it did no more than make him more hopeful that a way might somehow be found of developing a more sympathetic attitude to Islam: only later in his *'Wanderjahr'* did Gairdner discover such a road for himself.[89] Nevertheless, it should be noted that by September 1909 Gairdner was in friendly personal correspondence with Cairns, in which he was ready to concede that there was no ultimate contradiction between his own view that 'Islam is the greatest *direct* contradiction of Christianity in any form I know' and Cairns' inclination to stress the historical genesis of Islam as an offspring, albeit illegitimate, of Christianity.[90]

---

87. *Ibid.,* pp. 12-13, cited in *Report of Commission IV,* p. 153.

88. Gairdner, *'Edinburgh 1910',* pp. 134-5, 147.

89. Michael T. Shelley, 'The life and thought of W. H. T. Gairdner, 1873-1928: a critical evaluation of a scholar-missionary to Islam' (University of Birmingham PhD thesis, 1988), pp. 52-3, 109, 116-24, 146-51. See also Gairdner, *'Edinburgh 1910',* p. 148.

90. AUL, D. S. Cairns papers, MS 3384/3/3/1906-1933, W. H. Temple Gairdner to David S. Cairns, 17 Sept. 1909.

As Garvie's summary quoted above suggests, Gairdner's repudiation of any idea of Islam as constituting a *praeparatio evangelica* was in fact shared, to a greater or lesser extent, by almost all the respondents from the Muslim world. W. St. Clair Tisdall from the CMS Persia mission was equally emphatic that Islam could not be said to be a preparation for the older religion of Christianity, but was, on the contrary, one of the greatest hindrances to the spread of Christianity.[91] Two other CMS missionaries from northern Nigeria, W. R. Miller and T. E. Alvarez, declared roundly that 'only a superficial knowledge of Islam will ever lead missionaries to see many points of contact between it and our faith.'[92] Henry Jessup, from the American Presbyterian mission in Beirut, spoke for a number of respondents in his argument that the long-held supposition that Islam was 'a kind of quarantine of the nations previously pagan and idolatrous, through which they would the more readily pass on to Christianity' had been disproved by the reality that it was easier to convert a 'heathen' tribe to Christianity than one which had first converted to Islam.[93]

Several of the replies to question 6 from missionaries to the Muslim world did not deny that 'points of contact' between Christianity and Islam existed. Walter Rice of the CMS, working among the Shias of Persia, identified several areas of common doctrinal ground, which were 'valuable as a starting point' for Christian evangelism. Yet their role as a preparation for the actual reception of Christian truth was limited, for they manifestly did not make it any easier for Muslims to substitute the Christian versions of such doctrines for their own.[94] W. A. Shedd, an American Presbyterian missionary in Persia, went further than most in listing such points of commonality with a breadth of sympathy that commended itself to Garvie (who quoted him repeatedly) and in more recent times to Kenneth Cracknell, yet even Shedd admitted that almost all of his points of contact 'often seem to be hindrances rather than preparations', adding that 'one often longs to find minds without these ideas rather than to find minds filled with apparently similar but really perverted beliefs as compared with those of Christianity.'[95] 'Points of contact' which one longed to be rid of in order to clear the ground for effective Christian proclamation were

91. Commission IV replies, 271, p. 4, cited in Cracknell, *Justice, Courtesy and Love*, p. 236.

92. Commission IV replies, 300, p. 7.

93. Commission IV replies, 266, p. 4.

94. Commission IV replies, 270, pp. 20-1, cited in Cracknell, *Justice, Courtesy and Love*, p. 236.

95. Commission IV replies, 272, pp. 17-20; Report of Commission IV, p. 337 (index entries under Shedd); Cracknell, *Justice, Courtesy and Love*, pp. 233-5.

surely not quite what Cairns had in mind in drafting question 6. Although Cracknell is right to point out that few respondents explicitly denounced Islam as satanic,[96] the prevailing attitudes of respect, even sympathy, for Islam displayed by the respondents from the Muslim world did not extend to support for those theories of religious development that missionaries in contact with the 'higher Hinduism' had been so effective in promoting.

The Religions of Japan and China

Missionaries working in Japan were probably closer in their theological positions to their Indian colleagues than those in any other field. Japan in 1910 exhibited an impressive union of an ancient civilization with a rapidly modernizing economy and society, and the thesis that the Spirit of God was at work in the evolving processes of religious as well as social and economic change was an attractive one. Cracknell has documented several instances of Japan respondents who took this view.[97] He devotes sustained attention to Arthur Lloyd, a somewhat maverick Anglican who by 1910 was operating in Japan on a free-lance basis, having served previously as a missionary first with the SPG and then with the Protestant Episcopal Church of the USA.[98] Lloyd's questionnaire response alluded to his personal evolution 'from a more or less straight-laced Anglican to the nondescript Christian that I am now', and identified the Amitabha form of Mahayana Buddhism as a faith 'so wonderfully like Christianity that it is difficult to resist the inference that it was in the divine Providence intended as a Praeparatio Evangelica for the Gospel in Japan. It is theological, it recognises man as a sinner, it preaches the Gospel to the Poor, and it has a Salvation by Faith in a Saviour who has done everything for the soul.'[99]

Bishop C. F. D'Arcy, author of the Japanese section of the report, had been impressed by Lloyd's contributions to the Pan-Anglican Congress in 1908, and in 1909-10 he found Lloyd's replies 'the most interesting' of all those received from Japan; D'Arcy's text accordingly cited him more extensively than any of the other twenty-six respondents from Japan.[100] Probably more repre-

---

96. Cracknell, *Justice, Courtesy and Love*, p. 232.

97. *Ibid.*, pp. 214, 216-17, 221.

98. *Ibid.*, pp. 151-61.

99. Commission IV replies, 28A, pp. 7-9. Citations in *Report of Commission IV*, p. 118; Cracknell, *Justice, Courtesy, and Love*, pp. 158-9.

100. Cracknell, *Justice, Courtesy and Love*, pp. 152, 359; D'Arcy, *Adventures of a Bishop*, p. 170.

sentative of Japanese Protestantism as a whole, however, was the joint response of William Imbrie of the American Presbyterian Mission and Ibuka
Kajinosuke, the leading Japanese Presbyterian minister who was a delegate at
Edinburgh and the only non-western member of the influential business
committee.[101] They reported that among the indigenous Japanese ministry
were some who were

> quite well informed as to the new emphasis which is placed upon the el-
> ements of truth contained in the non-Christian religions. There is a
> conviction common among them that the non-Christian religions are
> not wholly of man. At times they think of them and speak of them as a
> preparation for Christianity; sometimes comparing them to Judaism, as
> shadows of the good things to come. Certainly they have no desire un-
> duly to cast discredit upon the national religions in which most of them
> were born.

Nevertheless, Imbrie and Ibuka went on to emphasize that 'the great majority of these men, even of those among them who would be accounted liberal in their views', followed the apostolic example of Paul on Mars Hill in
combining open-mindedness and tact with candour in speaking of the inad-
equacies of non-Christian belief. They exemplified what should be a model
for all Christian proclamation in their union of irenicism with polemi-
cism.[102] In addition to several other quotations from Imbrie and Ibuka, the
report cited the first part of this response, as far as 'the good things to come',
but pointedly omitted the second part. D'Arcy did, however, reproduce part
of their reply to question 6, which argued that the points of contact between
Shintoism or Buddhism and Christianity were no more than 'tapers flicker-
ing in the night and in the wind', being 'far outweighed by elements which
are fundamentally at variance with Christianity', and observed that their
view stood 'in very striking contrast' to that of Arthur Lloyd. The salvation
of Amida (or Amithaba), which Lloyd set such store by, was, in the view of
Imbrie and Ibuka, not a salvation from sin, but, like the Hindu *moksha*, a deliverance from the material world of sorrow and suffering.[103] Ibuka's individual response to the Commission III questionnaire on Christian education

101. On Ibuka (1854-1940) and his role at Edinburgh see Chapter 5 above, pp. 115-17. Although the response is listed as a joint one, the text seems in reality to have been written by
Imbrie.

102. Commission IV replies, 17/19, pp. 6-7; Cracknell, *Justice, Courtesy and Love*, p. 210.

103. Commission IV replies, 17/19, pp. 7-10; *Report of Commission IV*, p. 99; Cracknell,
Justice, Courtesy and Love, pp. 236-7.

makes it very clear that in his view the points of contact between Christianity and the traditional religious thought of Japan were less substantial than the points of contrast and opposition.[104] The Japan section of the Commission IV report again reveals a strong presumption in favour of the fulfilment thesis; though the existence of other views was given some attention, D'Arcy's preference for the position advanced by Arthur Lloyd left a clear imprint on the report.

The replies from China missionaries evidenced a similar variety of perspective. There were some enthusiastic advocates of fulfilment, and a few stalwart opponents of the whole idea. An example of the latter was the veteran CMS missionary, A. E. Moule.[105] Most notable among the former was Timothy Richard, the idiosyncratic Welsh Baptist who had found his missionary colleagues in the BMS too confining in their theology and discovered a more congenial home in the Christian Literature Society for China. Richard's response urged that 'we should rejoice greatly in the practice which the Chinese made of the revelation which God had given to them', making them 'superior to all civilized nations . . . even Christendom in the sixteenth and seventeenth centuries.' Richard identified truths in Confucianism, in what he termed 'advanced Buddhism' or 'Buddhist Christianity', and in Taoism, which found their fulfilment in Christianity. In Islam, however, Richard could locate no such truth other than 'loyalty to God'; he could see no future for a religion which 'assumes finality and refuses to grow', unless it were to be 'revived by the life-giving power of the Spirit of God.' Yet none of these religions, not even the best, was able to 'see the bearing of their creeds on the welfare of the human race as a whole. True Christianity alone, not the Greek form, not the Roman form, nor the Protestant form' possessed the capacity to win the allegiance of all religions and races, making them willing to 'unite in one Universal Kingdom of God.'[106]

A somewhat similar position was expounded by one of the three Chinese Christian respondents, C. T. Wang (Wang Cheng-Ting), who in 1915 became national secretary of the YMCA in China, and served on a number of occasions as minister of foreign affairs in the government of Nationalist China between 1922 and 1931. Wang was dismissive of older missionaries who could see no truth in Chinese religions, and was in no doubt that all great religious leaders had been sent by God. He insisted, however, that Confucianism was simply an ethical system rather than a religion, and stressed that the personality of God

104. Commission III replies, 5, pp. 148-9.

105. Commission IV replies, 82; cited in Cracknell, *Justice, Courtesy and Love*, p. 229.

106. Commission IV replies, 92, pp. 7-9. Richard had been seconded to the Christian Literature Society in 1891 by his original mission (the BMS), and retained a loose connection with the BMS. See Stanley, *History of the Baptist Missionary Society*, p. 195.

and the divinity of Christ were non-negotiable elements of Christianity which must be proclaimed despite their natural unacceptability to many Chinese.[107]

Probably the majority of China respondents were willing to regard the moral teachings of Confucius as in some sense a preparation for the acceptance of Christianity. Such was the view, for example, of Bishop James Bashford of the American Methodist Episcopal mission, James Beattie of the English Presbyterian mission, George Douglas of the United Free Church of Scotland mission in Manchuria, Frank Joseland of the LMS, and Henry M. Woods of the American Southern Presbyterian mission.[108] However, the precise theological meaning which such respondents attached to the principle of 'preparation' varied greatly. Paul Krantz was affiliated as an independent missionary to the Christian Literature Society in Shanghai, having broken his former connection with the Rheinische Mission on account of his opposition to their growing sympathy for higher criticism and the 'new theology', and his submission in 1906 to believer's baptism. Yet his response narrates how in 1902, four years *previously,* he had come to recognize as wrong his earlier rejoicing whenever he had discovered a flaw in Confucius' life or teaching. He now believed that missionaries should 'gather up the fragments of *original* revelation in the old religions and use them as *stepping stones* towards Christ'.[109] But this recognition should not place Krantz in the same theological camp as Slater, Farquhar, or even Richard (though Krantz acknowledges his indebtedness to Richard). His response expressed gratitude that higher criticism had not yet penetrated the Chinese churches, and emphasized that 'the high morality' of Confucianism 'saves nobody'; Confucianists were *'without hope',* though Krantz believed that they would not necessarily be subject to endless torment.[110]

Acceptance of 'points of contact' or preparation within Chinese ethical or religious ideas, and insistence on a respectful approach to Chinese religion and philosophy could thus exist within a conservative theological framework. Further evidence of this is supplied by the Canadian Presbyterian missionary

107. Commission IV replies, 104, pp. 1, 4-6. On Wang, who was in 1909 a student at Yale University, see Cracknell, *Justice, Courtesy and Love*, pp. 380-1; Howard L. Boorman and R. C. Howard (eds.), *Biographical Dictionary of Republican China*, 5 vols. (New York: Columbia University Press, 1967-79) III, pp. 362-4. He is not to be confused with Dr C. C. Wang, who attended the Edinburgh Conference as an unofficial delegate and spoke in the Commission VII debate.

108. Cracknell, *Justice, Courtesy and Love*, pp. 220-2.

109. Commission IV replies, 69, pp. 1, 5; Cracknell, *Justice, Courtesy and Love*, p. 243. Krantz drew the image of stepping-stones from an address by D. Z. Sheffield to the China Centenary Missionary Conference in 1907; see *Records: China Centenary Missionary Conference* (Shanghai: Centenary Conference Committee, 1907), p. 43.

110. Commission IV replies, 69, pp. 2, 8, 11, 12.

in Honan, Murdoch Mackenzie. Mackenzie made a list of ten such points of contact, and gave such pronounced emphasis to the importance of sympathy, attentiveness, and discrimination in missionary evangelism that Cracknell cannot resist hailing him as 'clearly a forerunner of contemporary theories of inter-religious dialogue.'[111] Yet Mackenzie professed himself just as disappointed with missionaries who were 'seemingly ever ready to see good in the non-Christian systems and ready to criticise their own' as he was with others who could 'see nothing worthy of attention in such systems.' 'As a matter of fact', he conceded, 'the non-Christian systems furnish but little of which we can make much practical use in our work.' Mackenzie found apparently irreconcilable contradictions between the Chinese belief in ancestors and a supreme being on the one hand, and their thorough-going materialism on the other. His answer to question 9 also suggests that he had no great enthusiasm for higher criticism.[112]

'Animistic' Religions and the Neglect of Africa

The report of Commission IV supplies perhaps the most striking evidence of the consistent marginalisation of Africa from the conference agenda at Edinburgh. The Commission sought (or at least *received*) responses from only 16 missionaries working in sub-Saharan Africa out a total of 187 responses from all fields; in addition to the 16, 11 missionaries submitted replies from other geographical contexts deemed by the Commission to be 'animistic' either in whole or in part. With the exception of T. E. Alvarez and W. R. Miller, who were listed in the Islamic rather than the animistic section of the report, the whole of the West African mission field was represented merely by one missionary from Sierra Leone (the Methodist, W. T. Balmer), one from the upper Congo (W. D. Armstrong of the Regions Beyond Missionary Union), and one retired missionary from Equatorial West Africa (the American Presbyterian, R. H. Nassau). East Africa had just two respondents — one from Uganda (Miss J. Elizabeth Chadwick), and one from Zanzibar (Canon Dale of the Universities' Mission to Central Africa). The remaining Africa respondents were all from southern Africa.[113]

---

111. Commission IV replies, 78, pp. 10-12, 13-16; Cracknell, *Justice, Courtesy and Love*, p. 207.

112. Commission IV replies, 78, pp. 12-13, 18, 20-1; see Cracknell, *Justice, Courtesy and Love*, p. 384; *Report of Commission IV*, p. 64.

113. *Report of Commission IV*, pp. xi-xii, xvi-xvii. In addition to the joint response from Alvarez and Miller, the Islam section of the report also considered responses from three

The problem which the Commission faced is that most of its respondents from Africa doubted the applicability of its predominant theology of religions to their own context, while some repudiated its validity altogether. The majority were unsure that African religiosity could supply any examples of what question 2 was looking for, as there was a conspicuous lack of formal acts of worship or 'religious observances' bringing what a European would have regarded as spiritual consolation or uplift. This was true even of respondents who were quite clear that what Africans possessed was indeed worthy of the label 'religion'. R. H. Nassau, a medical missionary who had worked for forty-five years in Equatorial West Africa, had published one of the earliest studies of traditional religion in West Africa, *Fetichism in West Africa* (1904). Although Nassau's book conceded that the religion of Africans came closer than that of any other people to being 'purely a superstition', his essential thesis was the universality of the 'sense of infinite dependence', an obvious allusion to Schleiermacher's famous identification of the essence of religion as 'the feeling of absolute dependence'. Africans in Nassau's view had a gravely defective knowledge of the character of the Supreme Being, and one that failed to influence their lives. Nonetheless, Nassau was prepared to call this imperfect knowledge of God a revelation from Jehovah himself: it was 'fearfully obscured and marred' because primal religion was a degeneration from original revealed monotheism.[114] In accordance with this interpretation, Nassau, in responding to the Edinburgh questionnaire, was more willing than most to recognise that even African religion contained 'at least a modicum of truth, and some fragments of a basis derived from forgotten traces of original light as God revealed it to our first parents'. Yet he was in no doubt that African religious thought was concerned only with physical well-being, and he could find 'nothing, in the Fetish Belief which was a religious help and consolation'. A poignant passage in which he described the desolation of African funeral rites was cited in the report as illustrative of the view of the majority of missionaries that traditional beliefs and rites were unable to supply 'any religious help or consolation'.[115]

Other respondents were in little doubt that the absence of such spiritual consolation meant that Africans, quite simply, had no religion. For example,

---

missionaries working in Cairo (Gairdner, George Swan of the Egypt General Mission, and Andrew Watson of the Presbyterian Church in the USA).

114. R. H. Nassau, *Fetichism in West Africa: forty years' observation of native customs and superstitions* (London: Duckworth, 1904), pp. 27, 32-7. On Nassau see *BDCM*; Friesen, *Missionary Responses to Tribal Religions*, pp. 122-4; and Cracknell, *Justice, Courtesy and Love*, pp. 381-2.

115. Commission IV replies, 303, pp. 1, 2, 5, cited in *Report of Commission IV*, p. 10.

W. D. Armstrong, who worked among the Balolo of the upper Congo, asserted bluntly that 'There is no religion in our district, simple [simply] heathenism. Religion is only represented by a few superstitions.'[116] His answer to question 2 began by reporting

> The people have no religious observances to speak of. They have a few tales or traditions which are quite apart from religion. They might be called stories with morals or perhaps fables, but they contain nothing of a consoling or helpful nature, nor have the native superstitions. . . . There is nothing in the beliefs of our people that is prized as a religious help or consolation.'[117]

In similar vein Elizabeth Chadwick, formerly of the CMS mission in Mengo, affirmed that 'The pagans of Uganda and surrounding tribes can scarcely be said to have any definite religion; certainly not set forms of religious observance.'[118]

Such observations cannot be dismissed as typical only of the conservative evangelical wing of the missionary movement, for almost identical verdicts were pronounced by the Anglo-Catholic missionaries of the SPG, whose incarnational theology might have been supposed to create greater sympathy for the possibility of divine presence in natural religion. The Revd Godfrey Callaway from Griqualand East began his response with the statement that 'There cannot be said to be any definite Non-Christian religions in this particular part of South Africa.' Callaway stressed that 'whatever belief in a supreme God the heathen people may give assent to in conversation, there is practically no sense of practical obligation due to such belief.'[119] Charles Johnson, archdeacon of Zululand, similarly insisted that 'Among the Zulus and Basutos there is nothing which could be called, strictly speaking, a religious system. . . . There are no doctrines or forms of religious observance which are helpful or consolatory to the Zulu mind. . . . The Zulu has probably no conception of spiritual consolation.'[120]

In reality the gap between an apparent 'progressive' such as Nassau and other respondents who hesitated to apply the term 'religion' to the African societies with which they were familiar, was quite narrow. The latter — for ex-

---

116. Commission IV replies, 284, p. 1, cited in part in *Report of Commission IV,* p. 6. See Friesen, *Missionary Responses to Tribal Religions,* pp. 117-21.

117. Commission IV replies, 284, p. 1.

118. Commission IV replies, 289, p. 1. See Friesen, *Missionary Responses to Tribal Religions,* pp. 118-19.

119. Commission IV replies, 287, pp. 1-2.

120. Commission IV replies, 298, p. 1.

ample, Godfrey Callaway — could be no less insistent that missionaries should adopt 'a sympathetic attitude . . . toward the heathen and toward the tribal life and customs which support it,' and could argue that African social systems displayed features of 'remarkable excellence' that provided the foundation for Christian social ethics.[121] W. T. Balmer in Sierra Leone regarded the points of contact between African religion and Christianity as 'very few and all perverted. I might mention the idea of sacrifice in fetishism. Anything else has seemed to me to be a wildering [sic] maze of superstition, which, but for its testimony to a spiritual world (of a kind) would be better left to die.' Nevertheless, Balmer insisted that the missionary's attitude to African religionists should be one of 'sympathy', and earnest striving to understand 'the native conception of things'.[122]

Almost all the Africa correspondents recorded the existence of a High Creator God figure in the cosmology of the peoples with whom they worked, as the report was eager to note.[123] Even Armstrong was prepared to give a positive answer to question 6, by reporting that the name of this God (Nzakomba in the case of the Balolo) had been adopted by the missions in their biblical translations, enabling missionaries to graft upon 'the imaginary "Nzakomba" the true and holy attributes of God.'[124] This implicit recognition of underlying religious continuity is in harmony with the emphasis of recent scholars, notably Andrew Walls and Lamin Sanneh, on the cultural and religious significance of the adoption by missionary translators of indigenous terms for the high God to describe the Christian deity.[125] However, most respondents, like Armstrong, saw little or no congruence between the attributes of the High God in African cosmologies and the Christian doctrine of God. Thus Donald Fraser of the Livingstonia Mission in what is now Malawi acknowledged that

> Our people believe in one supreme God. But the only thing they know about His character is that He is fierce. He is the creator, and is above all the forces of the world. But men have no access to him. No prayers or of-

121. Commission IV replies, 287, p. 3.

122. Commission IV replies, 285, pp. 5-6. (p. 5). Cracknell cites Balmer's commendation of sympathy as if it supplied evidence of theological progressivism, but ignores his virtual dismissal of 'points of contact' (*Justice, Courtesy, and Love*, pp. 199, 376).

123. *Report of Commission IV*, p. 25.

124. Commission IV replies, 284, pp. 3-4.

125. Andrew Walls, *The Missionary Movement in Christian History* (Edinburgh: T&T Clark, 1996), pp. 70-1; idem, *The Cross-Cultural Process in Christian History* (Edinburgh: T&T Clark, 2002), pp. 120-1; Lamin Sanneh, *Whose Religion is Christianity? The gospel beyond the West* (Grand Rapids and Cambridge: Eerdmans, 2004), pp. 18, 31-2.

ferings are made to Him. But He brings death into the home. And when a dear one is taken they say "God is fierce."[126]

Yet Fraser was happy to treat even such a belief as evidence that 'God has not left Himself without a witness among these people: that the God whom they ignorantly worship, we declare fully by the revelation of Christ.' The high God was indeed a valuable point of contact, but for Fraser, as for Gairdner in Egypt, the notion of 'points of contact' was to be understood primarily in an instrumental evangelistic sense. The deeper revelatory sense required by Cairns's theology posed a problem: if God had indeed chosen to reveal something of himself to the Ngoni and Tumbuka before the coming of Christianity, it seemed rather perverse that he should have disclosed his essential identity as being one of anger rather than of love. Fraser's solution was similar to Nassau's: what he was observing was the end-point of a process of religious decay, as his answer to question 2 put it:

> The two tribes among whom I work have less religion than any others possibly in Central Africa and there is now little of the old religious observances. What there is is not observable on the surface, and is rather disowned. But as far as my investigation has discovered there is practically no formal religion. What there is and was of the old type was genuine, for it was only remembered and observed in cases of necessity. There was no regular and formal worship of the spirits. . . . It is difficult to define what you mean by 'a religious help'. But I do not think I have found any one who sought or found elevation and purification of spirit in their religious rites. They were observed for purposes of religious necessity. But there was consolation. . . . To have a 'good spirit' was a relief and consolation.[127]

Professor W. P. Paterson, as the chief author of this section of the report, maintained that only a minority of respondents denied the existence of any religious content in animism and hence the possibility of any 'points of contact' with Christianity. This supposed minority view was ascribed to the 'idea that nothing deserves the name of religion which is false and unethical',[128] despite

126. Commission IV replies, 295, p. 9, cited in *Report of Commission IV*, p. 25.
127. Commission IV replies, 295, pp. 1-2. See Friesen, *Missionary Responses to Tribal Religions*, pp. 110-111.
128. *Report of Commission IV*, pp. 6, 24-25. Friesen, *Missionary Responses to Tribal Religions*, p. 117, accepts Paterson's statements uncritically. Cracknell, *Justice, Courtesy and Love*, p. 190, suggests that Warneck collaborated with Paterson in the writing of the animism section.

the fact that most missionaries in Hindu contexts at the time still regarded Hinduism as both false and ethically deficient, yet did not hesitate to call it a religion. Paterson instead gave prominence to those respondents, notably Nassau, who appeared closer to the theological stance of the Commission in being prepared to see the African belief in a creator God, personal immortality, occasional practice of prayer to the Great Spirit, and usage of sacrifice and religious ritual as bridging points for the teaching of Christian doctrine.[129]

Nassau, however, was in fact a stalwart *opponent* of evolutionary theories of religious development; as we have seen, he saw primal religions as representing an advanced stage of religious decay rather than an early stage of religious development. The report strained the evidence in its anxiety to accommodate Africa missionaries into the Commission's dominating theological paradigm which wished to show that, whatever errors needed correction by the light of the gospel, 'all that was noblest in the old religions was fulfilled in Christ'.[130] Charles Johnson, for example, was placed in the majority category of those who allegedly allowed for some form of contact on the slender basis of his recognition that the Zulus believed in 'a shadowy being who created the world and afterwards abandoned it.'[131] But Johnson's answer to question 6, 'I do not know of anything which could be regarded either as presenting points of contact with Christianity or as a preparation for it,' was ignored. So were his statements that the Zulu supreme being was 'so remote that they have no care for or respect for him', and that belief in such a being had no impact on everyday life or morals.'[132] Similarly, Elizabeth Chadwick's acknowledgement that 'Certain tribes, I think by no means all, seem to have had a vague idea of a supreme Creator' was quoted in the report (though without the qualification in parentheses) as evidently sufficient to reckon her on the side of the angels, whereas her robust answer to question 6 — advocating that 'the Christian teacher must almost ignore the old faiths in Uganda; and that there was very little point of contact, beyond their vague impression that there might be some sort of future life' — was omitted.[133]

Friesen's attempt to isolate five distinct models of theoretical relationship between primal religions and Christianity in the Commission IV responses is unpersuasive.[134] The differences between Nassau, Fraser, Armstrong, and

---

129. Commission IV replies, 303, pp. 8-9, 12-13. See *Report of Commission IV*, pp. 10, 15, 21-22, 24-5, 28-9, 32.

130. *Report of Commission IV*, p. 279.

131. *Ibid.*, p. 25.

132. Commission IV replies, 298, p. 5.

133. *Report of Commission IV*, p. 25; Commission IV replies, 289, pp. 1 and 3.

134. Friesen, *Missionary Responses to Tribal Religions*, pp. xiii-xiv and *passim*.

Johnson, for instance, lay not in degrees of cultural sympathy with Africans but in formal categories of analysis. Nassau thought Africans had religion, but that it offered no spiritual consolation. Fraser deemed the religion residual at best, but believed he could find evidence for consolation. Armstrong denied that Africans had religion, but identified belief in a Supreme Being as a useful point of contact. Johnson could find neither evidence of consolation nor points of contact, yet perceived more clearly than almost any other respondent that the real challenge then facing Christianity in Africa was not intellectual but rather its exotic status, being identified in the Zulu mind 'with the white man and his ways.'[135]

The confused and unsystematic nature of the spectrum of opinion reflects the uncertainty in European evaluation of 'primal' peoples during the high colonial period: were they defined in part by the absence from their societies of the Enlightenment category of 'religion', or were their beliefs to be organised, classified, and labelled by western theorists according to the extent of their consonance or dissonance with European norms of what 'religion' was? David Chidester contends that Europeans in the late nineteenth and early twentieth centuries constructed or even 'invented' the discrete religious systems of different African peoples as part of the process of systematising ethnographic knowledge that was essential to the consolidation of colonial control. Chidester argues that in southern Africa the transition from denying that Africans had any religion to the discovery that they had it after all was a function, not of growing European perception, but of growing European power: it was contingent on the closure of the colonial frontier with Xhosa, Zulu, and Sotho-Tswana peoples.[136] The evidence of the Commission IV replies throws Chidester's thesis into question, for by 1910 the frontier was closed in most, if not all of the contexts in which the African respondents worked, and yet some of them, as we have seen, continued to deny that African belief and practice merited the label 'religion'. Nevertheless, in an intellectual climate in which the new European 'science of religion' was straining to include a wider range of human societies in its categorisation, to deny that Africans possessed 'religion' was not necessarily evidence of racist myopia, nor was the contrary insistence that they had it automatically a sign of the theological progressivism that well-meaning modern commentators imagine. As Rosalind Shaw has pointed out, Africans themselves did not share the European view of 'religion' as a sphere of dogma or belief separate from this-

135. Commission IV replies, 298, p. 2.
136. D. Chidester, *Savage Systems: colonialism and comparative religion in southern Africa* (Charlottesville and London: University Press of Virginia, 1996), pp. 1-29, 219-25.

worldly concerns, and in most cases had no word in their languages to express such a concept.[137] Those respondents in 1909-10 who genuinely doubted whether Africans possessed any 'religious system' but who stressed the fundamental importance to African peoples of custom, tradition, and communal identity, may in fact have been the most discerning observers.[138]

Africa thus posed a dilemma to the authors of the Commission IV report. The final chapter, containing Cairns's 'General Conclusions', almost entirely ignored the African continent, with only three passing references in its sixty-seven pages.[139] The section which summarised the report's findings on 'animistic religions' was largely devoted to a discussion of Warneck's argument on the basis of his Sumatran experience that the Christian message to the animist must focus on the unity, omnipotence, and love of God. This was the emphasis which made the greatest appeal to the 'childlike faith' of the animist, and was the necessary foundation for Christian morality. Yet the report went on to admit that converts from animism displayed a simple faith in the capacity of God to intervene in the natural order that was closer to the Hebraic religion of the Psalms than it was to western Christianity, with its scientific view of nature 'as a closed system'.[140] Cairns seems to have been unsure about how to integrate primal religions into his theological system, torn between, on the one hand, Warneck's conviction that animism was a primitive and amoral worldview that had to be demolished, and, on the other, a sneaking admiration for the vitality and immediacy of faith that converts from such a background displayed.

Louis Brenner has argued that many academic studies of religion in Africa continue to demonstrate a similar set of assumptions to those displayed by the Commission IV questionnaire. They privilege knowledge and belief above communal participation, and persist in treating religion as 'an institutionally and conceptually distinct category of analysis'. 'Religious' activity in Africa does exactly the reverse, privileging ritual participation above knowl-

137. R. Shaw, 'The invention of "African traditional religion"', *Religion* 20:4 (1990), pp. 339-53.

138. See P. Landau, ' "Religion" and Christian conversion in African history: a new model', *Journal of Religious History* 23:1 (Feb. 1999), pp. 8-30; J. D. Y. Peel, review of P. McKenzie, 'Hail Orisha! a phenomenology of a West African religion in the mid-nineteenth century', *Journal of Religion in Africa* 30:3 (2000), pp. 401-3.

139. Report of Commission IV, pp. 218, 243, 271-2n. The final reference notes the forthcoming work by Henri Junod, published in two volumes in 1912 and 1913 as *The Life of a South African Tribe*. Friesen, *Missionary Responses*, p. 77, suggests that W. P. Patterson had access to a preliminary draft of Junod's work, but there is evidence only that Junod submitted a note on the tribes of Delagoa Bay: *Report of Commission IV*, p. 7.

140. *Report of Commission IV*, pp. 220-1.

edge or belief, and refusing to separate ritual activities from those various spheres which a European would label respectively as economics, agriculture, politics, or medicine.[141] Brenner cites with evident approval the leading Africanist, Jan Vansina, whose monograph on the Tio of the Congo concluded that 'one should not consider that the Tio had a system of beliefs in the supernatural. There was no system. Beliefs were linked to rituals and symbols and ritual was tied to specific situations. . . . The Tio had no sacred books, no dogma, no catechism, no compulsion to believe the same things as long as they participated fully in the same rituals.'[142]

There are, of course, major differences in cultural tone and assumption between the position of Vansina or Brenner and that expressed by Charles Johnson or Donald Fraser in 1909-10. Yet the denial of religious *system,* and of any body of orthodox *belief,* and the insistence on the priority of communal ritual, are remarkably similar. Vansina is prepared to use the word 'religion' when writing of Tio rituals, though he stresses that it is an integral part of a wider 'constellation' of knowledge, belief, and emotion common to all Tio.[143] Brenner also speaks of 'religion' and the 'religious' in Africa, but insists on placing the terms in inverted commas, 'in order to encourage a more open and questioning attitude about what might constitute "religion" in African societies'.[144] In 1909-10 Charles Johnson held back from calling what he observed of Zulu belief and ritual practice 'religion'; whilst Donald Fraser among the Ngoni discerned traces of what he thought was authentic religion, but believed them to be so fragmentary that one might say that he too deemed the Ngoni to have 'religion' only in inverted commas. In 1909-10 probably the majority of missionaries were still unsure whether whatever it was that Africans had, ought to be labelled 'religion'. There were, however, dissenting voices in the Christian community, whose influence was paramount in the writing of the Commission IV report. They tended to be those who did not know Africa, but felt on *a priori* theological grounds that the 'points of contact' with Christian truth which more liberal missionaries were eagerly identifying in Hinduism must surely be there in 'animistic' contexts as well.

141. Louis Brenner, '"Religious" discourses in and about Africa', in Karin Barber and P. F. de Moraes Farias (eds.), *Discourse and its Disguises: the interpretation of African oral texts*, Birmingham University African Studies series (Birmingham: University of Birmingham Centre of West African Studies, 1989), pp. 87-105.

142. Jan Vansina, *The Tio Kingdom of the Middle Congo 1880-1892* (London: OUP for the International African Institute, 1973), pp. 226-7, cited in Brenner, '"Religious" discourses', pp. 91-2.

143. Vansina, *The Tio Kingdom*, p. 221.

144. Brenner, '"Religious" discourses', p. 102.

Today the preponderance of opinion in Christian circles has been reversed. The majority view of African religiosity is now shaped by theologians and religious studies specialists who are concerned to validate the African past by insisting on the legitimacy of the notion of 'African traditional religion' (or, at least, 'religions'). Intellectually they are the descendants of those who in 1910 advocated searching for 'points of contact', for Geoffrey Parrinder's pioneering articulation of 'African traditional religion' in 1954[145] was rooted in the earlier writings of his fellow-Methodist (and PhD examiner), Edwin W. Smith, which themselves depended on an evolutionary model of development from supposedly primitive to advanced religious forms. Parrinder's presentation of African traditional religion emphasized diversity as well as commonality, and noted that not all African peoples had a High God figure; subsequent elaborations of the concept by E. B. Idowu, J. S. Mbiti, and others went much further in homogenizing African religion according to a monotheistic Judeao-Christian template.[146]

The modern dissenters from the resulting orthodoxy are mostly secular historians or anthropologists who question the unitary concept of 'African traditional religion' as a European construct and imposition. They range from overt secularists, such as the Ugandan poet and anthropologist, Okot p'Bitek, in his *African Religions in Western Scholarship* (1971),[147] to a few Christian scholars, such as the late Adrian Hastings, who believed the concept of 'African traditional religion' to be scarcely more meaningful than a generalized notion of 'African traditional politics' or 'African traditional culture' would be.[148] The essence of the attack on what Robin Horton called 'the Devout Opposition' is that the application of the methods of 'comparative religion' to African cultures has resulted in an illegitimate quest for homologies between Judeao-Christian understandings of religion and features of African religiosity. Horton challenges what he sees as a misguided preoccupation of

145. Geoffrey Parrinder, *African Traditional Religion* (London: Hutchinson, 1954).

146. Martin Forward, *A Bag of Needments: Geoffrey Parrinder and the study of religion* (Bern: Peter Lang, 1998), pp. 82-4, 94-5; Andrew Walls, 'Geoffrey Parrinder (*1910) and the study of religion in West Africa', in Frieder Ludwig and Afe Adogame (eds.), *European Traditions in the Study of Religion in Africa* (Wiesbaden: Harrassowitz Verlag, 2004), pp. 213-14.

147. Okot p'Bitek, *African Religions in Western Scholarship* (Nairobi: East African Literature Bureau, n.d. [1971]). See Henk J. van Rinsum, '"They became slaves of their definitions." Okot p'Bitek (1931-1982) and the European traditions in the study of African religions', in Ludwig and Adogame (eds.), *European Traditions in the Study of Religion in Africa*, pp. 23-38.

148. Adrian Hastings, 'Geoffrey Parrinder', *Journal of Religion in Africa* 21:3 (2001), pp. 354-9.

the 'Devout' with the supposed place of communion with the Supreme Being in African cosmologies, and insists instead on the centrality for African peoples of the everyday concerns of explanation, prediction, and control.[149] Although phrased in the language of a modern secular anthropologist, his argument bears comparison with Robert Nassau's response in 1909-10, which maintained that African religious thought was concerned with 'only a physical salvation', with 'the businesses of this Mortal Life, and Protection from the Machinations of human enemies and the malevolence of some disembodied spirits.'[150]

Assessing Edinburgh's Theology of Fulfilment

It is clear that the organisers of the conference were particularly impressed with the exceptional quality of the responses to the Commission IV questionnaire. The Continuation Committee in fact gave serious and protracted consideration to the possibility of publishing the entire set of responses, and only abandoned the idea with reluctance in May 1911.[151] The disproportionate attention that has been lavished by modern scholars on Commission IV, in contrast to the general neglect of the other seven Commissions, is an indication both of the foundational nature and contemporary resonance of its subject matter. Here, more than at any other point in the conference agenda, had to be faced the question of how to reconcile the universal compulsion of the Christian missionary imperative as traditionally understood with the searching challenges brought by the emerging 'science' of comparative religion, which to many outside the missionary movement appeared to call its essential rationale into doubt. The adulation which has been heaped on the Commission IV report, from Temple Gairdner's day down to such interpreters as Sharpe, Ariarajah, Cracknell, and Friesen in recent times, suggests that in the minds of these authors, David Cairns and his colleagues succeeded triumphantly in achieving this reconciliation. Whether or how far they did so, is for the reader to judge. The primary means whereby many of the Commission's respondents

---

149. Robin Horton, 'Judaeo-Christian spectacles: boon or bane to the study of African religions?', *Cahiers d'Études Africaines* 96:24-4 (1984), pp. 391-436, reprinted in his *Patterns of Thought in Africa and the West* (Cambridge: CUP, 1993), pp. 161-93.

150. Commission IV replies, 303, pp. 1-2.

151. UTS, MRL 12, WMC papers, series 1, box 15, folder 1, R. E. Speer to William Adams Brown, 26 September 1912; series 2, box 3, folder 1, minutes of the Continuation Committee, 24-25 June 1910, p. 9; series 2, box 3, folder 2, minutes of the Continuation Committee, 16 May 1911, p. 6.

effected that reconciliation was through the integration of the principle of evolutionary development into a Christian theology of providence and pneumatology. All religious phenomena were placed somewhere along a scale of progression from the 'lower' to the 'higher' forms of religion. The Spirit of God was said to be at work in all such phenomena, though less obviously so at the lower points of the scale. By revealing fragments of the light of divine truth to all peoples, God had, allegedly, prepared them to receive the full light of Christ. Although it was the high calling of Christian missionaries to bring that light, at the same time their own still partial apprehension of the light of Christ would burn more brightly as they absorbed into their understanding of truth the best insights of other religious traditions.[152] The presumed future trajectory of world religions was still one of the replacement of all other religions by Christianity, but that replacement was conceived of as a gradual process of absorption rather than an abrupt one of confrontation.

Whilst this synthesis between Christian theology and the evolutionary principle was clearly shared in some measure at least by many of those who responded to the Commission's questionnaire, this chapter has shown that it was far from universal. It was most widely accepted among those missionaries who worked, usually in educational roles, with the higher classes of India and Japan. Nevertheless, it was not shared by probably the most able India missionary of the day — A. G. Hogg — nor, if Imbrie and Ibuka are to be believed, was it owned, except in a heavily qualified sense, by the majority of Japanese Protestant ministers, who continued to believe that the elements of dissonance between their native religions and Christianity were much more numerous than the elements of consonance. In China, whose 'religion' often seemed to European observers to be a strange mixture of elevated Confucian ethics and degraded ancestral superstition, the concept of 'points of contact' was very widely accepted, but it did not necessarily imply adoption of a wider evolutionary philosophy of religious change. The sample of missionaries operating in a Buddhist context was far too small for meaningful conclusions to be drawn, but the few whose responses are recorded placed as much emphasis on the doctrinal dissonance between Buddhism and Christianity as on the existence of 'points of contact' (which were generally seen as more ethical than theological).[153] R. S. Fyffe of the SPG Burma mission was sympathetically inclined to a fulfilment approach that would 'plant the cross upon the pagoda', but had to admit that on closer inspection what appeared to be the obvious

152. Gairdner, 'Edinburgh 1910', pp. 137-8.
153. *Report of Commission IV*, pp. 285-6; Commission IV replies: 156, p. 6; 183, p. 4; 252, pp. 6-8.

points of contact between Buddhism and Christianity turned out to be points of contrast.[154] The theology of fulfilment was least persuasive of all to missionaries working in Islamic and primal religious contexts. To most of the former, the notion that Christianity could somehow present itself as the natural fulfilment of Islam seemed self-evidently absurd. To most of the latter, unsure as they were of whether tribal peoples possessed any identifiable 'religion', it had meaning only in a limited instrumental or strategic sense. Finally, it should be emphasized that the extent of David Cairns's own sympathy for the kind of fulfilment approach represented by Farquhar or Slater is doubtful. The wording of his questionnaire certainly encouraged answers along this line, while he remained fully persuaded of the necessity of a sympathetic approach to non-Christian religiosity, and included one section in the 'General Conclusions' to the report which used language characteristic of fulfilment theology.[155] Nevertheless, the evidence suggests that his extensive contact with A. G. Hogg in the months preceding the conference led Cairns to a more ambiguous position. Far from being sympathetic to a form of evolutionary naturalism, Cairns had been helped to adopt the conclusion that the future of Christianity lay with a bold re-appropriation of its original heritage of a radical dependence on the creative power of God who alone was able to conquer suffering and death.[156]

Those who had most doubts about the theology of fulfilment were those who could see that it patently did not work. Primal religionists did not move closer to accepting Christianity by first becoming Muslims or Hindus; rather, precisely the opposite was the case, as the conference's emphasis on the 'race' for the soul of the animist clearly implied. Conversely, adherents of the 'higher' Vedic forms of Hinduism did not find acceptance of the claims of Christ easier on account of their supposedly elevated position on the scale of religious development; on the contrary, it was those whose supposed 'Hinduism' was of the 'lowest' variety, characterized by 'superstition', who were flocking to the mass movements in India. Their simple faith in the power of the Christian God was probably closer to the style of apostolic faith advocated by Cairns or Hogg than either of them realized. The slender basis of missionary experience among the membership of the Commission is surely part of the explanation for the distortions and deficiencies in its analysis. For all Cairns's theological perspicacity and sophistication, Commission IV was unable to discern clearly the contemporary religious trends in Asia and Africa which in retrospect appear so transparent.

154. Commission IV replies, 158, pp. 13-14.
155. *Report of Commission IV*, pp. 267-8; see above, p. 226.
156. Cairns, *Autobiography*, pp. 24-7.

CHAPTER 9

Missions, Empire, and the Hierarchy of Civilization

Missions and Governments: The Membership of Commission VII

The selection of missions and governments among the eight constitutive themes of the 1910 conference was claimed as innovative and potentially controversial, not least because of the strain it might impose on the unity of the conference.[1] In fact the topic of missions and governments had received some brief attention at the Ecumenical Missionary Conference held in New York in 1900, but the decision to give the subject protracted attention at Edinburgh was certainly a bold one.[2] The report of Commission VII on 'Missions and Governments' is, however, much the slimmest volume of the nine produced by the conference: the central advisory committee recommended in June 1909 that Commissions VII and VIII would be permitted only 60,000 words for their reports, whereas all other Commission reports were given a maximum of 100,000 words, and this recommendation was endorsed by the executive committee on 30 June.[3] The report of Commission VII will also disappoint

1. *Report of Commission VII*, p. 173; Gairdner, '*Edinburgh 1910*', pp. 154-5. An earlier version of this chapter appeared in Andrew Porter (ed.), *The Imperial Horizons of British Protestant Missions, 1880-1914* (Grand Rapids, MI, and Cambridge: Eerdmans, 2003), pp. 58-84.

2. *Ecumenical Missionary Conference New York, 1900: Report*, 2 vols. (London and New York: Religious Tract Society and American Tract Society, 1900), I, pp. 335-46, 452-3; II, p. 365.

3. UTS, MRL 12, WMC papers, series 1, box 24, folder 6, minutes of central advisory committee, 7-8 June 1909, p. 4; ECG, minutes of executive committee, 30 June 1909, pp. 41-2. Each Commission was permitted an additional 20,000 words to record the debate on

any modern commentator who approaches the text in the hope that it might provide illumination on how Protestant missions during this period regarded the issues of ethical principle raised by missionary association with western imperialism. The report discussed at length the extent to which missionaries might legitimately appeal to the civil power, utilize the privileges of extra-territoriality, and claim compensation for loss of life or property. These topics, however, were treated as technical questions of international relations rather than as expressions of a fundamental disequilibrium of power between the western and non-western worlds. Moreover, the language and very structure of the report supplies plentiful ammunition for the case that the mainstream Protestant missionary enterprise as it neared its peak was saturated with the racial assumptions of the age of high imperialism. Nevertheless, this chapter will seek to show that there was more to Commission VII than meets the eye.

The decision taken at the Oxford meeting of the international committee in July 1908 to appoint a chairman and vice-chairman for each Commission from opposite sides of the Atlantic proved particularly significant for the construction of the report of Commission VII. The Oxford decision meant that in each case, those members who resided in the same country as the chairman of the Commission were to form an executive committee, with the members resident on the other side of the Atlantic forming an advisory and co-operative council under the guidance of the vice-chairman of the Commission.[4] It is clear from the example of Commission VII that this procedure, whether intentionally or not, operated so as to marginalize the continental European members of the Commissions: the report of Commission VII, as indeed of most of the others, was the product of a British-American axis (the only Commissions on which European continental members exerted significant direct influence were Commission I, where Julius Richter was one of two vice-chairmen, along with George Robson, and Commission V, one of whose three vice-chairmen was Friedrich Würz of the Basel Mission). It is equally clear that the numbers of serving missionaries on the Commissions were kept low, not simply by the practical difficulties of securing their attendance at the Commission's meetings, but also by a principled decision, which one suspects reflects the views of John R. Mott, that 'it was obviously desirable that the main body of each Commission should consist of those whose outlook upon the world field was detached from special experience or interest in a particu-

---

their report. The Commission VII report amounted to 191 pages, compared with Commission VIII's 243.

4. *History and Records of the Conference*, p. 10; see Chapter 2, p. 34.

lar country.'[5] In the case of Commission VII, that principle appears to have inclined Mott and Oldham to look first for distinguished laymen of wide experience in public and foreign affairs, and only secondarily for missionaries whose work had brought them into frequent contact with government.

The president of the conference, Lord Balfour of Burleigh, was appointed chairman of Commission VII. 'B. of B.', as he was frequently known, was a Tory grandee, a stout defender of the principle of church establishment, and of established institutions generally.[6] He was an old friend of Randall Davidson from student days in Oxford, and indeed got Davidson to write a letter of introduction on his behalf to E. G. Ingham, former bishop of Sierra Leone, who had been appointed as one of the British members of the Commission. Davidson's commendation of Balfour to Ingham is revealing:

> We were at Oxford together, and, as you are aware, he has been prominent in everything that is sound and sane and reasonable ever since, and all this upon the strongest religious lines. He is not an Evangelical or an enthusiast in religious matters, but he is a quiet and intelligent thinker — a convinced Presbyterian but in fullest harmony with the Church of England.[7]

Lord Balfour's presidential role in the conference as a whole was largely decorative, and his influence on the report of Commission VII appears to have been scarcely more substantial; nevertheless, his political and temperamental conservatism clearly left its mark on the Commission's work. Greater influence on the text of the report was, however, exercised by the secretary of the Commission, Dr Andrew Blair Wann of the Church of Scotland Foreign Mission Board. Wann had been educated for the Church of Scotland ministry at the University of Edinburgh under Robert Flint, a theologian who reconciled Calvinism with an optimistic and evolutionary view of human history as the story of humanity's progress towards truth, freedom, and justice.[8] Wann then served in India as a higher educational missionary from 1886, be-

5. *History and Records of the Conference*, p. 11.

6. On Lord Balfour of Burleigh see *ODNB*; N. M. de S. Cameron (ed.), *Dictionary of Scottish Church History and Theology* (Edinburgh: T&T Clark, 1993); Lady Frances Balfour, *A Memoir of Lord Balfour of Burleigh K.T.* (London: Hodder & Stoughton, n.d. [1924]).

7. LP, Davidson papers, vol. 269, fol. 9, Davidson to Bishop E. G. Ingham.

8. Wann took his MA in 1881, and BD in 1884; he received an honorary DD from Edinburgh in 1909. On Flint, professor of systematic theology at Old College, 1876-1903, see A. P. F. Sell, *Defending and Declaring the Faith: some Scottish examples 1860-1920* (Exeter: Paternoster, 1987), pp. 39-63.

coming principal of the Church of Scotland College in Calcutta in 1904, and then first principal of the united Scottish Churches College there from 1908 to 1909.[9] Wann wrote all of Part I and significant sections of Part II of the report. He was the author, for example, of the opening theoretical statement asserting that 'the consideration of the relations between Governments and Missions may be theoretically regarded as a study of one aspect of the great problem of the relation between the Church and the State, and the discrimination between their respective spheres'.[10] For Wann, as also, one suspects, for Lord Balfour, the topic of mission-government relations was primarily a geographical extension of the historic concern of western political theory with the lines of demarcation between church and state. The other British members of the Commission were not particularly noteworthy, with the exception of the Ulsterman, Sir Robert Hart, by now retired from his post as inspector-general of the Chinese imperial customs service.[11] There is, however, no evidence that Hart, by now seventy-five years of age, exerted any influence on the text of the report. The European continent was represented, somewhat unevenly, by three Germans with strong colonial connections and one Norwegian.[12]

With a British chairman, an American was required for vice-chairman to preside over the American 'advisory council'. Mott's choice (if, as seems probable, it was Mott who did the choosing) was Seth Low (1850-1916), a New York merchant and Episcopalian. Temple Gairdner described Low as 'a man whose name is honoured all over the States as one who has stood and fought for civic and political righteousness'.[13] Low, however, was no radical but a pillar of the municipal and mercantile establishment in New York. He had made his fortune

9. See A. B. Wann, *The Message of Christ to India: with a memoir and appreciations of the author,* edited by J. Morrison (Edinburgh and London: William Blackwood & Sons, 1925), pp. xii-xxii.

10. *Report of Commission VII,* p. 2.

11. On Hart see *ODNB.* Other British members included: Bishop Ingham; Wellesley Bailey, founder of the Mission to Lepers in India (now the Leprosy Mission); Sir Andrew Wingate, a retired member of the Indian civil service; George Cousins, a former LMS missionary in Madagascar, and joint foreign secretary of the LMS, 1898-1909; Lawson Forfeitt, a BMS missionary on the Congo from 1889 to 1909; and Marshall Hartley, a member of the WMMS secretariat since 1888, who had previously served in the Methodist home ministry.

12. The continental members were: Max Berner, president of the Berlin Missionary Society, and since 1903 'Private Counsellor of the German Government in Missionary Affairs'; Professor Gottlieb Haussleiter of Halle; Carl Mirbt, professor of church history at Marburg; and Lars Dahle, missionary in Madagascar, 1870-88, and from 1889 secretary general of the Norwegian Missionary Society.

13. Gairdner, *'Edinburgh 1910',* p. 53.

in the Far Eastern silk trade, and served as Republican mayor of Brooklyn from 1882 to 1885, and subsequently as mayor of New York from 1901 to 1903.[14] As vice-chairman, Low had responsibility for issuing a questionnaire to the North American mission boards and using the responses to present a report from the advisory council to the British executive committee. This American questionnaire (Appendix B, p. 276) differed significantly from that sent out by the Edinburgh conference office to selected individual missionaries (Appendix A, pp. 274-5).

Although Seth Low had an important role in determining the stance taken by Part II of the report on certain controversial points, a much more substantial contribution to the text of Part II came from another member of the American advisory council, rear-admiral Alfred Thayer Mahan (1840-1914), naval strategist, historian, and another Episcopalian. Mahan is remembered today as the architect of the strategic doctrine of American sea power, articulated through his highly influential work, *The Influence of Sea Power upon History, 1660-1783* (1890), and a string of later publications on British and American naval history.[15] He was a global political thinker who saw East Asia and the Pacific rim as the key to global security and the potential source of catastrophic conflict between East and West. That threat could be averted only by the extension of American power and its corollary, Christian civilization, to the Far East and the Pacific. Mahan was a fervent believer in the providential destiny of nations and consistently defended the use of force in international relations. Events such as the American annexation of the Philippines in 1898 were, in his view, part of a divine strategy for the incorporation of East Asia within Christendom.[16] In 1909, the same year in which he contributed so substantially to the Commission VII report, he published a devotional book, part of which argued that the English race, like Israel on her entry into Canaan, had been authorised by God to 'redeem' American territory from the Red Indian and set apart for a distinctive mission of universal salvation.[17] Mahan was, quite simply, an unashamed Anglo-American Christian imperialist.

14. *Dictionary of American Biography;* and B. R. C. Low, *Seth Low* (New York and London: G. P. Putnam's sons, 1925).

15. R. Seager, *Alfred Thayer Mahan: the man and his letters* (Annapolis, MD: Naval Institute Press, 1977).

16. R. N. Leslie, Jr., 'Christianity and the evangelist for sea power: the religion of A. T. Mahan', in J. B. Hattendorf (ed.), *The Influence of History on Mahan: the proceedings of a conference marking the centenary of Alfred Thayer Mahan's The Influence of Sea Power Upon History, 1660-1783* (Newport, RI: Naval War College Press, 1991), pp. 127-39.

17. A. T. Mahan, *The Harvest Within: thoughts on the life of the Christian* (Boston & London: Longmans, Green, 1909), pp. 118-24.

A letter Mahan wrote to Low on 12 August 1909, reflecting upon the replies from the American mission boards to Low's questionnaire, was the near-verbatim source for substantial sections of the report.[18] In addition, three of the eight findings of the Commission, with which the report concluded, owed their origin directly or indirectly to his letter.[19] The letter so impressed Low that he adopted it as the core of the advisory council's report to the British executive committee of the Commission, supplemented by a series of memoranda written by other members of the council in response to the letter. Portions of the memoranda also found their way into the final report. Though these memoranda, including Low's own, disagreed with Mahan on certain points, Mahan had thus set the agenda for the bulk of the interpretative section of the Commission VII report. It should also be noted that most of this section (Part II) reflected the responses of the North American mission boards alone: Mahan's letter and the memoranda it elicited were written without any knowledge of the other two sets of responses — those of the British and European missions and the forty-one individual missionaries — which were considered solely by the British executive committee.[20]

With a Part I based on an unusually small sample of missionary correspondents (only forty-one), and a Part II composed largely in ignorance of those correspondents' replies, the report of Commission VII was shaped as much by metropolitan perspectives as by those from the field. In comparison with the British members, the North American arm of the Commission was both more distinguished in political terms and also conspicuously lacking in those who had first-hand mission experience. In addition to Low and Mahan, it included R. L. Borden, leader of the Conservative opposition in the Canadian parliament and later prime minister of Canada; and John Watson Foster, the lawyer and diplomat who served briefly as American secretary of state in 1892-3 and a significant figure in the American annexation of Hawaii. Borden made virtually no contribution to the Commission. Foster, on the other hand,

18. UTS, MRL 12, WMC papers, series 1, box 23, folder 3 [microfilm in the Henry Martyn Centre, Cambridge]. Mahan's letter forms the first item in the printed report of the advisory council, entitled 'Documents submitted by the American members of Commission VII' [hereafter 'Documents submitted'], and is the source of pp. 97-104, 106-8, and 111-14 of the printed report.

19. These were No. 2, 'The right of entry for Christian missions' (p. 119); No. 7, 'The Belgian Congo' (p. 121); and No. 8, 'Preparation of a statement of principles' (p. 121).

20. Only four British missions replied to the questionnaire: the British and Foreign Bible Society; the China Inland Mission; the Presbyterian Church of England Foreign Missions Committee; and the Sudan United Mission. It is possible that the executive committee decided not to send questionnaires to the larger denominational missions, but rely on individual responses.

submitted a significant memorandum in response to Mahan's letter, and was instrumental in securing a statement from the solicitor to the US State Department on 'The Government of the United States and Foreign Missionaries', which was printed as Appendix A to the final report.[21] The American churches were represented by Bishop William Lawrence, bishop of Massachusetts, chairman of the house of bishops of the Protestant Episcopal Church, and a personal friend of Theodore Roosevelt; and by Rufus M. Jones, the historian of Quakerism. In contrast to the British arm of the Commission, there was only one representative of the American mission boards: the Revd Dr Thomas S. Barbour, foreign secretary of the American Baptist Missionary Union and the person chiefly responsible for introducing E. D. Morel's Congo Reform campaign to the United States.[22] His contribution to the report was considerable: a memorandum in response to Mahan was reproduced in the report, partly in the main text and partly as an appendix.[23] Of the seven North American members of the Commission, only Low, Bishop Lawrence, and Barbour attended the conference.

A Hierarchy of Civilization

Three themes stood out in the report of Commission VII. The first of these was that the question of how missions should relate to governments must be approached with reference to the degree of 'civilization' attained both by the people and by the government of the territory concerned. The introduction to the report lamented the difficulty of making meaningful generalisations about the variety of governments with which missions had to deal, and concluded with a passage whose very construction revealed the view taken of the hierarchical nature of the range of human societies and polities. It is worth quoting in full:

> In Japan, *e.g.,* a fully civilised native Government rules over a civilised and yet non-Christian people; in its neighbour, China, the Government

21. *Report of Commission VII*, pp. 123-34. On Foster see the *Dictionary of American Biography.*

22. W. R. Louis and Jean Stengers (eds.), *E. D. Morel's History of the Congo Reform Movement* (Oxford: Clarendon Press, 1968), pp. 154, 183. In 1910 the American Baptist Missionary Union changed its name to the American Baptist Foreign Mission Society.

23. UTS, MRL 12, WMC papers, series 1, box 23, folder 3, Documents submitted, pp. 26-36. Much of Barbour's memorandum appears in *Report of Commission VII*, pp. 108-110 (to the end of section 3), and as Appendix D, pp. 140-1.

is both antiquated in methods and defective in policy, according to European standards, and is therefore to some extent limited in its actions by European influences; in India a foreign Christian Government controls the destinies of 300,000,000 Hindus and Mohammedans; in Mohammedan lands the law of Islam, which, strictly interpreted, absolutely prohibits conversion to Christianity, is applied with various degrees of rigour; in European protectorates over uncivilised regions the amount of control varies infinitely, and Government policy varies with it; and in barbarous lands, still independent, the caprice of the chiefs, checked only by ancient usage and hereditary superstition, modifies the relations between them and the missionaries day by day.[24]

Part I of the report then proceeded to survey the different mission fields in the descending order of hierarchy set out by this sentence: Japan; China, India, and the Dutch East Indies; the Islamic world; and, finally, sub-Saharan Africa. The Caribbean and the Pacific islands were ignored altogether by Commission VII, and very largely by the other Commissions. The African population of the Caribbean was regarded as fully Christianised and hence outside of the terms of reference of the conference; the Pacific islands were described as a mixture of fully Christianised and heathen, but in practice attracted little attention from the Commissions.[25] Responsibility for both the text and construction of Part I lay with Dr Wann.[26] The concept of a hierarchy of civilization and polity appeared again in an alternative format in the opening sentences of Part II, which also were written by Wann: 'The differences in government with which the Commission is concerned are seldom political or constitutional, but arise from the nature of the religion and the stage of civilisation of the countries concerned.' Part II then proceeded to differentiate five categories of mission lands:

(a) those of low civilisation, but independent;
(b) those of higher civilisation, and independent;
(c) those of low civilisation, under Christian rule or influence;
(d) those of higher civilisation, under Christian rule or influence;
(e) those of the highest international rank.[27]

---

24. *Report of Commission VII*, p. 3.
25. See *Report of Commission I*, p. 132.
26. *Report of Commission VII*, pp. 147, 184.
27. *Ibid.*, p. 88.

The various mission fields surveyed in Part I were then allocated to these five categories. Japan belonged to group (e); India to (d); the European colonial empires in Africa to (c); whilst China and Persia were examples of group (b). But what of group (a)? Whereas the scale at the beginning of Part I had implied that 'barbarous lands, still independent' were a continuing reality in which missionaries had to cope with 'the caprice of the chiefs, checked only by ancient usage and hereditary superstition', Part II now declared category (a) to be vacant: 'The absolutely independent savage chief, representative of group (a), has disappeared; and the ethical and prudential rules governing the dealings of missionaries with such potentates, though intensely interesting as a study of character, need not occupy the attention of this Commission.'[28] It is a mark of just how comprehensive was the partition of the tropical world undertaken by the European powers since 1880 that such a bold statement could in 1910 be made without fear of challenge. The significance of the declaration that category (a) had vanished from view lay, however, primarily in its implications for category (c) — Africa under colonial rule.

Missions in African protectorates or colonies, according to Part II, could expect the encouragement of the civil power on the ground of the proven value of the missionary enterprise to civilization, peace, and humanity. In such countries, the report went on: '. . . there is no independent Government to be respected; there is no sensitive community, united by a great history or a great religion, to be approached with circumspection. Civilisation and religion come to them almost indistinguishably from the one power, and Missions and Governments may work in the closest sympathy.'[29] The fact that tribal authorities had failed to survive as independent political entities posed a question mark against the right of those that remained as dependencies of European powers to command the obedience due to sovereign 'governments'.[30] As Part I observed in relation to German East Africa, the 'legal powers' of subject native chiefs were 'somewhat indeterminate', confronting missionaries with the dilemma of deciding how far their authority was to be obeyed.[31] The report here was drawing on the testimony of Karl Axenfeld, *Missionsinspektor* of the Berlin Missionary Society. Axenfeld's reply to question II of the questionnaire had

28. *Ibid.*, pp. 88-9.
29. *Ibid.*, p. 90. Wann in an earlier draft had included after 'circumspection' the words 'and a voluntary abandonment of the prestige of the ruling race' (UTS, MRL 12, WMC papers, series 1, box 23, folder 6).
30. See W. Ross Johnston, *Sovereignty and Protection: a study of British jurisdictional imperialism in the late nineteenth century* (Durham, NC: Duke University Press, 1973), *passim*.
31. *Report of Commission VII*, p. 79.

discussed the delicacy of a situation in which some chiefs exerted real authority, and others a purely nominal one. If, for example, all orders from chiefs forbidding people to migrate to mission stations were to be respected, the labour
market would be sabotaged, and the industrial development of the protectorate imperilled. If, on the other hand, their orders were to be flouted with impu-
nity, mission stations would become asylums for the disaffected and the chiefs
rendered helpless as political authorities.[32]

Part II of the report gave some acknowledgement to the equilibrium
maintained by such views as Axenfeld's by asserting that those forms of native
chieftainship under European suzerainty which continued to command popular affection, preserve order, and 'conserve national and tribal life' were law-
ful powers which deserved respect.[33] The main drift of its discussion of Africa
was, however, in a contrary direction. Barbarous lands were, by definition,
those whose authorities had failed to meet the ends which the scriptures laid
down as the purpose of civil government, namely the maintenance of law and
order. In many cases, the report noted, it was missionaries who had stepped
into the governmental vacuum left by barbarism. Now that 'civilised rule' had
followed them, missionaries were well equipped to mediate between colonial
governments and 'the suspicious native races, resentful of interference with
their ancient ways, evil and good alike'.[34] The normal expectation in category
(c), therefore, was that missions and colonial governments should work in
harmonious partnership towards the civilization of the population; indigenous authorities had little role to play in the process.

Wann was typical of those whose mission experience was limited to Asia in
denying that African societies possessed any 'sensitive community, united by a
great history or a great religion'. However, such cultural and racial myopia was
not representative of responses to the questionnaire from Africa missionaries.
The most striking examples of insistence on respect for the integrity of African
cultures came in responses from French missionaries, and it may be that the
French colonial policy of cultural assimilation provoked missionaries to adopt
in reaction more self-conscious strategies of cultural indigeneity than many of
their colleagues working in British colonial contexts.[35] Part II of the report
took note of such statements, and indeed used them to claim that 'the re-

32. ECG, Commission VII replies, pp. 557-9. On Axenfeld see *BDCM;* H. Gründer,
Christliche Mission und deutscher Imperialismus 1884-1914 (Paderborn: Schöningh, 1982),
pp. 42-3, 102-3; and M. Wright, *German Missions in Tanganyika 1891-1941* (Oxford: Clarendon Press, 1971), pp. 121-5, 130.

33. *Report of Commission VII*, pp. 90-1, 93.

34. *Ibid.*, pp. 96-7.

35. ECG, Commission VII replies by E. Haug and F. Vernier, pp. 355-6, 415-16.

proach that missionaries desire to Europeanise the inhabitants of mission lands, if ever true, is now absurdly false.'[36] Yet such evidence from the replies was not permitted to affect the fundamental categorization of cultures which provided the organizing framework for the report itself.

The report's division of mission lands according to their supposed position on the scale of civilization and good government was seen by the British arm of the Commission to require clear emphasis.[37] The American advisory council, on the other hand, though not objecting to the hierarchy on principle, was anxious to stress that its validity was purely temporary: 'In the references made to existing social and political distinctions, we would be carefully on our guard against the peril of creating the impression that, in our judgment, or in the judgment of missionaries, the existing distinctions are in so far of divine appointment that genuine aspiration for advancement is to be repressed or regretted'.[38] This comment suggests that American Protestant thought may have been even more inclined than its British counterpart to filter evolutionary concepts of race through the mesh of a continuing firm commitment to ideals of a universal human capacity for progress. However, the majority of the Commission — whether American or British — viewed the purpose of the scale, not in didactic or theoretical terms, but as a pragmatic rule of thumb to guide missionaries in decisions about the exercise or voluntary suspension of their political rights. This was made most explicit in a section of the report taken from Barbour's memorandum. The lower the position on the scale of advancement occupied by the country in which missionaries worked, the less appropriate it would be for them to insist on recompense for injuries suffered. On the other hand, in higher civilizations where freedom of religious belief and practice was protected by law, to co-operate with government in its duty of exacting just reprisals was quite legitimate.[39] The way in which the report applied the idea of a hierarchy of civilization was indebted to the debate provoked among the American members by Mahan's letter to Low. Mahan subordinated American orthodoxy on the separation of church and state to an exalted view of the divinely imposed duties of governments. He argued in favour of missionaries appealing to the civil (i.e. imperial) power for protection and redress, and demanding indemnities from native authorities in compensation

36. *Report of Commission VII*, p. 94.

37. UTS, MRL 12, WMC papers, series 1, box 23, folder 4, Minutes of meeting of Commission VII, 17 Dec. [1909], pp. 1-2.

38. UTS, MRL 12, WMC papers, series 1, box 23, folder 9, Points submitted for consideration by Dr Low in preparing reply to British members of Commission VII, p. 2.

39. *Report of Commission VII*, p. 108; see also Lord Balfour's comments in *History and Records of the Conference*, pp. 144-5.

for loss of property or even life. Such action, he maintained, was necessary to satisfy the universal claims of justice and public order: for the sake of the community, 'evil forces' must be seen to be controlled.[40] Mahan's view, however, was not shared by the American members as a whole nor endorsed by the report. In what were termed the 'peculiar' circumstances of China, where missionary replies differed over the propriety of making use of the privileges secured by the 'unequal' treaties, the report came down on the side of discouraging appeals to the civil power.[41] By contrast, in countries where a high civilization guaranteed the rule of law in association, either with Christian rule, as in India, or with a commitment to religious liberty matching that of Christian nations, as in Japan, resort to the civil power was encouraged.[42] In practice, as the report acknowledged, 'vexatious questions' between missions and government were extremely rare in both India and Japan.[43] Hence the obligation to invoke the rule of law in support of religious freedom remained virtually redundant in 'civilized' countries; if they were civilized enough to make the appeal to the rule of law possible, they were civilized enough to make it largely unnecessary.

In practice, therefore, the concept of an evolutionary hierarchy of race and civilization was used to restrict rather than extend the contexts in which missions were encouraged to shelter under the umbrella of imperial power. The most blatant imperialist on the Commission — Mahan — made no use of the concept in his submission to Low, and indeed seems to have been unsympathetic to using such distinctions as a guide for policy: for him, there was one set of absolute moral and legal norms to be applied globally. Africa, however, remained the problem for the Commission's attempt to regulate missionary relations to government to the scale of civilization. According to Thomas Barbour's criteria, its indigenous authorities were insufficiently 'civilized' to attract the 'supporting public sentiment' which made it possible for missionaries to appeal to them to punish wrongs.[44] But equally those governmental structures were insufficiently 'civilized' to provide security for the Christian convert. In such extreme conditions, an appeal by the missionary to the colo-

40. UTS, MRL 12, WMC papers, series 1, box 23, folder 3, Documents submitted, pp. 8, 11-12. For Mahan's view of church-state relations see R. Seager and D. D. Maguire (eds.), *Letters and papers of Alfred Thayer Mahan volume III 1902-1914* (Annapolis, MD: Naval Institute Press, 1975), pp. 501-3, 507-9.

41. *Report of Commission VII*, pp. 7-22, 105.

42. *Ibid.*, p. 105.

43. *Ibid.*, pp. 4-5, 23.

44. UTS, MRL 12, WMC papers, series 1, box 23, folder 3, Documents submitted, pp. 31-33; *Report of Commission VII*, pp. 109-10.

nial power on behalf of the indigenous Christian community was sometimes, according to the report, the only avenue by which justice could be secured:

> . . . under some conditions even the intervention of the missionary to secure justice for the convert — a thing forbidden by European Ministers and deprecated by Mission Boards in the case of China — may be a necessary part of the missionary's work, as in European Protectorates over barbarous regions in cases where native chiefs tyrannise or European officials have not yet grasped the situation.[45]

Missionaries and Politics

The second recurring theme of the report was its claim that field opinion was 'practically unanimous' that missionaries, confronted with the awakening of political and social aspirations throughout the world, 'should have nothing to do with political agitation' but rather teach obedience to the 'settled government'. Although it was also reported that missionaries uniformly acknowledged their duty to press governments, particularly colonial ones, for the 'removal of gross oppression and injustice', the report added the qualification, 'provided that in so doing they keep clear of association with any political movement'.[46] These assertions of Dr Wann's were reinforced in still more absolute terms by Seth Low when he introduced the report to the conference on 20 June 1910:

> There is one . . . point on which . . . the missionaries are absolutely at one, and that is that everywhere a missionary is under a moral obligation to abstain entirely from politics. There is absolutely no exception, I think, to the expression of that opinion, and I am quite confident that the Conference will share it.[47]

Most answers to question VI of the British questionnaire (Appendix A) were predictably hostile to any overt identification by missionaries with movements professedly critical of established governments.[48] This was especially so among the ten China missionaries, most of whom cautioned against

---

45. *Report of Commission VII*, p. 105. This section was apparently written by Wann.
46. *Ibid.*, p. 95.
47. *Ibid.*, p. 149.
48. Low's American version contained no such question (cf. Appendices A and B).

any close association with the reform movement in the Chinese empire.[49] Yet there were minority voices — Gilbert Reid and Timothy Richard — who assessed the reform movement favourably.[50] Only six questionnaire replies were received from India missionaries.[51] Whilst they certainly counselled against any identification with 'agitation', most also revealed more active sympathy with national aspirations constitutionally expressed than might be deduced from the report. Thus Herbert Anderson, the BMS India secretary, warned against missionaries gaining a reputation for political activity, yet proclaimed his personal sympathy with the politicians of the 'Indian Moderate School'.[52] D. A. Rees, a British Wesleyan missionary in Bangalore, similarly advised missionaries to take no active part in politics themselves, but also stated that Indian Christians should have 'the fullest liberty to espouse any political cause they deem good'.[53] Perhaps the most remarkable of the India replies was that from Andrew Low, serving with the United Free Church of Scotland in Rajputana, who presented the case for a total severance of all mission schools from government grants-in-aid. Low argued not from principled commitment to voluntaryism, but from the standpoint of how Indians must inevitably perceive the funding of a foreign religion by a conquering government. Imagining a Buddhist power taking control of the British Isles, establishing Buddhist schools, and endowing them so lavishly as to overshadow entirely the ill-equipped existing schools, he concluded that, in such a situation, 'there is no doubt but that our sympathies would be most heartily with them in objecting to the *status quo*'.[54] No such attempt to adopt the perspective of the indigenous observer can be found in the report.

These expressions of sympathy with moderate nationalist aspirations may be thought to have little political significance, but in 1909-10 sufficient numbers of missionaries were declared supporters of the Indian National Congress for their presence to be hard to ignore, even by those to whom it was unwelcome.[55] Hence Wann's original draft of the section on social and political aspirations in India contained the observation:

49. E.g. Arnold Foster of the LMS; ECG, Commission VII replies, pp. 21-2.

50. *Ibid.*, pp. 105-6, 95.

51. Although it is possible that more questionnaires were sent out than were returned, the unusually small number of India correspondents for Commission VII suggests that the Commission may have decided in advance that in India the subject was too straightforward to need much investigation.

52. ECG, Commission VII replies, p. 177.

53. *Ibid.*, p. 196.

54. *Ibid.*, p. 207.

55. A. Mathew, *Christian Missions, Education and Nationalism: from dominance to com-*

In past days a few missionaries have thrown themselves with enthusiasm into the Congress movement; possibly they were more than balanced by others who regarded the Congress with suspicion, if not aversion. And certainly the approbation of the Missionary body, as a whole, was not with them.[56]

Wann's comment attracted the disapproving notice of members of the American advisory council, who made representations to Seth Low that it would be wise to avoid any reference to the 'attitude of missionaries to the movement in India for native independence' on the grounds that, from the perspective of American views of British colonial rule, it was desirable to avoid either 'championship of this rule on the one hand' or 'arraignment of it on the other.'[57] The objection in this instance was almost certainly to anything that might be construed as indicating missionary condemnation of British rule, though it is not easy to conceive how Wann's dismissive allusion to missionary support for the Congress could be read in this way. This section of the report ended by roundly applauding Indian Christians as a shining example of 'loyalty to a Government which they recognise as now ruling in India under God's Providence for the ultimate restoration of India to its place among the nations'. The Americans raised no objection to *that* markedly pro-British statement, whereas the offending passage about support for the Congress movement was omitted from the final report.[58] All that remained about missionary attitudes to Indian nationalism was an assertion that, whilst most missionaries agreed that 'a transfer of power to the natives of the soil should proceed *pari passu* with their advance in enlightenment and moral stability . . . very few indeed consider it part of their duty to spend any part of their time and thought in propagating the idea'.[59] Whilst this claim was doubtless accurate, it served to accentuate the monochrome tone of this section of the report in comparison with the more variegated character of the questionnaire replies from India.

---

promise 1870-1930 (New Delhi: Anamika Prakashan, 1988), pp. 125-44; G. A. Oddie, 'Indian Christians and the National Congress', *Indian Church History Review* 2:1 (June 1968), pp. 47-8; G. Thomas, *Christian Indians and Indian Nationalism 1885-1910: an interpretation in historical and theological perspectives* (Frankfurt: Peter Lang, 1979), pp. 123-33.

56. UTS, MRL 12, WMC papers, series 1, box 23, folder 5, Drafts by Dr Wann, pp. 41-2, and folder 7, Section C 'India', p. 19.

57. UTS, MRL 12, WMC papers, series 1, box 23, folder 9, Points submitted for consideration by Dr Low, p. 2.

58. *Report of Commission VII*, p. 35. The offending statement was removed from the end of the first paragraph on p. 34.

59. *Ibid.*, p. 34.

The majority of the Africa correspondents, like those from other fields, gave answers to question VI on the questionnaire which balanced respect for the authority of colonial governments with some form of statement of the priority of African interests.[60] In some replies the juxtaposition between imperial loyalty and higher Christian commitment was stark.[61] Where the colonial government was neither British nor Protestant, the missionary replies to question VI still maintained a similar equilibrium, although positive enthusiasm for empire was replaced by theological affirmations about the need to obey legitimate authority. Thus from Portuguese Congo (Angola), R. H. Carson Graham of the BMS referred to the intrinsic tendency of Protestantism to generate social and political freedom, while emphasizing that this could only be along lines of 'Christian Evolution rather than Revolution' (an interesting phrase coming from an Ulster Calvinist in the Spurgeonic tradition). Nonetheless, Graham was at pains to stress that Baptist missionaries in Angola had always taught obedience to the Portuguese government, and indeed claimed that, if the BMS mission were to be withdrawn, the Portuguese would require three times their present soldiery to hold the country and collect revenue. 'Yet it is said', commented Graham wryly, 'that Missionaries meddle unwarrantably with politics'.[62]

Two of the Africa responses were extensively cited in the report — those from Frederick B. Bridgman, an American Board missionary in Natal, and from Bishop Alfred Tucker of Uganda. Bridgman we shall consider below. Tucker's response reviewed the history of the CMS Uganda mission in order to explain how it was, 'through the necessities of the case, that the missionaries became mixed up with the politics of the country'. Tucker proclaimed that 'as a general principle I am entirely opposed to missionaries mixing themselves up in the political affairs of the country in which their lot is cast'. The Uganda circumstances were 'exceptional'. The natives were already bound to the missionaries by 'very close ties of affection and duty', and it would have been 'a grave dereliction of duty' on the part of the latter to refuse to offer the political guidance that was sought.[63] All this Wann reproduced in the report, as if Uganda could be presented to the conference as the single exception that proved the rule of 'no politics for missionaries'. What Wann did not include, however, were Tucker's answers to question VI about political aspirations:

60. E.g. Robert Laws of Livingstonia; ECG, Commission VII replies, p. 380.

61. E.g. W. R. Miller; ECG, Commission VII replies, pp. 391-2.

62. ECG, Commission VII replies, pp. 331-4. On Graham see his *Under Seven Congo Kings* (London: Carey Press, n.d.); also my *The History of the Baptist Missionary Society 1792-1992* (Edinburgh: T&T Clark, 1992), pp. 340, 343.

63. *Report of Commission VII*, pp. 73-5.

Sympathy with the political aspirations of the people among whom the Missionary is working, so long as it does not involve taking sides in political controversy, I should regard as almost a duty. The national spirit which has recently shown itself in Bunyow [Bunyoro] and Toro in Central Africa, is a case in point. The longing for the fullness of national life in these countries is all for good and involves no political controversy. The Missionery's [sic] duties and sympathies in a case like this are, in my view, really identical. But when political controversy is involved the Missionary should rigorously hold aloof. His mission is to both parties and to take sides would be to fail in one of the primary duties of his calling.[64]

Tucker, like many Christian imperialists of his generation, combined fervent enthusiasm for the British empire with a readiness to champion indigenous interests in a mixture that challenges modern preconceptions. He had recently, for example, successfully contested proposals from the governor of Uganda to introduce Indian settlers to Busoga which, he argued, would be fatal to the Basoga, who were still recovering from a sleeping sickness epidemic.[65] Tucker's prohibition on pastoral grounds of missionaries from taking partisan stances on disputed issues should not, therefore, be taken as evidence of absolute political quiescence. It has to be said that the Commission's bland reiteration of the 'no politics' rule failed to communicate to the conference the complex variety and not infrequent subtlety of the political responses displayed by those who had had to grapple first-hand with how to relate mission activity to colonial governments and their dependent indigenous authorities. It also reflected an extraordinarily narrow view of what constituted 'politics' and a deliberate blindness to the major role which missionaries frequently played in the introduction of western codes of law and order.

The Colonial View of Missions

The report's third predominant theme was articulated by Mahan in his letter to Low of 12 August 1909:

With the single glaring exception of the Congo State, and probably of the Portuguese African possessions, there can be elicited, I think, a

---

64. ECG, Commission VII replies, pp. 406-7. Tucker had toured Bunyoro and Toro earlier in 1909.

65. A. P. Shepherd, *Tucker of Uganda: artist and apostle 1849-1914* (London: SCM, n.d.), pp. 183-4.

concensus [*sic*] of opinion that the missionary cause on the whole has been gaining, and continues to gain, in the esteem and favour of Governments, both Christian and non-Christian.[66]

This confident assertion was incorporated in the report, apart from the opening clause, which was replaced by 'in spite of certain grievances, some of which have been illustrated in Part I. of this report'.[67] Conference delegates would certainly have left Edinburgh with the impression that almost all colonial governments viewed missionary activity with benevolent approval. The conference received an official message from the Imperial German Colonial Office, recording its 'satisfaction and gratitude that the endeavours for the spread of the Gospel are followed by the blessings of civilisation and culture in all countries'.[68] In the debate on Commission VII's report, delegates received reassurance from Seth Low that 'the good understanding between Missions and Governments is increasing', and were even told by Lord Reay, a former governor of Bombay Presidency, that 'missionaries in India, I consider, are auxiliaries of Government'.[69]

This picture of growing harmony between missions and governments had some basis in fact. The General Acts of the Berlin Conference of 1884-5 and the Brussels Conference of 1890 had committed the European powers, albeit in vague terms, to the support of missions as part of a wider programme for the civilization of Africa.[70] Now that colonial frontiers were largely settled, missionaries seemed more frequently an asset than a threat. Within the British empire, the main exceptions to this were in countries predominantly Muslim. The only sections of the report openly critical of British colonial policy were those relating to Egypt, the Egyptian Sudan, and northern Nigeria. In each case, the report complained, the administration was in practice inclined to favour Islam at Christianity's expense.[71] Similar views had been expressed by several of the American mission boards and in Mahan's letter to Low. Nevertheless, criticism of Lord Cromer's administration for excessive sensitivity to Muslim scruples proved too strong for most American members of the

66. UTS, MRL 12, WMC papers, series 1, box 23, folder 3, Documents submitted, p. 15.

67. *Report of Commission VII*, p. 112.

68. Gairdner, '*Edinburgh 1910*', p. 45.

69. *Report of Commission VII*, pp. 149, 154.

70. Article 6 of the Berlin Act, cited in A. B. Keith, *The Belgian Congo and the Berlin Act* (Oxford: Clarendon Press, 1919), p. 304; and Articles 1 and 2 (Clause 3) of the Brussels Act, in E. Hertslet (comp.), *A Complete Collection of the Treaties and Conventions . . . between Great Britain and Foreign Powers,* vol. XIX (London: Butterworth, 1895), pp. 281-2.

71. *Report of Commission VII*, pp. 51-7, 58-60.

Commission, who felt that such 'caustic criticism' was 'incongruous in the report of a joint Commission'.[72] These objections were over-ruled by the British, and the animadversions on Cromer remained. Low felt obliged in presenting the report to assure the conference that if the Commission's words on this subject gave pain, they were to be treated as 'the wounds of a friend'.[73]

There were, in addition, the more 'glaring exceptions' referred to by Mahan. Although his reference to the Congo and Portuguese Africa was cut from his opening summary of the replies to question VIII, the report still noted that 'the most crying scandals enumerated in the replies' occurred under the 'nominal Christian' governments of the Belgian Congo and Portugal. It also adopted verbatim Mahan's text recommending that the conference appeal to the signatories to the Berlin Act to take action to halt the continuing violation of the claims of humanity in the former Congo Free State.[74] Temple Gairdner recorded that 'almost the only real anger' manifested at the conference was in relation to the three 'great national wrongs' of the opium and liquor traffics and forced labour, which were allocated their own section in Part II of the report.[75] Similarly, one point at which the conference broke into 'very loud applause' during the debate of the report was when C. E. Wilson, foreign secretary of the BMS, promised that 'we are *not going to give up* our divinely appointed task to work for the emancipation and uplifting of the down-trodden and oppressed people of the Congo'.[76] The passion expended on the Congo and Portuguese Africa derived its force from a conviction that these so-called Christian nations had reneged on 'the only possible justification' of colonial annexations, namely the duty to adopt 'a deliberate, steadfast, and thorough policy' for the education and uplift of those described as 'the more backward races of mankind'.[77] Again, it should be noted that evolutionary concepts of racial hierarchy were foundational to the argument of this most outspoken and 'radical' section of the report.

Two qualifications must be added to the picture drawn by the report of a

72. UTS, MRL 12, WMC papers, series 1, box 23, folder 9, Points submitted for consideration by Dr Low, p. 2; see folder 3, Documents submitted, p. 16; and folder 12, series 6, *passim*; see also pp. 272-3 below.

73. *Report of Commission VII*, p. 148. The Americans had objected to a section of the draft criticising Lord Cromer's administration for its 'tender care for Moslem susceptibilities' (UTS, MRL 12, WMC papers, series 1, box 23, folder 5, pp. 69-71), but they appeared unamended in the final report.

74. *Report of Commission VII*, pp. 114, 121.

75. Gairdner, 'Edinburgh 1910', p. 168; *Report of Commission VII*, pp. 116-17.

76. Gairdner, 'Edinburgh 1910', p. 175; *Report of Commission VII*, p. 182.

77. *Report of Commission VII*, pp. 115-16.

generally harmonious relationship between missions and governments. First, the report itself gave no indication of the real divergences of view within the Commission on how far it was appropriate to include forthright criticism of colonial governments on any matters not self-evidently connected to religious liberty. Wann's early drafts, for example, were virtually silent on the question of forced labour. His section in Part I on Portuguese Africa had originally said that 'We have in this Commission nothing to do with troubles in connection with forced labour'. The American advisory council objected, and Wann revised his text to read 'We cannot discuss matters indirectly affecting mission work, such as the troubles in connection with forced labour, etc.'[78] Moreover, the section in Part II identifying the 'great questions' of national wrong on which missions had been compelled to make repeated representation to government had not originally mentioned forced labour alongside the opium and liquor trades.[79] The meeting of the British executive committee in December 1909 insisted that, in view of opinions expressed by members of the Commission, the section should be re-written by Wann and J. H. Oldham to include reference to forced labour (this, incidentally, appears to be the only point at which Oldham exerted any direct influence on Commission VII).[80]

Similarly, some of the American boards did not mince their words in condemning the British government for its 'political enthronement of Islam' in Egypt and the Sudan.[81] As seen above, the final report was a generally faithful reflection of such sentiments. Mahan and Barbour went further, voicing criticisms of British policy towards missions in India and China.[82] Such criticisms, however, failed to carry the majority support of the American members of the Commission.

A second and consequent qualification, therefore, is that the divergent political stances revealed in compiling the report corresponded only to a limited extent to divisions of nationality. Disagreements amongst the Commission's American members were as significant as those separating the Americans as a whole from their British colleagues. Yet it may not be coincidental that replies to the British questionnaire reporting quite serious ten-

78. UTS, MRL 12, WMC papers, series 1, box 23, folder 9, Points submitted for consideration by Dr Low, p. 2; *Report of Commission VII*, p. 72.

79. UTS, MRL 12, WMC papers, series 1, box 23, folder 7, draft report of section A, p. 17.

80. UTS, MRL 12, WMC papers, series 1, box 23, folder 4, minutes of meeting of Commission VII held on 17 Dec. [1909], p. 2.

81. UTS, MRL 12, WMC papers, series 1, box 23, folder 12, response 1 from Board of Foreign Missions of the United Presbyterian Church of North America.

82. UTS, MRL 12, WMC papers, series 1, box 23, folder 3, Documents submitted, pp. 16, 35.

sion or even confrontation with British officials, notably in Africa, came from non-British missionaries.[83]

The most comprehensive indictment of British colonial policy contained in the questionnaire replies was that of Frederick Bridgman. Bridgman, it is true, enjoined absolute loyalty to the colonial government; he also took pride in the fact that the ABCFM missionaries, as members of 'the great Anglo-Saxon family', had always been regarded by the British as 'fellow citizens of the Empire', and had thus been able to mediate between the native population and the authorities.[84] To dismiss Bridgman on this evidence as a typical Anglo-Saxon racist would be a grave mistake. Recent writing has identified him rather as a pioneer of a politically and socially aware approach to the problems of urban South Africa.[85] Alongside these markedly pro-imperial statements, his answers to the questionnaire contained a perceptive analysis of Ethiopianism in Natal and telling criticisms of British policy on African lands and the freedom of missions to operate in native reserves.[86]

Bridgman's indignant account was incorporated in the report, but in emasculated form, with the invective cut out. His advocacy of African land rights was grossly misrepresented by a mere passing reference to 'other difficulties' in Natal with 'mission lands'.[87] On the other hand, a passage in which he stressed missionaries' duty to 'inculcate absolute loyalty to Government' and teach the native 'the necessity of his proving his worthiness' to receive the privilege of political responsibility became virtually the entire section of the report devoted to political aspirations in South Africa.[88] The report did not print the immediately ensuing portion of Bridgman's text, in which he urged that *British* missionaries 'should be bold to declare themselves according to their convictions of truth and justice' on questions of African rights; missionaries who were not British subjects, whose status in the country was that of guests by courtesy of a government not their own, had to act with greater reserve and moderation.[89]

Bridgman also contributed to the conference debate on the Commission

83. See the case of Karl Cederquist in ECG, Commission VII replies, pp. 297-317, very selectively summarised in *Report of Commission VII*, pp. 57-8.

84. ECG, Commission VII replies, p. 278.

85. P. B. Rich, 'Albert Luthuli and the American Board mission in South Africa', in H. Bredekamp and R. Ross (eds.), *Missions and Christianity in South African History* (Johannesburg: Witwatersrand University Press, 1995), pp. 192-3.

86. ECG, Commission VII replies, pp. 279-92.

87. *Report of Commission VII*, pp. 82-3.

88. *Ibid.*, pp. 83-4.

89. ECG, Commission VII replies, p. 295.

VII report, spurred to his feet by the claim of the preceding speaker, a missionary of the Dutch Reformed Church, that missionaries in South Africa were able to proclaim the gospel 'without let or hindrance'.[90] This, Bridgman protested, had not been the case in Natal, though he was able to tell the conference that there were now hopes that government restrictions on native evangelists would soon be removed. The record of the South African colonies fell well short of the golden rule — 'they had not done to the natives as they would be done by. I feel in some respect that there has been a sad lack of a deep sense of responsibility on the part of the ruling race for the welfare of the weaker race'. From the new Union of South Africa, Bridgman hoped for better things, but he went on to spell out the agenda — beginning with the 'bed-rock issue' of the land question — which must be pursued if white responsibility to the black race were to be adequately discharged.[91] This conjunction between acceptance of race theory and accurate perception of the real political issues confronting the African population of South Africa is striking. It was precisely because blacks were the 'weaker race' that the standards of imperial duty had to be so strictly enforced. Bridgman's speech prompted Seth Low, in concluding the morning session of the debate, to hasten to correct the impression 'that I fear may have been created that the British Government is, in relation to Missions, either lukewarm or unfriendly'.[92]

The Impact of the Commission VII Report

How far the report of Commission VII shaped the subsequent relations between missions and governments is hard to establish. It made few specific recommendations. One that it did make — the proposal of an appeal to the European powers to take action over human rights in the Congo — was effectively stymied by the decision (taken at the Oxford meeting in July 1908) that no formal resolutions should be passed. As Gairdner observed, the conference debate on 'the red horror of the Congo' ended on a necessarily inconclusive note.[93] Public pressure for Congo reform was, in any case, ebbing following the death of Leopold II on 17 December 1909.[94] Some general observations are, however, appropriate.

90. *Report of Commission VII*, p. 169.
91. *Ibid.*, pp. 171-2.
92. *Ibid.*, p. 172.
93. Gairdner, '*Edinburgh 1910*', pp. 175-6.
94. S. J. S. Cookey, *Britain and the Congo Question 1885-1913* (London: Longmans, 1968), pp. 262-3.

The report's acceptance of A. T. Mahan's recommendation, that the conference should take steps for the appointment of a committee to draw up 'a brief statement of recognised principles which underlie the relations of Missions to Governments', bore fruit in the Continuation Committee's adoption of such a statement at its fifth meeting at The Hague in 1913. The statement was concerned primarily with defining the legal rights of missionaries, and differentiating these from spiritual obligations.[95] It said nothing about the moral obligations of governments towards subject peoples. Nevertheless, both the Conference of British Missionary Societies and the Foreign Missions Conference of North America established advisory committees on missions and governments in the wake of Edinburgh 1910. For all its deficiencies, Commission VII paved the way for the concerns of missionary statesmen with the questions of nationality and internationalism raised by the First World War and the post-war mandates. It is plausible to suggest that the Commission VII report laid the theoretical foundations for the campaigns waged so assiduously by J. H. Oldham on issues such as forced labour in Kenya after the war. The one section of the 1910 report which was in part Oldham's work was the one dealing with the 'public questions' of opium, the liquor trade, and forced labour. In 1919 Oldham intervened to ensure a reference was inserted in Article 22 of the League of Nations covenant to the peoples, 'especially those of Central Africa', who were 'at such a stage' that the mandatory powers must be prepared to guarantee 'freedom of conscience or religion, subject only to the maintenance of public order and morals'.[96] That statement owed its parentage to Article 6 of the Berlin Act of 1885.[97] It may also be indebted to the emphasis which Commission VII had placed on religious liberty as a distinguishing mark of civilization, yet a survey published in 1931 made no reference to the 1910 Commission.[98] Just how significant the Commission VII report was for the years that followed must, therefore, remain an open question.

The First World War made many of the report's assertions about the com-

95. The provisional statement was printed in *IRM* 2:7 (July 1913), pp. 563-6, and adopted without amendment by the Continuation Committee at its meeting from 14 to 20 Nov. 1913. ECG, IMC archives, microfiches H-10,000, 26.0003-4, minutes of the Continuation Committee of the World Missionary Conference 1910-1913, and papers for Continuation Committee, Nov. 1913. Members of Commission VII drafting the statement were Lord Balfour, Low, Mahan, Barbour, Max Berner, and Lars Dahle.

96. G. K. A. Bell, *Randall Davidson: Archbishop of Canterbury,* 2nd edn. (London: Oxford University Press, 1938), pp. 944-5.

97. See Keith, *The Belgian Congo and the Berlin Act,* p. 304.

98. M. Boegner, 'Missions et gouvernements: de l'acte de Berlin au traité de Versailles', *Le Monde Non-Chrétien* 1 (1931), pp. 59-78.

patibility between the respective objectives of missions and governments look threadbare, as the pressures of war exposed the profoundly self-interested national agenda concealed beneath the high-sounding professions by colonial governments that had so impressed the members of Commission VII. The war also marked the beginning of the end of the era in which subjects such as the relations of missions to governments could be debated out of earshot of representatives of the indigenous populations of Asia and Africa.[99] Even those missionaries who tried to see matters from the perspective of the indigenous populations among whom they worked, such as Andrew Low or F. B. Bridgman, were, as we have seen, given short shrift by the Commission report. Wann acknowledged at Edinburgh that 'there has been a great deal of combustible material which we have had to keep outside of the report', and admitted that 'a very large number of Missions and missionaries' had used the questionnaires to vent particular grievances against governments.[100] The Commission's decision to omit such material resulted in a document which can easily mislead historians who have not consulted the sources that lie behind it.

It remains the case that the disagreements which we have uncovered rumbling beneath the dominant harmonies of the Commission VII report were all variations on an agreed imperial theme. Those variations of view cannot be neatly arranged into patterns determined by nationality. Whilst it is possible to conclude that non-British missionaries were more likely than British ones to find fault with British colonial administration, it is also true that most American members of Commission VII were less prepared than their British counterparts to criticise British colonial governments in the text of the report, despite considerable evidence in replies from the American boards justifying such criticism. This reluctance is to be explained less by national affiliation than by the fact that the American arm of the Commission tended more towards governmental perspectives and the British members more towards the missionary viewpoint. The Christian imperialism of the missionary movement was primarily an international rather than a national ideology, even though it was frequently seduced by the rhetoric of those whose agenda was a nationalistic one.

Of greater significance for the historiography of the missionary relation to imperialism is the complex relationship between political stances and racial theory apparent among both Commission members and their missionary cor-

99. Only one non-western voice was heard in the debate on Commission VII — that of Dr C. T. Wang of China — in a speech which Gairdner described as 'a revelation of the Chinese point of view': Gairdner, '*Edinburgh 1910*', p. 164; *Report of Commission VII*, pp. 154-6.
100. *Report of Commission VII*, p. 173.

respondents. This chapter has suggested that the Commission employed the concept of a hierarchy of race and civilization to insist that missionaries grade their political expectations and claims to civil rights according to the degree of 'civilization' possessed by the people and government of the field in which they worked. The report argued that appeals by missionaries to governments to grant redress for contravention of rights of freedom of religious belief and practice were least appropriate in countries towards the bottom end of the scale of civilization. This might appear to imply that the report anticipated that the relations of missions and governments would be at their most distant in the African continent. In point of fact, of course, it took the opposite view. The paradox is explained by the way in which concepts of race were put to political use. Those missionaries who were most outspoken in their assertion of indigenous interests — such as Bridgman — often defended their position by appeal to the extent of moral obligation created by the differential between the 'higher' and the 'lower' races. For such missionaries, the utility of evolutionary race theory was precisely that it could be used to enforce the obligations owed by colonial governments to haul their subject populations up the rungs of the ladder of civilization. Bridgman contrasted his own position with that of Natal's white settlers, concerned to keep the native 'down and under' in perpetuity.[101] Similarly, Wann, for all his deeply conservative instincts, employed categories of racial development in the section of the report on 'National duties to the more backward races of mankind' to argue against those who doomed the 'coloured' races to 'perpetual national servitude', and insist on policies of 'native uplift' as the only possible justification for empire.[102]

It was thus no accident that most of the report's more politically radical statements related to Africa. Here, where racial differentials were held to be widest, lay the most pressing need for the vacuum of civilization to be filled by the closest possible co-operation between missions and colonial governments. Missionaries in Africa were indeed not to expect much from governments in defence of their own civil rights, but they were to expect open acknowledgement of the civilizing imperative. In the minds of mission theorists, Africa should have supplied the most admirable examples of government collaboration with the missionary enterprise. The fact that not infrequently the reverse was the case led Commission VII to abandon its prevailing timidity and adopt more adventurous political pronouncements. The paragraph on forced labour, inserted into the concluding section of the report at a late stage, condemned the practice as one tending 'to the oppression

101. ECG, Commission VII replies, p. 279.
102. *Report of Commission VII*, pp. 115-16, 119.

and virtual enslavement of helpless races', and called on all 'civilized Governments' to aim at its speedy and complete suppression.[103] Whilst the report of
Commission VII failed at crucial points to reflect the range and passion of
missionary opinion from the field, it still in some measure set the direction
for the more fundamental Christian challenges to the operation of colonial
rule in Africa led by Oldham in the inter-war years. Philip Curtin long ago
pointed out that evolutionary racism could lead to diametrically opposed colonial policies. He suggested, however, that the missionary movement by the
early twentieth century had succumbed to notions of the intrinsic inferiority
and hence permanent wardship of the African race.[104] Much recent writing
similarly blames pseudo-scientific theories of racial hierarchy for the frac-
tures of mission-church relationships on the field in this period. The evidence from Edinburgh 1910 points in a different direction: these same unpal-
atable theories, albeit cast in developmentalist form, were intrinsic to the
missionary endeavour to hold colonial governments true to their professions
of imperial trusteeship. As Oldham's *Christianity and the Race Problem* (1926)
would make clear, the argument over imperial trusteeship was not over the
centrality of the category of race — which almost all accepted — but over the
relative importance of 'nature' and 'nurture' in determining the perceived
pattern of racial development.[105] The Protestant missionary movement absorbed theories of racial hierarchy into its existing paradigm of progress and
civilization without fundamental readjustment of mental categories.

103. *Ibid.*, p. 117.

104. P. D. Curtin, '"Scientific" racism and the British theory of empire', *Journal of the
Historical Society of Nigeria* 2:1 (1960), pp. 49-50.

105. J. H. Oldham, *Christianity and the Race Problem* (London: SCM, 1926), p. 75 and
passim.

British Questionnaire

I. What subjects have led in recent years to important communications between your Mission and the Government authorities in the district in which it is working? Kindly state the result of any such negotiations and the way in which that result affects missionary work.

II. To what extent and in what circumstances is it advisable for missionaries to appeal to the civil authorities for protection and assistance in such matters as danger to life and property, persecution of converts, compensation for damage to property or loss of life, etc.?

If your Mission acting as a body, or if a United Conference of Missionaries working in your field, has made any pronouncements regarding the attitude of missionaries to the civil authorities in these or similar questions, kindly send us a copy of such pronouncements.

Is it possible, in your judgment, to lay down any clear guiding principle in the matter?

In countries in which there is a native Government, kindly distinguish clearly between appeals to the native authorities and appeals to the representatives of the Government of which the missionary is himself a subject.

In discussing the advisability of such appeal, kindly quote in illustration as many definite instances as possible, showing favourable or unfavourable results.

III. Is there anything in the attitude, policy, or regulations of the Government under which you are working which restrict or hinder [sic] the success of Missions?

Have you any practical suggestion to offer as to the way in which a remedy should be sought?

Kindly deal as fully as possible with particular instances.

IV. Is it desirable that there should be some representative missionary body in each field through which matters of common interest can be laid before the local Government and which can advise individual missionaries in important cases?

V. To what extent have missionaries been able to exert any influence in the shaping of legislation in such matters as education, marriage laws, the language question, etc.?

VI. What attitude, in your judgment, should be taken by missionaries towards the social and political aspirations of the people among whom they are working?

VII. Can you give instances in which missionaries have been able to render important services to Governments through geographical exploration, scientific research, linguistic work, or through facilitating the conduct of the administration?[106]

---

106. UTS, MRL 12, WMC papers, series 1, box 23, folder 2, Instructions to correspondents.

American Questionnaire

I. What are the chief matters which have led, in recent years, to important communications between your Board and the Government authorities in the various districts in which it is working?

II. In matters affecting converts and their property, do you advocate resort to the civil authority, and, if so, in what cases? What should be the guiding principle? In what cases ought the missionary to resort to the civil power for help or protection?

III. Discuss the limits of Government interference with missionary activity, either by general prohibition or on particular occasions. How far is Government justified in forbidding a missionary to cross a frontier? Discuss instances.

IV. Should missionaries take advantage of extra-territorial rights?

V. Is it advisable to claim or accept compensation for damage to mission property, or loss of life?

VI. What are the circumstances which, in your opinion, justify missionaries in extending protection to religious or other refugees?

VII. Is it not desirable that there should be some representative missionary body in each field through which matters of common interest can be laid before the local government, and which can advise individual missionaries in important cases?

VIII. Is the attitude of any government under which you are working in any respect inimical or unfavourable to missionary work? Or does the attitude in any way militate against its success? If so, what government, and in what respects?[107]

107. UTS, MRL 12, WMC papers, series 1, box 23, folder 13, summary of replies from missionary boards and churches, pp. 1-13.

CHAPTER 10

Missionary Co-operation:
Its Limits and Implications

The Dilemma of Edinburgh:
Missionary Co-operation or the Promotion of Christian Unity?

'Edinburgh 1910' is frequently remembered, and will no doubt be commemorated in 2010, as a milestone along the road towards the elusive goal of Christian unity. As was emphasized in Chapter 1, this characterization of the World
Missionary Conference is both selective in its memory and somewhat mis-
leading in its implications. It was pointed out in Chapter 2 that at an early
date in the planning of the conference, in October 1908, J. H. Oldham had to
reassure an anxious Bishop Charles Gore that Commission VIII on 'Co-
operation and the Promotion of Unity' would not be permitted to infringe
the decision taken by the international committee at its meeting in Oxford
the previous July that 'no resolution shall be allowed which involves questions of doctrine or Church polity with regard to which the Churches or Societies taking part in the Conference differ among themselves'.[1] Oldham's ruling on this question aroused the disquiet of the American executive
committee, and in particular of the Episcopalian layman, Silas McBee, whose
expansive vision for the conference was that it should not merely discern the
mind of Christ for the co-operation of mission agencies on the field, but also
as a result 'find a message from Him through the field to the home Church'.[2]

---

1. ECG, World Missionary Conference (1910), minutes of executive committee, 11 Dec.
1908, pp. 22-23, citing Oldham to the bishop of Birmingham, 5 Oct. 1908. See Chapter 2, p.
38.
    2. See Chapter 2, pp. 38-9.

McBee's controversial stance on this issue may have been the reason why Oldham, on behalf of the British executive committee, soon afterwards asked him to step aside from his original position as the nominated chairman of Commission VIII, to serve instead as vice-chairman under Oldham's father-in-law, Sir Andrew Fraser.[3] If McBee had been permitted a free hand, the ironic result would probably have been the withdrawal from the conference of his fellow-Anglicans from the Church of England. In introducing the Commission VIII report to the delegates at Edinburgh eighteen months later, Fraser made very clear that the conference, and hence the Commission, were precluded from all discussion of 'different schemes of union between different sections of the Church of Christ'.[4]

It is nevertheless the case that the work of Commission VIII had a far greater impact on subsequent ecumenical history than that of all the other Commissions put together. This chapter will trace the origins of the Continuation Committee which was the most tangible product of the conference and the most obvious source of subsequent ecumenical formations. It will argue that the most significant ecumenical development at Edinburgh was the extension to the British context of formal instruments of co-operation that were already well established between Protestant mission agencies in both North America and the European continent, particularly in Germany. The initiative taken at Edinburgh was neither widely anticipated nor immediately recognized by all participants as of enduring importance for the mutual relationships of Christian churches. Nevertheless, it represented at least the partial fulfilment of the expectations which a number of Christian leaders — most notably J. H. Oldham and Silas McBee — had attached to the conference. The militant campaigning rhetoric which enveloped and justified the work of Commission VIII, calling the allied missionary forces of western Protestantism to a more 'concerted policy', a more 'adequate combination', and a more efficient 'generalship' in the 'gigantic task' of world evangelization which confronted them, was nothing new.[5] What broke new ground at Edinburgh was the decision to embody missionary co-operation in a structured form and on a global scale which imposed on wholly autonomous voluntary missionary agencies an obligation to take much more seriously than hitherto a broader ecumenical view of the missionary task.

When the central advisory and executive committees in June 1909 fixed the

---

3. See NCE, Oldham papers, box 22, folder 2, unpublished manuscript on Oldham by Kathleen Bliss, pp. 80-1; Clements, *Faith on the Frontier*, p. 95.

4. *Report of Commission VIII*, p. 187.

5. *Ibid.*, p. 7.

maximum permitted length of the Commission reports, the fact that Commission VIII (as also Commission VII) was limited to only 60,000 words of main text, rather than the 100,000 words allocated to Commissions I to VI, does not suggest that there was a clear corporate vision among the organisers of the conference that the promotion of Christian unity was to be uppermost in its concerns.[6] It may also be significant that the number of correspondents for Commission VIII was, at ninety-five, rather smaller than for most of the other Commissions, a fact which the report acknowledged.[7] The accent of the Commission's questionnaire was on the nature and limits of the practical interdenominational co-operation which missionaries had experienced on the field. Only one question out of the six asked about what steps had been taken towards the achievement of 'closer ecclesiastical union' on the field.[8] For many, perhaps most, participants, the World Missionary Conference was simply that and nothing more: a conference about world mission in which like-minded Protestants would consult about more effective common strategies for the evangelization of the world. The promotion of unity between Christians was a means to the end of co-operation in mission, rather than the other way round. Nevertheless, the cumulative weight of evidence supplied by many questionnaire respondents from China, Japan, and India forced the question of how to expedite the visible unity of indigenous national churches (as opposed to the mere collaboration of foreign missionary agencies) higher up the Commission's agenda than was originally envisaged. Respondents from Japan or South India were able to cite the formation of the Church of Christ in Japan *(Nihon Kirisuto Itchi Kyokai)* in 1877 or the South India United Church in 1908 as examples of united churches that were already in existence, though these unions were modest in ecclesiastical scope, being entirely Presbyterian-Reformed in the first case and Presbyterian-Congregational in the second.[9] From North In-

6. UTS, MRL 12: WMC papers, series 1, box 24, folder 6, minutes of central advisory committee, 7-8 June 1909, p. 4; ECG, minutes of executive committee, 30 June 1909, pp. 41-2. Each Commission was permitted an additional 20,000 words to record the debate on their report.

7. *Report of Commission VIII*, pp. ix-xiii, p. 2. Commission VII, however, had only forty-one correspondents.

8. Question 4 asked 'Have any steps been taken towards closer ecclesiastical union? If so, kindly describe them as fully as possible, and send a copy of any printed matter relating to them. Wherever possible, please distinguish clearly between the foreign and the native view of the question.' Question 6, a general inquiry about what steps were in contemplation for securing co-operation in any of the directions mentioned in the other questions, also elicited some replies that made mention of plans of church union.

9. ECG, Commission VIII replies. See, for example, the answers to questions 4 and 6 from: J. Campbell Gibson (30), pp. 134-7, 144-6; Bishop L. H. Roots (52), pp. 227-34; Wil-

dia, the BMS missionary, George Howells, was in no doubt that the pattern of Indian church government in the future would combine the advantages of congregationalism, presbyterianism, and episcopacy — and, Baptist though he was, he welcomed the prospect.[10] The Commission report acknowledged that on the mission field, especially in Asia, the fact of Christian disunity was a scandal inhibiting the progress of the gospel, particularly in the light of strengthening national sentiment in Asian countries. The report accepted without reservation the judgment of regional missionary conferences, such as the Centenary Missionary Conference held in Shanghai in 1907, that the goal of Christian missions should be to plant one undivided church of Christ in any nation.[11]

There was thus an imperfectly recognized disjunction in the Commission's thinking in relation to its dual brief to examine 'Co-operation and the Promotion of Unity': the report actively encouraged western missionary societies in their pursuit not simply of 'co-operation' but also of 'the promotion of unity' on the field; but any discussion of how church unity might be promoted in the sending countries was ruled out of order as an infringement of the terms of the conference. The 1908 ruling that prohibited the conference from discussing 'different schemes of union between different sections of the Church of Christ' was scrupulously observed so far as the Church in Europe or North America was concerned. However, one speaker in the Commission VIII debate, Arthur Wellesley Pain, the Anglican bishop of Gippsland, did report to the conference on the current state of negotiations on church unity between Anglicans and Presbyterians in Australia, and even ventured to suggest that piecemeal reunions 'at the circumference' might be the eventual means of securing 'organic union between the Presbyterian Church and the Church of England'.[12] Moreover, the longest chapter of the Commission VIII report was Chapter Five, which dealt with the supposedly forbidden subject of 'different schemes of union between different sections of the Church of Christ' in relation to schemes of federation and union among the Protestant churches of Asia; Africa, where moves towards even federal unity had hardly begun in 1910, received only a few lines of attention by comparison.[13] Silas McBee and some of his American colleagues were aware of the inconsistency, and wished to eliminate it by extending the discussion to the necessity for a

liam Imbrie (7), pp. 285-99; L. B. Chamberlain (63), pp. 362-4; J. S. Chandler (64), p. 371; George Howells (70), pp. 397-405; and J. H. Maclean (74), p. 425.

10. ECG, Commission VIII replies, No. 70, George Howells, p. 402.
11. *Report of Commission VIII*, pp. 9-10.
12. *Ibid.*, pp. 228-9.
13. *Ibid.*, pp. 83-118. Africa receives a few lines on p. 115.

more united Christian witness in 'the home base'. Oldham, one suspects, was also aware of it, but was determined to maintain it as the necessary price of the success of the conference.

Existing Instruments of Missionary Co-operation

Contrary to what is often supposed, the concept of creating a permanent body to promote missionary co-operation among Protestants was not conjured out of the Edinburgh air in June 1910. George Robson's narrative of the conference gives some credence to this misapprehension by locating the proposal of Commission VIII to establish a Continuation Committee in the context of the doubt in the minds of many delegates over whether the conference would be permitted simply come to an end with no permanent legacy other than the text of the reports.[14] John Mott's account, published in the opening issue of the *International Review of Missions* in 1912, correctly related the decision of the conference to establish a Continuation Committee to the views expressed by many respondents to the questionnaires of the various Commissions, yet gave no hint that this apparently bold initiative was an interim response to pressure from various sources which originated prior to, and largely independently of, the World Missionary Conference.[15] At national level various forms of Protestant missionary co-operation already existed. In England the London Secretaries' Association had met regularly since 1819. In North America in January 1883, twenty-three Protestant foreign missionary societies of the United States and Canada had formed an annual conference.[16] Two years later twelve German overseas missions formed a committee (known as the *Ausschuss der deutschen evangelischen Missionen*) primarily to co-ordinate their relations with the German Colonial Office, but also to organise a national German mission conference every four years in Bremen. Similar bodies were formed in Scandinavia (1863) and the Netherlands (1887).[17] With such embryonic national structures in place, it was not surprising that some began to think in terms of international co-ordination. At the Centenary Missionary Conference held in London in 1888 a plan was submitted (in absentia) by the founding father of missiology, Professor Gustav Warneck of

14. *History and Records of the Conference*, p. 25.

15. John R. Mott, 'The Continuation Committee', *IRM* 1:1 (Jan. 1912), p. 62.

16. Ruth Rouse and Stephen C. Neill (eds.), *A History of the Ecumenical Movement 1517-1948* (London: SPCK, 1954), p. 374.

17. W. Richey Hogg, *Ecumenical Foundations: a history of the International Missionary Council and its nineteenth-century background* (New York: Harper, 1952), pp. 53-74.

Halle, for the formation of a standing central committee, to be based in London, with representatives elected by national missionary conferences in 'every Protestant nation'. It would promote co-operation, arbitrate in comity disputes, and organise an international missionary conference every ten years. This proposal was not discussed at the 1888 conference, though it was printed in the conference report.[18] However, at the quadrennial meeting of the German *Ausschuss* held in Bremen in 1909, a resolution was passed to enlarge the organization into one that in principle spanned the European continent: a 'committee of continental missions'. A conference of representatives of mission boards from Germany, Denmark, Finland, France, the Netherlands, Norway, Sweden, and Switzerland had in fact been in existence since 1866, generally meeting every four years.[19] In Britain, the London Secretaries' Association first raised the idea of forming a conference of British missionary societies in December 1909, prompted by Dr Herbert Lankester, home secretary of the CMS, who had visited the United States in 1906 and been impressed by the example of the Foreign Missions Conference of North America. The Association resolved to ask its secretary, J. H. Ritson (who was a member of Commission VIII), to try to arrange a meeting of secretaries of British missionary societies during the Edinburgh conference, with a view to forming a conference of British missionary secretaries on the model pioneered in America.[20] A considerable momentum in favour of new forms of Protestant missionary co-operation had thus been generated before the World Missionary Conference or the publication of any of its reports.

By the early years of the twentieth century the Foreign Missions Conference of North America was a well-established feature of the North American Protestant landscape, representing over fifty missionary societies; it had also initiated and organised the Ecumenical Missionary Conference in New York in 1900. As seen in Chapter 2, the Foreign Missions Conference played a crucial role in the origins of Edinburgh 1910, having in 1905 first raised the possibility of holding a series of such conferences as the one held at New York in 1900 on a decennial basis, commencing in 1910.[21] At its January 1907 meeting, the Foreign Missions Conference took a significant step towards more struc-

18. James Johnston (ed.), *Report of the Centenary Conference on Protestant Missions of the World*, 2 vols. (London: James Nisbet, 1889), II, p. 437; Rouse and Neill (eds.), *History of the Ecumenical Movement*, p. 329.

19. Hogg, *Ecumenical Foundations*, pp. 60-67; *Report of Commission VIII*, pp. 121-2.

20. CUL, BSA/F4, microfilm minutes of London Secretaries' Association, 1893-1924, minutes of 17 Oct. 1906 and 15 Dec. 1909; BSA/F4/3/1, fol. 108, J. H. Ritson to J. H. Oldham, 16 Dec. 1909.

21. See Chapter 2 above, pp. 19-21.

tured forms of co-operation by setting up a committee on reference and counsel, with responsibilities that included liaison with the Scots in preparations for the next ecumenical conference. By 1910 the committee comprised eleven members (among them being John Mott and five others who were involved in the work of the World Missionary Conference as members of different Commissions) and had concerned itself with some questions that were of international and not merely American import, such as the Congo rubber atrocities, the anti-opium movement, and the labour traffic in Melanesia.[22] It is not coincidental that three of the Commissions in which members of the committee on reference and counsel were prominently involved took careful note of these developments in North America and would later conclude their reports with specific recommendations in favour of the formation of an international co-operative missionary body. Commission I, under Mott's chairmanship, recommended 'that an International Committee should be formed for the consideration of international missionary questions'.[23] The concluding section of the report of Commission VI on the Home Base, chaired by James L. Barton, foreign secretary of the ABCFM, alluded to the Foreign Missions Conference of North America, and suggested that similar conferences be formed within convenient geographical and language zones in Europe; it also proposed that representatives from such regional conferences should constitute 'an International Committee of Reference and Counsel' to represent what was grandly but inaccurately described as 'the missionary work of Christendom'.[24] Commission VIII, of which Arthur J. Brown of the Presbyterian Board of Foreign Missions was a member, considered at its extended meeting in London from 21 to 23 December 1909, at which the initial drafts of the report were discussed, the question of whether it should recommend 'the formation in Britain of any such Conference or Committee as those in America and on the Continent'.[25] Although the Commission VIII report in its final form did not in fact include such a recommendation, it described at length the work of the Foreign Missions Conference and committee of reference and

22. UTS, MRL Pamphlets North America, *Printed Circular Letter to the Foreign Missionary Societies of Great Britain, from the Committee on Reference and Counsel Representing the Boards of Foreign Missions in the United States and Canada . . . 26 January 1910*. The other five who were members of WMC Commissions were Arthur J. Brown, Thomas S. Barbour, James L. Barton, Walter R. Lambuth, and Charles R. Watson.

23. *Report of Commission I*, p. 368; see also pp. 297 and 394.

24. *Report of Commission VI*, pp. 278-80.

25. UTS, MRL 12, WMC papers, series 1, box 23, folder 15, Sir A. H. L. Fraser to Silas McBee, 13 Dec. 1909. Brown was not present at this meeting, though Silas McBee as American vice-chairman was.

counsel, and, as is well known, unanimously recommended that the work of the Conference should be followed up by forming an international continuation committee.[26]

The German Proposal for an International Missionary Commission

Commission VIII found itself faced with two originally distinct but ultimately converging proposals for an international coordinating body for Protestant missionary activity, one from continental Europe and the other from North America. The first originated in the German *Ausschuss,* which drew up a formal memorandum or 'memorial' addressed to 'the Edinburgh World Missionary Conference, 1910' in or before September 1909. The document was accompanied by a lengthy covering letter from the venerable chairman of the *Ausschuss,* Dr Theodor Oehler (1850-1915), *Direktor* of the Basel Mission. Although originating in an initiative from the *Ausschuss,* the memorandum had by mid-September 1909 received the official endorsement of eight Scandinavian missions in addition to eighteen German ones, and hence Oehler's covering letter claimed, somewhat disingenuously, that the memorandum came from 'The Missionary Societies of the Continent of Europe'. His letter referred to the 'papers pouring in' in answer to the questionnaire prepared by Commission I, of which Richter was co-vice-chairman: Oehler stated that the replies (which Richter had evidently shown him) made proposals for 'a more definite and new form of missionary co-operation' 'on every side', and cited three such proposals, all of which hailed from India — those from the CMS missionary in the Punjab, H. U. Weitbrecht; from V. S. Azariah in his capacity as general secretary of the National Missionary Society of India; and from Nicol Macnicol of the United Free Church of Scotland mission in Pune.[27]

The German memorandum was quite explicit in its acknowledgement that the primary motive behind the proposal to form an international commission for the treatment of missionary questions was to address, and prevent any repetition of, the perceived injustices that German missions had ex-

---

26. *Report of Commission VIII,* pp. 122-6, 145-8.

27. UTS, MRL 12, WMC papers, series 1, box 24, folder 4, memorandum on appointment of a standing international committee, submitted by the missionary societies on the continent of Europe: covering letter from Dr Oehler, 15 Sept. 1909. The responses of Weitbrecht, Azariah, and Macnicol are to be found in UTS, MRL 12, WMC papers, series 1, boxes 3 and 4. For a brief account of the memorandum see Hogg, *Ecumenical Foundations,* pp. 117-18.

perienced as a result of the South African or Boer War of 1899-1902. The memorandum began by referring to the severe losses suffered by the Berlin Missionary Society during the war, amounting to some £20,000 in value, and to the principled refusal of the British government to contemplate the payment of compensation to German missions. The Hermannsburg Mission had also suffered serious loss to its property as a result of the war. The memorandum argued that the only hope of persuading the British government to change its mind lay in the formation of an international commission that could 'bring intelligent influence and expert knowledge to bear'. What the Germans wanted was a body that could make legal and political representations on behalf of Protestant missions (and of German Protestant missions in particular), whenever imperial power (and specifically British imperial power) operated in a way that threatened their interests. The memorandum requested the Edinburgh conference to authorize the establishment of an international commission that would have two functions: to assist and represent missionary societies in their dealings with foreign governments; and to represent the united body of Protestant missions at international conferences or other gatherings concerned with such moral issues as the opium and liquor traffics, or the Congo rubber atrocities. The Commission was to be composed partly of active missionaries and partly of 'statesmen with experience of missions'. It was to number no more than 20 members, with a suggested allocation of 6 from Great Britain, 6 from the United States, 4 from the European continent, 1 from Canada, 1 from South Africa, and 1 from Australia. No representatives of the 'younger churches' were envisaged, and no explicit mention was made in the proposed terms of reference of promoting co-operation in evangelism. The Commission was to work in close collaboration with the existing united missionary bodies, such as the *Ausschuss* and the committee of continental missions.[28]

The Commission VIII Meeting of 21-23 December 1909

The German memorandum, with Oehler's covering letter, appears to have been entrusted to Professor Gustav Warneck, who was a member of Commission VIII, to convey to Sir Andrew Fraser, chairman of the Commission, for

28. UTS, MRL 12, WMC papers, series 1, box 24, folder 4, memorandum on appointment of a standing international committee, submitted by the missionary societies on the continent of Europe. An alternative and probably earlier draft version of this document is to be found in UTS, MRL 12, WMC papers, series 1, box 8, folder 12.

consideration at the Commission's London meeting from 21 to 23 December 1909, which was convened to discuss the first rough drafts of the Commission's report. Warneck, then seventy-five years of age, was prevented by infirmity from attending the meeting, and posted the document to Fraser. Fraser, in a letter to his American vice-chairman, Silas McBee, written on 13 December, declined to offer any opinion on it until he had received the instructions of the Commission at the meeting.[29] Unfortunately the minutes of Commission VIII are not extant, so no direct evidence is available of the reception given to the German proposal. Clements suggests that the prospect of the British missionary societies having to take the lead in interceding with the British government on behalf of the interests of non-British missions aroused strong reservations.[30] Nevertheless, it is clear that the December meeting, at which Silas McBee was present to represent the desire of the American wing of the Commission to see tangible progress towards structured co-operation, took some kind of decision in principle to explore ways in which the co-operative spirit of the conference could be perpetuated beyond June 1910. It was almost certainly at this meeting that McBee made a suggestion that two of the English members of the Commission, Walter H. Frere and J. H. Ritson, be deputed to draft a practical proposal, remarking that 'If they agree, doubtless the Conference would accept the proposal'.[31] If the father superior of the Community of the Resurrection at Mirfield and the Methodist secretary of the Bible Society could come to a common mind on the shape of an ecumenical instrument, there was a good chance that they could carry both the Anglo-Catholic minority and the evangelical majority of the conference with them. Oldham, however, was under no illusions about the difficulties that lay in the way of a solution. He felt privately (even after 1910) that McBee had 'no notion of the real complexity of the subject as it affects missionary societies in the different countries' and above all in England.[32] Nevertheless, Oldham was in no doubt of the necessity of a new initiative in Protestant missionary co-operation: 'I recognise', he wrote to McBee on 12 January 1910,

> that on all human calculations, the difficulties in the way of any important steps in advance are insuperable and decisive. But the issues are so

29. UTS, MRL 12, WMC papers, series 1, box 23, folder 15, Fraser to McBee, 13 Dec. 1909, and Oldham to McBee, 14 Dec. 1909 [both letters also in NCE, Oldham papers, box 1, folder 4].

30. Clements, *Faith on the Frontier*, p. 96.

31. John H. Ritson, *The World is Our Parish* (London: Hodder & Stoughton, 1939), p. 278, cited in Hogg, *Ecumenical Foundations*, p. 119.

32. NCE, Oldham papers, box 1, folder 7, Oldham to Mott, 9 Feb. 1912.

great and the resources of God so incalculable, that I think we ought prayerfully to wait upon Him to know whether it is His will to bring us to something to which we cannot imagine a way.[33]

Recognizing the importance of the question, McBee took this letter to Mott, and then sent a reply to Oldham, assuring him that:

> We are in entire accord with your feeling that we have not yet seen all that we are meant to see. This has been much on my mind, and in view of the spirit that controlled our conferences in London and the frankness with which we endeavored to meet the duty upon us, I am not without hope of further progress, but the controlling principle must be that we shall see together and progress together. A short way together is better than a long way with provocation to difference and definition.[34]

Nonetheless, McBee could still inform Oldham on 25 February of his hope that the next draft of the report would be less apologetic and more 'constructive, aggressive and comprehensive' than were the initial drafts considered at the London meeting in December 1909.[35] There is little doubt that it was the American members of the Commission who were setting the pace, and the British who were at best cautious and at worst sceptical about the possibilities for a viable international organ of missionary co-operation. The American view was that the Commission had at first been too vague in differentiating between what McBee did not hesitate to call 'methods of approach to unity'. William Croswell Doane, bishop of Albany, was deputed by the American wing of the Commission to prepare alternative proposals. Precisely what these were, is not known, though McBee reported to Oldham Doane's conclusion, which he endorsed, that 'perhaps the indefiniteness which we felt at first makes the conclusion all the more catholic.'[36]

In the course of January 1910 John Ritson and Walter Frere engaged in correspondence on their allotted task to consider what form of international missionary body might command universal acceptance. Their views at first

33. UTS, MRL 12, WMC papers, series 1, box 23, folder 15, Oldham to McBee, 12 Jan. 1910 [also in NCE, Oldham papers, box 1, folder 5].

34. UTS, MRL 12, WMC papers, series 1, box 23, folder 15, McBee to Oldham, 28 Jan. 1910.

35. UTS, MRL 12, WMC papers, series 1, box 23, folder 15, McBee to Oldham, 25 Feb. 1910.

36. UTS, MRL 12, WMC papers, series 1, box 23, folder 15, McBee to Oldham, 15 March 1910.

diverged markedly. 'I quite see that the difference between your scheme and mine is fundamental', Ritson wrote to Frere: 'I am aiming at more than you are and am possibly too hopeful as regards unity'. Ritson wanted a body that was in some sense representative, just as the conference itself was; Frere appears to have feared the creation of any body that could collectively commit its member societies to actions of which individually they might disapprove.[37] Their initial negotiations on how to go about forming an international missionary committee appear to have been inconclusive.

The American Circular Letter

On 29 January 1910 the North American committee of reference and counsel issued a circular letter, addressed to the foreign missionary societies of Great Britain, suggesting that it would be 'highly advantageous' for the American committee to secure 'united conference, and, when desirable, united action' with similar committees in Britain and on the European continent. The letter expressed the view that the time had come for the creation of 'some regular means of conference' on matters which affected the missionary cause as a whole, and spoke in terms of the formation of an 'International Committee'. It also reported the independent proposal for united missionary action made by the German *Ausschuss,* which Dr Julius Richter had presented in person to the Foreign Missions Conference of North America at its meeting in New York earlier that month. However, the North Americans doubted the expediency of referring the idea of an international missionary committee to the forthcoming Edinburgh conference, since no formal votes were to be taken at Edinburgh, and the conference would have no power to act. The Foreign Missions Conference had accordingly resolved unanimously that the committee on reference and counsel should be empowered to act as the American section of an international committee and to confer with representatives of British missionary societies in the hope that a similar national body to the North American and German ones should be formed in Britain, thus making possi-

---

37. CUL, BSA/F4/3/1, fol. 124, Ritson to Frere, 18 Jan. 1910; and fols. 119-20, Ritson to Oldham, 14 Jan. 1910; see also fol. 114, Ritson to Frere, 4 Jan. 1910. There is no mention of Frere's role in the origins of the Continuation Committee in either C. S. Phillips et al., *Walter Howard Frere: Bishop of Truro* (London: Faber & Faber, 1947), or Alan Wilkinson, *The Community of the Resurrection: a centenary history* (London: SCM Press, 1992). However, E. K. Talbot in Phillips et al., *Walter Howard Frere,* p. 52, does comment on the impact which Frere made at Edinburgh when he led the conference in extempore prayer. Oldham also comments on this; see Clements, *Faith on the Frontier,* p. 92.

ble the formation of an international committee. The letter also noted that, after the conclusion of the New York meeting, word had reached the committee of the fact that two of the Edinburgh Commissions had been impressed by the need to form an international committee of some kind. The letter concluded by suggesting that the British societies might appoint their own representatives to attend a preliminary meeting on the subject to be held in Edinburgh on 13 June prior to the opening of the World Missionary Conference.[38]

No such meeting would ever take place. What in fact followed was rather a gradual convergence of the three strands of the American proposal for an international committee, the German suggestion of an international missionary commission, and the strengthening conviction of the members of Commission VIII that they should agree on some recommendation for permanent co-operative action. On 16 February 1910 the London Secretaries' Association at its regular meeting, held on this occasion at the China Inland Mission headquarters in Newington Green, welcomed Dr Julius Richter of the Berlin Missionary Society, who gave an address on the formation of an 'International Committee of Foreign Missions'. Richter reported on the 'strong consensus of opinion in favour of such an organisation' which he had found on his recent visit to the United States. He outlined the changes which had taken place in the mutual relations of missionary societies during the last twenty-five years, and stressed 'the consciousness of unity and of nationalism growing up in many lands'. He then presented to the meeting the circular letter from the committee of reference and counsel, which may in fact have been written at his own suggestion.[39] A 'prolonged discussion' ensued on the subject of how the British section of an international committee might be formed, in view of the fact that the London Secretaries' Association possessed no authority to take such action. It was noted that Commission VIII of the World Missionary Conference was likely to draft a resolution on the subject for presentation to the conference, and it was accordingly agreed to leave the matter in the hands of the Commission and report to the Association at its April meeting.[40]

38. UTS, MRL Pamphlets North America, *Printed Circular Letter to the Foreign Missionary Societies of Great Britain, from the Committee on Reference and Counsel Representing the Boards of Foreign Missions in the United States and Canada . . . 26 January 1910.*

39. Clements, *Faith on the Frontier*, p. 95, suggests that it was Richter who persuaded the committee of reference and counsel to send the circular letter.

40. CUL, BSA/F4, microfilm minutes of London Secretaries' Association, 1893-1924, minutes of 16 Feb. 1910.

British Hesitations Overcome: Walter H. Frere, John H. Ritson, and the Birth of the Idea of the Continuation Committee

Sir Andrew Fraser and J. H. Oldham succeeded in producing a draft of the first six chapters of the Commission VIII report for dispatch to the members by the end of February. The North American members met on 8 March and after careful consideration gave a general welcome to the draft. Silas McBee informed Oldham that 'we accept the six chapters sent us, being deeply impressed with the fairness, comprehensiveness and irenic spirit of the entire work'.[41] The British, however, were not yet at a sufficient stage of agreement to formulate clear and united proposals regarding an international missionary committee, which was why chapter seven of the report had to be held back. A letter from Julius Richter to John Mott, written on 4 March after his return to Germany from his travels in America and Britain, sheds further light on the varying British reactions to the idea of an international missionary committee. Contrary to what might have been expected, Richter reported that Bishop Montgomery of the SPG had shown himself to be an ardent supporter of the plan, and was confident that the Edinburgh conference would create such a powerful impression on the SPG delegates that he would be able to carry his society with him in support of a proposal congruent with that contained in the letter of the American committee of reference and counsel. This was despite the fact that the SPG standing committee did not finally approve the society's official participation in the conference until 14 April.[42] To Richter's surprise, the strongest reservations had been expressed by Herbert Lankester of the CMS and John Milton Brown of the WMMS.[43] Both were personally in favour of the idea, but had been instructed by their societies to raise official objections, which Richter summarized as follows:

> In Britain we know too little of each other, of our methods and aims, really to have confidence in each other. We have so long gone our own way without regard of any other society's operations that we find it hard to combine in action of an intersociety — much less of an international kind. And: we do not yet see how such an international committee could

41. UTS, MRL 12, WMC papers, series 1, box 23, folder 15, McBee to Oldham, 15 March 1910; McBee to Sir Andrew Fraser, 23 March 1910.

42. Oxford, Rhodes House, USPG Archives, minutes of SPG standing committee, vol. 60 (1909-), pp. 1752-4; LP, Davidson papers, vol. 269, fol. 61, H. H. Montgomery to Randall Davidson, 14 April 1910.

43. John Milton Brown had served for many years as a missionary in Ceylon and Calcutta before becoming a secretary of the WMMS in 1905.

be of any real profit of our own society. And we fear, our Board will be very reluctant to pledge its authority or its official prestige in any international committee which is not absolutely under its own control, because it would fear to become compromised by unwise actions of such a committee.[44]

In the British context, the concept of structuring international missionary co-operation in a formal representative body proved more threatening to some evangelical societies long accustomed to total independence of operations than it did to the secretary of the SPG, the leading High Church missionary agency, which had never wholly subscribed to the voluntary society ideal. Oldham therefore had to inform Silas McBee on 24 March that 'the proposals regarding practical outcome have a little hung fire', and suggested that the report be dispatched to delegates with the final two to three pages, dealing with practical outcomes, omitted. It had been arranged that the Commission would meet as a whole in Edinburgh on the eve of the conference, and Oldham proposed that the decision on the concluding section of the report should be left to that meeting, which could then print and circulate the final paragraphs in time to reach delegates three or four days before the debate on the report, which was scheduled for 21 June.[45]

The British members of Commission VIII, plus Silas McBee,[46] assembled in London on 7-8 April for a meeting to consider the draft report. Ritson still entertained hopes that considerable time would be given at the meeting to the subject of the formation of the international committee. He wrote to Fraser beforehand that 'This is a matter of supreme importance, and many outsiders are expecting us to do something practical'.[47] There is no direct evidence of how far Ritson's hopes for the meeting were fulfilled, but it is at least clear that the meeting commissioned Frere and Ritson to do more work on the final section of the report; and that they were specifically instructed to produce a definite scheme for the establishment of a continuation committee.[48] Ritson's

44. YDS, RG45, John R. Mott papers, Richter to Mott, 4 March 1910.

45. UTS, MRL 12, WMC papers, series 1, box 23, folder 15, McBee to Oldham, 24 March 1910.

46. McBee's presence can be deduced from Fraser's remarks in *Report of Commission VIII*, pp. 187-8, and also from LP, Davidson papers, vol. 269, fol. 70, Randall Davidson to Silas McBee, 20 April 1910.

47. CUL, BSA/F4/3/1, fol. 201, Ritson to Fraser, 6 April 1910.

48. Ritson immediately produced two paragraphs for the report at the request of the meeting, but it seems unlikely that these related to the idea of a continuation committee: see CUL, BSA/F4/3/1, fol. 202, Ritson to Fraser, 8 April 1910. It is clear from CUL,

World Missionary Conference letter-book indicates that the proposal to establish a continuation committee (rather than an international missionary committee) was drafted by Frere and refined by Ritson in the course of correspondence over the following six weeks. On 11 April Frere sent Ritson some 'draft paragraphs regarding continuation Committees' for insertion in the closing section of the report. On a first reading, Ritson found himself in agreement with what Frere had written, yet he wondered 'whether we can go a little further'.[49] After careful reflection, Ritson suggested a few verbal changes to Frere's 'admirable' draft, which he sent to him for approval on 19 April.[50]

On the following day, 20 April, the London Secretaries' Association met and returned to the subject of the World Missionary Conference. Ritson as secretary of the Association was able to give an up-to-date insider's report on 'the trend of the discussions of Commission VIII'. It was necessarily somewhat tentative in view of the fact that the Commission as a whole had not yet given formal approval to the proposal that the conference should set up a continuation committee. He accordingly informed the Association that 'possibly they [the Commission] would advise the Edinburgh Conference to appoint a Continuation Committee on an International and representative basis'; the duties of such a Continuation Committee would include the development of a permanent International Committee, such as envisaged by the American proposal. The meeting resolved after some discussion to postpone further consideration of the matter until after the Edinburgh conference.[51] Ritson's unofficial report to the Association reflected the brief which had been entrusted to him and Frere at the meeting on 7-8 April, namely to produce proposals whereby the Commission could recommend the appointment by the conference of a representative international body to be called 'The Continuation Committee'.[52] It would not itself be the international committee for which the Americans and the Germans had in their different ways been campaigning, and which had met with such a hesitant response from various sources in Britain; it would rather be the necessary modest first step towards the formation of such a permanent body.

BSA/F4/3/1, fols. 260-2, Ritson to Frere, 18 May 1910, and fol. 271, Ritson to Fraser, 21 May 1910, that Frere and Ritson were given a brief by the Commission meeting to draft a scheme for a Continuation Committee.

49. CUL, BSA/F4/3/1, fol. 208, Ritson to Frere, 15 April 1910; and fol. 219, Ritson to Fraser, 18 April 1910.

50. CUL, BSA/F4/3/1, fol. 220, Ritson to Fraser, 19 April 1910.

51. CUL, BSA/F4, microfilm minutes of London Secretaries' Association, 1893-1924, minutes of 20 April 1910.

52. Ritson, *The World is Our Parish*, p. 278.

A month later, Ritson sent Frere a further and more substantial set of amendments to what may have been a revised draft of Frere's. Ritson's amendments were designed, *inter alia,* to distinguish more clearly the 'permanent' nature of any 'International Missionary Committee' that might in future be formed from the role of the Continuation Committee, which, he was anxious to emphasize, would cease to exist on the formation of such an international committee.[53] These amendments are exactly reflected in the final text of the report, which would in turn become the basis of the resolution establishing the Continuation Committee.[54] Frere readily agreed to Ritson's amendments, and on 21 May Ritson sent Fraser the final draft of the paragraphs in chapter seven of the report relating to the Continuation Committee.[55]

On 9 June Bishop Montgomery penned a lengthy memorandum to the archbishops of York and Canterbury on the subject of 'the proposed "International Committee" of Missions'. It should be observed that at this stage he was apparently unaware of the idea of a conference continuation committee. The most likely source of Montgomery's information was his membership of Commission I, whose report in three places recommended the formation, not of a continuation committee, but rather a permanent international committee of missions.[56] The final conference *Monthly News Sheet* for May 1910 also printed a letter to the editor from Dr H. U. Weitbrecht of the CMS Simla mission, proposing that the conference should initiate a systematic international effort for the study and teaching of 'the science of Foreign Missions' and establish a 'general Missionary Council' on the model of the *Ausschuss;* an accompanying editorial comment noted that the idea of setting up 'a General Council or International Committee' had already received support on the European continent and in America, and was 'engaging the careful attention' of Commission VIII.[57] However, a later comment by Montgomery suggests that he had not seen the May *Monthly News Sheet.*[58]

Montgomery's memorandum informed the archbishops that an informal meeting of leaders of missionary societies was planned for the close of the conference on 24 June 'to consider a *Worldwide International Committee of*

53. CUL, BSA/F4/3/1, fols. 260-2, Ritson to Frere, 18 May 1910.

54. *Report of Commission VIII,* pp. 145-7; *History and Records of the Conference,* p. 96, paragraphs I (6) and II.

55. CUL, BSA/F4/3/1, fol. 271, Ritson to Fraser, 21 May 1910.

56. *Report of Commission I,* pp. 297, 368, 394.

57. World Missionary Conference 1910, *Monthly News Sheet* 8 (May 1910), pp. 159-60, 168. For Weitbrecht's enthusiasm for interdenominational co-operation see above, p. 284 and n. 27.

58. LP, Davidson papers, vol. 269, fol. 87, Montgomery to Oldham, n.d. [14 June 1910].

Missions.' He was in no doubt that the American, continental European, and British Protestant societies would all join before the year was out. Montgomery had been asked privately 'what the possibilities were of the Anglican Church joining'. His answer was unequivocal: 'I do not think we dare to stand out'. It was imperative that 'this new force' should be 'kept straight'. That meant appointing as Anglican representatives neither Low Churchmen (whom, he complained, were regarded by Nonconformists as 'their own people within the Anglican fold' whom they could 'play with' as they liked), nor even an unstable mixture of Low and High Churchmen (which would fatally weaken the Anglican witness), but rather a phalanx of 'wise High Churchmen'. Montgomery nominated the bishops of Birmingham and Southwark as just the men for the task, though he suggested to the archbishops that he and his evangelical counterpart, Cyril Bardsley, the newly appointed honorary clerical secretary of the CMS, could act as a private committee of 'fags' to do the necessary work behind the scenes.[59] Montgomery's memorandum confirms Richter's report to Mott that in principle he was a firm supporter of the idea of an international missionary committee. However, it suggests that his understanding at that point was that the initiative to establish an international missionary committee would be taken at an informal meeting outside of the conference itself, and that there would accordingly be no question of the SPG delegates having to act in a formal capacity within the conference to commit the society to participate in an ecumenical body. It also implies that he expected the Church of England as such to be represented on the proposed international committee. The first assumption was, to his great consternation, about to be proved false; the second, though not formally correct, would in fact be substantially true.

At some point between 21 May and the opening of the conference on 14 June, Commission VIII met for the last time — most probably in Edinburgh itself during the weekend of 11-12 June.[60] At Oldham's suggestion, Ralph Wardlaw Thompson was invited to the meeting to lend his considerable weight to the proposals.[61] The meeting was also attended not simply by Silas McBee but also by a majority of the other North American members.[62] The meeting approved the paragraphs in chapter seven which Frere and Ritson

59. LP, Davidson papers, vol. 269, fols. 80-83, memorandum by H. H. Montgomery, 9 June 1910.

60. Ritson did not travel to Edinburgh until the afternoon of Friday 10 June: CUL, BSA/F4/3/1, fol. 338, Ritson to G. Graham Brown, 7 June 1910.

61. CUL, BSA/F4/3/1, fol. 204, Ritson to Oldham, 14 April 1910.

62. *Report of Commission VIII*, pp. 187-8. The precise date of the meeting is not known. Not all the American members of Commission VIII attended the conference.

had written, and formulated the text of a resolution to be moved in the conference on 21 June. The 'general conclusions' of the Commission VIII report
now included a recommendation that the conference should establish on an
international and representative basis a Continuation Committee, whose responsibilities were to include the maintenance of the co-operative work and
spirit of the conference, and, crucially, 'to confer with the Societies and
Boards as to the best method of working towards the formation of such a permanent International Missionary Committee as has been already recommended by this and other Commissions and by various missionary bodies
apart from the Conference.'[63] As we know that the full set of printed Commission reports was available by 24 May at the latest,[64] it would appear that
Oldham's suggested mode of proceeding was adopted, and that the section of
the final chapter of the Commission VIII report containing these crucial
paragraphs (and conceivably the entire chapter) was not made public until
the conference itself opened, possibly at the same time as the resolution itself
was circulated.[65] This helps to explain the impression given in the published
accounts by Mott and Robson that the proposal to establish the Continuation
Committee emerged in the course of the conference itself. It also explains the
alarm evinced by Bishop Montgomery in letters written to Oldham and to
Randall Davidson on 14 June on learning that the conference was, after all, to
be asked to pass a resolution. Montgomery complained to Oldham that this
undercut all the assurances which had been given to the standing committee
of the SPG in April when the Society was undecided on whether it could be
officially represented at Edinburgh. 'It is a very bold step indeed', he reminded
Oldham,

> to invite Christian people not in communion with one another to dis-
> cuss great Christian questions for a fortnight. It can only be a question
> of Conference but not of Resolutions.
>
> You will realise the perplexity I feel. It borders on dismay.
>
> I am quite clear that in the name of the S.P.G. I am not able to con-
> sent to the passing of any Resolution whatsoever, except of course in re-
> gard to details of the business of the Conference.[66]

63. *Ibid.*, pp. 146-7.
64. See CUL, BSA/F4/3/1, fol. 283, A. Taylor to Oldham, 24 May 1910.
65. In introducing the resolution to the conference on 21 June, Sir Andrew Fraser
noted that the resolution to establish the Continuation Committee had been in the hands
of delegates for 'several days': *Report of Commission VIII*, p. 202.
66. LP, Davidson papers, vol. 269, fols. 85-7, Montgomery to Oldham, n.d. [14 June
1910]; see also fol. 84, Montgomery to Davidson, 14 June 1910.

No response from Oldham to Montgomery's sombre letter is extant. It is clear that during the first week of the conference Montgomery scurried around trying to rally support for an attempt to block the passing of any resolution on any substantive matter; he claimed to have recruited both Silas McBee and Bishop D'Arcy of Ossory to his cause.[67] By Sunday 19 June, however, his anxiety was abating: according to Tissington Tatlow, Montgomery had agreed to the idea of a resolution and was 'less nervous' than on the first day of the conference.[68] On Monday the 20th, Montgomery himself informed Davidson that although he was skating 'on thin ice', he was 'agreeing to a *"Continuation Committee"* to carry on conference — I see nothing but good in that'.[69] Montgomery was unaware that on Sunday Tatlow had written to Davidson, enclosing the text of the proposed resolution, seeking the archbishop's confidential advice and his permission to share it with Oldham, on who should be nominated as a High Churchman to accompany one of the CMS secretaries (Tatlow thought, incorrectly, that it would be Bardsley) among the ten British members envisaged for the Committee. Tatlow confessed to the archbishop that 'Bishop Montgomery w^d be the obvious man in some ways but he is timid & is inclined at times through being over anxious to have his judgment impaired. Oldham rather favours trying to get either the Bishop of Southwark or Rev. W. H. Frere.'[70] Davidson replied immediately, on Monday the 20th, agreeing that it would be unfair to Montgomery as secretary of a body that was so divided on these subjects to place him in such an exposed position, expressing his clear preference for Bishop Talbot, and giving his permission for Tatlow to show his letter privately to Oldham.[71] For a second time, the archbishop of Canterbury had exercised a decisive influence on the course of the conference.

67. LP, Davidson papers, vol. 269, fol. 84, Montgomery to Davidson, 14 June 1910, and fol. 91, Montgomery to [Davidson], 16 June 1910.

68. LP, Davidson papers, vol. 269, fols. 95-6, Tatlow to Davidson, 19 June 1910.

69. LP, Davidson papers, vol. 269, fol. 100, Montgomery to Davidson, 20 June 1910.

70. LP, Davidson papers, vol. 269, fols. 95-6, Tatlow to Davidson, 19 June 1910.

71. LP, Davidson papers, vol. 269, fols. 98-99, Davidson to Tatlow, 20 June 1910. Davidson commended Talbot as someone who was universally respected, but also as chairman of the UMCA, a mission which was not even officially represented at Edinburgh. He no doubt felt that Talbot, as a diocesan bishop and only an honorary officer of the UMCA, would be less exposed to criticism than Montgomery would have been as secretary of the SPG if he had been appointed to the Continuation Committee.

The Commission VIII Debate and the Creation
of the Continuation Committee

The debate on the Commission VIII report on Tuesday, 21 June is the only one which George Robson felt important enough to summarize in his brief 'general account of the conference', the first official report of the conference proceedings which was printed in volume 9 of the conference reports and published soon afterwards.[72] It also figures prominently in newspaper and periodical accounts of the conference. The first morning session was devoted to discussing the report as a whole. Speakers included Cheng Jingyi, whose eloquent speech on the impulse towards Christian unity in China was discussed in Chapter 5, Bishop Charles H. Brent, and the Bishop of Southwark. Brent's contribution was a bold plea, born of his own experience as missionary bishop of the Protestant Episcopal Church in the Philippines, for co-operation with Roman Catholics wherever that was possible. He had consulted Bishop Gore in advance about what he should say, and noted in his diary that though his task was a difficult one, he had been well received: 'men of every type and creed came to me by scores and thanked me. It was most moving.'[73] In his old age, Oldham claimed that Brent had gone still further, and called for another conference to tackle those questions of faith and order that had been excluded from the Edinburgh agenda, but the evidence suggests that Oldham's memory was at fault; no such reference is recorded in the reports of Brent's address, and his diary records that the idea of a world conference on faith and order in fact came to him vividly at a morning eucharist in Cincinnati on 5 October 1910 at the opening of the Convention of the Protestant Episcopal Church.[74] Bishop Talbot qualified Cheng Jingyi's call for a united church in China by reminding the conference that no Christian unity could be complete which ignored the Roman Catholic and Orthodox communions. Talbot's carefully phrased exposition of the Anglo-Catholic contention that an Anglican understanding of church, ministry, and sacraments was an integral part of the church's witness to the incarnation received a mixed response. One CMS delegate, who on the whole was annoyed that the

---

72. *History and Records of the Conference*, pp. 25-6. The intention was to publish the reports by about the end of September 1910; see World Missionary Conference, *Monthly News Sheet* 3 (Dec. 1909), p. 68.

73. Washington, Library of Congress Manuscripts Division, papers of C. H. Brent, box 53, diary of C. H. Brent, p. 406, entries for 18 and 21 June 1910.

74. Washington, Library of Congress Manuscripts Division, papers of C. H. Brent, box 53, diary of C. H. Brent, p. 415, entry for 5 Oct. 1910; W. Richey Hogg, 'Edinburgh 1910 — Perspective 1980', *Occasional Bulletin of Missionary Research* 4:4 (Oct. 1980), pp. 148-9.

Anglo-Catholics at Edinburgh had so successfully commandeered Anglican identity, voiced his admiration for Talbot's realistic appraisal of the problem of Christian unity.[75] Others felt that Talbot had transgressed the very limitations excluding doctrinal and controversial matters from debate which the Anglo-Catholic party had made the condition of their participation.[76] The correspondent of the Nonconformist *Christian World* wrote an unenthusiastic report of the speech under the heading 'Bishop of Southwark's cold water', and observed that the various Anglo-Catholic contributions to the debate had 'caused the greatest astonishment among Continental and American delegates, who did not know what established High Anglicanism means'.[77]

Immediately after the mid-morning act of worship, Mott invited Sir Andrew Fraser as chairman of the Commission to move the resolution to establish the Continuation Committee. Fraser took great pains to emphasize that what was being proposed was not an international missionary committee, since the conference had no authority to act for the various mission boards in that respect: the conference was merely being invited to vote on whether it should establish a Continuation Committee which would in due time invite the societies and boards to consider the larger question of whether a permanent international and fully representative body should be formed.[78] Right up to the last, there was intense nervousness that the idea of the Continuation Committee would be the subject of misrepresentation and attack. Oldham later reflected that until the eleventh hour the issue hung in the balance and that 'but for the unclouded vision and exceptional force of conviction of John R. Mott the decision would have gone the other way'.[79] Mott's decision to use his authority from the chair to delay the vote on the resolution until one hour into the afternoon session is evidence of the seriousness with which he viewed the resolution and the potential implications of its failure.[80]

The resolution was seconded by Arthur J. Brown, chairman of the American committee of reference and counsel which had done so much to put the question of international missionary co-operation on the agenda. Supporters of the resolution included Julius Richter and Bishop Handley Moule of Dur-

75. 'A C.M.S. Delegate', 'The World Missionary Conference, 1910. II. Further Impressions', *Church Missionary Review* 61:736 (Aug. 1910), pp. 454-6.

76. Howard B. Grose, 'The Edinburgh conference: a pen picture of the world meeting', *Missions* 1:9 (Sept. 1910), p. 572.

77. *Christian World*, 23 June 1910, p. 11 and supplement, p. 24.

78. *Report of Commission VIII*, pp. 203-4.

79. J. H. Oldham, 'Reflections on Edinburgh, 1910', *Religion and Life* 29:3 (Summer 1960), p. 335.

80. *History and Records of the Conference*, p. 26.

ham. Richter assured the conference that 'all the leading Missionary Societies on the Continent of Europe' were deeply sympathetic to the resolution, and referred, somewhat disingenuously, to the memorandum submitted by the *Ausschuss* as 'a comprehensive petition to establish such a Committee, binding together the different missionary organizations into united action' — a claim which tended to blur the distinction that Fraser had been at such pains to stress between the Continuation Committee and a future international missionary committee.[81] What Richter could not say in public was that the German delegates, although in favour of a Continuation Committee, had privately informed Oldham that their support was conditional upon his agreement to serve as its secretary; unless this were so, they feared being swamped by the Anglo-American majority.[82]

When the conference re-assembled after lunch, the Revd Lord William Gascoyne-Cecil, one of the SPG delegation, confessed that his initial doubts over the wisdom of presenting a formal resolution on the question had been overcome only because all that was being proposed was the choosing of a committee to study the question of whether an interdenominational missionary body should subsequently be established.[83] John Campbell Gibson, on the other hand, gently criticized the resolution for not going far enough, insisting that 'we are prepared for more thoroughgoing and united action than is fully shadowed here'.[84] The note of Anglo-Catholic caution was, however, immediately resumed by Bishop Montgomery, whose much-quoted metaphor of belonging to 'a little band of lions in an enormous den of Daniels' was designed to put the conference in good humour before he delivered his main and more disturbing point, namely that 'undenominationalism' was dead and that respect for distinctive denominational convictions offered the only hope for the future.[85] Anglo-Catholic support, like that of the Germans, had in fact been bought at a price: Oldham disclosed many years later that Walter Frere had told him in the course of the conference that Anglo-Catholics (no less than the Lutherans) would consent to take part in a continuing body only if he were its secretary: the participation of Frere, Gore, Montgomery, and Kelly in the work of the Commissions had given them a confidence in Oldham that they were not prepared to place in anyone else.[86] What was equally crucial was that Tatlow had fed Archbishop Davidson's advice to

81. *Report of Commission VIII*, p. 206.
82. Oldham, 'Reflections on Edinburgh, 1910', p. 335.
83. *Report of Commission VIII*, p. 209.
84. *Report of Commission VIII*, p. 211.
85. *Report of Commission VIII*, pp. 213-14.
86. Oldham, 'Reflections on Edinburgh, 1910', p. 335.

Oldham, and Bishop Talbot's name was there on the list of British members of the proposed committee.[87]

Mott allowed nine speakers in all to make their contribution that afternoon before asking the conference whether it was ready to vote. It unanimously declared itself so ready. The vote on the resolution was then passed by a resounding 'Aye' of acclamation. When Mott asked for votes to the contrary, not a single 'No' was heard in the assembly. The conference, apparently spontaneously, began to sing the doxology in relief and jubilation.[88] The World Missionary Conference had taken its one and only decision. 'This', recalled Oldham fifty years later, 'was the turning point in the history of the ecumenical movement'.[89] His words were not simply the inflated verdict of hindsight. The report of the conference in the *Missionary Record of the United Free Church of Scotland* claimed that 'one of the momentous decisions that make history' had been passed, a decision that would have been impossible ten years previously.[90] The American Congregationalist, Cornelius H. Patton, writing in the Boston *Missionary Herald,* agreed that 'the significance of this action can hardly be overstated. It makes international the large measure of comity which has existed for years among the American societies, and is big with promise for a general movement looking to the reunion of Christendom'.[91]

The remainder of the session was devoted to discussing chapter six of the report, concerned with the possibilities and principles of co-operation at the home base. Only now, with the vote safely in the bag, was Silas McBee permitted to read the famous but controversial letter of greeting from Bishop Bonomelli of Cremona; the business committee had privately encouraged McBee to read the letter as part of his speech, but declined to take any official responsibility for it.[92] Fittingly, the final speaker of the afternoon was John Ritson, who summed up the mood of the conference by urging the importance of looking for the best in other Christian traditions: referring to a saying of the late Dr John Watson (better known by his *nom de plume* of 'Ian Maclaren') that it would be unfair of a visitor to Edinburgh to search out the Cowgate and then to leave and slander 'one of the fairest cities on earth', he

87. LP, Davidson papers, vol. 269, fols. 101-2, Tatlow to Davidson, 22 June 1910.

88. *History and Records of the Conference,* p. 98; Gairdner, 'Edinburgh 1910', p. 209; *Missionary Herald* (Boston) 106 (1910), p. 354.

89. Oldham, 'Reflections on Edinburgh, 1910', p. 333.

90. 'The World Missionary Conference: impressions and lessons', *Missionary Record of the United Free Church of Scotland* 116 (Aug. 1910), p. 352.

91. *Missionary Herald* (Boston) 106 (1910), p. 354.

92. UTS, MRL 12, WMC papers, series 1, box 23, folder 15, Oldham to McBee, 18 June 1910; see above, Chapter 1, p. 11.

enjoined, 'we must look for the Princes Street in the churches and in the lives of one another'.[93]

The resolution establishing the Continuation Committee left the business committee of the conference to nominate its members. The nominations were brought forward on the afternoon of 22 June, and were unanimously adopted. Britain, North America, and the continent of Europe were each given ten members; South Africa, Australasia, Japan (Bishop Honda), China (Cheng Jingyi), and India (K. C. Chatterjee) had one each, making thirty-five members in all — the membership was both larger and more geographically inclusive than that proposed by the *Ausschuss* in 1909 for an 'International Missionary Commission'. The bishop of Southwark was joined by two other Anglicans of Catholic sympathies: Silas McBee and Louise Creighton (widow of Bishop Mandell Creighton, and a member of the SPG delegation); she was the sole woman among the thirty-five. Bishop Talbot later confessed that he had 'very grave doubts whether he could on ecclesiastical and other grounds' consent to be a member, but he did so and never regretted it.[94] Julius Richter as chairman of the *Ausschuss* and Arthur Brown as chairman of the American committee of reference and counsel were obvious choices. So were Sir Andrew Fraser, Ralph Wardlaw Thompson, and Mott himself. It was no coincidence that John Ritson was also one of those appointed, though there was no place for Walter Frere, who had played the greater part in the drafting of the text of the proposal to establish the Committee. The *Christian World* took pleasure in reporting 'a dash of amusement' among the American delegates who felt that Mott had been 'exceptionally anxious to corral the S.P.G. in order to round the Conference circle' but who now had the distinct and probably accurate impression that the Anglo-Catholic voice on the Continuation Committee was not going to have its own way.[95]

It should be noted that Oldham himself was not one of the thirty-five. On the recommendation of the business committee, the Continuation Committee was given power to appoint its own officers. At its inaugural meeting, held at 1 p.m. on Thursday 23 June while the conference was still in session, Mott was elected as acting chairman, and it was agreed to invite Oldham to serve the Committee as its acting secretary. A sub-committee comprising George Robson, Arthur Brown, Mott, and Oldham was elected to prepare the agenda

93. *Report of Commission VIII*, p. 230. On Watson see *ODNB*.

94. Basil Mathews, *Dr Ralph Wardlaw Thompson* (London: Religious Tract Society, 1917), p. 143. The other Anglican members were Canon Norman Tucker from Canada, Eugene Stock (formerly editorial secretary of the CMS), and Arthur Pain, bishop of Gippsland (Australia). On Louise Creighton see *ODNB*.

95. *Christian World*, 23 June 1910, p. 11.

for the meeting that was to convene on the following day. A further sub-committee comprising Fraser, Richter, and James L. Barton was appointed to prepare proposals on the constitution and officers of the Committee.[96] The Committee met again for four extended sessions, lasting for eleven and a half hours in all, on the Friday and Saturday immediately after the close of the conference. The agenda sub-committee proposed moving immediately 'to the discussion of the formation and functions of a permanent International Committee', but after discussion it was agreed to proceed more cautiously and concentrate initially on matters left over from the work of the Commissions and the discussions of the conference. In the course of these sessions, the Committee determined its own organization of sub-committees, the priorities on its agenda, and appointed its officers; Oldham was confirmed as its full-time salaried secretary. An executive committee of nine members was created, with Oldham as non-voting secretary. A series of eight special committees, with membership drawn from a much wider body of people than the Continuation Committee itself, was also set up to carry forward many of the practical proposals and policies of co-operation recommended by the eight Commissions.[97] Within thirty-six hours of the conclusion of the conference on the evening of 23 June, the framework of an ecumenical missionary structure had been erected. Eleven years later, in 1921, it would lead to the formation of the International Missionary Council, thus fulfilling the visions first elaborated by the *Ausschuss* in September 1909 and the Foreign Missions Conference in January 1910.

96. ECG, minutes of Continuation Committee, 23 June 1910, p. 2.
97. ECG, minutes of Continuation Committee, 24-25 June 1910, pp. 4-11.

CHAPTER 11

The Legacy of Edinburgh 1910

Missionary Perceptions of East, West, and South

The thinking of delegates to the World Missionary Conference was dominated by the conceptual juxtaposition of east and west. From the east arose the pressing questions of how to respond to the singular opportunities created for Christian missions by western imperial might and movements of modernizing national reform, as well as to the more ominous trends of the resurgence of the great non-Christian religions or the rise of newly strident forms of Asian nationalism. From the Christian west, so it was assumed, the answers would have to come, in the form of missionary strategies of intensified zeal, broader sympathies, and closer co-operation. The conference, as explained in Chapter 3, was premised on the working assumption that Christian mission had to be treated as a movement from the Christian world of the western hemisphere to the non-Christian world of the east. Even if not all of the conference delegates in actuality believed this (many of the Americans, it should be remembered, represented societies which operated in Latin America or in the countries bordering the eastern Mediterranean), they had to accept that a crudely geographical division between Christendom and heathendom was the only basis on which the fragile ecumenical consensus at Edinburgh could be maintained. For most delegates at Edinburgh such a territorial understanding of Christendom was a deeply ingrained feature of their understanding of the world. For others it may have been no more than a rough, even regrettable, working assumption. In the former category were a group of American mission secretaries, led by Robert E. Speer, who assembled for two unofficial sessions at Edinburgh to consider the Latin American missions which had been excluded from the agenda. Speer, though believing that 'there certainly is such a thing as Christendom which is different from paganism', held that 'nevertheless, there is a great deal of paganism in what we call Christendom'.[1] The unofficial Latin American sessions led eventually to a conference on missions in Latin America, held in New York in March 1913 under the auspices of the Foreign Missions Conference of North America, which established a permanent body to co-ordinate American Protestant work on the continent, the Committee on Co-operation in Latin America. The Committee convened a major Congress on Christian Work in Latin America, organised along similar lines to the Edinburgh conference, which took place in Panama in February 1916.[2]

The World Missionary Conference's division of the world into two sharply delineated geographical sectors — Christian and non-Christian — is the aspect of the conference that became outdated more quickly than any other, and which strikes the twenty-first-century observer as most obviously unacceptable. The first insistent question marks to be placed over the conceptual juxtaposition of Christian west and non-Christian east appeared within a few years of the conference, with the outbreak of war in Europe. J. H. Oldham, when writing his missionary survey of the year 1914, published in the January 1915 number of the *IRM*, had to resort to the geological analogy of 'some gigantic prehistoric catastrophe', twisting and breaking the rock strata, in order to convey the magnitude of the 'tremendous upheaval of the war', which had opened up 'a huge fault' in the apparent unity of the Christian west expressed at Edinburgh. 'All facts are in a new setting', mused Oldham: 'their proportion and significance is changed'. The war upset missionary plans, interrupted communications, and threw over a supposedly Christian Europe the menacing shadow of 'the evil and ruin' wrought by human sin.[3] It also brought the work of the Continuation Committee to a shuddering halt. Although initially Oldham had some success in his attempts to keep the Committee independent of either side in the conflict, by July 1917 the German mission leaders, including all four German members of the Continuation Committee, had issued a declaration dissociating themselves from Mott's leadership as chairman and from one of the Scottish members, J. N. Ogilvie, on account of strongly anti-German statements they had both made.[4] Although the rift in ecumenical fel-

---

1. Princeton Theological Seminary, Special Collections, Robert E. Speer papers, box 6, vol. 17, fol. 308, R. E. Speer to Paul Barnhardt, 13 June 1910.

2. Hogg, *Ecumenical Foundations*, p. 132. *Addresses and Papers of John R. Mott Volume Five: the International Missionary Council* (New York: Association Press, 1947), pp. 179-217.

3. 'A missionary survey of the year 1914', *IRM* 4:1 (Jan. 1915), pp. 3, 60-1, 65.

4. Oldham, *Faith on the Frontier*, pp. 135-44; Hogg, *Ecumenical Foundations*, pp. 174-5;

lowship caused by the war was gradually healed after 1919, the war had thrown into question the assumption, so foundational to the Edinburgh conference, that Christian mission could be understood as a movement from the Christian nations of the west to the non-Christian nations of the east. In Oldham's book, *The World and the Gospel*, published in 1916, the first questionings of the idea of the Christian nation can be discerned: western civilization, complained Oldham, had become 'materialistic, vulgar, feverish and unsatisfying'; mission, therefore, must embrace within its scope a challenge to the prevalence of secular values within the public life of the western nations that were supposed to exemplify the Christian gospel.[5] Two decades later, in an article written for the *IRM* in 1935, the doubts had become more insistent. Oldham looked back at 1910, and reflected that what had since changed was not so much the fracture of Christendom as the dissolution of the very notion:

> . . . the startling fact which confronts us is the emergence in what has hitherto been known as Christendom of a new paganism openly repudiating the whole Christian understanding of life. The frank determination to base public policy on pagan ideas and pagan values is opening our eyes to the extent to which western thought and society as a whole has become secularized and paganized. The dividing-line between Christian and non-Christian countries is tending to disappear, and we have to accustom ourselves more and more to thinking of the one universal (though unhappily divided) Christian Church confronting a world which notwithstanding its differences is at one in the repudiation of the authority of the Christian revelation.[6]

By 1935 the binary language of 'the Christian world' and 'the non-Christian world' was losing its force. The idea of Europe as in some sense the distinctive embodiment of Christian cultural values was not yet extinct. In 1940 the darkest days of the battle against Hitler provoked a temporary renaissance in Britain of the vocabulary of 'Christian civilization', but the fact that this grave challenge to Christian ideas of humanity came from within Europe itself made impossible the continuation of any simple equation between the west and the

---

R. V. Pierard, 'John R. Mott and the rift in the ecumenical movement during World War I', *Journal of Ecumenical Studies* 23:4 (Fall 1986), pp. 601-20.

5. J. H. Oldham, *The World and the Gospel*, 3rd edn. (London: United Council for Missionary Education, 1917), pp. 20-24 (quotation at p. 22); see Oldham, *Faith on the Frontier*, pp. 133-5.

6. J. H. Oldham, 'The International Review of Missions after twenty-five years', *IRM* 24:95 (July 1935), pp. 300-1.

Christian world.[7] After 1945, the concept of Christendom limped on among some Christian conservatives. Ironically it was strongest in parts of the African continent, in the white enclaves of South Africa and Rhodesia before the coming of majority rule, where it was used as a justification for white supremacy. In Europe itself, the Roman Catholic Church continued to make appeal to the Christian roots of European civilization as a necessary resource in the struggle with secularism. Some recent publications by Josef Ratzinger, now Pope Benedict XVI, are a contemporary example: Benedict has argued that the very idea of Europe emerged in contradistinction to the encircling threat of Islam, and that only a return to its roots in Christian values will save Europe from decline and fall.[8] But for Pope Benedict Europe's Christendom status is a lost heritage to be reclaimed, not a present reality, whilst among Protestant leaders the notion of Europe as a continent defined by its Christian identity holds even less plausibility, even if it remains ingrained in much popular Christian thinking. The assumption made by the organisers of the 1910 conference that the division between the Christian and non-Christian worlds could be delineated in simple geographical terms has long since capitulated to the mounting evidence to the contrary.

The other implication of the east-west language that shaped the mentality of Edinburgh 1910 was its covert relegation of the south — Latin America, Oceania, and Africa — to a decidedly secondary place on the missionary agenda, well behind the Asian Orient, where it was believed that the most decisive battles of missionary confrontation with other religions and ideologies would be fought. The almost total exclusion of Latin America from consideration evoked structural responses in both North America and Britain: respectively, the formation of the Committee on Co-operation in Latin America, and the formation in 1911 of the Evangelical Union of South America (now Latin Link) by a group of British evangelical missionary leaders. Oceania was not formally excluded from the Edinburgh agenda in this way, but in practice received very little attention, despite the recognition in the Commission I report that there was still 'a vast work to be accomplished', particularly in Melanesia.[9] The relatively slight attention given to Africa in the Commission re-

7. Keith Robbins, 'Britain, 1940 and "Christian civilization"', in Derek Beales and Geoffrey Best (eds.), *History, Society and the Churches: essays in honour of Owen Chadwick* (Cambridge: CUP, 1985), pp. 279-99.

8. Josef Ratzinger (Pope Benedict XVI), and Marcello Pera, *Without Roots: the West, relativism, Christianity, Islam* (English translation, New York: Basic Books, 2006); Josef Ratzinger, *Europe Today and Tomorrow: addressing the fundamental issues* (San Francisco: Ignatius Press, 2007).

9. *Report of Commission I*, p. 132.

ports and debates was congruent with the racial assumptions of the day and with the fact that Africa took second place to India and East Asia in the respective priorities of British and American missions for many years to come. It may also reflect the relative ignorance of the African continent that characterised both Oldham and Mott at this stage of their careers. Oldham had, of course, served in India with the YMCA from 1897 to 1901; his interest in questions of land and forced labour in East Africa did not develop until 1923, and his first visit to Africa was not until 1926. Mott, by June 1910, had already made three extended tours of parts of Asia, but only one brief visit to South Africa in 1906. It is noteworthy also that the impulse towards church unity was, if not less powerful in theory, certainly less effective in practice in Africa than in Asia, both because in 1910 the mission churches in Africa were generally much younger than those in Asia, and also because after 1914 the church in Africa grew with an ease and rapidity that undermined the insistent rationale for Christian unity which motivated the small and often harassed minority Christian communities of Asia.

It would be a long time before western Christianity lost its preoccupation with Asia and woke up to the realities of movements of religious conversion in Africa which were to a considerable extent independent of external missionary initiative or leadership. The enforced missionary exodus from China in 1951 played its part on the one hand, as did the cumulative evidence of African independent church and revival movements on the other. However, it was only after the era of independence had come virtually to a close, in the mid-1970s, that both scholars and Christian leaders came to the full realization that for several decades a profound religious transformation had been under way in the African continent that was clearly destined to outlive European colonial rule: as a seminal gathering of African scholars and Christian leaders on Christianity in independent Africa put it in September 1975, 'during the modern colonial period nowhere else in the world witnessed so rapid and extensive a process of Christianization'.[10]

Race and Culture

Concepts of racial distinctiveness and variation were integral to the language of the Edinburgh reports. The Commission I report observed the 'enormous influence' currently wielded by the white man among 'the primitive races',

10. E. Fasholé-Luke, R. Gray, A. Hastings, and G. Tasie (eds.), *Christianity in Independent Africa* (London: Rex Collings, 1978), p. 3.

and in this light reviewed the advantages and disadvantages of reliance on native rather than foreign agency in evangelistic work. Although it warned of such drawbacks as native evangelists importing into their presentation of Christianity 'ideas and practices derived from heathenism', it was emphatic that these disadvantages were far outweighed by the evangelistic benefits that only native agency could supply, above all that instinctive appreciation of what subsequent generations have learned to call 'culture':

> . . . the native understands the mind of the non-Christian people. He knows the native ways of thinking, the values they attach to different things, the modes of argument that influence them, the illustrations that appeal to them, the beliefs, traditions, customs, etiquette that instinctively shape the movement of thought or the play of feeling — in short, the whole mental world in which the native dwells, and from which he looks out on new claimants for belief and obedience.[11]

The World Missionary Conference did not, by and large, use the language of 'culture' when making such statements, though there were undoubtedly some among its delegates, notably from Germany, who were beginning to apply the term to the particularities of human society. The conference regularly referred instead to the particularities of race, and accepted without apparent question the contemporary ranking of different human 'races' on an evolutionary scale from barbarism to civility. R. E. Speer's principal disappointment in relation to the presence at Edinburgh of the Asian delegates was that they had not signalled more clearly what might be 'the contribution by the great Asiatic races to our apprehension of that revelation of God in Christ which is richer than any one people's confessions or any one race's experience.'[12] John Campbell Gibson's Commission II report attributed the contrast between Chinese and Indian rates of progress towards a three-self church to the differential in their racial characteristics, and yet argued that the firm hand of missionary control was most needed when dealing with the most 'primitive' races. It also diagnosed the essence of the problem of dependency in mission-church relations as being the result of a disparity between the supposedly 'vigorous and progressive' races of the west, and the 'contemplative and mystical' spirituality of the oriental races.[13] Bishop Gore's compelling vision of global Christian catholicity, as set out in the report of

11. *Report of Commission I*, pp. 319, 326, 323.
12. See Chapter 5, p. 130.
13. See Chapter 6, pp. 147-8, 150, 162.

Commission III, similarly depended on the assertion that 'each separate race' was fitted by providence to bring out some particular aspect of the truth and grace of the gospel. Christian missions in Asia, urged Gore, should be committed to the goal of cultivating 'an oriental type of Christianity, or as many oriental types as the varieties of national life and spirit shall demand'.[14] Our study of Commission IV in Chapter 8 has made clear that the low status accorded to the African race in contemporary thinking was related in part to the uncertainty over whether Africans had anything that Europeans could recognize as 'religion'. Chapter 9 has argued with respect to Commission VII that acceptance of the notion of a 'hierarchy' of race was intrinsic to the conference's attempts to hold colonial governments to policies that would place the welfare of 'native races' above all other concerns of the colonizing power, especially in Africa, whose vulnerable peoples were placed on the bottom rung of the hierarchy.

The records of the World Missionary Conference thus supply ample evidence that questionable assumptions of racial essentialism and differentiation were foundational to the very aspects of the conference's pronouncements which present-day Christians are inclined to view with greatest sympathy, namely its consistent enthusiasm for indigenous agency and cultural diversity in the expression of the Christian faith, and its opposition to imperial exploitation of indigenous peoples. The same pseudo-scientific theories of race which, with some justification, have been blamed by historians for the weakening of the mid-nineteenth-century missionary commitment to the creation of self-governing indigenous churches, supplied the intellectual apparatus which enabled missions in the early twentieth century to develop theories of cultural plurality and hence of 'accommodation' or 'indigenization', theories that were the necessary precondition for the development of Asian, and later African theologies. Racial theory was a plastic tool with the potential to be used for a variety of contradictory ideological purposes, as recent work by Werner Ustorf and Colin Kidd has made clear.[15] Modern concepts of plural cultures have emerged from the soil of concepts of plural races, and in principle are vulnerable to similar critique on the basis of either their tendencies to anthropological essentialism or an implicit moral relativism.

---

14. See Chapter 7, pp. 193-7.

15. Werner Ustorf, *Sailing on the Next Tide: missions, missiology and the Third Reich* (Frankfurt: Peter Lang, 2000); Colin Kidd, *The Forging of Races: race and scripture in the Protestant Atlantic world, 1600-2000* (Cambridge: CUP, 2006).

The Pursuit of Church Union in Asia

Probably the most significant aspect of the legacy of Edinburgh 1910 was the fillip which it gave to Asian Christians in their quest for forms of church life and organization that would be free of western denominational labels. This was despite the fact that some leaders of western denominational missions after 1910 remained wary of proposals for church union in the mission fields. The general committee of the WMMS, for example, issued a statement of policy in April 1914 which committed the society to co-operation with other Protestant missions, but expressed caution about the dangers of 'hurried union' of churches on the field. The statement advised 'the younger growing Churches of the Mission Field that they should for some time to come maintain their connexion with the Churches that under God have given them birth and nurture, and that they should cherish in perpetuity the consciousness of a Catholic rather than a national Christianity.'[16] According to the WMMS, therefore, the cause of catholic ecumenicity would be better served by Methodists in Asia and Africa retaining their distinctive identity in connection with British Methodism than by subsuming that identity within new national church unions. National Christian leaders in India and China, and some individual missionaries, took a different view. On their journey back to India from Edinburgh, V. S. Azariah, G. S. Eddy, and the ABCFM missionary, J. P. Jones, conferred on what immediate steps could be taken towards church union in India. The result was a three-day unofficial meeting at Henry Whitehead's episcopal residence in Madras, attended by Azariah, K. T. Paul, J. P. Cotelingam, and seven missionaries (including Eddy and Jones) to discuss a possible basis for union between the South India United Church and the Anglican Church. Although these discussions had no immediate structural consequences, Bengt Sundkler, in his history of the movement towards church union in South India, argued that the Madras meeting swung the emphasis of the first Continuation Committee regional conferences, held in Ceylon and India under Mott's chairmanship in November and December 1912, from the discussion of mere co-operation towards the issue of church union.[17] It also seems that Azariah had persuaded Bishop Whitehead before the end of 1910 that nothing less than organic union would serve the needs of Christian mission in India.[18] The road which led eventually to the for-

16. G. G. Findlay and W. W. Holdsworth, *The History of the Wesleyan Methodist Missionary Society,* 5 vols. (London: Epworth Press, 1921-4), I, p. 181.

17. Bengt Sundkler, *Church of South India: the movement towards union 1900-1947,* revised edn. (London: Lutterworth Press, 1965), p. 67. Sundkler notes (p. 364), that there is some doubt over the date of the Madras meeting, but late 1910 seems the most likely.

18. Harper, *In the Shadow of the Mahatma,* p. 237.

mation of the Church of South India in 1947, and of the Church of North India in 1970, began at Edinburgh.

A similar story can be told from China. On his return from Edinburgh to Beijing, Cheng Jingyi was ordained to be the pastor of the newly planted church at Mi-shih Hutung, which, though related to the LMS, was independent of it and rapidly established a reputation as the leading example of the independent Chinese church movement.[19] Cheng's appointment as joint secretary (alongside an American Presbyterian, Edwin C. Lobenstine) of the China Continuation Committee at the first Continuation Committee conference in China, held in Canton from 30 January to 4 February 1913, ensured that in China also the consequences of Edinburgh would not be limited to the pursuit of co-operation between western missions. The six conferences of the Continuation Committee held in China in early 1913 consistently stressed the goal of the three selves and encouraged the idea of federation as a first step towards full union.[20] The Continuation Committee in China led to the formation of the National Christian Council of China in 1922, of which Cheng was appointed secretary. In 1927 the Church of Christ in China was formed, uniting some sixteen denominational groups, mainly of Presbyterian or Congregational affiliation, but also including the BMS-related Baptist churches of Shandong province; those of Shanxi and Shaanxi provinces joined in 1933.[21] Cheng served as the first moderator, and later (from 1934 to 1939) as general secretary, of the new united church. The vision of a single three-self non-denominational church, which the Communists forcibly imposed on the Chinese Protestant churches after 1951, thus saw a partial realization over twenty years earlier, a fact which is often forgotten. The Edinburgh conference had played an important part by giving Cheng Jingyi and other Chinese spokesmen the platform for the initial articulation of that vision.

Similar trends towards the formation of federal or united Protestant churches can also be discerned in Japan, where eight denominations, accounting for some 80% of all Protestant Christians in Japan, combined in late 1911 to form the Japanese Federation of Churches, a precursor to the foundation of the United Church of Christ in Japan in 1941. The Federation predated by some eighteen months John Mott's visit to Japan to promote Continuation

19. Boorman and Howard (eds.), *Biographical Dictionary of Republican China*, I, p. 284; *IRM* 2:1 (Jan. 1913), pp. 18-19; *Chinese Recorder*, Dec. 1939, pp. 692-3; Hans-Ruedi Weber, *Asia and the Ecumenical Movement 1895-1961* (London: SCM Press, 1966), pp. 144-5.

20. *Addresses and Papers of John R. Mott Volume 5*, pp. 82, 116-19; Cheng Ching-yi, 'The Continuation Committee Conferences in China: a Chinese view of the conferences', *IRM* 2:7 (July 1913), pp. 509-10. A seventh conference was held in Moukden, Manchuria.

21. See Stanley, *History of the BMS*, pp. 316-17.

Committee work there, which took place in April 1913. In Korea, the momentum towards church union was weaker, owing in part to the divisions created by the Japanese annexation of 1910.

Even before 1910 Asian Christian leaders were seeking solutions to the problem of how to develop patterns of church life and structure that were congruent with current aspirations for national unity and cultural authenticity. Because that search raised questions of faith and order, it could not be reflected formally in the agenda of the World Missionary Conference, although, as the previous chapter has emphasized, the Commission VIII report did in fact pay sustained attention to moves towards church federation or union in the Asian context. Participation in the conference gave Azariah and Cheng Jingyi, and doubtless some of the other Asian delegates, the confidence and determination to push for a more urgent implementation of their vision. The conference had a similar impact on Charles Brent, deeply influenced as he was by the questions raised for Protestant missions by the Philippine context, where national identity was so closed linked to the Roman Catholic tradition. Although it was not until October 1910, at the Cincinnati Episcopal Convention, that Brent formalized his idea of summoning a world conference on faith and order, there is no doubt that the experience he had gained at Edinburgh was foundational to his proposal: the conference, he testified, had made him into 'an apostle of church unity'.[22] The World Missionary Conference, whose viability depended on the formal exclusion of discussion of faith and order, paradoxically thus became, as is well known, the parent of the Faith and Order movement.

The Role of Women in Mission

One of the least obvious yet conceivably most far-reaching consequences of the World Missionary Conference relates to a theme that has not so far been discussed in this book. Even before 1910, pressure was being applied by the Protestant denominational mission boards on their autonomous women's societies or semi-autonomous auxiliaries to consider full integration within their respective denominational societies, which were run by men. Separate women's missionary organizations seemed increasingly to male society administrators to promote inefficient duplication of philanthropic effort and frequently provoked envy on the grounds of their lower costs of administra-

22. Hogg, 'Edinburgh, 1910 — ecumenical keystone', *Religion and Life* 29:3 (Summer 1960), p. 349; see Chapter 10, p. 297.

tion, owing to their greater reliance on volunteer labour and lower missionary salary levels.[23] One American women's mission board, that of the United Brethren Church, accepted integration in 1909. The formative meeting of the international committee at Oxford in July 1908 considered whether to appoint a separate Commission for women's work, but decided instead to 'have women's help on all of the Commissions, and so not draw any line between work for men and work for women'.[24] In fact, Commissions VII and VIII had no female members; and only Commissions III (three women out of twenty) and V (four women out of twenty-four) had more than two women members.[25] Commission VI on 'The Home Base of Missions' invited its questionnaire respondents from missions which had autonomous women's boards to identify 'any weakness or difficulty arising from the existence of separate women's boards', and devoted a whole chapter of its report to the subject of women's missionary societies and women's auxiliaries. The Commission's chairman, James L. Barton, informed the British section of the Commission at its meeting in London in December 1909 that 'the American evidence pointed to the fact that the tendency was to closer co-operation between Societies and Women's Boards, but that it was not felt that the time was ripe to dispense with Women's Boards entirely. If this were done the funds would seriously diminish.'[26] Although the Commission had as one of its members Helen Barrett Montgomery, a Baptist who was the most prominent figure in the American women's missionary movement and a stalwart defender of the autonomy of the women's boards, she was the sole woman among twenty men, and appears to have been prevented by pressure of other engagements from attending most, if not all, of the Commission's North American meetings.[27] The Com-

23. R. Pierce Beaver, *All Loves Excelling: American Protestant women in world mission* (Grand Rapids: Eerdmans, 1968), pp. 178-80.

24. UTS, MRL 12, WMC papers, series 1, box 22, folder 6, J. L. Barton to Mrs H. B. Montgomery, 23 Nov. 1908.

25. Commission VIII originally had one woman member, Mary Morley of the Committee of the World's YWCA, but she resigned in October 1909; *Report of Commission VIII*, p. vii.

26. UTS, MRL 12, WMC papers, series 1, box 22, folder 3, minutes of meeting of Commission VI at Bible House, London, 7-9 Dec. 1909, p. 2.

27. ECG, Commission VI questionnaire, question VII.7; *Report of Commission VI*, pp. 222-34; UTS, MRL 12, WMC papers, series 1, box 22, folder 6, correspondence of J. L. Barton and H. B. Montgomery, 1908-10. On Montgomery (1861-1934) see *BDCM*; Beaver, *All Loves Excelling*, p. 181; Dana L. Robert, *American Women in Mission: a social history of their thought and practice* (Macon, Georgia: Mercer UP, 1996), pp. 261-82; and Dana L. Robert (ed.), *Gospel Bearers, Gender Barriers: missionary women in the twentieth century* (Maryknoll, NY: Orbis, 2002), pp. 8-9.

mission VI report noted the gradual disappearance of 'the old hard and fast lines' that separated the work of women's (often 'zenana') missionary societies from their male counterparts, and raised the question of 'whether the time has not arrived when an effort can wisely be made to unite more closely the women's foreign missionary societies or organisations and the general or parent or denominational society, without sacrificing anything that is valuable.'[28] Although this recommendation was not included in the final chapter of 'Conclusions and Recommendations', it provided the male advocates of integration with valuable ammunition. Helen Montgomery's sole complaint with the draft report concerned the section dealing with the relations of the women's boards to the parent societies; she protested to James Barton that it was based on opinion rather than evidence, and 'that no attempt had been made to get the facts from the Women's Boards'.[29] The recommendation, however, was allowed to stand in the final version of the report.

Some missionary agencies responded almost immediately. In the United States, the Methodist Episcopal Church, South, integrated its general home and foreign, and women's home and foreign, mission boards into a single mission board before the end of 1910. Although the other major American denominations followed more slowly, the trend was almost irresistible. By the 1960s the elimination of the women's missionary societies was virtually complete.[30] In Britain there was a greater variety of relationship between women's missions and their male counterparts, but a similar trend is evident after 1910. The BMS and the Baptist Zenana Mission, for example, began joint discussions of the issue in the light of the Commission's report as early as 1911, and by 1914 had decided to incorporate the Zenana Mission within the BMS as its Women's Missionary Association. This was despite evidence submitted to the Edinburgh Commission by the officers of the Baptist Zenana Mission to the effect that 'a greater amount of work was done at less cost, and a larger amount of money raised than would be the case under one Board'.[31] The decision to amalgamate was not universally welcomed by British Baptist women.[32] Other women's societies, however, were more successful in resisting

28. *Report of Commission VI*, pp. 228-9.

29. UTS, MRL 12, WMC papers, series 1, box 22, folder 6, H. B. Montgomery to J. L. Barton, 24 Feb. 1910.

30. Beaver, *All Loves Excelling*, pp. 182-90; Robert, *American Women in Mission*, pp. 302-3.

31. *Report of Commission VI*, p. 225.

32. Stanley, *History of the BMS*, pp. 373-4; Karen E. Smith, 'Women in cultural captivity: British women and the Zenana Mission', *Baptist Quarterly* 42:2 (April 2007), pp. 103-13, and 42:3 (July 2007), pp. 245-8. The Baptist Zenana Mission originated in 1867 as 'The La-

integration for a time. In the Presbyterian Church of England, the Women's Missionary Association remained independent of the Foreign Missions Committee until 1925.[33] The Church of England Zenana Missionary Society (formed in 1880) continued as an entirely separate body from the CMS until as late as 1957.[34] Where women's missionary organizations had a lesser degree of existing autonomy, the pressure for change in the wake of Edinburgh was rather less insistent. In British Wesleyan Methodism, for example, the Women's Auxiliary of the WMMS (established in 1858) was run from rooms within the Mission House in Bishopsgate, and women missionaries on the field worked under the authority of circuit and district officials in exactly the same way as their male colleagues. The Auxiliary continued after 1910 to operate as a separate agency for the raising of funds from women and for the selection of women candidates. Nevertheless, by 1922 it was apparent that the society was considering the desirability of closer co-ordination between its male and female branches, and at the time of Methodist union in 1932 the Auxiliary was absorbed into the WMMS as its 'Women's Work' department.[35] The LMS was distinctive in never having had a separate women's organization, and in 1910 women were able to serve on the Board of Directors and on all committees, with the notable exception of the finance committee.[36]

Edinburgh 1910 undoubtedly contributed to the decline of the women's missionary societies as an autonomous movement in the course of the twentieth century. Although the concept of gender-specific mission organizations now appears decidedly archaic, it should be emphasized that women themselves were consistently opposed to the mergers with the male-dominated societies which took place. As the opportunities for women's leadership in foreign mission agencies diminished, Dana Robert argues that the attention of leading Christian women in the west turned instead to women's rights and the quest for formal recognition, and ultimately ordination, in the churches at home. She suggests that such a re-orientation of Christian women's cam-

---

dies' Association for the support of Zenanah work, and Bible women in India in connection with the Baptist Missionary Society'.

33. Edward Band, *Working His Purpose Out: the history of the English Presbyterian Mission 1847-1947* (London: Presbyterian Church of England Publishing Office, 1948), pp. 579-80.

34. Jocelyn Murray, *Proclaim the Good News: a short history of the Church Missionary Society* (London: Hodder & Stoughton, 1985), p. 271.

35. Findlay and Holdsworth, *The History of the Wesleyan Methodist Missionary Society*, I, p. 178, and IV, pp. 68-9; N. A. Birtwhistle, 'Methodist missions', in R. Davies, A. R. George, and G. Rupp (eds.), *A History of the Methodist Church in Great Britain*, 4 vols. (London: Epworth Press, 1965-88), III, p. 96.

36. *Report of Commission VI*, p. 225.

paigning enthusiasm from global to domestic concerns may have been one of the causes of the weakening of commitment to overseas missions in the mainline churches as the century proceeded.[37] If this is indeed the case, the World Missionary Conference will have had precisely the opposite effect in the long term to that which its promoters intended.

New Patterns of Missionary Study and Training

Despite the ambiguous consequences of the conference's questioning of the rationale for women's mission agencies, it is undeniable that Edinburgh 1910 made a valuable contribution to the provision of new opportunities for missionary study and training, especially for women. The most significant and enduring means by which it did so was through the foundation of the *International Review of Missions* in January 1912 as a high-quality quarterly journal of 'missionary science', under the editorship of J. H. Oldham; Georgina Gollock, formerly literature secretary of the CMS, was appointed assistant editor. The journal was the official organ of the Continuation Committee, and fulfilled a need identified by the report of Commission VI on 'The Home Base', but its creation owed much to Oldham's personal vision of a periodical which would put on a permanent basis the fertile dialogue between serving missionaries and scholars which he had sought to achieve in the Edinburgh Commissions.[38] The journal, of course, continues to this day, under the slightly modified title of the *International Review of Mission*: the 's' was dropped in April 1969 as a visible sign of the post-colonial shift to a *Missio Dei* as opposed to a Eurocentric view of mission.

By 1910 single and married women formed the majority of the work-force of Protestant missions. The Commission V report on 'The Preparation of Missionaries' drew attention to the haphazard and unsatisfactory nature of existing provision for the training of missionary candidates on both sides of the Atlantic, and in particular to the need to systematize and raise the educational standards of the missionary training offered to women, which was frequently in small, privately run, and poorly resourced institutions.[39] In the United States one immediate response was the formation in 1911 of the Hartford School of Missions (later known as the Kennedy School of Missions) at Hart-

---

37. Robert, *American Women in Mission*, pp. 303-4, 306-7.

38. *Report of Commission VI*, pp. 53-4; Clements, *Faith on the Frontier*, pp. 105-8.

39. *Report of Commission V*, pp. 82-94, 146-54. The Commission V report is entitled 'The Preparation of Missionaries' on the spine but, oddly, 'The Training of Teachers' appears on its title-page.

ford Seminary in Connecticut. It was not accidental that the Seminary's president was Dr W. Douglas Mackenzie, the chairman of Commission V, and that one of the Commission's members, Edward Capen of Boston, was secretary of the new School. The School proudly advertised itself in the early numbers of the *IRM* as 'an interdenominational graduate school for Special Missionary Preparation as recommended by Commission V. of the Edinburgh Missionary Conference'.[40] Through the expertise of Duncan Black Macdonald, professor of Semitic languages in the seminary, the Kennedy School of Missions became a leading centre for the study of Islamics, a subject that had received scant attention in missionary training prior to 1910. By the early 1950s the Kennedy School had more missionary candidates or missionaries on furlough enrolled in its courses than any other theological school in the United States.[41] It is also not accidental that in the years following 1910, chairs of missions were established in a number of leading American seminaries or university schools of theology, including Boston University (1910), Drew Theological Seminary, Madison (1914), Emory University (1914), Princeton Theological Seminary (1914), and Union Theological Seminary, New York (1918).[42]

In Britain the most significant response to the Commission's recommendation was the opening in 1912 of Carey Hall as an addition to the Selly Oak colleges in Birmingham, on land leased by Edward Cadbury, of the Quaker chocolate manufacturing family. Carey Hall was a pioneering collaborative venture involving three missionary societies from different denominations: the BMS (specifically its new Women's Missionary Association), the LMS, and the Women's Missionary Association of the Presbyterian Church of England. Carey Hall trained the majority of women candidates for these three missions until 1966, when it amalgamated with the neighbouring St Andrew's Hall, which opened as an institution for the training of male missionary candidates in 1946.

Co-operation in Mission: New Initiatives in Britain

The story of the Continuation Committee and the various initiatives in missionary co-operation which it engendered has been well and fully told by a

40. E.g., *IRM* 2:6 (April 1913), p. ix; and 3:12 (Oct. 1914), p. iii. The Hartford School was a development of an existing 'Special course of instruction in foreign missions', begun in 1904.

41. Olav G. Myklebust, *The Study of Missions in Theological Education*, 2 vols. (Oslo: Egede Instituttet, 1955, 1957), II, p. 93.

42. *Ibid.*, II, pp. 71-2.

number of previous writers, most notably W. Richey Hogg, H.-R. Weber, and, most recently, Keith Clements.[43] Readers desiring a detailed account of the Continuation Committee meetings and the process which led to the formation of the International Missionary Council at Lake Mohonk in October 1921 are referred to these standard sources. The purpose of this brief section is to emphasize the particular consequences for church relations in Britain of the initiatives taken after Edinburgh. In North America, with its already well-established Foreign Missions Conference, or in continental Europe, which had the *Ausschuss* and similar national missionary bodies in Scandinavia and the Netherlands, the immediate ecumenical implications of the Edinburgh conference were not so far-reaching.

In Britain the most important step taken in the light of the World Missionary Conference was the decision in June 1911 to hold an annual Conference of British Missionary Societies (CBMS) on the lines of the Foreign Missions Conference of North America. The origins of the CBMS, however, go back beyond the Edinburgh conference to the meetings of the London Secretaries' Association held in February and April 1910. As described in the previous chapter, it was at its meeting in Newington Green on 16 February 1910, in response to Julius Richter's address, that the Association first gave its attention to the idea of creating a British equivalent to the Foreign Missions Conference or the *Ausschuss*. The Association took no action at that point, deciding to leave the matter in the hands of Commission VIII.[44] When the Association met again, on 20 April 1910, it discussed not simply the appointment of an international missionary committee, but also 'the co-operation of British missionary societies on the lines of the Committee on Counsel and Reference in America, and of the Executive Committee of Continental Missionary Societies'. Although the meeting again decided to await developments from Edinburgh, it is clear that before June 1910 there was already an emerging consensus in favour of the formation of a British conference of missionary societies.[45] Hence at the next meeting of the Association, on 19 October 1910, Oldham was present as a visitor and spoke about the outcome of the Edinburgh conference, the work of the Continuation Committee, and 'the proposal to hold an annual conference of British societies'. Although there was evident reluctance on the part of the secretaries to take any action which might commit their respective societies, the members present,

43. Hogg, *Ecumenical Foundations*, pp. 143-201; Weber, *Asia and the Ecumenical Movement*, pp. 135-42; Clements, *Faith on the Frontier*, pp. 101-19.

44. CUL, BSA/F4, microfilm minutes of London Secretaries' Association, 1893-1924, minutes of 16 Feb. 1910; see Chapter 10 above, p. 289.

45. CUL, BSA/F4, microfilm minutes of London Secretaries' Association, 1893-1924, minutes of 20 April 1910.

'speaking in their personal capacity', unanimously requested J. H. Ritson to communicate with the Continuation Committee and ask its British members 'to take steps for the summoning of a Conference on the lines suggested, in the early part of June 1911.'[46] Ritson raised the matter at the second meeting of the Continuation Committee in May 1911, and a conference of British missionary societies duly took place in York on 14-15 June 1911. A constitution for the CBMS, drafted by Ritson as chairman of the business committee of the Continuation Committee, was adopted, and an interim standing committee was appointed. The CBMS came into formal existence a year later, at an inaugural conference at Swanwick from 12 to 14 June 1912. Ritson served for six years as chairman of the standing committee, and in 1915 and 1916 presided over the conference itself.[47]

The SPG was not represented at the crucial meeting of the London Secretaries' Association in October 1910. The Kikuyu controversy of 1913 compelled Bishop Montgomery to accentuate the distinctive High Church identity of the Society in his final years as secretary, and the SPG did not join the CBMS until 1918, when Montgomery was on the eve of retirement.[48] Nevertheless, from that point on the principal missionary representative of High Anglicanism played a full part in an institution which was destined to have a long history. Montgomery's successor, Bishop George L. King, with the crucial support of Charles Gore, steered the SPG into more whole-hearted involvement in the ecumenical bodies set up after 1910: he oversaw the founding of the College of the Ascension in Selly Oak in 1923 for the training of SPG women missionaries, thus bringing to an end the initial hesitation of the SPG to be involved in the Selly Oak colleges, which until then had been entirely Nonconformist (and predominantly Quaker) in their ecclesiastical complexion.[49] The decisions

---

46. CUL, BSA/F4, microfilm minutes of London Secretaries' Association, 1893-1924, minutes of 19 Oct. 1910. Ritson's memory was at fault in suggesting in *The World is Our Parish*, p. 281, that the proposal to establish a conference of British societies was first raised by the Continuation Committee at its Bishop Auckland meeting in May 1911.

47. Ritson, *The World is Our Parish*, p. 282. Ritson succeeded George Robson as chairman of the business committee of the Continuation Committee on Robson's death in 1912.

48. Steven Maughan, 'An archbishop for Greater Britain: Bishop Montgomery, missionary imperialism, and the SPG, 1897-1915,' in O'Connor, *Three Centuries of Mission*, p. 369; Thompson, *Into all Lands*, p. 487. Montgomery announced his resignation in 1918, but did not leave office till April 1919.

49. O'Connor, *Three Centuries of Mission*, p. 88. The CMS was not represented at Selly Oak until the opening of Crowther Hall in 1969. The first two Selly Oak colleges, Woodbrooke (1903) and Westholme (1905), were Quaker institutions. Westholme, a missionary training college, moved in 1906 to Kingsmead, and from 1915 began accepting Methodist women missionaries for training. West Hill College (1907) and Fircroft

taken by the SPG in 1918 and 1923 marked the culmination of what Oldham had worked so hard to achieve in 1909-10, namely the full participation of High Anglicans in the emerging ecumenical missionary movement.

Western Ecclesiastical Divisions and the Changing Contours of World Christianity

The World Missionary Conference was unique in modern Christian history in that its delegates spanned the full theological spectrum of non-Roman western Christianity from the most conservative of evangelical Protestants to committed Anglo-Catholics. Unlike its predecessors in London in 1888 or New York in 1900, the Edinburgh conference was intended to be representative of all sections of the Protestant and Anglican churches, and not merely of those that were happy to style themselves as 'evangelical'. Unlike its successors in Jerusalem in 1928 or Tambaram in 1938, the World Missionary Conference included representatives of the so-called 'faith missions', such as the China Inland Mission, the Africa Inland Mission, or the Regions Beyond Missionary Union. By 1928 very few of these conservative nondenominational agencies were participating in ecumenical missionary gatherings.[50] In 1910 the broad evangelical consensus that had characterized the nineteenth-century missionary movement still held, even though the cracks were beginning to show.

The delicate ecumenical consensus displayed at Edinburgh was modelled on principles that had been successfully trialled on a smaller scale within the British Student Christian Movement. Anglicans of Catholic sympathies had been progressively drawn in to the SCM from 1900 onwards, and especially after the Church Congress of 1908, when a number of High Churchmen gave their blessing to the movement.[51] Such inclusiveness was founded on what Tissington Tatlow called 'the interdenominational position', which insisted that the first duty of Christian students was 'loyalty to their own denomina-

---

Working Men's College (1909) also had strong Quaker influence through the Cadbury family, but were more broadly based Nonconformist institutions. On Carey Hall (1912) see above, p. 317. The College of the Ascension united in 1996 with Kingsmead College to form the United College of the Ascension, which closed in 2006.

50. One representative of a faith mission, the Christian and Missionary Alliance, H. M. Shuman, was present at Jerusalem in 1928; see *Addresses and Records: report of the Jerusalem meeting of the International Missionary Council March 24th-April 8th, 1928* (London: Oxford University Press, 1928), p. 213.

51. Tissington Tatlow, *The Story of the Student Christian Movement of Great Britain and Ireland* (London: SCM Press), pp. 386-92.

tion'; co-operation with those of different churchmanship was only for 'certain definite aims and activities' and was to be viewed as an opportunity to share with others the truth for which their own denomination stood.[52] This was also the basis on which Talbot, Gore, Montgomery, and other Anglo-Catholic leaders were persuaded to participate in the World Missionary Conference. As Talbot remarked over a private lunch held during the conference at the home of Alexander Whyte, 'We [the Anglo-Catholics] would not have been here had it not been for the Student Christian Movement'.[53] Although there were times when continuing Anglo-Catholic participation in the Edinburgh conference hung by a slender thread, notably from February to April 1909, Oldham and Tatlow achieved their objectives, and in so doing set the Anglo-Catholic leadership (though not all their followers) on an enduring course of participation in the emerging ecumenical movement. The majority of those who would jump ship from organised ecumenism in the twenty years after 1910 were not Anglo-Catholics but those who became known after the First World War either as 'fundamentalists' or as 'conservative evangelicals'. It was a trajectory that in retrospect can be seen to be anticipated in the decision in March 1910 of the conservative-controlled Cambridge Inter-Collegiate Christian Union to disaffiliate from the SCM,[54] but this Cambridge rupture had no obvious repercussions at Edinburgh three months later. Many of decidedly conservative theology were delegates at the conference, and there is no surviving evidence of their being uneasy at supposedly liberal tendencies displayed by the Commission reports, even though the Commission IV report, for example, might be thought to have supplied obvious grounds for such a complaint. Where there was unease expressed by some English delegates, both evangelical Anglican and Nonconformist, it was directed at the extent of the concessions that had been made to Anglo-Catholic ecclesiastical sensitivities, but such unease issued from the specific context of English ecclesiastical politics and was not interpreted by evangelicals from across the Atlantic as an example of the response that conservatives ought to make to the growing threat of liberal theology.[55]

A few of those who would subsequently be designated as 'conservative evangelicals' were not simply delegates at Edinburgh but were also involved in the preparatory work of the conference. The proposal to hold a third ecumenical conference in the wake of those held at London in 1888 and New York

52. *Ibid.*, p. 400.
53. *Ibid.*, p. 410.
54. *Ibid.*, pp. 380-5.
55. See the comments of the American evangelical periodical, *The Missionary Review of the World* 33:8 (Aug. 1910), pp. 561-2.

in 1900 was first made in the letter from W. H. Grant of the Foreign Missions Conference to Walter B. Sloan, home director in Britain of the China Inland Mission, written on 16 September 1905.[56] Three CIM leaders were appointed to membership of Commissions: Sloan to Commission II; Marshall Broomhall, editorial secretary of the British CIM, to Commission I; and Henry W. Frost, North American director, to Commission V. Frost is partly remembered for his imposition on the mission of a strict doctrinal statement that subsequently became a standard formula for many fundamentalist institutions.[57] Prebendary H. E. Fox, the resolutely conservative honorary clerical secretary of the CMS, served as a member of the international committee from its inception in 1908; in 1922 he would be one of the leaders of the conservative secession from the CMS that led to the formation of the Bible Churchmen's Missionary Society. On the invitation of W. H. Griffith Thomas, the decisive planning meeting for the Edinburgh conference took place in July 1908 at Wycliffe Hall in Oxford, later to become renowned as a centre of Anglican 'conservative evangelicalism'.[58] As described in the previous chapter, the proposals that eventually issued in the formation of the Continuation Committee were first aired in Britain by Julius Richter at the meeting of the London Secretaries' Association in February 1910 held at the British office of the CIM.[59]

The formation of the Continuation Committee was welcomed by some evangelicals of conservative inclination. The second extended meeting of the Committee was held in May 1911 at Auckland Castle, the official residence of Handley Moule, bishop of Durham, supporter of the Keswick Conventions and the most senior figure in Anglican evangelicalism at the time: Moule seems to have been glad to offer his home for the purpose and the experience was evidently a congenial one for both host and guests, without any sense of theological discomfort. Moule even contemplated celebrating a service of Holy Communion for all the members, but according to his biographers 'wisely abandoned the idea in view of possible misunderstanding outside.'[60] If Moule had persisted with his bold notion of an ecumenical eucharist, it is highly likely that Bishop Talbot and Louise Creighton, if no others, would

56. See Chapter 2 above, p. 19.

57. Alvyn Austin, 'Only connect: the China Inland Mission and transatlantic evangelicalism', in Wilbert R. Shenk (ed.), *North American Missions 1810-1914: theology, theory, and policy* (Grand Rapids and Cambridge: Eerdmans, 2004), p. 300.

58. See Chapter 2, pp. 30-1.

59. See Chapter 10, p. 289.

60. J. B. Harford and F. C. Macdonald, *Handley Carr Glyn Moule Bishop of Durham: a biography* (London: Hodder & Stoughton, 1922), pp. 327-9.

have declined to participate: two years later, Talbot's reaction to the Kikuyu conference of June 1913, which appeared to commit Anglican missions in East Africa to a limited measure of intercommunion, and closed with a united communion service held according to the Anglican rite, was to condemn the Kikuyu proceedings as a contravention of the principles scrupulously observed at Edinburgh and to attempt (unsuccessfully) to persuade the Continuation Committee as whole to take the same view.[61]

It was not immediately apparent in the wake of the Edinburgh conference that conservative evangelicals would stand aside from the more inclusive ecumenical co-operation in mission that the Edinburgh conference initiated. The CIM was strongly represented at the China national conference in Shanghai in March 1913 which established the China branch of the Continuation Committee.[62] The CIM was a member of the National Christian Council of China from its formation in 1922 until 1926, after which the CIM ceased to participate in any broadly-based ecumenical organizations.[63] Under the pressure of the fundamentalist controversies of the 1920s, the Protestant consensus that was held intact in 1910 fell apart, opening up the divergence between 'ecumenical' and 'evangelical' Protestants which has largely endured to the present day.

From the perspective of a century later, the ecclesiastical and theological divisions which the organisers of the World Missionary Conference worked so hard to bridge appear rather less significant than they did at the time. Questions such as whether the Anglican Church should collaborate or even deign to converse with representatives of non-episcopal communions are, happily, no longer the most pressing items on the agenda of world Christian discourse, and Edinburgh 1910 must be granted some of the credit for that fact. There were no representatives at the Edinburgh conference of the infant Pentecostal movement, or of Ethiopian or 'African independent' churches from South or West Africa. The conference displayed very little awareness of the cultural, political, and theological issues which were to fuel the extraordinary growth of these and similar movements over the next century. Despite David Cairns's impassioned concluding appeal in the Commission IV report for a renewal of faith in the 'illimitable potencies of the Divine Spirit' who

61. Stuart P. Mews, 'Edinburgh and Kikuyu: the interaction of attitudes to two conferences', in G. J. Cuming and Derek Baker (eds.), *Councils and Assemblies, Studies in Church History*, vol. 7 (Cambridge: CUP, 1971), pp. 347-8, 357.

62. *Addresses and Papers of John R. Mott Volume 5*, pp. 145-9.

63. Alvyn J. Austin, 'Blessed adversity: Henry W. Frost and the China Inland Mission', in Joel A. Carpenter and Wilbert R. Shenk (eds.), *Earthen Vessels: American evangelicals and foreign missions, 1880-1980* (Grand Rapids: Eerdmans, 1990), p. 68.

empowered the early church, the conference paid very little attention to the pentecostal dimension of Christian theology.[64] One of the few speakers who did in some measure was Father Walter Frere, whose evening address on 16 June on the subject of 'medieval missions in their bearing on modern missions' urged the conference to lay aside the relics of eighteenth- and nineteenth-century scepticism, and consider sympathetically the apparent reliance of medieval missionaries on miracles and exorcisms:

> Are we not right to expect more of the same sort of manifestation at the present time? We are only working at half power. The kingdom of God comes with power, and when we see how in the old days those signs and wonders were perfectly direct motives for conversion, may we not again believe, in people of the same sort, and in circumstances of a similar sort, that some force may be imparted, and God may give us this wonderful manifestation, so that quite evidently the kingdom of God may be coming in power? Ought not the sick still to be healed? Are there no demoniacs now from whom the man of God by the finger of God should cast out the devil? That is the question I ask.[65]

It took an Anglo-Catholic outsider to the Protestant family, with a vivid sense of the long sweep of Catholic history and the continuing power of the holy to transform material reality, to ask such an uncomfortable question. Frere's understanding of the coming of the kingdom of God with power was not what Archbishop Davidson had in mind when he referred to the same theological motif in his opening address to the conference, but hindsight suggests that it was a more accurate anticipation of the remarkable course that world Christianity was very soon about to take.

64. *Report of Commission IV,* p. 263.
65. *History and Records of the Conference,* pp. 193-4.

Bibliography

1. Archival Collections

In the United Kingdom

Aberdeen
Aberdeen University Library, Special Collections:
    D. S. Cairns papers.
    World Missionary Conference, Commission IV, questionnaire replies.

Birmingham
University of Birmingham Library, Special Collections:
    Church Missionary Society archives, G2 I 7/0 and Acc215 Z1.
    Student Christian Movement archives, Tissington Tatlow papers and Student Volunteer Missionary Union papers.

Cambridge
Cambridge University Library, Bible Society archives:
    Letter-books of John H. Ritson.
    Microfilm minutes of London Secretaries' Association, 1893-1924.
Henry Martyn Centre, Westminster College:
    Copies of Commission IV questionnaire replies.
    Microfilm of World Missionary Conference papers held in Union Theological Seminary, New York, box XVIII (now series 1, box 23).

Edinburgh
University of Edinburgh, New College Library, J. H. Oldham papers.

St Colm's International Centre, 23 Inverleith Terrace, *Journal of Women's Mission-ary Training Institute, June 1910.*

Glasgow

International Christian College, Bible Training Institute archives:
Bible Training Institute Annual Report for 1908-09.
Student record register, volume 4 (1904-10).
Student fees register, 1905-14.

London

Lambeth Palace Library:
Davidson papers.
School of Oriental and African Studies, University of London:
Council for World Mission archives, LMS Home Office outward letters and LMS Board minutes.

Oxford

Bodleian Library, Rhodes House, USPG archives:
Minutes of SPG standing committee.
H. H. Montgomery letters (X 266).

York

University of York, Borthwick Institute for Archives, Mirfield Deposit, Gore papers.

In Switzerland

Geneva

Ecumenical Centre Library:
Third Ecumenical Missionary Conference (later World Missionary Conference), minutes and memoranda of general, international, and executive committees.
World Missionary Conference, Commissions III, IV, VII, and VIII: questionnaire replies (also available on microfiche from IDC Publishers of Leiden).
Continuation Committee of the World Missionary Conference, minutes and pa-pers (also available on microfilm from 10C Publishers of Leiden).

In the United States

Chicago

University of Chicago Library, Department of Special Collections, Ernest deWitt Burton papers.

New Haven
> Yale Divinity School, Special Collections, Record Group 45, John R. Mott papers.
> Yale Divinity School, Special Collections, Record Group 38, R. P. Wilder papers.

New York
> The Burke Library archives (Columbia University libraries) at Union Theological Seminary, MRL 12, World Missionary Conference papers, series 1 and 2.

Princeton
> Princeton Theological Seminary, Special Collections, Robert E. Speer personal letters.

Washington
> Library of Congress Manuscripts Division, papers of C. H. Brent, box 53, diary of C. H. Brent.

In Australia

In personal possession of Mrs Birgitta Sharpe of Sydney:
> A. G. Hogg collection: Transcripts of correspondence of A. G. Hogg and David S. Cairns, 1909-10, though at the time of publication these have not been located.

2. Printed Primary Sources: Newspapers and Periodicals

The Baptist Times and Freeman
Chinese Recorder
Christian World
The Chronicle of the Convocation of Canterbury
The Chronicle of the London Missionary Society
Church Missionary Review
Church Times
Congregational Year Book
Daily Graphic
Delhi Mission News
The East and the West
The Harvest Field
International Review of Missions
Life and Work: the Church of Scotland Magazine and Mission Record
London Quarterly Review
Missionary Herald (Boston)
Missionary Herald (London)

Missionary Herald of the Presbyterian Church of Ireland
Missionary Record of the United Free Church of Scotland
Missionary Review of the World
Missions
Presbyterian Messenger
Record of Christian Work
The Scotsman
The Student Movement
Women's Missionary Magazine of the United Presbyterian Church
World Missionary Conference 1910, *Conference Daily Paper*
World Missionary Conference 1910, *Monthly News Sheet*

3. Printed Primary Sources: Articles, Reports, Books, and Pamphlets

Addresses and Records: report of the Jerusalem meeting of the International Missionary Council March 24th–April 8th, 1928 (London: Oxford University Press, 1928).

Beach, H. P., et al. (eds.). *World Statistics of Christian Missions* (New York: The Committee on Reference and Counsel of the Foreign Missions Conference of North America, 1916).

Brown, A. J. *The Korean Conspiracy Case* (Northfield, MA: Northfield Press, 1912).

———. *The Mastery of the Far East: the story of Korea's transformation and Japan's rise to supremacy in the Orient* (London: G. Bell & Sons, 1919).

Christian Education in China: a study made by an educational commission representing the mission boards and societies conducting work in China (New York: Committee of Reference and Counsel of the Foreign Missions Conference of North America, 1922).

Church Missionary Society. *Register of Missionaries and Native Clergy from 1804 to 1904* (CMS, n.p., n.d.).

Conference on Missions Held in 1860 at Liverpool (London: James Nisbet, 1860).

Ecumenical Missionary Conference New York, 1900, 2 vols. (London and New York: Religious Tract Society and American Tract Society, 1900).

Foreign Missions Conference of North America. *Thirteenth Conference of the Foreign Missions Boards in the United States and Canada, February 27 and 28, 1906* (New York: Foreign Missions Library, n.d. [1906]).

Foreign Missions Conference of North America. *Fourteenth Conference of the Foreign Missions Boards in the United States and Canada, January 9 and 10, 1907* (New York: Foreign Missions Library, n.d. [1907]).

Foreign Missions Conference of North America. *Fifteenth Conference of the Foreign Missions Boards in Canada and in the United States at New York January 29th and 30th 1908* (New York: Foreign Missions Library, n.d. [1908]).

Foreign Missions Conference of North America. *Printed Circular Letter to the Foreign Missionary Societies of Great Britain, from the Committee on Reference and*

Counsel Representing the Boards of Foreign Missions in the United States and Canada . . . 26 January 1910 (New York: Foreign Missions Library, n.d. [1910]).

Fraser, Sir Andrew. *Among Indian Rajahs and Ryots: a civil servant's recollections & impressions of thirty-seven years of work & sport in the central provinces & Bengal* (London: Seeley, 1911).

Gairdner, W. H. T. *The Reproach of Islam* (London: CMS, 1909).

———. *'Edinburgh 1910': an account and interpretation of the World Missionary Conference* (Edinburgh and London: Oliphant, Anderson & Ferrier, 1910).

Graham, R. H. C. *Under Seven Congo Kings* (London: Carey Press, n.d.).

Hanna, R. K. *The World Missionary Conference: some impressions* (Belfast: R. Carswell & Son, Ltd., 1910).

Harada Tasuku. 'The present position and problems of Christianity in Japan', *IRM* 1 (1912), pp. 79-97.

———. *The Faith of Japan* (New York: Macmillan, 1914).

Hayford, Mark C. *West Africa and Christianity* (London: Baptist Tract and Book Society, n.d. [1903]).

Hogg, A. G. *Karma and Redemption: an essay toward the interpretation of Hinduism and the re-statement of Christianity* (Madras: Christian Literature Society, 1909).

Johnston, James (ed.). *Report of the Centenary Conference on the Protestant Missions of the World,* 2 vols. (London: James Nisbet, 1888).

[Lindsay, A. D. (chairman)]. *Report of the Commission on Christian Higher Education in India: an enquiry into the place of the Christian College in modern India* (London: Oxford University Press, 1931).

Mahan, A. T. *The Harvest Within: thoughts on the life of the Christian* (Boston and London: Longmans, Green, 1909).

Montgomery, H. H. (ed.). *Mankind and the Church: being an attempt to estimate the contribution of great races to the fullness of the church of God* (London: Longmans, Green & Co., 1907).

Moore, Edward Caldwell. *West and East: the expansion of Christendom and the naturalization of Christianity in the Orient in the XIXth century, being the Dale lectures, Oxford, 1913* (London: Duckworth, 1920).

Mott, John R. *Addresses and Papers of John R. Mott Volume Five: The International Missionary Council* (New York: Association Press, 1947).

Murray, Andrew. *The Key to the Missionary Problem,* 3rd edn. (London: James Nisbet & Co., 1902).

Nassau, R. H. *Fetichism in West Africa: forty years' observation of native customs and superstitions* (London: Duckworth, 1904).

Oldham, J. H. *The World and the Gospel,* 3rd edn. (London: United Council for Missionary Education, 1917).

———. *Christianity and the Race Problem* (London: SCM, 1926).

The Relations between the Younger and Older Churches: report of the Jerusalem meeting of the International Missionary Council March 24th–April 8th, 1928 Volume III (London: Oxford University Press, 1928).

Report of the Fourth Decennial Indian Missionary Conference Held in Madras December 11th–18th, 1902 (London and Madras: Christian Literature Society, n.d. [1903?]).

———— *Records: China Centenary Missionary Conference Held at Shanghai, April 25 to May 8, 1907* (Shanghai: Centenary Conference Committee, 1907).

Slater, T. E. *The Higher Hinduism in Relation to Christianity,* 2nd edn. (London: Elliott Stock, 1903).

Smellie, Alexander. *At the World Missionary Conference: a little narrative for friends who were not there* (Dundee: James P. Mathew & Co., 1910).

Wann, A. B. *The Message of Christ to India: with a memoir and appreciations of the author,* edited by J. Morrison (Edinburgh and London: William Blackwood & Sons, 1925).

World Missionary Conference, 1910. *Reports of Commissions I to VIII and vol. IX, The History and Records of the Conference Together with Addresses Delivered at the Evening Meetings* (Edinburgh and London: Oliphant, Anderson & Ferrier; and New York, Chicago, and Toronto: Fleming H. Revell Company, n.d. [1910]).

————. *Statistical Atlas of Christian Missions* (Edinburgh: World Missionary Conference, 1910).

————. *World Missionary Conference 1910, Edinburgh, June 14-23 Official Handbook* (Edinburgh: World Missionary Conference Office, 1910).

Yun Ch'iho. *Yun Ch'iho Ilgi* (Diary of Yun Ch'iho), 7 vols. (Seoul: Kuksa p'yonch'an wiwonhoe, 1971-86).

4. Works of Reference

Anderson, Gerald H. (ed.). *Biographical Dictionary of Christian Missions* (New York: Simon and Schuster Macmillan, 1998).

Boorman, H. L., and Howard, R. C. (eds.). *Biographical Dictionary of Republican China,* 5 vols. (New York and London: Columbia University Press, 1967-79).

Cameron, N. M. de S. (ed.). *Dictionary of Scottish Church History and Theology* (Edinburgh: T&T Clark, 1993).

Dictionary of American Biography.

Lodwick, Kathleen (comp.). *The Chinese Recorder Index: a guide to Christian missions in Asia, 1867-1941,* 2 vols. (Wilmington, DE: Scholarly Resources Inc., 1986).

Oxford Dictionary of National Biography.

Sunquist, Scott (ed.). *A Dictionary of Asian Christianity* (Grand Rapids: Eerdmans, 2001).

5. Secondary Sources

Aizan, Y. *Essays on the Modern Japanese Church: Christianity in Meiji Japan* (Ann Arbor, MI: Center for Japanese Studies, University of Michigan, 1999).

Ariarajah, S. Wesley. *Hindus and Christians: a century of Protestant ecumenical thought* (Amsterdam and Grand Rapids, MI: Editions Rodopi and Eerdmans, 1991).

Askew, Thomas A. 'The 1888 London Centenary Missions Conference: ecumenical disappointment or American missions coming of age?', *IBMR* 18:3 (July 1994), pp. 113-18.

———— 'The New York 1900 Ecumenical Missionary Conference: a centennial reflection', *IBMR* 24:4 (Oct. 2000), pp. 144-54.

Austin, Alvyn. 'Blessed adversity: Henry W. Frost and the China Inland Mission', in Joel A. Carpenter and Wilbert R. Shenk (eds.), *Earthen vessels: American evangelicals and foreign missions, 1880-1980* (Grand Rapids, MI: Eerdmans, 1990), pp. 47-70.

————. 'Only connect: the China Inland Mission and transatlantic evangelicalism', in Wilbert R. Shenk (ed.), *North American Missions 1810-1914: theology, theory, and policy* (Grand Rapids, MI, and Cambridge: Eerdmans, 2004), pp. 281-313.

————. *China's Millions: the China Inland Mission 1832-1905 and Late Qing Society* (Grand Rapids, MI, and Cambridge, 2007).

Ayandele, E. A. *Holy Johnson: pioneer of African nationalism, 1836-1917* (London: Frank Cass, 1970).

Ayandele, E. A. *A Visionary of the African Church: Mojola Agbebi, 1860-1917* (Nairobi: East African Publishing House, 1971).

Badley, Brenton T. *The Making of a Bishop: the lifestory of Bishop Jashwant Rao Chitambar, Bishop of the Methodist church* (Lucknow: Lucknow Publishing House, 1949).

Balfour, Lady Frances. *A Memoir of Lord Balfour of Burleigh K.T.* (London: Hodder & Stoughton, n.d. [1924]).

Band, Edward. *Working His Purpose Out: the history of the English Presbyterian Mission 1847-1947* (London: Presbyterian Church of England Publishing Office, 1948).

Beaver, R. Pierce. *All Loves Excelling: American Protestant women in world mission* (Grand Rapids. MI: Eerdmans, 1968).

Beckerlegge, Oliver A. (comp.). *United Methodist Ministers and their Circuits* (London: Epworth Press, 1968).

Bell, G. K. A. *Randall Davidson Archbishop of Canterbury*, 2nd edn. (London: OUP, 1938).

Birtwhistle, N. A. 'Methodist missions', in R. Davies, A. R. George, and G. Rupp (eds.), *A History of the Methodist Church in Great Britain*, 4 vols. (London: Epworth Press, 1965-88), III, pp. 1-116.

Bitton, Nelson. 'Cheng Ching-yi: a Christian statesman', *IRM* 30 (1941), pp. 513-20.

Boegner, Marc. 'Missions et gouvernements: de l'acte de Berlin au traité de Versailles', *Le Monde Non-Chrétien* 1 (1931), pp. 59-78.

Boynton, C. 'Dr Cheng Ching-Yi', *Chinese Recorder* 70 (1939), pp. 689-98.

Brain, J. B. *Christian Indians in Natal 1860-1911: an historical and statistical study* (Cape Town: Oxford University Press, 1983).

Brenner, Louis. '"Religious" discourses in and about Africa', in Karin Barber and P. F. de Moraes Farias (eds.), *Discourse and its Disguises: the interpretation of African oral texts*, Birmingham University African Studies Series (Birmingham: University of Birmingham Centre of West African Studies, 1989), pp. 87-105.

Cairns, David S. *An Autobiography: some recollections of a long life, and selected letters, edited by his son and daughter, with a memoir by Professor D. M. Baillie* (London: SCM Press, 1950).

Ceuster, Koen de. *From Modernization to Collaboration, the Dilemma of Korean Cultural Nationalism: the case of Yun Ch'i-ho*, 2 vols. (Leuven: Katholieke Universiteit Leuven, 1994).

Chidester, David. *Savage Systems: colonialism and comparative religion in southern Africa* (Charlottesville and London: University Press of Virginia, 1996).

Clements, Keith. *Faith on the Frontier: a life of J. H. Oldham* (Edinburgh and Geneva: T&T Clark and WCC Publications, 1999).

Coakley, J. F. *The Church of the East and the Church of England: a history of the Archbishop of Canterbury's Assyrian Mission* (Oxford: Clarendon Press, 1992).

Cookey, S. J. S. *Britain and the Congo Question 1885-1913* (London: Longmans, 1968).

Cox, James L. 'The development of A. G. Hogg's theology in relation to non-Christian faith: its significance for the Tambaram meeting of the International Missionary Council, 1938' (University of Aberdeen PhD thesis, 1977).

Cox, Jeffrey. *Imperial Fault-Lines: Christianity and Colonialism in the Punjab* (Stanford, CA: Stanford University Press, 2001).

Cracknell, Kenneth. *Justice, Courtesy and Love: theologians and missionaries encountering world religions, 1846-1914* (London: Epworth Press, 1995).

Curtin, P. D. '"Scientific" racism and the British theory of empire', *Journal of the Historical Society of Nigeria* 2:1 (1960), pp. 40-51.

D'Arcy, C. F. *The Adventures of a Bishop* (London: Hodder & Stoughton, 1934).

Drummond, R. H. *A History of Christianity in Japan* (Grand Rapids, MI: Eerdmans, 1971).

Elliott, Ivor Elliott (ed.). *The Balliol College Register Second Edition 1833-1933* (Oxford: Oxford University Press, 1934).

Ewing, J. C. R. *A Prince of the Church in India: being a record of the life of the Rev. Kali Charan Chatterjee, D.D., for forty-eight years a missionary at Hoshyarpur, Punjab, India* (New York: Fleming H. Revell, 1918).

Farrimond, K. J. T. 'The policy of the Church Missionary Society concerning the development of self-governing indigenous churches 1900-1942' (PhD thesis, University of Leeds, 2004.

Findlay, G. G., and Holdsworth, W. W. *The History of the Wesleyan Methodist Missionary Society,* 5 vols. (London: Epworth Press, 1921-4).

Fasholé-Luke, E., Gray, R., Hastings, A., and Tasie, G. (eds.). *Christianity in Independent Africa* (London: Rex Collings, 1978).

Forward, Martin. *A Bag of Needments: Geoffrey Parrinder and the study of religion* (Bern: Peter Lang, 1998).

Friesen, J. S. *Missionary Responses to Tribal Religions at Edinburgh, 1910* (New York: Peter Lang, 1996).

Gaitskell, Deborah. 'Power in prayer and service: women's Christian organizations', in Richard Elphick and Rodney Davenport (eds.), *Christianity in South Africa: a political, social and cultural history* (Oxford and Cape Town: James Currey and David Philip, 1997), pp. 253-67.

Garrett, Shirley S. *Social Reformers in Urban China: the Chinese Y.M.C.A., 1895-1926* (Cambridge, MA: Harvard University Press, 1970).

Goodall, Norman. *A History of the London Missionary Society 1895-1945* (London: Oxford University Press, 1954).

————. *The Ecumenical Movement,* 2nd edn. (London: Oxford University Press, 1964).

Grayson, James Huntley. *Korea — A Religious History,* revised edn. (London: RoutledgeCurzon, 2002).

Grier, Lynda. *Achievement in Education: the work of Michael Ernest Sadler 1885-1935* (London: Constable, 1952).

Gründer, Horst. *Christliche Mission und deutscher Imperialismus 1884-1914* (Paderborn: Schöningh, 1982).

Haliburton, G. M. 'Mark Christian Hayford: a non-success story', *Journal of Religion in Africa* 12:1 (1981), pp. 20-37.

Harford, J. B., and Macdonald, F. C. *Handley Carr Glyn Moule Bishop of Durham: a biography* (London: Hodder & Stoughton, 1922).

Harper, Susan B. *In the Shadow of the Mahatma: Bishop V. S. Azariah and the travails of Christianity in British India* (Grand Rapids, MI, and Richmond, Surrey: Eerdmans and Curzon Press, 2000),

Hastings, Adrian. *A History of English Christianity 1920-2000,* 4th edn. (London: SCM Press, 2001).

————. 'Geoffrey Parrinder', *Journal of Religion in Africa* 21:3 (2001), pp. 354-9.

Hayward, V. E. W. *Christians and China* (Belfast: Christian Journals Ltd., 1974).

Hedges, Paul. *Preparation and Fulfilment: a history and study of fulfilment theology in modern British thought in the Indian context* (Bern: Peter Lang, 2001).

Heimsath, Charles H. *Indian Nationalism and Hindu Social Reform* (Princeton: Princeton University Press, 1964).

Hertslet, E. (comp.). *A Complete Collection of the Treaties and Conventions . . . between Great Britain and Foreign Powers,* vol. XIX (London: Butterworth, 1895).

Hewitt, Gordon. *The Problems of Success: a history of the Church Missionary Society 1910-1942,* 2 vols. (London: SCM Press, 1971).

Hodge, J. Z. *Bishop Azariah of Dornakal* (Madras: Christian Literature Society for India, 1946).

Hollister, J. N. *The Centenary of the Methodist Church in Southern Asia* (Lucknow: Lucknow Publishing House, 1956).

Hood, George. *Mission Accomplished? The English Presbyterian Mission in Lingtung, South China: a study of the interplay between mission methods and their historical context* (Frankfurt: Verlag Peter Lang, 1986).

Hopkins, C. H. *John R. Mott 1865-1955: a biography* (Grand Rapids: Eerdmans, 1979).

Hogg, W. Richey. *Ecumenical Foundations: a history of the International Missionary Council and its nineteenth-century background* (New York: Harper & Bros., 1952).

———. 'Edinburgh, 1910 — ecumenical keystone', *Religion and Life* 29:3 (Summer 1960), pp. 339-51.

———. 'Edinburgh 1910 — Perspective 1980', *Occasional Bulletin of Missionary Research* 4:4 (Oct. 1980), pp. 146-53.

Horton, Robin. 'Judaeo-Christian spectacles: boon or bane to the study of African religions?', *Cahiers d'Études Africaines* 96:24-4 (1984), pp. 391-436, reprinted in his *Patterns of Thought in Africa and the West* (Cambridge: Cambridge University Press, 1993), pp. 161-93.

Howes, John F. 'Japanese Christians and American missionaries', in Marius B. Jansen (ed.), *Changing Japanese Attitudes Toward Modernization* (Princeton: Princeton University Press, 1965), pp. 337-68.

Hudson-Reed, S. (ed). *Together for a Century: the history of the Baptist Union of South Africa 1877-1977* (Pietermaritzburg: South African Baptist Historical Society, n.d. [1977]).

Ingleby, J. C. *Missionaries, Education and India: issues in Protestant missionary education in the long nineteenth century* (Delhi: ISPCK, 2000).

Iremonger, F. A. *William Temple Archbishop of Canterbury: his life and letters* (London: Oxford University Press, 1948).

Jabavu, Davidson D. T. *The Life of John Tengo Jabavu: editor of Imvo Zabantsundu, 1880-1921* (Lovedale: Lovedale Institution Press, 1922).

Johnston, W. Ross. *Sovereignty and Protection: a study of British jurisdictional imperialism in the late nineteenth century* (Durham, NC: Duke University Press, 1973).

Jones, Kenneth W. *Arya Dharm: Hindu consciousness in 19th-century Punjab* (Berkeley: University of California Press, 1976).

Kalu, Ogbu. 'To hang a ladder in the air: talking about African education in Edinburgh in 1910', in Chima J. Korieh and Raphael Chijoke Njoku (eds.), *Missions, States and European Expansion in Africa* (New York and London: Routledge, 2007), pp. 101-26.

Karanja, John. 'The role of Kikuyu Christians in developing a self-consciously African Anglicanism', in Kevin Ward and Brian Stanley (eds.), *The Church Mission Society and World Christianity, 1799-1999* (Grand Rapids, MI, and Richmond, Surrey: Eerdmans and Curzon Press, 2000).

Keith, A. B. *The Belgian Congo and the Berlin Act* (Oxford: Clarendon Press, 1919).

Kent, John. *The Unacceptable Face: the modern church in the eyes of the historian* (London: SCM Press, 1987).

Kidd, Colin. *The Forging of Races: race and scripture in the Protestant Atlantic world, 1600-2000* (Cambridge: Cambridge University Press, 2006).

Kim, Hyung-chan. 'Portrait of a troubled Korean patriot: Yun Ch'i-ho's views of the March First Independence Movement and World War II', *Korean Studies* 13 (1989), pp. 76-91.

King, Hazel. 'Co-operation in contextualization: two visionaries of the African Church — Mojola Agbebi and William Hughes of the African Institute, Colwyn Bay', *Journal of Religion in Africa* 16 (1986), pp. 2-21.

Landau, Paul. ' "Religion" and Christian conversion in African history: a new model', *Journal of Religious History* 23:1 (Feb. 1999), pp. 8-30.

Latourette, K. S. 'Ecumenical bearings of the missionary movement and the International Missionary Council', in Ruth Rouse and Stephen Charles Neill (eds.), *A History of the Ecumenical Movement 1517-1948* (London: SPCK, 1954), pp. 353-402.

Leslie, R. N., Jr. 'Christianity and the evangelist for sea power: the religion of A. T. Mahan', in J. B. Hattendorf (ed.), *The Influence of History on Mahan: the proceedings of a conference marking the centenary of Alfred Thayer Mahan's The Influence of Sea Power Upon History, 1660-1783* (Newport, RI: Naval War College Press, 1991), pp. 127-39.

Lin, J. J. E. van. *Protestantse Theologie der Godsdiensten van Edinburgh naar Tambaram 1910-1938* (Assen: Van Gorcum and Comp., B.V., 1974).

Louis, W. R., and Stengers, Jean (eds.). *E. D. Morel's History of the Congo Reform Movement* (Oxford: Clarendon Press, 1968).

Low, B. R. C. *Seth Low* (New York and London: G. P. Putnam's Sons, 1925).

Lutz, Jessie G. *China and the Christian Colleges 1850-1950* (Ithaca and London: Cornell University Press, 1971).

McCracken, John. *Politics and Christianity in Malawi 1875-1940: the impact of the Livingstonia Mission in the Northern Province* (Cambridge: Cambridge University Press, 1977).

MacDonald, Alec. *A Short History of Repton* (London: Ernest Benn, 1929).

Maclagan, P. J. *J. Campbell Gibson, D.D. Missionary of the Presbyterian Church of England: a biographical sketch* (London: Religious Tract Society, n.d. [1922]).

Martin, Hugh. *Beginning at Edinburgh: a jubilee assessment of the World Missionary Conference 1910* (London: Edinburgh House Press, 1960).

Mathew, A. *Christian Missions, Education and Nationalism: from dominance to compromise 1870-1930* (New Delhi: Anamika Prakashan, 1988).

Mathews, Basil. *Dr Ralph Wardlaw Thompson* (London: RTS, 1917).

——— *John R. Mott: world citizen* (New York and London: Harper Bros., 1934).

Maughan, Steven. 'An archbishop for Greater Britain: Bishop Montgomery, missionary imperialism, and the SPG, 1897-1915,' in D. O'Connor, *Three Centuries of*

Mission: the United Society for the Propagation of the Gospel (London and New York: Continuum, 2000), pp. 358-70.

———. 'Imperial Christianity? Bishop Montgomery and the foreign missions of the Church of England, 1895-1915', in Andrew Porter (ed.), *The Imperial Horizons of British Protestant Missions, 1880-1914* (Grand Rapids, MI, and Cambridge: Eerdmans, 2003), pp. 32-57.

Maw, Martin. *Visions of India: fulfilment theology, Aryan race theory, and the work of British Protestant missionaries in Victorian India* (Bern: Peter Lang, 1990).

Menzel, Gustav. *Die Rheinische Mission: aus 150 Jahren Missionsgeschichte* (Wuppertal: Verlag der Vereinigten Evangelische Mission, 1978).

Mews, Stuart P. 'Edinburgh and Kikuyu: the interaction of attitudes to two conferences', in G. J. Cuming and Derek Baker (eds.), *Councils and Assemblies, Studies in Church History,* vol. 7 (Cambridge: Cambridge University Press, 1971), pp. 345-59.

M. M. [Montgomery, Maud]. *Bishop Montgomery: a memoir* (London: SPG, 1933).

Morris, Jeremy. *The Church in the Modern Age* (London and New York: I. B. Tauris, 2007).

Murray, Jocelyn. *Proclaim the Good News: a short history of the Church Missionary Society* (London: Hodder & Stoughton, 1985).

Myklebust, Olav G. *The Study of Missions in Theological Education,* 2 vols. (Oslo: Egede Instituttet, 1955, 1957).

Neill, Stephen. *Men of Unity* (London: SCM Press, 1960).

Ng, Peter Tze Ming. *Changing Paradigms of Christian Higher Education in China, 1888-1950* (Lewiston, Queenston, and Lampeter: Edwin Mellen Press, 2002).

Nutt, Rick L. *The Whole Gospel for the Whole World: Sherwood Eddy and the American Protestant mission* (Macon, GA: Mercer UP, 1997).

O'Connor, Daniel, et al. *Three Centuries of Mission: the United Society for the Propagation of the Gospel* (London and New York: Continuum, 2000).

O'Connor, Daniel. *A Clear Star: C. F. Andrews and India 1904-1914* (New Delhi: Chronicle Books, 2005).

Oddie, Geoffrey A. 'Indian Christians and the National Congress', *Indian Church History Review* 2:1 (June 1968), pp. 45-54.

———. *Imagined Hinduism: British Protestant Missionary Constructions of Hinduism, 1793-1900* (New Delhi, Thousand Oaks, and London: Sage, 2006).

Oldham, J. H. 'The International Review of Missions after twenty-five years', *IRM* 24:95 (July 1935), pp. 297-313.

———. 'John R. Mott', *Ecumenical Review* 7:3 (April 1955), pp. 256-9.

———. 'Reflections on Edinburgh, 1910', *Religion and Life* 29:3 (Summer 1960), pp. 329-38.

Parker, F. C. *The Southern Baptist Mission in Japan, 1889-1989* (Lanham, MD: University Press of America, 1991).

Parrinder, Geoffrey. *African Traditional Religion* (London: Hutchinson, 1954).

Payne, Ernest A. *The Growth of the World Church* (London: Edinburgh House Press and Macmillan, 1955).

p'Bitek, Okot. *African Religions in Western Scholarship* (Nairobi: East African Literature Bureau, n.d. [1971]).

Peel, J. D. Y. Review of P. McKenzie, *Hail Orisha! a phenomenology of a West African religion in the mid-nineteenth century, Journal of Religion in Africa* 30:3 (2000), pp. 401-3.

Phillips, C. S., et al., *Walter Howard Frere: Bishop of Truro* (London: Faber & Faber, 1947).

Pierard, R. V. 'John R. Mott and the rift in the ecumenical movement during World War I', *Journal of Ecumenical Studies* 23:4 (Fall 1986), pp. 601-20.

Piper, John F., Jr., *Robert E. Speer: prophet of the American church* (Louisville, KY: Geneva Press, 2000).

Porter, Andrew. 'Scottish missions and education in nineteenth-century India: the changing face of "trusteeship"', *Journal of Imperial and Commonwealth History* 16:3 (May 1988), pp. 35-57.

——— (ed.). *The Imperial Horizons of British Protestant Missions, 1880-1914* (Grand Rapids, MI, and Cambridge: Eerdmans, 2003), pp. 58-84.

Prestige, G. L. *The Life of Charles Gore: a great Englishman* (London: Heinemann, 1935).

Ratzinger, Josef (Pope Benedict XVI). *Europe Today and Tomorrow: addressing the fundamental issues* (San Francisco: Ignatius Press, 2007).

Ratzinger, Josef (Pope Benedict XVI), and Pera, Marcello. *Without Roots: The West, Relativism, Christianity, Islam* (New York: Basic Books, 2006).

Rich, P. B. 'Albert Luthuli and the American Board mission in South Africa', in H. Bredekamp and R. Ross (eds.), *Missions and Christianity in South African History* (Johannesburg: Witwatersrand University Press, 1995), pp. 189-209.

Rinsum, Henk J. van. '"They became slaves of their definitions." Okot p'Bitek (1931-1982) and the European traditions in the study of African religions', in Frieder Ludwig and Afe Adogame (eds.), *European Traditions in the Study of Religion in Africa* (Wiesbaden: Harrassowitz Verlag, 2004), pp. 23-38.

Ritson, John H. *The World is Our Parish* (London: Hodder & Stoughton, 1939).

Robbins, Keith. 'Britain, 1940 and "Christian civilization"', in Derek Beales and Geoffrey Best (eds.), *History, Society and the Churches: essays in honour of Owen Chadwick* (Cambridge: Cambridge University Press, 1985), pp. 279-99.

Robert, Dana L. *American Women in Mission: a social history of their thought and practice* (Macon, GA: Mercer University Press, 1996).

———. *Gospel Bearers, Gender Barriers: missionary women in the twentieth century* (Maryknoll, NY: Orbis, 2002).

Roberts, David. 'Mission: home and overseas. Richard Glover of Bristol', *Baptist Quarterly* 35:3 (July 1993), pp. 108-20.

Roe, James Moulton. *A History of the British and Foreign Bible Society 1905-1954* (London: British & Foreign Bible Society, 1965).

Romanes, Ethel. *The Story of an English Sister* (London: Longmans, Green & Co., 1918).

Rouse, Ruth. 'William Carey's "pleasing dream"', *IRM* 38:150 (April 1949), pp. 181-92.

Rouse, Ruth, and Neill, Stephen Charles (eds.). *A History of the Ecumenical Movement 1517-1948* (London: SPCK, 1954).

Sadler, Michael. *Michael Ernest Sadler . . . : a memoir by his son* (London: Constable, 1949).

Sanneh, Lamin. *Whose Religion is Christianity? The gospel beyond the West* (Grand Rapids and Cambridge: Eerdmans, 2004).

Schäfer, Richard (ed.). *A Muslim who Became a Christian: the story of John Avetaranian (born Muhammed Schükri Efendi)*, transl. John Bechard (Hertford: AuthorsOnLine, 2002).

Seager, R. *Alfred Thayer Mahan: the man and his letters* (Annapolis, MD: Naval Institute Press, 1977).

Seager, R., and Maguire, D. D. (eds.). *Letters and Papers of Alfred Thayer Mahan volume III 1902-1914* (Annapolis, MD: Naval Institute Press, 1975).

Sell, A. P. F. *Defending and Declaring the Faith: some Scottish examples 1860-1920* (Exeter: Paternoster, 1987).

Sharpe, Eric J. *Not to Destroy but to Fulfil: the contribution of J. N. Farquhar to Protestant missionary thought in India before 1914* (Uppsala: Gleerup, 1965).

———. *From Faith to Faith: some Christian attitudes to Hinduism in the nineteenth and twentieth centuries* (London: SCM Press, 1977).

———. *Alfred George Hogg* (Chennai: Christian Literature Society, 1999).

Shaw, Rosalind. 'The invention of "African traditional religion"', *Religion* 20:4 (1990), pp. 339-53.

Shepherd, A. P. *Tucker of Uganda: artist and apostle 1849-1914* (London: SCM, n.d.).

Shelley, Michael T. 'The life and thought of W. H. T. Gairdner, 1873-1928: a critical evaluation of a scholar-missionary to Islam' (University of Birmingham PhD thesis, 1988).

Sinclair, Margaret. *William Paton* (London: SCM Press, 1949).

Smith, Edwin. *Aggrey of Africa: a study in black and white* (London: SCM Press, 1929).

Smith, George. *The Life of Alexander Duff, D.D., LL.D.,* 2 vols. (London: Hodder & Stoughton, 1879).

Smith, Karen E. 'Women in cultural captivity: British women and the Zenana Mission', *Baptist Quarterly* 42:2 (April 2007), pp. 103-13, and 42:3 (July 2007), pp. 245-8.

Sondheimer, Janet. *Castle Adamant in Hampstead: a history of Westfield College, 1882-1982* (London: Westfield College, 1983).

Sorabji, Cornelia. *India Calling: the memories of Cornelia Sorabji* (London: Nisbet, 1934).

Stanley, Brian. *The History of the Baptist Missionary Society 1792-1992* (Edinburgh: T&T Clark, 1992).

———. 'The re-shaping of Christian tradition: western denominational identity in a non-western context', in R. N. Swanson (ed.), *Unity and Diversity in the Church* (*Studies in Church History,* vol. 32, Oxford: Blackwell, 1996), pp. 399-426.

———. 'Hunting for souls': the missionary pilgrimage of George Sherwood Eddy', in Pieter N. Holtrop and Hugh McLeod (eds.), *Missions and Missionaries,* Studies in Church History Subsidia 13 (Woodbridge: Boydell Press, 2000), pp. 127-41.

———. 'Edinburgh 1910 and the *Oikumene*', in Anthony R. Cross (ed.), *Ecumenism and History* (Carlisle: Paternoster Press, 2002), pp. 89-105.

———. 'Church, State, and the hierarchy of "civilization": the making of the Commission VII report, "Missions and Governments" Edinburgh, 1910', in Andrew N. Porter (ed.) *The Imperial Horizons of British Protestant Missions, 1840-1914: The Interplay of Representation and Experience* (Grand Rapids, MI, and Cambridge: Eerdmans, 2003), pp. 58-84.

———. 'Twentieth-century world Christianity: a perspective from the history of missions', in Donald M. Lewis (ed.), *Christianity Reborn: the global expansion of evangelicalism in the twentieth century* (Grand Rapids, MI, and Cambridge: Eerdmans, 2004), pp. 52-83.

———. 'Africa through European Christian eyes: the World Missionary Conference, Edinburgh 1910', in Klaus Korschorke (ed.), *African Identities and Global Christianity in the Twentieth Century* (Wiesbaden: Harrassowitz Verlag, 2005), pp. 165-80.

———. "Defining the boundaries of Christendom: the two worlds of the World Missionary Conference, 1910," *International Bulletin of Missionary Research* 30:4 (October 2006), pp. 171-6.

———. 'The Church of the Three Selves: a perspective from The World Missionary Conference, Edinburgh, 1910', *Journal of Imperial and Commonwealth History* 36:3 (Sept. 2008), pp. 435-51.

Stephenson, Gwendoline. *Edward Stuart Talbot 1844-1934* (London: SPCK, 1936).

Stock, Eugene. *The History of the Church Missionary Society,* 4 vols. (London: 1899-1916).

Sundkler, Bengt. *Church of South India: the movement towards union 1900-1947,* revised edn. (London: Lutterworth Press, 1965).

Tatlow, Tissington. *The Story of the Student Christian Movement of Britain and Ireland* (London: SCM Press, 1928).

Taylor, Mrs Howard. *Pastor Hsi (of North China): one of China's Christians* (London: Morgan & Scott, n.d. [1904]).

Thomas, G. *Christian Indians and Indian Nationalism 1885-1910: an interpretation in historical and theological perspectives* (Frankfurt: Peter Lang, 1979).

Thompson, David M. 'The unity of the Church in twentieth-century England: pleasing dream or common calling?', in R. N. Swanson (ed.), *Unity and Diversity in the Church, Studies in Church History,* vol. 32 (Oxford: Blackwell, 1996), pp. 507-31.

Thompson, H. P. *Into All Lands: the history of the Society for the Propagation of the Gospel in Foreign Parts 1701-1950* (London: SPCK, 1951).

Tikhonov, Vladimir. 'Social Darwinism in Korea and its influence on early modern Korean Buddhism', *International Journal of Korean History* 2 (Aug. 2002), pp. 65-97.

Tinker, Hugh. *The Ordeal of Love: C. F. Andrews and India* (Delhi: Oxford University Press, 1979).

Underwood, Elizabeth. *Challenged Identities: North American missionaries in Korea, 1884-1934* (Seoul: Royal Asiatic Society, Korea Branch, 2003).

Ustorf, Werner. *Sailing on the Next Tide: missions, missiology and the Third Reich* (Frankfurt a.m.: Peter Lang, 2000).

Vansina, Jan. *The Tio Kingdom of the Middle Congo 1880-1892* (London: Oxford University Press for the International African Institute, 1973).

Vidler, A. R. *The Church in an Age of Revolution: 1789 to the present day* (Harmondsworth: Penguin, 1961).

Visser 't Hooft, W. A. (ed.). *The First Assembly of the World Council of Churches Held at Amsterdam August 22nd to September 4th, 1948* (London: SCM Press, 1949).

Walls, Andrew F. *The Missionary Movement in Christian History: studies in the transmission of faith* (Edinburgh: T&T Clark, 1996).

———. *The Cross-Cultural Process in Christian History: studies in the transmission and appropriation of faith* (New York and Edinburgh: Orbis Books and T&T Clark, 2002).

———. 'Geoffrey Parrinder (*1910) and the study of religion in West Africa', in Frieder Ludwig and Afe Adogame (eds.), *European Traditions in the Study of Religion in Africa* (Wiesbaden: Harrassowitz Verlag, 2004), pp. 207-15.

Wardin, A. W. (ed.). *Baptists around the World: a comprehensive handbook* (Nashville, TN: Broadman & Holman, 1995).

Weber, Hans-Ruedi. *Asia and the Ecumenical Movement 1895-1961* (London: SCM Press, 1966).

Webster, J. C. B. *The Christian Community and Change in Nineteenth-Century North India* (Delhi: Macmillan, 1976).

———. *A History of the Dalit Christians in India* (San Francisco: Mellen Research University Press, 1992).

Wells, Kenneth M. *New God, New Nation: Protestants and self-reconstruction nationalism in Korea, 1896-1937* (Honolulu: University of Hawaii Press, 1990).

Williams, C. Peter. *The Ideal of the Self-Governing Church: a study in Victorian missionary strategy* (Leiden: E. J. Brill, 1990).

Willison, Sir John. *Sir George Parkin: a biography* (London: Macmillan, 1929).

Wood, H. G. *Henry T. Hodgkin: a memoir* (London: SCM Press, 1937).

Woolverton, John F. *Robert H. Gardiner and the Reunification of Worldwide Christianity in the Progressive Era* (Columbia and London: University of Missouri Press, 2005).

Worrall, B. G. *The Making of the Modern Church: Christianity in England since 1800* (London: SPCK, 1998).

Wright, David F., and Badcock, Gary (eds.). *Disruption to Diversity: Edinburgh divinity 1846-1996* (Edinburgh: T&T Clark, 1996).

Wright, Marcia. *German Missions in Tanganyika 1891-1941* (Oxford: Clarendon Press, 1971).

Yates, T. E. 'Edinburgh revisited: Edinburgh 1910 to Melbourne 1980', *Churchman* 94:2 (1980), pp. 145-55.

————. *Christian Mission in the Twentieth Century* (Cambridge: Cambridge University Press, 1994).

Zetzsche, Jost O. *The Bible in China: the history of the Union Version or the culmination of Protestant missionary Bible translation in China* (Nettetal: Monumenta Serica Institute & Steyler Verlag, 1999).

6. Websites

http://www.ccel.org/s/schaff/encyc/encyc09/htm/iv.vii.cxlvii.htm
http://www.ccrc.or.kr/englishchanwon/koreacycle.jsp
http://www2.hawaii.edu/-georgeo/ipr/HARADA.htm
http://www.nahste.ac.uk/cgi-bin/viewisad.pl?id=GB-0248-DC-080&view=basic
http://www.theglasgowstory.com/image.php?inum=TGSA05160

Index

Adams, J. E., 143

Africa, 207, 209; lack of representation at Edinburgh, 97-102; marginalisation of, 235-45, 306-7; missions and education in, 178-79, 180-81, 187, 197, 198, 199; relations of missions and governments in, 255, 256-58, 259, 263-64, 266, 267-69; religion in, 236-45; remuneration of national workers in, 137, 138

Africa Inland Mission, 320

African-American participation in conference, 99-100

African Methodist Episcopal Church, 76

African Methodist Episcopal Church Zion, 101; Foreign Missionary Society of, 99

Agbebi, Mojola, 98, 143, 158

Aggrey, James E. K., 101

Ah Sou, L. T., 91, 106

Allen, Young J., 119

Alvarez, T. E., 230, 235

American Baptist Foreign Missionary Society, 96, 100, 106

American Baptist Missionary Union, 61, 158, 254

American Board of Commissioners for Foreign Missions (ABCFM): administrators of, 172, 283; as Commission re-

spondents, 174; missionaries associated with, 34, 150, 215, 263, 268, 310; non-Western representation at Edinburgh, 106, 112; remuneration of native workers, 144

American executive committee, 25, 78; Commission I and scope of statistics, 56-57, 59-62, 63; conference guests of, 106, 115, 120; conference planning and organization, 36, 37, 41-42, 44, 47-48; exclusion of 'faith and order', 38-41, 277

Andersen, Hans P., 58, 59, 61, 71

Anderson, Herbert, 145, 163, 261

Andrews, C. F., 105, 215, 218, 226

Anglo-Catholics, Anglo-Catholicism, 5, 11, 169, 237, 301; and formation of Continuation Committee, 286, 299; participation in conference, 10, 13, 33, 38-41, 50-68, 71, 86, 297-98, 321

Archbishop of Canterbury. *See* Davidson, Randall

Archbishop of York. *See* Lang, Cosmo

Ariarajah, Wesley, 206, 245

Armstrong, W. D., 235, 237, 238, 240, 241

Asia: 13, 16, 52, 80, 112, 145, 156, 247, 252, 307, 309; church union in, 280, 310-12; missions and education in, 173, 178,